G000125936

THE GOOD
web site
GUIDE 2008

THE GOOD
web site
GUIDE 2008

THE GOOD
web site
GUIDE 2008

graham edmonds

HARPER

Harper

An Imprint of HarperCollins*Publishers*

77–85 Fulham Palace Road,

Hammersmith, London W6 8JB

www.harpercollins.co.uk

A Paperback Original 2007

1

A catalogue record of this book is
available from the British Library

ISBN-13 978 0 00 722516 3
ISBN-10 0 00 722516 4

Printed and bound in Great Britain by
Clays Ltd, St Ives plc

Mixed Sources
Product group from well-managed
forests and other controlled sources
www.fsc.org Cert no. SW-COC-1806
© 1996 Forest Stewardship Council
FSC

Contents

The Good Web Site Guide's
Top 10s of the Internet

Introduction

Ten of the Best

The Good Web Site Guide's Top 10s
of the Internet

1. **www.bbc.co.uk** – TV, news and many free services
2. **www.google.co.uk** – not just a search engine
3. **www.wikipedia.org** – the people's encyclopedia
4. **www.ebay.co.uk** – for some a way of life, for others the best online auction site
5. **www.amazon.co.uk** – not just a book store any more
6. **www.apple.com** – an absolute must for all Apple users
7. **www.24hourmuseum.org.uk** – access to all our galleries and museums
8. **www.imdb.com** – if anyone has appeared on screen, they're listed here at the Internet Movie Database
9. **www.shockwave.com** – for games and graphics, they don't come any better
10. **www.howstuffworks.com** – if you want to find out how something works, start here

Welcome to the latest edition of *The Good Web Site Guide*. We've now sold over 350,000 copies to date. This edition is fully updated, all the sites have been checked and rechecked, and I've added over 500 more this year. The book now contains well over 5,000 sites in all.

I review the very best sites in each category, and then look for those sites that offer something unique or have features that make them stand out and recommend those too. I also list alternatives, especially in the popular genres such as music, shopping or finance. Essentially I concentrate on what's really useful, and would like to encourage people to see the Internet as a tool like any other and not be intimidated by it.

Timewasters

The Good Web Site Guide's Top 10s
of the Internet

1. **www.millionsofgames.com** – more games than you can shake a stick at
2. **www.bored.com** – when you've time on your hands, there's nowhere better
3. **www.youtube.com** – you're an addict – admit it …
4. **http://wikipedia.org** – once you start looking, it's difficult to stop
5. **www.ebay.co.uk** – addictive buying and selling
6. **www.queendom.com** – welcome to the land of tests
7. **www.myspace.com** – games, friends, gossip – what more do you want??
8. **www.sudoku.com** – who said the game was dead?
9. **www.googlefight.com** – enter two search phrases, see who wins – my money is on Paris Hilton for overall champion
10. **www.google.com/Top/Games** – there are some 100,000 game sites listed on Google

So what else has changed in a year since the last edition? The number of blogs we're including has increased dramatically; we've found that they can be a really good source of information, especially when it comes to technology. They are great too for allowing you to have your say about something you're passionate about. There are also sections on emerging technologies such as BitTorrent, Peer-to peer (P2P), RSS and Web 2.0.

Quality is still a big issue. The costs and time involved in maintaining a good site are sometimes prohibitive, so that many sites don't seem to be updated as frequently as they should be, while others just die through lack of interest and funding. Still hundreds of sites go live every day, showing that creativity and entrepreneurialism are alive and kicking on the Net.

Lack of time and resources often result in site names (URLs) being turned over to directories, search engines or even adult entertainment sites. Please do let me know if you find any major changes to the sites recommended in this book. I can assure you that all the reviews are accurate at the time of writing. Send comments to: **goodwebsiteguide@hotmail.com**

Keeping Safe

Some people are worried about using their credit card to shop on the Net. In theory it's safer than giving credit card details over the phone, because on most sites the information is encrypted. Before giving out card details, check that you are on a secure line, a small padlock icon will appear on your toolbar, and the http:// prefix will change to https://. Providing you shop from UK sites, you are fully covered by the same fair-trade laws that cover every form of shopping in the UK, but buying from abroad could have some risks attached. If in doubt, shop from reputable firms and known brand names.

There's still a great deal of concern about cookies. A cookie is the popular name of a file which holds some information about your machine and, only if you give out that information, about you. They have a sinister reputation but they enable web site owners to monitor traffic and find out who is visiting their sites. In theory, this means they can tailor their content to their customers or provide a better service. If you're worried about cookies, you can easily delete them or set your computer not to receive them. Be aware, however, that many sites do need cookies to function, especially shopping sites. Check out **www.cookiecentral.com** for more information.

Spyware and Malware are a real issue, especially for Microsoft users, despite their attempts to make Windows more secure, let's hope the new operating system will prove a tougher nut to crack. With many sites using Spyware for sinister purposes such as obtaining credit card details, you should always ensure your system is clean of it, especially if you have an 'always on' broadband connection. Check out our security section on page 423 if you need more information.

Using the Book

Ratings

Standards are now so high that nearly all the sites included in the book follow the key rules on web design; however, some deserve extra recognition.

 Information merit – this is awarded when the site content goes beyond what would normally be considered reasonable and provides a level of information that is exceptional.

 Service merit – awarded to those sites that offer something unique or something that you'd otherwise have to pay for, it's not a reflection of how good the staff are or how quickly they deliver.

 Design merit – given to those sites that ignore the web site sausage-factory approach to design and produce something definitive or use the technology in an original way.

 GWSG **Top Site Award** – reserved for those exceptional sites that offer a combination of quality design, service and content.

In this guide I'm not pretending to be a judge and jury; these ratings are just my opinion, that of a customer and consumer.

Origin

A site's country of origin is not always obvious. This can be important, especially if you are buying from abroad. There may be restrictions or taxes that aren't obvious at the time of purchase. Also, information that is shown as general may apply to one part of the world and not another. For instance, gardening advice on a US site may not be appropriate in the UK. It's also important to know the origin if you're shopping, as import duties and taxes may apply if you're buying something from abroad. Often these are not mentioned and you could end up with a hefty bill which negates the advantage of going there in the first place.

Shopping Note – we have checked all the shopping sites in this book and all appear to be reputable traders. However, *The Good Web Site Guide* cannot be held responsible for transactions or purchases which are unsatisfactory.

Most Useful

The Good Web Site Guide's Top 10s
of the Internet

1. **www.google.co.uk** – the world's most used search engine
2. **www.kelkoo.co.uk** – for finding the best price for everything
3. **www.yell.com** – the yellow pages
4. **www.met-office.gov.uk** – we all need to know about the weather
5. **www.expedia.co.uk** – for all your travel needs
6. **www.newsnow.co.uk** – create your own news channel
7. **www.which.net** – when you want to know which is the best
8. **www.direct.gov.uk** – government information
9. **www.nhsdirect.nhs.uk** – help from the NHS
10. **www.pti.org.uk** – transport information, route finding and more

If you have any suggestions as to how I can improve *The Good Web Site Guide* or have a site you think should be included in the 2008 edition, then please e-mail me at **goodwebsiteguide@hotmail.com**

Acknowledgements

I'd just like to end by thanking a few important people:

Firstly, a big thank you to all those people who have written in with suggestions and sites for me to check out, several hundred sites have been included in the book as a result of people e-mailing me. Particular thanks to Margaret Dickinson.

To the excellent team at HarperCollins.

All my many friends and colleagues for their support and suggestions.

Anyone who bought the first books and the booksellers who supported them.

Especially to Deborah Gray for her great patience and excellent advice and ever increasing contributions to the book.

And to Michaela.

Aircraft and Aviation

The Internet has proved a great resource for pilots, those with an interest in the history of aviation, those who fly and those who just like to watch.

Information and Links

www.aeroseek.com   US
> AVIATION LINKS
> An excellent portal offering over 10,000 aviation-related links in 24 categories – a good place to start for any enthusiast.

www.flyer.co.uk   UK
> AVIATION IN THE UK
> A good and well-established portal site from *Flyer* magazine devoted to all things aviation in the UK, it offers information on the weather, news, a shop plus chat and forums too. It's excellent for links and there's a slightly pricey ISP facility too.
>
> *See also:*
> **www.aeroflight.co.uk** – clearly laid-out 'information stop' for all aviation enthusiasts.
> **www.caa.co.uk** – the Civil Aviation Authority.
> **www.landings.com** – use the directory to navigate this massive but unwieldy site.
> **www.risingup.com** – includes performance information on over 500 aircraft.

For Pilots

www.pilotweb.co.uk   UK
> PILOT WEB
> An excellent overview of the aviation scene with lots of features, help and information, the site is well laid out and easy to navigate with lots of interaction, although you need to subscribe to get the best out of it. See also **www.pilotfriend.com** which is excellent for information, flight planning and links, also **www.pilotweb.aero** which is equally informative.

www.gliderpilot.net   UK
> GLIDER PILOT NETWORK
> Weather, news, links and information on all forms of gliding,

A

plus chat and classified ads. You need to register to get the best out of the site.

www.aviationconsumer.com   US
EQUIPMENT RATED
A consumer site dedicated to the aviation world with reviews and tests done on everything from planes to sunglasses. To get the best out of it you need to subscribe. Unfortunately, the dull layout makes it tedious to use.

See also:
www.aerobatics.org.uk – the British Aerobatic Association.
www.aerostationery.co.uk – maps for aviators.
www.airsupply.co.uk – a Yorkshire-based shop supplying equipment and maps, online ordering available, shipping costs vary.
www.aopa.co.uk – home of the Aircraft Owners and Pilots Association and a dull affair it is too.
www.babo.org.uk – the British Association of Balloon Operators.
www.bmaa.org – the British Microlight Aircraft Association.
www.eballoon.org – comprehensive ballooning encyclopaedia including history, clubs, technical information and where to find a ride.
www.flightstore.co.uk – if want to look the part go here …
www.iac.org – site of the International Aerobatic Club.
www.intotheblue.co.uk/flying-lessons.shtml – flying lessons and aerial experiences.
www.pprune.com – gossip, news and trivia from the Professional Pilot's rumour network.
www.start-flying.com – here you can get an overview of what it takes to start flying.

Devoted to Aircraft

www.aircraft-info.net

THE WEB'S NO.1
A fact based site listing all the world's major aircraft, their specifications, performance and also what's in development.

www.airliners.net   UK

THE WINGS OF THE WEB
With nearly 700,000 photos, this is a huge site; it has a good search facility and should appeal to photographers as well as plane spotters. It also offers a shop, news, chat, links and a huge amount of information.

See also:
http://avia.russian.ee – a not that up-to-date overview of the world's helicopters.
http://exp-aircraft.com – all you need to find out about experimental aircraft and where to buy one.
www.airchive.com – a labour of love with masses of material posted by someone who is clearly a commercial aviation aficionado possibly without equal ...
www.aircraft-photos.net – hundreds of photos to download but you have to subscribe.
www.airspacemag.com – the magazine of the Smithsonian Air and Space Museum has a few really interesting articles.
www.flightglobal.com – industry news, jobs and more.
www.globalaircraft.org – a vast site with information primarily on US aircraft with lots of information and interactivity.
www.helicoptermuseum.co.uk – OK site with good links.
www.rotor.com – helicopter industry news plus information and links.
www.zap16.com – excellent site that offers fact sheets and pictures on both military and civil aircraft.

Military and Defence

www.janesonline.com   US
JANES
Janes is *the* authority on defence forces world-wide and for a price you can buy books and CD-ROMs which contain all the information you'll ever need about the world's military might.

www.raf.mod.uk   UK
ROYAL AIR FORCE
This site features lots of information on the RAF – you can locate a display or fly past, find career advice, check out a squadron, download pictures or get technical information. The history section is particularly good with data covering aircraft from the very first planes to the latest illustrated by a gallery of pictures.

www.wpafb.af.mil/museum   US

US AIR FORCE MUSEUM
A superbly detailed site with masses of data on the aircraft and their history from the first planes to space flight. The archive section is particularly good with features on particular types of aircraft and weapons, and information about their development.

A

See also:
www.rafmuseum.org.uk – the RAF museums at London and Cosford.
www.fas.org – the Federation of American Scientists has a fascinating if somewhat scary site (e.g. nuclear bomb blast calculator), it contains a listing of the world's military aircraft too.
www.fighter-planes.com – lots of stats and information about the world's fighter planes.
www.hazegray.org/navhist/carriers – all you need to know about aircraft carriers.
www.mar.co.uk – home of the Military Aviation Review and lots of photos.

History

www.century-of-flight.net   US

AVIATION HISTORY
A good overview of the history of flying with background on the planes and pilots, excellent for school projects and a general browse for anyone interested in the history of flight.

http://theaerodrome.com   UK

FIRST WORLD WAR
Devoted to the aircraft and aces of the First World War, this site offers lots of background information, personal experiences and details about the pilots who fought above the trenches.

See also:
www.battle-of-britain.com – an overview of the battle, the aircraft and those who fought in it.
www.battleofbritain.net – home of the Battle of Britain Historical Society.
www.historicaircraftcollection.ltd.uk – home to a collection of WW2 planes, beautifully restored.
www.spitfiresociety.demon.co.uk – all you need to know about Spitfires.
www.thunder-and-lightnings.co.uk – a site devoted to British post war military aircraft, with lots of detail, but not updated that often.
www.vintageaircraft.org – Vintage Aircraft Association's site with events, information and photos.

Air Crashes

A

www.airdisaster.com US

NO.1 AVIATION SAFETY RESOURCE
A rather macabre site that reviews each major air crash, and looks into the reasons behind what happened. It's not for the squeamish, but the cockpit voice recordings and eyewitness accounts make fascinating, if disturbing listening and reading. There are some really annoying adverts on this site. For more crashes see **www.1001crash.com** which may be a little gratuitous for some. See also **www.aaib.gov.uk** for the Air Accident Investigation Branch, which has a monthly bulletin with details of crashes and current investigations.

Antiques and Collectibles

The Internet is a great place to learn about antiques, it's also full of specialist sites run by enthusiastic collectors. If you want to take the risk of buying over the Net, then the best prices are found on the big auction sites such as eBay, see page 39.

www.invaluable.com UK

SEARCH THE WORLD'S AUCTION CATALOGUES
The aim of this site is to provide 'impartial electronic information on antiques, fine art and premium collectibles to dealers, private buyers, museums and other institutions'. It proves to be a great resource providing contact details and links to hundreds of dealers, catalogues and auction houses worldwide. Use the 'iFind' section to search dealers' stock. The links section is particularly good. They have links to live auctions (via eBay) that enable you to participate in international sales.

www.antiquesbulletin.co.uk UK

INTERACTIVE BULLETIN
A site with good information and links to more specialist sites and dealers. It aims to be comprehensive and does a great job, there are details on auctions, advice on buying and selling, and a bookshop. You can also buy and sell from the site. To access the articles archive, you need to purchase a site licence.

www.finds.org.uk UK

THE PORTABLE ANTIQUITIES SCHEME
An interesting site devoted to volunteered archaeological and

antiquity finds made by individuals who offer to register them so that they can be researched properly.

www.chinasearch.co.uk   UK
REPLACING LOST CHINA
A company specialising in finding china to match services and lost pieces, they also buy unwanted tableware. The site is easy to use and they have items in over 2,500 different designs in stock so they should be able to help.

www.studiopottery.com   UK

THE POTTERY STUDIO
Divided into three sections (pots, potters and potteries), this site gives information on the history of studio pottery. It's a huge site with over 5,400 pages and it's continually being updated. Everything is cross-referenced with good explanations and photographs.

Useful specialist sites:
www.antique-furniture.co.uk – attractive site from a specialist dealer offering a wide range of furniture, good photography and the promise of a high level of service to match.
www.antiqueprintshop.co.uk – a good selection of antique prints.
www.antiques-atlas.com – an interactive regional listing of dealers and fairs.
www.antiquesworld.co.uk – the latest news, details on major and local fairs, book a course or indulge your interests by linking to a specialist online retailer or club. The links and information are very good.
www.atg-online.com – home of the Antiques Trade Gazette. It's comprehensive and wide-ranging, covering all aspects of antique buying. You have to subscribe to get the best out of it.
www.bada.org – another association, this time the British Antique Dealer's Association, a listing site for antique dealers in the UK, grouped in 16 categories, it's easy to find a specialist in a particular area of interest.
www.bafra.org.uk – The British Antique Furniture Restorer's Association site is a useful place to visit as it helps you find the right restorer. Apart from the usual links page, there's also information and articles on caring for antiques and how to find a course if you want to become a restorer.
www.claricecliff.com – a must for fans of Clarice Cliff pottery. There is information on auctions, biographical details, patterns,

shapes, also a newsletter and forum for related chat. The site offers reproductions and related merchandise for sale.

www.collectingchannel.com – a good US site with excellent links.

www.collectingnetwork.com – links to collectors around the world.

www.collectorcafe.com – portal site which is great for classified ads links, articles and chat covering most of the major areas of collecting.

www.dmgantiquefairs.com – DMG run the largest fairs in the UK, their attractive site gives details of each fair, including dates, location and local tourist information.

www.lapada.co.uk – home to the Association of Art and Antique Dealers.

www.oldbear.co.uk – antique teddy bears … ah.

www.tademagallery.com – to-kill-for art deco and art nouveau jewellery, most prices on application.

www.worldcollectorsnet.com – great for discussion groups, collectors' message boards, links and general chat about collecting.

www.wwii-collectibles.com – mainly WW2 stamps, covers, posters and coins.

Antiques on TV

www.bbc.co.uk/antiques   UK

BBC

A typically excellent site from the BBC with links to the major shows and a very useful price guide covering some 5,000 antiques, plus expert guidance and tips.

See also:
www.david-dickinson.net – all you need to know about the man …

www.pbs.org/wgbh/pages/roadshow – home of the US version of the Antiques Roadshow.

A

Apple Mac Users

The following sites specialise in Apple Mac technology and programs.
See also the general sections on Computers, Software and Games that
may also have relevant information.

www.apple.com/uk   US/UK

 HOME OF THE ORIGINAL
Get the latest information and advances in Apple computers at
this beautifully designed site. You can buy from the Applestore,
they do offer finance deals and help for businesses, so software
is surprisingly good value.

Hardware

www.cancomuk.com   UK

APPLE MAC HARDWARE AND SOFTWARE
A messy site offering a wide selection of hardware, peripherals
and software all developed for Apple computers. There are
plenty of deals and choice.

www.macwarehouse.co.uk   UK

GREAT PRICES ON MACS
Part of the Microwarehouse group, they specialise in mail-order
supply with a reputation for excellent service. Good prices and a
wide range make this a good first port of call if you need a new
Mac or an upgrade.

See also:
www.macassist.co.uk – buy the Mac that's right for you.
www.macreviewzone.com – more reviews and buying help.
www.mrsystems.co.uk – a London-based specialist store.

Software

www.versiontracker.com   US

 SOFTWARE FOR MACS
A software specialist that's a great place for downloading the
latest programs, it has a huge selection and many are free. You
have to subscribe to get the best out of it, but it's well worth the
effort although it can feel like a bit of a minefield at times.

A

See also:
www.macupdate.com – good for the latest hot software and updates.
www.theapplecollection.com – a huge site with lots of information and downloads but principally a collection of all things sporting the apple logo.

Information and Help

www.macintouch.com   US

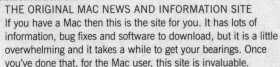
THE ORIGINAL MAC NEWS AND INFORMATION SITE
If you have a Mac then this is the site for you. It has lots of information, bug fixes and software to download, but it is a little overwhelming and it takes a while to get your bearings. Once you've done that, for the Mac user, this site is invaluable.

www.macdirectory.com   US
KEEP UP TO SPEED
Good-looking and well-organised, maybe not as comprehensive as some Mac sites but much easier to use, particularly good for software.

See also the following:
http://thinksecret.com – the latest information and predictions about what's going on at Apple.
www.applelust.com – a site devoted to forums discussing all things Apple.
www.everymac.com – another good guide to the world of Macintosh.
www.everythingmac.com – great for links.
www.google.com/mac.html – Google's excellent and very useful Mac-only search engine, with downloads and widgets.
www.macfixit.com – go troubleshooting and fix your problems.
www.macinstein.com – a good directory and Mac search engine.
www.macnn.com – the Mac News network, lots of ratings and useful articles.
www.macrumors.com – a great place to find the latest information and ideas about what could be on the way from Apple, good for tips too.
www.securemac.com – information on how to keep your Mac updated, safe and secure.

A

Music for Macs

Here's a selection of sites that offer the Mac owner a place to go to download the latest digital music files. Please be aware that downloading some types of files may be illegal (see page 317).

www.apple.com/itunes – the original.
www.dailytunes.com – linking to iTunes and Macrumors, here you can get recommendations and tips on what to download and buy.
www.limewire.com – a very popular and fast file-sharing program that is suitable for Mac users, more stable than some.
www.macband.com – a well-categorised site covering free music donated by bands.
www.macidol.com – news, discussions and even free downloads.
www.macjams.com – an Apple Garageband community site.
www.macmusic.org – keep up to date with the latest music news, software and hardware. There are over 3,500 music-related links and also forums and advice.

Games for Macs

Here are some great sites to help you if you feel restricted by having an Apple Mac, watch out for spyware though.

www.macgamer.com   US
MAC GAMER MAG
A very good online magazine with all the usual features we've come to expect: news, reviews, links and even a few giveaways. It's all neatly packaged on an attractive website.

www.macgamefiles.com   US
MAC GAME FILE LIBRARY
To quote them: 'Macgamefiles.com is the one-stop source for Macintosh game files, the site features lively libraries of Macintosh demos, shareware, updaters, tools, add-ons, and more'. And they're right; it's a very useful site with some really good games and software.

See also:
www.apple.com/games – worth checking out Apple's games site.
www.insidemacgames.com – good magazine.
www.gamedb.com/ssps – a huge number from which to choose.

Mac Fans and Miscellaneous sites ...

Here are a few sites dedicated to specific Apple products and enthusiasts ...

> **www.byodkm.net** – the Mac Mini enthusiast's network.
> **www.cubeowner.com** – discussion for users of Apple's Cube.
> **www.macvisionaries.com** – for visually impaired Mac users.
> **www.theapplemuseum.org** – home of the Mac Museum.

Architecture and Buildings

www.greatbuildings.com   US
ARCHITECTURE ONLINE
This US-oriented site shows over 800 buildings and features hundreds of leading architects, with 3-D models, photographic images and architectural drawings, commentaries, bibliographies and web links. It's all well packaged, easy to use and you can search by architect, building or location.

www.emporis.com   US
SKYSCRAPERS AND MORE ...
An excellent technical and entertaining resource covering high rise and many historical buildings, it is industry-oriented but has good search facilities and is always being added to. It's run by a company who specialise in the field so the data is pretty authoritative, but spoiled by the amount of extraneous information. See also **www.glasssteelandstone.com** which is a growing architecture encyclopaedia with details of some 1,500 buildings.

www.architecture.com   UK
 THE ROYAL INSTITUTE FOR BRITISH ARCHITECTS
A massive site from the RIBA with some 250,000 pages on all aspects of architecture including history, jobs, events and features on great buildings.

www.buildingconservation.com   UK
CONSERVING ASSETS
They claim to be the online information centre for the conservation and restoration of historic buildings, churches, gardens and landscapes; the site seems to live up to its billing providing plenty of quality information and links.

A

www.implosionworld.com   US
DEMOLITION
If watching buildings going down instead of up turns you on,
then you should visit this site which offers videos and pictures of
demolitions plus lots of information on explosive demolition.
There's also an educational side to the site and a FAQ section
covering the World Trade Center disaster too.

Also check out the following sites:
http://architecture.about.com – some excellent articles and
features at About.com.
http://content.lib.washington.edu/buildingsweb/index.html – a
searchable picture database featuring some 10,000 buildings.
http://en.wikipedia.org/wiki/Architecture – Wikipedia's well put
together overview about architecture and its history.
http://www.culture.gov.uk/what_we_do/Architecture_design –
the government's pages on architecture.
www.aabc-register.co.uk – the register of architects accredited
in building conservation.
www.archiseek.com – good for news and forums.
www.architecturemag.com – *Architecture* magazine.
www.arcspace.com – photos, opinions and features on the most
important architects and their work.
www.bbc.co.uk/history/programmes/restoration – get the low
down on the BBC's architectural salvage projects.
www.english-heritage.org.uk – some of England's finest
buildings.
www.galinsky.com – informative site on modern architecture.
www.landmarktrust.org.uk – saving national treasures.
www.nationaltrust.org.uk – home to many of our finest
buildings.
www.spab.org.uk – home of the charity The Society for the
Protection of Ancient Buildings.

Art and the Arts

*One of the best things about the Internet is the ability to showcase things
that otherwise would be quite obscure or inaccessible. Now working
artists are able to show their wares to excellent effect and we can view
their art before we buy. In addition, we can now 'visit' some of the world's
great galleries and museums. Here are the best sites for posters, online
galleries, museums, cartoons, exhibitions, and showcases for new talent
and how to get the best clip art for your own use.*

Visual Treats

The Good Web Site Guide's Top 10s
of the Internet

1. **www.nationalgeographic.com** – beautiful photography and writing too
2. **www.apple.com/uk** – proving that computers need not be dull
3. **http://uk.fmagazine.com** – the gorgeous Flash 8 Forum music magazine
4. **www.scifi.com** – makes the best of all those effects
5. **http://hubblesite.org** – stunning pics from the Hubble space telescope
6. **www.liveplasma.com** – information on any artist graphically presented and linked
7. **www.noggin.com** – great for young kids
8. **www.thebanmappingproject.com** – stunning site on the history of Thebes and the Pharoahs
9. **www.yoox.com** – make fashion shopping a pleasure
10. **www.edible.com** – unusual food – not for all but the site is cool

Resources and Encyclopaedias

www.artlex.com   US

THE VISUAL ARTS DICTIONARY
From abbozzo to zoomorphic, there are some 4,000 definitions of art-related terms with links to related articles on other sites. The cross-referencing is excellent.

www.artcyclopedia.com   CANADA

THE FINE ART SEARCH ENGINE
A popular resource for finding out just about anything to do with art, it's quick, nicely designed and informative. At the time of writing they had indexed 2,100 leading arts sites and offer links to an estimated 180,000 works by over 8,000 different artists.

http://wwar.com   US

THE WORLD-WIDE ART RESOURCE
This is an effective search vehicle with links to artists,

A

exhibitions, galleries and museums, it now offers over 100,000 works of art from over 22,000 'masters'. Excellent.

www.artchive.com   UK
MARK HARDEN'S ARTCHIVE
Incredible, but seemingly the work of one art fanatic, this superb site not only has an excellent art encyclopaedia, but also the latest art news and galleries with special online exhibitions. The quality of the pictures is outstanding. There's also a section on theory, good links too, great for homework.

See also:
http://www.artindustri.com – huge portal site offering information and the portfolios of over 4,000 artists. You can browse by image too.
www.abcgallery.com – Olga's Gallery is hugely informative and well illustrated.
www.askart.com – a massive directory on art and artists, US-oriented.
www.bbc.co.uk/arts/art – high quality pages from the BBC covering their latest programmes, prizes and education.
www.chart.ac.uk/vlib – excellent for links.
www.ibiblio.org/wm – the web museum offers background and information on art movements and artists.

Art in the UK

http://www.culture.gov.uk/about_us/culture   UK
THE GOVERNMENT'S VIEW
A dense site giving information on how the government is supporting the arts and museums, there are plenty of facts, figures and reports to download, as well as links and information on libraries, the creative industries and architecture.

www.design-council.org.uk   UK
PROMOTING THE EFFECTIVE USE OF DESIGN
This good-looking site effectively promotes the work of the Design Council through access to their archives of articles on design and details of their work with government; it also gives feedback on design issues.

www.britisharts.co.uk   UK
COMPREHENSIVE UK LISTING
A well-categorised and comprehensive listing site aimed at artists, buyers and regional art.

For information on grants, funding and events see also:
www.artscouncil.org.uk –Arts Council of England
www.artscouncil-ni.org – Arts Council of Northern Ireland
www.artswales.org.uk – Arts Council of Wales
www.scottisharts.org.uk –Scottish Arts Council

What's On in the UK?

www.artguide.org/uk   UK
> THE ART LOVER'S GUIDE TO BRITAIN AND IRELAND
> Organised by artist, region, exhibition or museum with more
> than 4,500 listings in all. This site is easy to navigate with a
> good search engine and cross-referencing making it simple to
> find out about events in a particular region, aided by annotated
> maps. See also **www.artsfestivals.co.uk** where you can search
> for festivals by date or alphabetically.

Art Styles, Periods, Schools, Most Popular Artists and Countries

www.impressionism.org   US
> LEARN ABOUT IMPRESSIONISM
> An overview of the movement with a tutorial all contained on a
> well-illustrated site.

www.surrealism.co.uk   UK
> ONLINE GALLERY
> Not as way out as you'd expect, this site gives an overview of
> surrealism and features contemporary artists. The online gallery
> is OK without being that exciting, but as a showcase it works.

www.graffiti.org   UK
> THE WRITING ON THE WALL
> If you're fascinated by graffiti, then here's the place to go. It's got
> a gallery of the best examples, history and links to other graffiti
> sites.

www.wga.hu   HUNGARY

> THE RENAISSANCE AND MORE
> The Web Gallery of Art is a virtual museum dedicated to
> European painting and sculpture of the 12th–18th centuries. It
> is nice to look at and contains a phenomenal number of
> paintings; however, it takes a little time to get the knack of

navigating the site. There is the option to listen to related music while browsing.

www.the-artists.org UK
20TH CENTURY ART
This site is easy to use, with minimalist design and details of every major artist of the last century.

www.dlc.fi/~hurmari/preraph.htm UK

PRE-RAPHAELITES
An exhaustive listing of sites and links to pages on the Pre-Raphaelites, their paintings, lives and even those who posed for them.

For biographical information on a huge number of artists see the entries under Resources and Encyclopaedias. The following have pages devoted to the particular artists:
http://arthistory.about.com/od/artistsaz – biographies of over 150 artists plus loads of art history information.
http://essentialvermeer.20m.com – Vermeer
http://picasso.tamu.edu/picasso – Picasso
www.chez.com/renoir/indexe.html – Renoir
www.daliuniverse.com – Dali
www.diegorivera.com – Diego Rivera
www.expo-degas.com – Degas
www.expo-klimt.com – Klimt
www.ibiblio.org/wm/paint/auth/rembrandt – Rembrandt
www.lucidcafe.com/library/96jun/gauguin.html – Gauguin
www.marmottan.com/uk – Monet
www.mos.org/leonardo – Da Vinci
www.musee-matisse-nice.org – Matisse
www.vangoghgallery.com – Van Gogh
www.warhol.org – Andy Warhol

World Art

www.asianart.com US
ART IN ASIA
All you need to know on Asian art. Basically, it covers all the major cultures in four sections: exhibitions, articles, associations and galleries. It's not very well cross-referenced which makes it hard to navigate, although there is a pretty good search engine.

www.japaneseart.org   FRANCE
JAPAN
A virtual tour of the best in Japanese art, with links to antique
dealers, galleries and museums, it's quite information light so for
more go to **www.kanzaki.com/jinfo/jart.html** where you find
links to numerous aspects of Japanese culture and arts. You can
also try **http://web-japan.org/museum** but we found the site
unreliable.

http://depts.washington.edu/chinaciv   US
CHINESE CIVILISATION
Essentially an educational resource, this site provides a good
general introduction to the arts and culture of China. Maps and
a good timeline help to make sense of it all. For a snapshot of
contemporary Chinese art visit **www.newchineseart.com**

www.latinart.com   US
THE LATIN AMERICAN ARTS SCENE
A magazine-style site dedicated to emerging and established
artists in Latin America. There is a guide to international
exhibitions showcasing Latin American art and some good
resources available on the site.

www.lonker.net/art_african_1.htm   US
AFRICAN ART
A good-looking site dedicated to mainly sub-Saharan cave and rock
paintings. It's well illustrated and authoritative, there's also a sister
site on Aboriginal Art at **www.lonker.net/art_aboriginal_1.htm**

The Major Museums and Galleries

www.museums.co.uk   UK
MUSEUM SEARCH
MuseumNet is a simple search engine which allows you to
search either by subject or location, each entry has a short
description and a map. There's also industry information and a
jobs page for those who want to work in a museum, however it
doesn't list many of the smaller museums.

http://vlmp.museophile.com   UK/US
MUSEUMS WORLD-WIDE
Provides links to the world's museums which have an online
presence and indicates which languages they use. Information
on galleries, museums and libraries is listed separately.

A

www.museumstuff.com US
 MUSEUM GATEWAY
An outstanding portal devoted to American museums. There's
information on virtually any topic you can name plus thousands
of links to specialist sites and museums. They also provide a list
of museum shops, chat rooms and forums plus links to the fun
sections on museum sites.

www.coudal.com/moom.php US
 THE MUSEUM OF ONLINE MUSEUMS
An excellent place to go if you want to see what the world's
museums have to offer, the site is very well designed and it's
easy to get immersed in what's on offer here.

www.24hourmuseum.org.uk UK
 CELEBRATING UK CULTURE
Run by the Campaign for Museums, this site aims to give high
quality access to the UK's galleries, museums and heritage sites
– and it succeeds. The graphics are clear, it's easy to use and
really informative. There are a selection of online exhibitions,
web features, a museum finder, links, news and a link to
www.show.me.uk which is the excellent sister site for children.

http://digitalgallery.nypl.org/nypldigital/index.cfm US
NEW YORK DIGITAL LIBRARY
The library's attempt to make accessible online 'the accumulated
wisdom of the world, without distinction as to income, religion,
nationality, or other human condition', and with some 500,000
images and a great search facility, it largely succeeds.

*Below are listed the sites owned by the major museums and
galleries; all are of a high standard and offer insights into their
collections, exhibitions and history. Many have associated
shops, which while generally expensive (especially shipping)
do offer the chance to find gifts that would be unavailable
elsewhere.*
www.courtauld.ac.uk – The Courtauld Collection.
www.guggenheim.org – The Vanguards of Architecture and
Culture.
www.hermitagemuseum.org – The Russian State Hermitage
Museum.
www.louvre.fr – The Louvre, France's Treasure House
www.metmuseum.org – The Metropolitan Museum Of Art, New
York.

www.moma.org – The Museum Of Modern Art in New York.
www.natgalscot.ac.uk – National Gallery for Scotland.
www.nationalgallery.org.uk – The National Collection.
www.npg.org.uk – The National Portrait Gallery.
www.royalacademy.org.uk – Royal Academy, where art is
made, seen and debated.
www.si.edu – The Smithsonian.
www.tate.org.uk – Tate Gallery.
www.thebritishmuseum.ac.uk – British Museum, great site.
www.vam.ac.uk – Victoria & Albert Museum.

Clip Art

*These sites are loaded with pop-ups and advertising which is really
irritating. You may just try Google which has an excellent image search
facility. If you know of a site that is ad free please let me know.*

www.clipart.net   US
  THE PLACE TO START IF YOU NEED CLIP ART
  With this clip-art search facility you should quickly find the
  perfect image. Many linked sites have free art for use, otherwise
  cost varies enormously depending on what you want.

  See also:
  http://classroomclipart.com – a wide selection good for projects.
  http://office.microsoft.com/en-us/clipart/default.aspx?lc=en-us
  – Microsoft's selection of free clip art and images.
  www.321clipart.com – some 12,000 images.
  www.barrysclipart.com – a huge resource with hundreds of
  categories.
  www.clipartcastle.com – sections on web graphics, photos and
  animation as well as clip art. Registration is a right pain though.
  www.kidsdomain.com/clip – nice selection by topic.

Cartoons and Drawing

www.cartoonbank.com   US
  WORLD'S LARGEST CARTOON DATABASE
  Need to find a cartoon for a particular occasion? Then there's a
  choice of over 20,000, mostly from *New Yorker* magazine. You
  can send e-cards and you can now get some products delivered
  to the UK (at reasonable shipping rates). For a massive set of
  links to cartoon and humorous sites then try the excellent
  Norwegian search **www.cartoonstock.com**

www.cartoon-factory.com   US
BUYING CARTOON CELS
Buy cartoon cels, mainly from Disney and Warner cartoons; you
can search by subject or artist. Delivery is expensive, although
they are flexible about payment. See also the Open Directory
Project's section on Animation. It offers nearly 14,000 links at
http://dmoz.org/arts/animation

www.drawingpower.org.uk   UK
THE BIG DRAW
A bid to get us all drawing, the Big Draw happens every October
and here you can get encouragement and details on events and
programmes.

http://drawsketch.about.com/od/cartooning   US
DRAWING AND SKETCHING
A good set of links, articles and web pages devoted to all aspects
of drawing from About.com.

Buying Art

www.theartsource.org   UK
BUYING ART THE EASY WAY
A well designed online gallery offering a wide selection of art at
'fair' prices, it's mainly contemporary in style but there's plenty
to choose from and a 14 day money back guarantee.

www.eyestorm.com   UK
BUYING CONTEMPORARY ART
A really attractive and well-designed site which showcases
contemporary art and photography, you can buy online as well.

www.whitecube.com   UK
WHITE CUBE GALLERY
Although this gallery is influential in developing the careers of
some of the best artists working today, you can buy art here at
reasonable prices too.

www.artnet.com   UK

FINE ART ONLINE
Possibly the largest gallery network featuring work from some
18,000 artists, the site is well put together and the information
on offer is extraordinary with an encyclopaedia, price database,
links and a comprehensive directory.

www.commissionaportrait.com   UK
PORTRAITS
If you fancy immortalising yourself in a painting or sculpture,
then this is a good place to go. There are over 100 artists to
choose, whether they specialise in people or dogs.

Other online art showcase sites and stores worth visiting:
www.artandparcel.com – a messy site that shows the work of
120 artists.
www.artcapitalgroup.com – borrow against your work of art or
borrow funds to buy something for the living room.
www.artlondon.com – a well-designed art store with an
emphasis on the UK, Russia and the Ukraine – value for money
and quality.
www.artprice.com – a subscription service that allows the
subscriber to check on the value of the work from over 300,000
artists world-wide. There's also help and a good links section.
www.axisartists.org.uk – a very good showcase site for
contemporary artists with lots of content and information as well
as links and exhibitions.
www.britart.com – a good-looking, well-stocked site
concentrating on the work of British artists.
www.fineart.co.uk – the home of the Fine Art Trade Guild.
www.modernbritishartists.co.uk – a gallery and shop catering
for those of us who love and covet the work of modern British
artists, including those from early in the last century.
www.newbritishartists.com – well-designed gallery, wide variety
of artists and paintings.
www.redraggallery.co.uk – another good gallery specialising in
British, and in particular, Scottish art.

www.artloss.com   US
THE ART LOSS REGISTER
The register of stolen and lost art. Featured thefts and recoveries;
makes for interesting if rather sad reading.

Posters

www.artrepublic.co.uk   UK
BOOKS, POSTERS AND WHAT'S ON WHERE
A nicely designed, easy-to-use site with thousands of art posters
and prints to choose from, there is also an option to have posters
framed and free shipping world-wide. There is also a glossary of
art terms and biographical data on an impressive number of

artists. 'What's On World-wide' provides details of the latest exhibitions, competitions and travel information for over 1,250 museums around the world.

www.barewalls.com   US
INTERNET'S LARGEST ART PRINT AND POSTER STORE
This site backs its claim with a huge range, it's also excellent for gifts and unusual prints and posters but be aware that the shipping costs are high. There's also a gift voucher scheme.

See also:
www.art.co.uk – excellent selection and a great line in movie posters as well as art.
www.easyart.co.uk – an excellent art shop selling posters, limited editions, photographs, etchings and now, canvas art too. They provide inspiration too with advice on the best place to hang art in your home and a custom art section where you can turn pictures of your friends into pop icons.
www.postershop.co.uk – huge selection of fine art posters, there's also a framing service and a good user-friendly search facility where you can search by subject as well as artist.
www.thebigartcompany.com – turn your photos into modern art.
www.totalposter.com – excellent poster store, specialising in photographic posters with a very wide and topical selection.

Creating Art

www.kurzweilcyberart.com   US
CYBER ART
Once you download the program, watch in fascination as art is created for you as a screen saver. It's free and great fun too. See also **www.storyabout.net/typedrawing** where you can create your own art with an excellent drawing program.

www.saa.co.uk   UK
THE SOCIETY FOR ALL ARTISTS
Help, advice, forums, tuition and a good shop make this a useful site for any artist, amateur or professional. There's also a gallery if you're looking for art to buy. Additional services and discounts are on offer for those who join.

www.watercolor-online.com   US
  ALL FORMS OF WATERCOLOUR
Very good site devoted to all aspects of watercolour painting; it

A

has tutorials, advice, links and provides a good place to start when searching for information on the subject.

For more watercolour sites try:
http://painting.about.com/cs/watercolours/index.htm – pages of advice from the excellent www.about.com
www.1art.com – online art courses from $120.
www.learntodo.co.uk – an online painting course from Andy Walker.
www.wasp-art.skynow.co.uk – a simple online course by Peter Saw.
www.watercolorpainting.com – a US-based portal site with some good tutorials.

www.accessart.org.uk   UK
MAKING ART ACCESSIBLE
A really good, colourful site dedicated to helping students, children and teachers get to grips with the art world and the meaning behind art. There are good online workshops on topics such as sculpture, use of colour and photography.

www.simplypainting.com   UK
FRANK CLARK
Learn how to paint with leading art teacher Frank Clark, the site has free lessons and tips plus a shop and gallery.

For more inspiration try:
www.interactiveartschool.com – 10 free lessons for you to try.
www.learn-to-draw.com – text dense, a bit American but sound. You have to subscribe (about £10) to get the best out of it.
www.thesunneversets.talktalk.net/calligraphy/index.htm – an introduction to calligraphy.

Astrology and Prediction

Mostly these sites offer a huge range of predictions and not surprisingly adverts and all sorts of ways for you to part with your money. Some seem genuine enough in their aims though and we've listed the best of them.

www.astrology.com   UK
ALL ABOUT ASTROLOGY
Part of the iVillage site, here you can find celebrity horoscopes, and learn about the history and techniques of astrology as well

A

as get your own reading. See also **www.horoscope.co.uk** home of *Horoscope Magazine.*

www.live-astro.com   UK
RUSSELL GRANT
Now is your chance to buy a horoscope from a real celebrity. This site has been expanded to include dream interpretations, tarot and other astrological resources as well as the various horoscopes. There are articles by celebrities on the various aspects of the predictive arts.

www.easyscopes.com   US
ASTROLOGY SEARCH ENGINE
Here you can get as many different free horoscopes as you can handle, the site contains direct links to the daily, weekly, monthly and yearly horoscopes for each zodiac sign. You just have to select your zodiac sign and you are presented with a large list of horoscopes to choose from. It's amazing how different they all are for the same sign!

See also:
www.astro.com – a comprehensive offering with every major aspect of astrology covered and explained.
www.astroadvice.com – astrology, palmistry and err bingo …
www.freewillastrology.com – good-looking site with lots of predictions about future events, usual star signs and much more from astrologer Rob Brezsny.
www.tarot.com – tarot, astrology, numerology and the I Ching all on one site, to cater for all problems, obviously.
www.thezodiac.com – a fairly amateur site but it's clear and easy to use with lots of fun astrological things to do.

Auctions and Classified Ads

Before using these sites be sure that you are aware of the rules and regulations surrounding the bidding process, and what your rights are as a seller or purchaser. If they are not properly explained during the registration process, then use another site. They should also offer a returns policy as well as insurance cover. Whilst there are plenty of bargains available, not all the products on offer are cheaper than the high street or specialist vendor; it's very much a case of buyer beware. Having said that, once you're used to it, it can be fun and you can save a great deal of money.

A

www.ukauctionhelp.co.uk
UK

HELP WITH USING AUCTIONS
A site dedicated to giving the low-down on auctions. It's informative and genuinely helpful – shame about the design, which makes it difficult to use and it's cluttered with lots of adverts. See also **www.auctionseller411.com** which has lots of good advice.

www.eBay.co.uk
UK

THE WORLDS BIGGEST AUCTION
eBay is one of the internet's greatest success stories and is one of the most visited sites on the web. With millions of items listed, you are likely to find what you want, from cars to musical instruments. If it's sellable, it's sure to be here. There is a 24-hour support facility, loads of online help and automatic insurance cover on all items up to £250 using PayPal. Previous clients have reviewed many of those who have something to sell, so you can check up on their reliability too. Buying and selling on eBay can be addictive and many businesses now rely on it as a good source of income. It's also easy to fall into the trap of believing that if it's on eBay then it must automatically be cheap.

Here are some top tips for using eBay (and any auction site for that matter) ...

1. Don't rely solely on the 'good feedback' reports, they can be bought.
2. Do your research, check out the product you're buying on a price check website such as Froogle or, if it's a specialist product, look it up at the various forums and discussion groups, or on a search engine. Research what you are buying thoroughly.
3. Be cautious, know your rights. Does the seller actually trade as a trader or is it a private individual? It's a case of buyer beware. If you buy via the 'buy it now' button you should have the same rights as if you buy from any shop as long as they are a UK-based trader, but check!
4. Only bid on tangible things, not schemes or anything you can't physically hold.
5. Read the small print and especially the descriptions – they may not be all they appear to be.
6. If anyone asks you to do a deal outside eBay after advertising their products on the site, walk away.
7. Pay electronically, through PayPal or by credit card, you'll be better protected. Never use a seller's finance or escrow services.

A

8. If it seems too good to be true then it probably is.
9. Check out **www.scamdex.com** for the latest information on scams.

See also:
www.rummaging.org – an amusing blog run by someone who keeps track of all the unusual stuff that ends up on eBay, among other things.
www.startups.co.uk/YemqYqE.html – good advice on how to start a business using eBay.
www.stuffusell.co.uk – a company that will do all the work for you and sell your stuff on eBay for a commission.
www.vendio.com – a comprehensive service for eBay sellers.

www.huntforit.co.uk   UK
FREE SELLING, LOW COMMISSION
A good UK-based auction site, which is cheaper than many of its rivals, it has the added benefits of a system whereby you can bid by text message. The same system can be used to alert potential buyers when something that they have registered an interest in comes up for sale.

www.ebid.co.uk   UK
NO CHARGE TO LIST AN ITEM
Divided into auctions, wanted and swap sections. The auctions can easily be accessed and browsed; its strengths are in computing, electronics and music, although there has been a great increase in the number of collectibles available. There is a special section dedicated to raising money for charity if you want to donate the proceeds of your auction.

www.icollector.com   US
REDEFINING THE ART OF COLLECTING
An attractive site bringing together the wares of hundreds of auction houses and dealers, icollector is an ambitious project that works well. The emphasis is on art, antiques and collectibles. Be sure that the auction house you're dealing with ships outside the US. Another site worth checking out is **www.CQout.co.uk** – it had some 250,000 lots when we visited, a wide selection of categories and a nice design.

www.sothebys.com   UK/US
QUALITY ASSURED
Details of their auctions and information on what they do, plus

A

you can buy catalogues and search for items that may be
coming up for sale.

www.christies.com UK
FOR THOSE WITH DEEP WALLETS
Christies have a classic site with info on their programme of
auctions and on how to buy and sell through them, but you
can't carry out transactions from the site. The LotFinder service
searches their auctions for that special item – for a fee. There's
also a good specialist bookstore and lots of information on how
to buy and sell.

www.bid-up.tv UK
BID UP.TV
Linked to the TV channel of the same name, this site shows the
auctions they have on TV. You can bid online or call their
hotline.

www.ad-mart.co.uk UK
AWARD WINNING
Excellent design and ease of use makes this site stand out; there
are fourteen sections, all the usual suspects plus personal ads,
boating and pets. See also **www.nettrader.co.uk** which is also
really well designed and easy to use.

www.loot.com UK
FREE ADS ONLINE
A redesigned site with a clean look and access to thousands of
classified ads in 12 categories, it has an excellent search engine
and many bargains.

www.bumblebeeauctions.co.uk UK
UK POLICE PROPERTY DISPOSAL
Ever wondered what happened to all those umbrellas, bicycles
and paraphernalia that gets handed in and the Police just don't
know what to do with? Well if no one claims them, here's where
they get sold off.

Beauty

B

Beauty product retailers are popular on the Internet so we've featured a few of the best ones for advice, help and shopping including organic or natural products.

www.beautybible.com UK

THE BEAUTY BIBLE
They claim to have the largest product directory and it certainly looks very comprehensive. There's also good advice, product reviews, a newsletter and a selection of offers and no adverts.

http://avonshop.co.uk UK

AVON CALLING
A very good-looking, popular and easy-to-use site selling a wide range of cosmetics. They also sell health products and lingerie, and a range for men and kids.

www.lookfantastic.com UK

ALL A GIRL DESIRES
A well-designed retailer offering some really good discounts and a wide range of products, it also offers advice guides on how to use make-up, shampoo and conditioners – in fact, virtually everything a girl needs. Oh yes, there's a section for men too.

www.osmoz.com US

MUSICAL PERFUMES
An unusual fragrance store with an encyclopaedia devoted to fragrances, plus reviews and analysis of the latest products. You can use a quiz to find your perfect perfume and there are also links to help you in your search. See also **www.perfume4u.co.uk** who offer a huge choice, some good deals, plus guidance on which is the best perfume to suit you or whoever you're buying for.

www.halfpriceperfumes.co.uk UK

HALF PRICE …
Well, they are not all half price but there are certainly some fantastic discounts to be had. You have to take the delivery charge into consideration too although this is often free if you purchase over a certain amount, so you may want to compare prices with **www.supaperfume.com** who also offer great discounts and deliver for free.

For a Beautiful You

The Good Web Site Guide's Top 10s
of the Internet

1. **www.lookfantastic.com** – more hair and beauty products than you'll ever need
2. **www.beautyconsumer.com** – sort out your skin, nails and body
3. **www.netfit.co.uk** – tone that body
4. **www.allcures.com** – for all those pills and potions
5. **www.yoox.com** – the place to go for the top designers
6. **www.net-a-porter.com** – what's hot from the catwalk
7. **www.asos.com** – look like your favourite celebrity
8. **www.figleaves.com** – it's a one stop shop for underwear
9. **www.jewellers.net** – accessorise
10. **www.shoe-shop.com** – what's more important than shoes?

See also:
www.fragrancenet.com – US-based store who claims to be the world's largest discount fragrance store, but remember to check the international delivery charges.
www.sendmescent.com – who have some good offers and a no quibble returns policy, particularly good on men's smellies.

www.mankindonline.co.uk   UK
MALE GROOMING
Innovative and contemporary men's shaving, skincare and hair products. There's lots of help on understanding skin type, good advice and assistance in finding products for specific problems. There's a nice range of gifts both for him and for her, and they'll do the wrapping for you. See also **www.maleorder.co.uk** who offer a wide range of products on a well designed 'lifestyle' site.

See also:
http://uk.loccitaine.com – home of the popular L'Occitaine range.
www.allbeautyproducts.com – excellent site from the Allcures camp.
www.beautyexpert.co.uk – stocking a range of professional beauty products for home use.

B

www.benefitcosmetics.com – trendy cosmetics from the US, reasonable shipping costs means that it might be cheaper to buy here than in the UK.

www.buycosmeticsdirect.com – a wide range and lots of excellent offers, jewellery as well as cosmetics.

www.creativenailplace.com – specialist shop covering nail art and beauty.

www.escentual.com – good looking site with plenty of offers, free delivery and gift wrapping too.

www.magicmakeup.co.uk – great for special offers, also sell sunglasses and handbags

www.saveonmakeup.co.uk – certainly good savings to be had here.

www.skinstore.com – good-looking US site selling premium skincare products.

www.spacenk.co.uk – nicely designed store featuring their excellent cosmetics.

www.virgincosmetics.com – Virgin Vie online or arrange to have a party at home.

www.wellbeing.com – strong offering from Boots, easier to shop than at the real store!

Hair

www.ukhairdressers.com   UK

HAIR STYLES DATABASE
Some 1,000 styles illustrated including celebrity styles and virtual makeovers, also with advice and fortune telling.

See also:
www.folica.com – great US site on hair care.
www.hairstyling.co.uk – plenty of advice and products too.
www.hqhair.com – magazine-style online store including tips.
www.jazma.com – great advice on black hair care and on the products the celebrities use. Sells beauty products too.
www.salonproducts-direct.com – products the hairdressers use.
www.salonsales.co.uk – a wide selection of hair products to choose from.

Natural Beauty

www.thinknatural.com   UK

THINK NATURAL
A good looking site with a wide range of natural health products,

B

the beauty section has lots of choice, all products made from natural ingredients.

www.lizearle.com   UK
NATURALLY ACTIVE SKINCARE
They select the best natural ingredients, organic wherever possible, to create award-winning beauty products. If you've ever wondered what frankincense is, there is a helpful guide to ingredients and they've included a few fact sheets too.

www.nealsyardremedies.com   UK
NATURALLY COMMITTED
One of the country's most established and respected providers of natural beauty products. Covers all the body parts, for men, women and children, while also selling the ingredients for you to make your own cosmetics.

www.lush.co.uk   UK
SOAP WITHOUT THE SCENT
Lush offer a wide range of soaps and associated products from their site, it's easy to shop and if you like their soap but find the smell of the high street shops overpowering, then it's perfect.

See also:
www.bodyshop.co.uk – balancing the rights of the underprivileged with the demands of a commercial cosmetics company. Lot's of offers, much more commercial than it used to be.
www.gentlebodycare.co.uk – for organic hair dyes, baby care and skin products.
www.jerseylavender.co.uk – specialists in lavender based products.
www.luxuriousmoments.co.uk – a wide range of soaps and bath products to choose from as well as a face care range.
www.naturalsoap.co.uk – soap and related products made naturally.
www.whiteginger.co.uk – good range of organic products.

www.acne-advice.com   UK
HELP IS AT HAND
A web site dedicated to advice on treating acne naturally. There is loads of information on acne, its causes and what you can do about it.

Blogging

*Keeping a web log or 'blog' is one of the more recent and largest
Internet crazes; it allows you to effectively set up your own site cheaply
and to a high standard. Its commonest form is that of an online diary
covering a specific interest, usually with lots of links to related web
sites. Pages are added chronologically and there's usually a facility for
visitors to leave comments. Some blogs are very informative and
entertaining, they allow people to have their say or groups to exchange
ideas and information. Others are used as a means of keeping up-to-
date with friends and family. Here are some sites that can help you on
your way and give you all the advice you're likely to need. A good
jumping off point is Wikipedia's excellent information pages about
blogging and how to get started: **http://en.wikipedia.org/wiki/Blogging***

www.blogger.com   US
> THE MOST POPULAR
> The original blogger's site, owned by Google, it's easy to
> use and free, there are step-by-step instructions and plenty of
> support.

www.bloglines.com   US
> ONE STOP BLOG SHOP
> A search facility, subscription service and publishing tool all on
> one site. It's owned by ask.com so you can be sure it's a quality
> offering.

> *Other sites and software to get you started:*
> **http://b2evolution.net** – one of the best blog programs.
> **http://blogs.guardian.co.uk/index.html** – from the *Guardian*, a
> blog covering the latest in technology and the Internet, news,
> culture and games.
> **http://blogsearchengine.com** – search for content on blogs.
> **http://moblog.net** – blog services for people with mobiles,
> camera phones and PDAs.
> **http://quacktrack.com** – a massive database of blogs, some
> 135,000 in 1,500 categories. However, many seem to be in
> Chinese or languages other than English.
> **www.20six.co.uk** – here you can even send photos to your blog
> via a mobile, the site is nicely designed but only the minimum
> service is free to use.
> **www.blog.co.uk** – easy to use and it's British …
> **www.blogarama.com** – a directory of some 40,000 blogs.

For Sharing

The Good Web Site Guide's Top 10s
of the Internet

1. **www.flickr.com** – great for sharing photos
2. **www.mercora.com** – create your own radio station
3. **www.friendster.com** – organise your social life
4. **www.furl.net** – save web pages and share them with your friends
5. **www.wikipedia.org** – share your knowledge
6. **www.dudecheckthisout.com** – put together your own set of favourites and share them with your network
7. **www.friendsreunited.co.uk** – get in touch with old friends
8. **www.feedster.com** – get the latest news, make it relevant to you and your friends
9. **www.linkedin.com** – create a business network
10. **www.meetup.com** – share your interests with like minded people

www.livejournal.com – home of the very flexible *Live Journal* which can be used in a number of creative ways.

www.mydeo.com – share your videos with family and friends.

www.sixapart.com – offers two beautifully designed blog services: go to 'typepad' for an easy-to-use blog service with lots of options to help you get underway, or for the more advanced user, 'moveable type' which, if you take the time to learn how to use it, will offer some features for customising your blog.

www.vidblogs.com – video blogs are said to be the 'latest thing'. Although most are just rubbish or plain boring, there are some gems to be found if you search hard enough. Be aware that there's adult content here.

www.youtube.com – world famous, here you can post virtually any video recording, tasteful or tasteless.

www.technorati.com   US
EXPLORE THE BLOGOSPHERE
Here at what has become a pretty commercial affair, you can discover over 30 million blogs, explore by topic or just use the search engine.

Books

Books were the first products to be sold in volume over the Internet, and their success has meant that there are many online booksellers, all boasting about the speed of their service, what great discounts are available and how many titles they can get. In the main, the basic service is the same wherever you go, just pick the bookshop that suits you. It's an area that's crying out for some individuality and a bit of innovation.

Finding a Book

www.bookbrain.co.uk UK

BEST PRICES FOR BOOKS
All you do is type in the title of the book and BookBrain will search out the online store that is offering it the cheapest (including postage). You then click again to get taken to the store to buy the book – simple, however it did seem a little out of date when we last visited, hopefully it's not been allowed to lapse. See also **www.bookfinder4u.com** as a reliable alternative that covers some 130 bookstores.

See also:
http://amaztype.tha.jp – a book search engine with a difference: type in the title and the results appear in the form of book covers, which you click on to get more results. It's linked to Amazon and it's great fun.
www.book-shops.net – a directory of internet bookshops.

Booksellers

*To find a book shop near you go to **www.booksellers.org.uk** or if you're visiting abroad try **www.bookweb.org/bookstores**. For virtual booksellers see the list below.*

www.amazon.co.uk UK

 MORE THAN JUST A BOOKSTORE
Amazon is the leading online bookseller and most online stores have followed their formula of combining value with recommendation. Amazon has spent much on providing a wider offering than just books and now has sections for music, gifts, travel, games, software and DVD/video. It also offers an auction service, there's an excellent kids' section aimed at parents, and

you can download e-books to read on your PC or handheld computer. It also offers used goods for sale via third party retailers, which can offer great value for money (although watch out for high postage charges). For books, there are better prices elsewhere, although they have the odd very good offer and the 'search inside' facility is useful.

www.waterstones.co.uk   UK
ON THE HIGH STREET AND ONLINE
Waterstones have reversed their rather strange decision to hand over all their online business to Amazon and have launched their own site. It's very clearly laid-out and easy to find your way around, the look is functional rather than fun but some of the good features from the old Ottakar's site (which it supersedes), such as the ability to e-mail a bookseller for advice, still remain. Although there are some good discounts and offers to be had, there is better value to be had elsewhere and at time of writing postage was free for orders over £15.

Other online bookstores worth checking out ...
http://bookshop.blackwell.co.uk – Blackwells are best known for academic and professional books, their site offers much more, with the emphasis on recommendation and help finding the right book rather than value for money.
www.bn.com – Barnes and Noble's site boasts more books than any other online bookseller. It looks very similar to Amazon and has a good out-of-print and used book service; you can also buy software, prints and posters as well as magazines and music. Unusual features include a 'meet the writers' section and their excellent book club.
www.bookfellas.co.uk – good, unfussy design, easy to navigate and well categorised too, with the promise of good service including order tracking and cheap delivery charges.
www.booksdirect.co.uk – some great offers from the UK's leading book clubs, but you have to join to get them.
www.borders.com – defaults to Amazon.
www.countrybookshop.co.uk – one of the more enjoyable bookseller's sites, here you can get signed copies, magazine subscriptions, information on festivals as well as the usual crop of best sellers and discounts.
www.dymocks.com.au – excellent Australian bookstore.
www.powells.com – huge and impressive site which is well designed and relatively easy to use, Powells seems to occupy most of Portland in Oregon and for once the cost of shipping

B

isn't prohibitive for UK customers. A good place to go if you're looking for something unusual or rare.

www.samedaybooks.co.uk – not so many discounts but speedy delivery from High Street stores.

www.thebookpeople.co.uk – the online version of this popular mail-order bookseller offers the expected huge discounts and incentives. The range isn't huge but enough to satisfy most book lovers, they also sell more copies of this book than any other retailer!

www.thebookplace.com – if you like a bit more background and information on the books before you buy then it's worth coming here, especially as you get the usual discounts too.

Specialist Booksellers and Sites

The following sites specialise in one form or genre of book. For science fiction and fantasy see page 415.

www.compman.co.uk – computer manuals.

www.crimetime.co.uk – good overview of what's going on in the crime fiction world.

www.dancebooks.co.uk – if you need a book on dance, here's where to start.

www.dhmb.co.uk – a good site from a military history specialist.

www.firstbookshop.com – one of the few to offer book tokens, terrible site design though.

www.francisfrith.com – local books.

www.gamblingbooks.co.uk – excellent selection from the High Stakes bookshop.

www.greenbooks.co.uk – a specialist publisher on environmental issues.

www.historybookshop.com – how a specialist bookshop should be.

www.nhbs.com – the excellent Natural History Bookshop.

www.ospreypublishing.com – more military history.

www.poems.com – home of *Poetry Daily*.

www.poetrybooks.co.uk – the Poetry Book Society.

www.poetrybookshoponline.com – very good specialist poetry shop.

www.soccer-books.co.uk – features over 1400 books on football.

www.stanfords.co.uk – excellent site from the UK's leading travel and map retailers.

Second-hand Books and Book Finding

www.abebooks.co.uk   UK
ADVANCED BOOK EXCHANGE
A network of some 13,500 independent booksellers from
around the world claiming access to 80 million used, rare and
out-of-print books. Just use the excellent search engine to find
your book and they'll direct you to the nearest bookseller.

www.booklovers.co.uk   UK
QUALITY SECOND-HAND BOOKS
If you can't find the book you want, then this is worth a try.
There is an excellent search facility or you can leave them a
request. They will then give you a quote if you want to sell a
book or arrange a swap. There's also an events listing for book
fairs.

www.greenmetropolis.com   UK
GOING GREEN
An interesting take on the bookselling theme, here all (mainly
good condition second-hand) books are one price £3.75 with
free delivery and there's a donation towards planting a tree. You
can sell your books at this site too. Great idea.

See also:
www.bibliofind.com – a search engine from Amazon devoted to
second-hand and rare books.
www.bookfinder.com – a more detailed search facility than
Bibliofind and you can use it in French, German and Italian.
www.hp-bookfinders.co.uk – UK-based book-finding service
with an easy-to-use site.
www.shapero.com – a specialist in natural history and travel
related, second-hand books.

Audio Books

www.talkingbooks.co.uk   UK
THE TALKING BOOKSHOP
A talking website for these specialists in books on tape. They
have around 6,000 titles in stock and can quickly get another
20,000. They also stock CDs and a good selection of MP3
downloads. Search the site by author or reader, as well as by
title. There are some offers, but most stock is at full price.

B

See also:

www.audible.co.uk – many audio books and podcasts to download, the advantage here is that you can listen to them using iTunes; however, it's not cheap and there aren't many offers.

www.audiobooksforfree.com – only free for downloading files which they describe as of 'bearable quality', for anything better there is a charge, but it is still not expensive and files are available in a number of formats.

www.listen2books.co.uk – strong selection of audio books in various formats, some good prices too.

www.payperlisten.com – a pay-as-you-go service which saves a huge amount on the usual audio book formats.

www.isis-publishing.co.uk – who have thousands of unabridged audio books and more in the way of CDs.

E-books

These are no longer the preserve of a few classical and out-of-copyright authors. There is a wide range of contemporary literature available, albeit not at the free sites. Many of the sites are online libraries and provide a useful source of information for educational and reference purposes.

www.free-ebooks.net   US
E-BOOKS FOR FREE
A straightforward site devoted to making the most of free e-books with recommendations and the encouragement to produce your own e-book. Available in MP3 format for subscribers. See also **http://ebookdirectory.com**

www.sacred-texts.com   US

HISTORICAL AND ANCIENT TEXTS
An amazing collection of historic documents and books presented electronically, it covers mythology, religions, folklore and the occult. Many have been translated into English and are well presented with links to related sites and to Amazon.

www.gutenberg.org   US
PROJECT GUTENBERG
This is one of the most famous Internet projects ever and one of the first web sites to post free e-books. There are over 20,000 listed. You can't do it justice in a small review, suffice to say it's well worth a visit for any book lover. If you're hooked on it, then there is the chance to become a volunteer proof-reader too.

See also:

http://en.wikipedia.org/wiki/Sony_Reader – learn about the Sony Reader and how it will change the way we read and buy books.

http://labs.adobe.com/technologies/digitaleditions/library – lots available but you have to have the Adobe reader to access them.

http://onlinebooks.library.upenn.edu – over 20,000 books to download with a huge bias towards American titles; it's especially strong on history.

www.bartleby.com/ebook – lots of classics and other free books to choose from. Also provides access to the encyclopaedia as well as American dictionaries and thesauruses.

www.fictionwise.com – a massive range of e-books from non-fiction to fiction and they seem to cover all the formats too.

www.manybooks.net – a good selection of free e-books mainly taken from Project Gutenberg.

www.questia.com – claiming to be the world's biggest online library with over 60,000 books plus one million journals and other articles, covering thousands of research topics. You have to subscribe, though some content is free.

Literature and Authors

www.wordswithoutborders.org   US
INTERNATIONAL LITERATURE

An attractive e-zine devoted to world literature with reviews, recommendations and articles on books and writers. It's well categorised, interesting and you're bound to find something new.

http://classics.mit.edu   US
THE CLASSICS ONLINE

A superb resource offering over 440 free books to print or download, there's also a search facility and help with studying. If that's not enough, try **http://etext.lib.virginia.edu** with 1,800 publicly-available e-books including classic British and American fiction, major authors, children's literature, American history, Shakespeare, African-American documents, the Bible.

www.william-shakespeare.info   US
COMPLETE WORKS

This is a straightforward site featuring historical and biographical details plus a dictionary explaining the language of the time. Annoying adverts.

B

See also:

www.artsfestivals.co.uk – for a literature festival near you.

www.bronte.org.uk – home of the Parsonage Museum in Haworth with information about the place and an overview of the Brontes and their lives.

www.ciconline.org/bdp1 – a new look at Shakespeare, excellent site design.

www.dickensmuseum.com – home of the Dickens Museum in London with details about what you can see and links.

www.fantasticfiction.com – biographies of over 10,000 authors on over 200,000 books … phew.

www.fantasticsherlockholmes.com – buy illustrations, download the stories, good for links too.

www.fidnet.com/~dap1955/dickens – a superb resource dedicated to Dickens: a real labour of love.

www.janeausten.co.uk – the Jane Austen Centre in Bath with a good online magazine offering information on everything from fashion to biographical details.

www.hardysociety.org – the Thomas Hardy Society with good contextual links.

www.lang.nagoya-u.ac.jp/~matsuoka/Bronte.html – all you need to know about the Bronte sisters and more.

www.meettheauthor.com – here you can download video clips of authors talking about their work.

www.pemberley.com – a pretty obsessive site devoted to everything Jane Austen with discussion groups too.

www.sherlock-holmes.org.uk – home of the Sherlock Holmes Society of London.

www.yale.edu/hardysoc – award-winning site on Thomas Hardy.

Reading Groups

www.bookgroup.info   UK

READING GROUP GUIDE

An attractive and informative site on how to run a book group and choose titles, with an archive of titles and how they've rated them. There's also a forum, and a directory in the process of being built.

See also:

http://readers.penguin.co.uk – run by Penguin books. You can get discounts for your group and use the directory, but you have to register first.

www.complete-review.com – reviews of over 1,600 books plus news, links and a reader's rating too.

www.readinggroupguides.com – an American site offering information and guidance on books and how to run a reading group.

www.readinggroups.co.uk – a neat site run by publisher HarperCollins with news, advice and competitions.

www.thereadinggrouponline.co.uk – a good bookshop and forum aimed at reading groups, run by The Book People.

Children's Books

www.cool-reads.co.uk   UK

CHILDREN'S BOOK REVIEWS
Books for 10- to 15-year-olds, reviewed by 10- to 15-year-olds. An outstanding site both for its design and for its content. The books are well categorised and reviewed using a star rating system. If you're stuck for something to read, then a trip here is well worthwhile. There are also games, quizzes and chat.

www.achuka.co.uk   UK
CHILDREN'S BOOKS
Achuka are specialists in children's books and offer a comprehensive listing of what's available. There's plenty of information on the latest news and awards as well as reviews, author interviews, a chat section and links to booksellers. For shopping you are directed to Amazon.

www.wordpool.co.uk   UK
FOR PARENTS, TEACHERS AND WRITERS
A very useful resource devoted to children's books with lots of advice and recommendations. See also their sister site **www.ukchildrensbooks.co.uk** which is a list of links to sites listed by author, illustrator, publisher and a miscellaneous section.

www.sevenstories.org.uk   UK
SEND A STORY
Sevenstories is a centre for children's books and a museum celebrating the rich and diverse world of British children's books. There is a facility for children to write and illustrate a story online and send it to a friend or an online gallery. Online bookshop still under development.

B

Other children's book sites:

http://childrensbooks.about.com – excellent as ever from About.com with reviews, guidance and more …

www.booktrusted.co.uk – information for parents and professionals on all aspects of children's books from the Book Trust.

www.carolhurst.com – good for links, great for book reviews, too many adverts.

www.childrensbookshop.com – very traditional site from a shop based in Hay on Wye.

www.myhomelibrary – Anne Fine encouraging children to build a library of their own (with the aid of charity shops), loads of bookplates to download.

www.redhouse.co.uk – a good bright and breezy site devoted to children's books with lots of discounts and recommendations.

www.ucalgary.ca/~dkbrown/ – home of the excellent Children's Literature Web Guide.

www.worldbookday.com – find out about this great event that happens every March.

Resources for Writers

www.writersservices.com   UK

THE WEBSITE FOR WRITERS

A slightly messy site but compensates by having over 1,700 pages of help, advice and information for writers updated weekly. It's certainly worth a visit if you are thinking of pouring your heart out in print. See also **www.writewords.org.uk** which is a useful community resource for writers.

www.lulu.com   US

SELF PUBLISHING THE EASY WAY

Lulu enables you to take advantage of the latest printing technology to produce books in very small numbers, so dust off that manuscript! They will even host your work and sell it too and you get royalties. It's a relatively cheap and pain-free way to get published. See also **www.lightningsource.com**, **www.selfpublishing.co.uk** and **www.authorhouse.com** (highly recommended by a friend) who all have their various approaches.

See also:

www.cremedelacrime.com – specialist crime publisher who wants to encourage new talent.

www.thecwa.co.uk – home of the Crime Writers Association.
www.thenewwriter.com – magazine for writers.
www.theromancereader.com – lots of romantic reviews and links.
www.openwriting.com – an open writing web magazine for writers.

Best Publisher's Websites

www.bloomsbury.com – an attractive site, home of Harry Potter, Scott's Miscellany and more.
www.dk.com – excellent site from one of the leading reference publishers, some good offers too.
www.faber.co.uk – an interesting site from the most literary of publishers.
www.harpercollins.co.uk – now a word from our sponsors – a wide-ranging site from the publishers of this book with sections on Tolkien and plenty of celebrities as well as fiction and reference.
www.madaboutbooks.co.uk – a cool site from Hodder Headline.
www.penguin.co.uk – a bright and breezy site from Penguin with plenty to see, information on author events and readers' groups too.
www.randomhouse.co.uk – nice design from one of the biggest publishers, particularly good kids' section.
www.thefridayproject.co.uk – an attempt to turn some of the most creative websites into books.
www.virago.co.uk – an interactive and imaginative site from this publisher of women's literature.

Other book-related sites worth checking out …

www.bookaid.org   UK
BOOKS FOR CHARITY
A charity dedicated to giving unwanted books to places where books are scarce and needed. Find out about their activities and how you can get involved.

www.bookcrossing.com   UK
RELEASE A BOOK
1. Read your book.
2. Say what you think about the book on the site with a reference number.
3. Release the book, give it to a friend or leave it somewhere.

B

You can then get e-mails from anyone who reads the book. Members have released over 2.6 million books so far, so the odds on finding one are increasing daily.

Broadband

As access to ADSL or broadband becomes common, more and more sites are cropping up. Here are some useful sites where you can start your broadband experience. For information on downloading music, TV or movies go to the relevant section in the book, where you'll find more information.

www.thinkbroadband.com   UK

ALL YOU NEED TO KNOW

A good place to start, here you'll find advice and reviews all dedicated to help you make the most out of your broadband experience. See also **www.broadband-help.com** which is just as informative albeit from a less attractive site.

www.broadbandchecker.co.uk   UK

BROADBAND AVAILABILITY

A neat and easy-to-use site; you just type in your postcode and phone number and the site will tell you whether broadband is available in your area. You can also compare providers, prices too.

www.jonnybroadband.com   UK

BROADBAND SEARCH

Entertaining and a bit messy, it's a massive resource and a very useful guide to what's available on Broadband once you get your head around it. See also **www.razav.com** which is cleaner and great for links but less fun.

www.broadbandweek.com   UK

ALL THE LATEST DEVELOPMENTS

Keep abreast of all the latest technology and increasing download speeds at this business-like site.

www.btopenworld.com   UK

BRITISH TELECOM

Here you can establish whether you can get access to broadband and, if not, they'll tell you more or less when it will be coming your way. There are details of the various BT packages, other suppliers and also information for business users too.

Other sites worth checking out are:
www.broadband4britain.co.uk – information from this broadband pressure group.
www.ispreview.co.uk/broadband.shtml – informative pages from the excellent *ISP Review*.
www.theregister.co.uk – the latest telecom and broadband news, if you can find it …

Browsers

We're often asked about alternatives to Internet Explorer. Here are the best:

www.caminobrowser.org – another Mozilla product, here's an alternative to Apple's Safari browser.
www.mozilla.org – home to Firefox, certainly one of the fastest browsers and it works on all operating systems. It's easy to use and set up too.
www.netscape.com – the earliest real alternative to IE, it offers a huge amount of content and plenty of extra features.
www.opera.com – another claimant for the fastest browser, it's certainly flexible and easy on the eye and has lots of features. There is a mobile version too.

Business

Here are a few essential and helpful business sites; see also the finance section on page 150 for share dealing and other related sites. Be aware that many official-looking sites offering advice are often companies out to make a profit or are part of a larger organisation, so may not be impartial.

www.economist.com   UK

THE *ECONOMIST* MAGAZINE
The airports' best-selling magazine goes online with a wide-ranging site that covers business and politics world-wide. You can get access to the archive and also their excellent country surveys. If you're in business, you need this in your 'favourites' box.

See also:

www.better-business.co.uk – a helpful site from this magazine including tips on starting up and even what to do when things get boring.

www.businessweek.com – offering a wide range of business news and information.

www.managementtoday.co.uk – one of the leading business magazines.

www.businesslink.gov.uk   UK

THE NATIONAL BUSINESS ADVICE SERVICE

An outstanding government-run site which has a comprehensive set of helpful guides and links, backed up by a hotline. It has to be the first port of call for any small business needing advice or help.

See also:

www.business.com – a US-oriented business search engine.

www.dti.gov.uk – here you'll find a great deal of wide-ranging information from the Dept of Trade and Industry

www.sbs.gov.uk – the UK government's small-business service.

www.startinbusiness.co.uk   UK

AN ONLINE BUSINESS STARTER KIT

An excellent portal site on all things to do with business including a good guide to help you start a business. There are plenty of links plus listings of businesses for sale, property, services and potential opportunities.

www.startups.co.uk   UK

BUILD A BETTER BUSINESS

An excellent and comprehensive site designed to help businesses start up and get going. It has basic advice on finances and covers aspects like planning, tax, employment and insurance.

See also:

www.advertopedia.com – all you need to know about advertising.

www.bankexperts.co.uk – a good place to start if you need financial advice for your business.

www.bawe-uk.org – home of the British Association of Women Entrepreneurs.

www.bized.ac.uk – aimed at students and teachers but a great resource for business people too.

www.business-ethics.com – believe it or not, a magazine devoted to the finer arts of corporate responsibility.
www.bvca.co.uk – the public face of venture capitalism.
www.ecademy.com – a messy business networking and community site.
www.ecourier.co.uk – an online courier management system.
www.fsb.org.uk – home of the Federation of Small Businesses.
www.iba.org.uk – contact a qualified business adviser.
www.linkedin.com – create your own business network.
www.payontime.co.uk – excellent advice on how to manage payment.
www.plaxo.com – a service devised to help you keep your business contacts up to date.
www.uktradeinfo.com – from HM Customs and very useful if you are going to trade overseas.
www.whichfranchise.com – a slightly messy site that offers the information you need on all the available franchises in the UK, and how to go about getting one.

www.companies-house.gov.uk   UK
COMPANY REGISTRATION
A hugely useful site, for information on setting up a company, providing all of the forms you need (all downloadable). There is also access to information and guidance on most aspects of business and the regulations surrounding it. The site also has the facility to research companies: here you can check-up on whether companies really exist or not, plus download their last set of accounts for a small fee.

www.hoovers.com   UK
COMPANY RESEARCH
Get basic information on any UK and US company plus related links and advice; a very useful research tool. See also **www.carolworld.com** or Company Annual Reports Online; a useful free service.

www.sage.co.uk   UK
BUSINESS SOFTWARE
If you need accounting software to solve virtually any sort of problem or provide a new service, you should find it here. Sage has a good reputation for helping small businesses. See also **www.myob.com** who offer similar products.

Cars

Whether you want to buy a car, check out your insurance or even arrange a service, it can all be done on the Internet. If you want to hire a car see page 517, while for information on road travel go to page 560.

Motoring Organisations, Campaigning Sites and Government Agencies

www.theaa.co.uk
UK

THE AA

A comprehensive motoring site with a route planner (with speedtrap information), new and used car info, travel information, insurance quotes, shop and a car data checking facility.

www.rac.co.uk
UK

RAC

This site has a very good route planner and traffic news service. There's also information about buying a car, getting the best finance and insurance deals, and a shop.

www.greenflag.co.uk
UK

GREEN FLAG

A high quality route planner and car buying advice all packaged on a nice-looking and very green site; there's a particularly good section on European travel and motoring advice. See also **www.internationalbreakdown.com** which offers a wide range of cover across the UK and Europe.

www.dvla.gov.uk
UK

DRIVER AND VEHICLE LICENSING AGENCY

Excellent for the official line in motoring; the driver's section has details on penalty points, licence changes and medical issues. The vehicles section goes through all related forms and there's also a 'What's New' page. It's clearly and concisely written throughout and information is easy to find but be warned, some pages talk to you. See also **www.direct.gov.uk/en/ Motoring/index.htm** where you can apply for your tax disc online, book theory and practice tests and find out about vehicle recalls. There are also sections on MOTs, crime,

Petrolheads

The Good Web Site Guide's Top 10s
of the Internet

1. **www.autoindex.org** – home of the highly detailed Global Auto Index
2. **www.autoexpress.co.uk** – excellent online mag …
3. **www.autocarmag.com** – … and another
4. **www.parkers.co.uk** – find out how much your car is worth.
5. **www.conceptcar.co.uk** – the latest in car design
6. **www.speed-trap.co.uk** – the site is a mess, but at least you'll know where they are
7. **www.bbc.co.uk/topgear** – the site of the popular show
8. **www.modify.co.uk** – bored with your car, then modify!
9. **www.classicmotor.co.uk** – the first place to go for classic motoring
10. **www.uglycars.co.uk** – laugh at the worst

buying and selling cars and information for learner drivers.

www.rmif.co.uk   UK
RETAIL MOTOR INDUSTRY FEDERATION
A rich source of information covering all aspects of buying and selling cars for both industry and consumers alike. It's great as a starting place if you want to find out about legislation and the latest news, it also has an excellent links section.

www.smmt.co.uk   UK
SOCIETY OF MOTOR MANUFACTURERS & TRADERS
The SMMT support the British motor industry by campaigning and informing the trade and public alike. Here you can get information on topics like the motor show, the tax regime, the latest industry standards, as well as links to other industry sites.

www.abd.org.uk   UK
CAMPAIGNING FOR THE DRIVER
The Association of British Drivers aims to be the lobbying voice of beleaguered drivers in the UK. Here you can find out about

their campaigns against road user charging, speed limits, the environment and the road infrastructure.

www.rospa.co.uk UK

 ROYAL SOCIETY FOR THE PREVENTION OF ACCIDENTS
An excellent site from ROSPA with loads of information about road safety with fact sheets available on most issues and problems that affect every driver and pedestrian. See also **www.cic.cranfield.ac.uk** where all the crash testing goes on.

www.roadpeace.org UK

SUPPORT FOR CRASH VICTIMS
RoadPeace, the UK's national charity dedicated to supporting bereaved and injured road crash victims and the only national helpline for road victims – 0845 4500 355. Join a campaign or use the extensive links section. Salutary stuff.

www.euroncap.com

HOW SAFE IS YOUR CAR?
Euroncap is responsible for testing the safety of cars sold in Europe. Results are posted for each car on its safety performance in a crash and how 'friendly' it is if you happen to hit a pedestrian.

www.secureyourmotor.gov.uk UK

SECURITY TIPS FOR MOTORISTS
Pretty straightforward site from the Home Office detailing the best steps to guard against your car, bike or truck being stolen. You find out which models of car and bike are most at risk too.

www.carplus.org.uk UK

RIDE SHARING
Promoting responsible car use; join a car club, help the environment and aid congestion by sharing your journey with others; plus info on car sharing and alternative fuels. See also **www.citycarclub.co.uk** and also **www.mystreetcar.co.uk**, plus **www.carshare.com** which is a directory site for regional schemes.

www.cclondon.com UK

LONDON CONGESTION CHARGES
All you need to know about the congestion charge and how to pay it.

www.speed-trap.co.uk   UK
  THE SPEED TRAP BIBLE
  While not condoning speeding, this site gives the low-down on
  speed traps, the law and links to police forces. There's even data
  on the types of camera used and advice on dealing with the
  courts and police. However, they are sponsored by a speed trap
  detector company. See also **www.speedcamerasuk.com**

www.parkingticket.co.uk   UK
  PARKING PROBLEMS
  This site gives details regarding parking and free advice on how
  to challenge a parking ticket that you feel has been issued
  unfairly.

Cheaper and Greener Fuels

www.est.org.uk/fleet   UK

  CONVERTING TO CLEANER FUELS
  A well-put-together and informative site aimed at encouraging
  drivers to shift to cleaner fuels such as LPG. You can find out
  how to convert your car, where the fuel stations are and the
  latest government information such as grants and future
  proposals.

www.spongecars.com   UK

  LPG CONVERSIONS
  Excellent overview and information site covering all aspects of
  converting a car to LPG, an explanation of what it is, how to get
  a conversion quote and the latest news.

  See also:
  www.bath.ac.uk/~en2bwp/gaspower.htm – learn about gas-
  powered cars.
  www.cbev.org – the Campaign for Battery Vehicles has a very
  informative site.
  www.evuk.co.uk – not just milk floats and golf carts, it's serious
  stuff, the electric car business.
  www.evworld.com – environmentally friendly vehicles need not
  be boring.
  www.goingreen.co.uk – home of the G Whiz electric car.
  www.lpga.co.uk – information from the Liquid Petroleum Gas
  Association.
  www.toyota.co.uk/prius – home of the successful hybrid
  electrical petrol car.

Car Information and Buying Guides

www.globalautoindex.org   US

WORLD CAR CATALOGUE
An amazing directory of the world's car makers illustrated using
thousands of pictures. There is detailed information on each
manufacturer and what they produce. You can search by maker,
country, and category or body style.

www.carsurvey.org   UK

CAR REVIEWS BY THEIR OWNERS
Don't let the basic design fool you; this is an impressive
collection of reviews on hundreds of cars, by those most
important people – their owners. It's easily searchable and
genuinely useful if you're looking for unbiased opinion.

www.parkers.co.uk   UK

REDUCING THE GAMBLE
The premier buying guide with a clear, readable site, this covers
all the information you'll need to select the right car for you.
However, these days you have to register and pay to get the
more detailed information. See also **www.glass.co.uk** which
offers similar information but with a valuing system which
involves typing in your number plate; there is a charge.

www.jdpower.com/autos   US

J.D.POWER RELIABILITY
It's only geared to the US market but some models are the same
and you can get a great deal of safety and reliability information
here.

Magazine and E-zine Sites

www.autoexpress.co.uk   UK

THE BEST MOTORING NEWS AND INFORMATION
Massive database on cars, with motoring news and features on
the latest models, you can check prices too. It also has classified
ads and a great set of links. You have to register to get access to
most of the information; lots of advertising makes the site a bit
annoying to use.

www.whatcar.co.uk   UK

WHAT CAR? MAGAZINE
A neatly packaged, one-stop shop for cars with reviews and data

on every car, there's a 'cars for sale' section and an easy-to-use search facility.

www.autocarmag.com UK

AUTOCAR MAGAZINE
A fine and well designed site from this popular weekly with plenty of interactive features including videos and even a blogging service; there is news, reviews, advice and shopping too.

www.carnet.co.uk UK

ONLINE CAR MAGAZINE
Car Net is a well-designed and fun site with the latest news and new car reviews as well as feature micro-sites and links to deals on cars and insurance, statistics (on over 6,000 cars) and classifieds. You can also visit the specialist forums and have a go at the trivia quizzes.

www.carkeys.co.uk UK

INFORMATION SERVICE STATION
A wide-ranging and entertaining magazine-style site with lots of data on current and new models, as well as launch reviews and motoring news.

www.pistonheads.com UK

SPEED MATTERS
Pistonheads is a British site dedicated to the faster side of motoring and is great for reviews of the latest cars and chat. It's passionate and very informative.

www.womanmotorist.com US

MOTORING ISN'T JUST FOR MEN
A well-laid-out and interesting American magazine site that dispels the myth that motoring is just for men. Lots of advice, buying information, a glossary and car reviews.

TV Tie-in Sites

www.topgear.com UK

TOP GEAR
A site to go along with the TV series, it has everything you'd expect along with features on new and used cars, competitions, classifieds and a shop. For a site designed to give motoring information go to **www.bbc.co.uk/motoring/ontheroad/**

C

www.channel4.com/4car   UK
DRIVEN
News, sport, reviews, advice, chat and games – it's all here, and
you can find out what's been and is being featured on their main
motoring programmes.

Traders and Car Finding Services

www.autobytel.co.uk   US/UK
WORLD'S LEADING CAR BUYING SERVICE
The easy way to buy a car online, just select the model you want
then follow the online instructions. Good information on used
and nearly new cars and will get quotes from local dealers. All
cars featured have detailed descriptions and photos. There's also
financial information and aftercare service.

www.jamjar.com   UK
DIRECT LINE
Jam Jar is owned by Direct Line Insurance and they want to
make it work well. The design is OK, and if you persevere there
are some fantastic offers. They offer personal leasing and
insurance and encourage you to call them at every opportunity!

For more car buying information and cars for sale try:
http://cars.kelkoo.co.uk – the car price checking pages at Kelkoo.
http://carsguide.news.com.au – all you need to know about
cars down under.
http://uk.cars.yahoo.com – the excellent Yahoo has a used car
search engine, car comparison facility and directory.
www.autolocate.co.uk – great for links, good new car guide and
review section, also good for used cars.
www.autopoint.ie – Ireland's leading online car retailer and
auction house.
www.autoseek.co.uk – thousands of cars for sale, great for links.
www.autotrader.co.uk – claiming to be Britain's biggest car
showroom with over 300,000 listed. Nice, clear design.
www.broadspeed.com – car import specialists with a nicely
designed and fast site.
www.carseller.co.uk – free advertising if selling and good links.
www.car-supermarkets.com – a useful list of the UK's car
supermarkets with lots of information and how to find them.
www.cartalk.com – a good US magazine site that is something
of a cult stateside. It's worth following the links and listening to
the radio show.

www.drive.com.au – high quality offering from Australia.
www.easyvan.com – excellent if you just want to hire a van.
www.fish4cars.co.uk – over 150,000 cars on their database, plus hundreds of other vehicles. Comprehensive.
www.milweb.net – the place to go to buy a military vehicle.
www.new-car-net.co.uk – informative and well-illustrated car review site.
www.oneswoop.com – from Norwich Union, not the site it was.
www.showroom4cars.com – bright, brash and fast, with lots of deals.
www.thevanwebsite.co.uk – vans and more vans.
www.topmarques.co.uk – luxury vehicles only, part of Autotrader.
www.vanbuyer.com – vans and more vans of all shapes and sizes.

Car Auctions

www.british-car-auctions.co.uk   UK
CAR REMARKETING
The leading car auction company uses its site to inform rather than sell online, there are catalogues of upcoming auctions plus information on buying and selling.

Online auction sites

These seem much the same so find the one that suits you, if you are happy buying a car in this way:

http://motors.ebay.co.uk – the motor pages from the popular auction site with a vast array of cars, bikes and accessories to choose from.
www.autobyauction.co.uk – one of the easier sites to use but it's amazing how few cars are illustrated with photos.
www.autorola.co.uk – a simple way to sell your car to some 1,000 dealers.
www.raw2k.co.uk – buy a wreck, do it up or take the parts.

www.hpicheck.com   UK
 DON'T BE RIPPED OFF ...
Before you buy a second-hand car it's wise to pay out £39.95 for an HPI check which will tell you about what mileage the car should have, whether it's been in an accident or damaged and also if there's any outstanding finance against it. See also

www.ukstolencars.co.uk, a simple search of the UK stolen cars database offering helpful information and advice.

Disabled Motorists

www.mobilise.info   UK

DISABLED DRIVERS MOTOR CLUB
A campaigning site from the DDMC who are devoted to improving the lot of disabled motorists. It has lots of useful information and you can find out about and support their latest campaigns.

www.motability.co.uk   UK

GET MOBILE
A scheme for helping disabled people get mobile by contract hiring a car, the site is very clear and easy to use too.

See also:
http://www.direct.gov.uk/en/DisabledPeople/index.htm – lots of information on transport schemes and adapting cars.
www.aixam-cars.co.uk – a leading supplier of quadricycles and adapted cars.
www.dft.gov.uk – the Department for Transport; follow links for disabled people.
www.motability.royalsun.co.uk/fullsite/index.html – a motability scheme from an insurance company.

Car Registrations

www.dvla-som.co.uk   UK

CHERISHED AND PERSONALISED NUMBERS
Here's the first port of call if you want that special number plate. They sell by auction but there's plenty of help and you search for un-issued, select registrations in both new and old styles, you can even view your plate on a car. Order over the phone using their hotline.

For more sites offering car registrations try:
www.carreg.co.uk
www.newreg.co.uk
www.northumbriannumbers.com
www.regtransfers.co.uk

Insurance and warranties

*Most of the general finance sites (page 151) and motoring
organisations (page 62) will offer links to insurance companies, but
these are worth a try.*

www.easycover.com   UK
> CAR INSURANCE
> Quotes from a large number of insurance suppliers, you just fill
> in the form, and they get back to you with a quote. See also
> **www.quotelinedirect.co.uk** who have an excellent website and
> **www.cheapest-motor-insurance.co.uk** who don't but you may
> find a good deal.

www.warrantyguide.co.uk   UK
> WHICH WARRANTY?
> A guide from New Car Net that guides you through the pitfalls of
> buying a warranty.

www.warrantydirect.co.uk   UK
> WARRANTIES
> One of the leading warranty suppliers has a site that offers a
> wide range of options, and it's easy to use – don't forget to
> haggle though. See also **www.warrantywise.co.uk**

Looking After and Repairing Your Car

www.ukmot.com   UK

> M.O.T.
> Find your nearest M.O.T. test centre, get facts about the test and
> what's actually supposed to be checked, there's also a reminder
> service. You can also run an HPI check from the site and find
> out about the foibles of specific models.

www.haynes.co.uk   UK
> HAYNES MANUALS
> Unfortunately they've stopped the download service, so now you
> have to buy the books – there's 2,500 available so there should
> be one for you.

www.partsgateway.co.uk   UK
> FIND THE PART YOU NEED
> An excellent place to go if you want to find a particular part for
> your car but don't want to pay dealer prices. If you don't know

what it's called then you can upload a digital photo and they'll use that to identify exactly what you want.

See also these other sites, all offer a way to get cheaper car and bike parts ...
www.247spares.co.uk
www.atozmotorspares.co.uk
www.breakeryard.com
www.carparts-direct.co.uk
www.eurocarparts.co.uk

Car Accessories and Kits

www.halfords.com   UK
DRIVING DOWN PRICES
A fairly wide range of products for your car and bike at good prices and sold from a very good site, there's advice and a store locator too.

www.modify.co.uk   UK
COMPREHENSIVE LISTING SERVICE
Outstanding source for information on those companies that can help you improve your car. There's a directory of specialists – everything from tuners to insurance, articles on how to modify your motor and lastly statistics on virtually every modern car.

www.autofashion.co.uk   UK
ACCESSORISE YOUR CAR
An entertaining site where you can buy body kits and accessories for many makes of car, including custom made. Turn the sound off unless you want it loud ...

See also:
www.autostore.co.uk – specialists in car storage solutions, slow site though.
www.caralarms.org – every type of car alarm and security device.
www.gttowing.co.uk – for tow bars, roof racks and trailers, good site.
www.motech.uk.com – specialists in performance enhancement.
www.roofbox.co.uk – roof boxes and most other storage solutions.
www.saveanddrive.co.uk – for roof boxes, cycle carriers and radar detectors.

www.caraudiocentre.com   UK
IN CAR AUDIO SYSTEMS
Here you can get loads of advice and offers on a wide range of
stereos with a price promise and low delivery costs. See also
www.toade.com who have a highly interactive site and can also
supply security, multi-media and navigation equipment on top of
audio.

www.mytyres.co.uk   UK
TYRES
A site where you can save money buying tyres for your car. It
pays to know what you want but the prices appear competitive
and they'll find a fitter for you too.

See also:
www.kwikfit.co.uk – very good site with mobile fitting service,
although you can get cheaper deals by visiting them.
www.tyresafety.co.uk – home of the Tyre Industry Council with
advice on safety.
www.tyres-online.co.uk – basic web site but some good prices.

Specialist Car Sites

www.classicmotor.co.uk   UK

FOR CLASSIC CARS
By far the best classic car site. Design-wise it's a jumble (it's
better to use the no frames version), but it's comprehensive,
including clubs, classifieds and books; here you can buy
anything from a car to a headlight bulb.

www.motorbase.com   UK
FOR THE CAR ENTHUSIAST
A very comprehensive site with plenty of information, links, a
forum and a chance to buy everything from cars, tools, books
and models.

See also:
www.classic-car-directory.com – a well-categorised links site.
www.hireaclassiccar.com – classic car hire specialist.
www.kitcarnet.com – from *Kit Car* magazine, great for links.
www.oldclassiccar.co.uk – amazing amount of information, plus
advice and links, even a section of future classics.
www.vintage-car-world.com – a German owned site offering
news, event information and classifieds.

C

www.britishmm.co.uk UK
HISTORY OF BRITISH CARS TO 1960
An amateur site with a good make-by-make history of the British
car industry, it includes a glossary and information on tax and
other historical references.

www.conceptcar.co.uk UK
AUTOMOTIVE DESIGN
A really interesting, comprehensive and well-laid-out site
devoted to car design and new concepts, it's great for links and
you can tell that it's used by the industry itself.

www.uglycars.co.uk UK
UGLY CARS
There's been a spate of books published about the worst cars
sold in the UK and this site goes along with that trend and our
fascination with all things that are rubbish. Here you can relish
some of the worst excuses for car design and even suggest some
candidates to be added.

Learning to Drive

www.learners.co.uk UK
LEARNER'S DIRECTORY
The point of this site is to help you find the right driving school.
Just type in your postcode and the schools will be listed along
with helpful additional information such as whether they have a
female instructor or whether they train for motorway driving.
There is plenty of supplementary information on things like
theory tests and how to buy a car.

www.2pass.co.uk UK
 THEORY AND PRACTICAL TESTS
A learner driver's dream, this site helps with your tests in giving
advice, mock exams plus other interesting snippets of
information such as why the British drive on the left. There are
also articles on driving abroad, on motorbikes and driving
automatics. There's also help finding insurance, plenty of fun
with top stories, quizzes and RSS feeds.

www.driving-tests.co.uk UK
THE DSA
Get the official line from the Driving Standards Agency where
you can now book both the theory and practical test online, get

advice for learners and instructors and learn about government schemes to promote better driving. For the Highway Code faithfully reproduced as a website and more theory tests go to **www.highwaycode.gov.uk**

See also:
www.bsm.co.uk – one of the UK's biggest driving schools.
www.iam.org.uk – home of the Institute of Advanced Motorists.

Celebrities

Find your favourite celebrities and their web sites using these sites.
A word of caution though – there are many celebrity search engines available on the web and while it's easy to find your favourite, it's also very easy to unwittingly access adult-orientated material through them.

www.celebhoo.com   US
FOR EVERYTHING CELEBRITY
A very good fan site directory plus information, birthdays, chat and gossip. At Links for Kids you'll find a selection of sites that have been checked for safety, so hopefully there will be no nasty surprises – **www.links4kids.co.uk/celebrities.htm**

www.thespiannet.com   UK
ACTORS AND ACTRESSES
Lots of actors and actresses listed with links and details including e-mail addresses. It's also a good resource for aspiring thespians.

www.celebrityemail.com   US
E-MAIL THE STARS
E-mail addresses to over 22,000 of the world's most famous people. It's quite biased towards Americans but give it a try anyway, you might get a reply.

www.hellomagazine.com   UK
THE WORLD IN PICTURES
Hello magazine's web site features pictures and articles from current and previous issues with loads of celebrities. You can't search by celebrity but you can have fun trawling through the pictures.

Gossip

The Good Web Site Guide's Top 10s
of the Internet

1. **www.popbitch.com** – the first stop for conjecture
2. **www.salon.com** – excellent and up-to-the-minute e-zine
3. **www.hollywood.com** – over 1 million pages to choose from
4. **www.aintitcoolnews.com** – the latest film gossip and reviews
5. **www.bollywoodworld.com** – all you need on the world's biggest film industry
6. **www.celebhoo.com** – find all the info on your favourite star at this directory
7. **www.debretts.co.uk** – posh celebrity gossip
8. **www.thesmokinggun.com** – if it's sleaze you're looking for, it's probably here
9. **www.mykindaplace.com** – gossip and celebrity news for teenagers
10. **www.teamtalk.com** – sports gossip

---

www.eonline.com   US
> E!
> Entertainment Online features all the latest gossip mainly
> oriented towards the US and Hollywood in particular. It's fun
> and irreverent and has a reputation for being first with the news.

www.glamourmagazine.co.uk   UK
> LOSE YOURSELF IN GLAMOUR
> Gossip, fashion, beauty tips, chat, competitions and, of course,
> celebrities are the mainstay of *Glamour* magazine's site. Its main
> function though is to plug the real magazine. See also the
> similar **www.moremagazine.co.uk** and
> **www.graziamagazine.co.uk**

www.amiannoyingornot.com   US
> VOTE FOR MOST ANNOYING CELEBRITIES
> You can spend ages on this site; it's easy to vote and fun to use.
> Each celeb gets a page with biographical details and reasons
> why they could be annoying or not …

www.mugshots.com US

WHEN IT ALL GOES WRONG

This could only happen in America, mug shots of the rich and famous when, once in a while, they break the law. There's also a serious side with sections covering national US events and the FBI's most wanted list. Ghoulish but fascinating too.

www.thesmokinggun.com US

FINDING THE SLEAZE – ALLEGEDLY

Devoted to finding skeletons in cupboards, Smoking Gun has everything from confidential documents and incriminating evidence to mug shots. If your favourite celeb has done something wrong, even a small thing, it'll be here.

www.bbc.co.uk/celebdaq UK

CELEBRITY STOCK EXCHANGE

The BBC's celebrity stock exchange show now lives on in the form of this web site. It monitors the rise and fall of many celebrities and allocates a stock price to them – it's fun to see who's on the up and who's on the slide. See also the Hollywood Stock Exchange at **www.hsx.com**

www.famousbirthdays.com US

WHO SHARES YOUR BIRTHDAY

A comprehensive listing of celebrity birthdays. Click on any celebrity and you get sent to a Google search page featuring your chosen one.

Charities

The Internet offers a great opportunity to give to your favourite charity or support a cause dear to your heart. There are so many that we're unable to list them all, but here are some top sites with directories to help you find the ones that interest you. For charity cards see page 231 and for health-related charities see page 240.

Charity Information

www.charitychoice.co.uk UK

 ENCYCLOPAEDIA OF CHARITIES

An advert-laden but very useful and well-put-together directory of charities with a good search facility, there's also the excellent

'Goodwill Gallery' where you can post up a service or a donation you're willing to give to charity.

www.caritasdata.co.uk UK

CHARITIES DIRECT

A support site for charities with information on how to raise funds and run a charity, there's also a good directory of UK charities (via **www.charitiesdirect.com**) and you can rank them by expenditure, revenue and fund size. See also **www.charitynet.org** which is a useful database covering charities and non-profit organisations world-wide, it has sections on education, government, IT, legal issues and jobs too.

www.charitycommission.gov.uk UK

THE CHARITY COMMISSION

The Charity Commission's mission is to give the public confidence in the integrity of charities in England and Wales and their site lists over 166,000 charities. There's also lots of advice for charities, a list of their publications and links to related sites.

See also:
www.bcconnections.org.uk – businesses can find out how they can get involved in charity donations and charities can find out how they can get businesses involved in their work.
www.charities.org – information about American charities.
www.helplines.org.uk – the Telephone Helplines Association with a useful search facility.

Giving

www.justgiving.com UK

GIVE EFFECTIVELY

A newsy and informative site devoted to making the process of giving to charity as easy as possible whether you're an individual donor, a charity or a company. The site is divided into three sections: Fundraise, Donate and Sponsor so you can go directly to the area that interests you. See also **www.cafonline.org** which is especially informative about unusual ways of donating such as using tax and shares.

www.thehungersite.com US

CLICK AND GIVE

Just one click and you'll donate a cup of food to the world's hungry via registered sponsors, a brilliant idea and one that works: last year the site funded nearly 44 million cups of food. Sign up and they'll send you a reminder to visit every weekend. There are also sister sites for breast cancer, saving rain forests, animal rescue, child health and a new literacy site. See also **www.freedonation.com** which has similar aims and works along the same lines.

www.careinternational.org.uk   UK
HELPING THE WORLDS POOREST

Care are all about helping the world's most stricken people, here you can learn about their work and donate.

www.missionfish.org.uk   UK
CHARITY AUCTIONS

Make money for charity when you auction your goods through eBay. Various major charities are supported and it's easy to use. See also eBay's pages at **http://pages.ebay.co.uk/community/charity/index.html**

See also:
www.50ways.org – an outstanding American site devoted to ways of giving money to save the world's children from suffering.
www.charitychallenge.com – raise money for your chosen charity by taking an adventure holiday through Charity Challenge.
www.dec.org.uk – donate to emergency appeals and track how the money has been spent.
www.ecpat.net – working to eliminate all forms of child abuse.
www.givewater.org – help get water to where it's most needed.
www.sendacow.org.uk – get livestock to those who really need it in East Africa.

Chat and Virtual Worlds

There are literally thousands of chat sites and rooms on the web covering many different topics. However, this is the area of the Net that people have the most concerns about. There have been loads of cases where people have been tricked into giving out personal information and even arranged unsuitable meetings. But at its best, a chat program is a great way to keep in contact with friends, especially if they live miles away. So chat wisely by following our top tips for keeping safe.

Chat – Our Top Tips

1. Be wary, just like you would be if you were visiting any new place.
2. Don't give your e-mail address out without making sure that only the person you're sending it to can read it.
3. People often pretend to be someone they're not when they're chatting; unless you know the person, assume that's the case with anyone you chat with online.
4. Don't meet up with anyone you've met online – keep your online life separate. Chances are they'd be a let down anyway, even if they were genuine.
5. If you like the look of a chat room or site but you're not sure about it, get a recommendation first.
6. If you want to meet up with friends online, arrange a time and place beforehand.
7. If you don't like someone, just block 'em.
8. Check out the excellent **www.chatdanger.com** (see below) for more info on how to chat safely.

www.chatdanger.com   US

KEEP SAFE IN CHAT ROOMS
A great site devoted to the perils of using chat rooms, full of advice and sensible information, it can be a little slow though, but it's worth persevering. See also **www.thinkuknow.co.uk** who provide advice for young people.

www.aim.com   UK

AOL INSTANT MESSENGER
One of the most popular, it's pretty safe and you can easily block people who are a nuisance, or just set it up so that only friends can talk to you.

http://web.icq.com   US

ICQ – I SEEK YOU
There are lots of chat rooms here. It's quick and easy to use combined with a mobile phone. There are lots of features such as games, money advice, music and lurve.

www.mirc.com   US

IRC – INTERNET RELAY CHAT
A straightforward chat program that is easy to use. Generally it's been overtaken by the likes of AOL but some web sites may opt to use it.

www.trillian.cc US

COMMUNICATE WITH FLEXIBILITY AND STYLE
Trillian enables connections to all the major chat programs
through one interface. The reader looks good and you can
personalise it too.

www.paltalk.com US

VERSATILITY
A feature-laden system with everything from video conferencing
to instant messaging – all free!

Virtual World

*A Virtual World or Meta-universe is a program, also known as an
MMOSG (Massively Multiplayer Online Social Game), that enables you
to create a separate personality that lives in a separate world. You can
live your life in this alternative reality and it's becoming increasingly
popular with companies, who use these sites to advertise, sponsor and
even do business.*

www.virtualworldsreview.com US

START HERE
A good place to start as it gives an overview of each site, their
costs and benefits, which will help you find the one you feel
most comfortable to join.

*It's a matter of opinion of course but here are some of the best virtual
world sites …*

http://secondlife.com US

YOUR WORLD
With some three million 'inhabitants', Second Life boasts that
it is entirely built by its own 'residents'. It even has its own
currency, which can be traded for real dollars (guides are
available to help you do business on the site), which means it's
a pretty commercial place. If you've ever played games like Sim
City, you'll get the picture and once you get your head around it,
it's fun and relatively straightforward. Enjoy! See also
http://teen.secondlife.com which is aimed at 13–17 year olds.

www.habbo.co.uk FINLAND

FOR UK TEENS
Lots of recommendations from users has meant the inclusion of
this site in the book. Flexibility, fun graphics and an excellent

monitoring policy make it popular. This is the new UK site for
www.habbohotel.com. The basics are free but additional
services are not.

C

www.there.com   US
  3-D CHAT
  Create your avatar or virtual identity, join in one of the
  conversations or play a game with your new friends, it's
  entertaining and as with all these sites best used in broadband.

Children

*You can save pounds on children's clothes and toys by shopping over
the Net; it's easy and the service is often excellent. The Internet is also
a great way to educate and entertain children; they are fascinated by it
and soon become experts, often quickly overtaking their parents. We've
put together a selection of the very best sites here but for ideas for days
out with children see the British travel listings page 553, for educational
sites see page 117 and for parenting concerns see page 361.*

Shopping for Children

www.toy.co.uk   UK
  FIND THAT TOY
  A very useful toy search engine, you can search by type,
  company or age. Once searched, it lists the toys with details,
  price and where you can buy them online, sometimes a little out
  of date but the search engine works well.

www.elc.co.uk   UK
  EARLY LEARNING CENTRE
  A well-designed and user-friendly site that offers a wide range of
  toys for the under-fives in particular, it's strong on character
  products and traditional toys alike.

www.hamleys.co.uk   UK
  FINEST TOY STORE IN THE WORLD
  At the Hamley's site you can search for toys by gender, price or
  age. There's also an okay selection of character areas within the
  store as well as the more traditional range, which is their main
  strength. Children can leave a wish list on the site and they do a
  birthday reminder service.

For Young Children

The Good Web Site Guide's Top 10s
of the Internet

1. **www.mamamedia.com** – great for encouraging communication skills
2. **www.bonus.com** – excellent, great looking and fun
3. **www.yucky.com** – learn about science the fun way
4. **www.nickjr.com** – a superb site from Nickelodeon
5. **www.sesamesworkshop.org** – still going strong
6. **www.bbc.co.uk/cbeebies** – great for the very young
7. **www.disney.co.uk** – despite the overt commerciality, it's still worth a visit
8. **www.barbie.com** – heaven for 5-year old girls
9. **www.lego.co.uk** – a little gem featuring the little bricks
10. **www.citv.co.uk** – more games and program links

www.toysrus.co.uk   UK
   NOT JUST TOYS
   Good site with all the key brands and 'in' things you'd expect.
   Has links to key toy manufacturers' sites and a sister site called
   www.babiesrus.co.uk which covers younger children.

www.theentertainer.com   UK
   THE ENTERTAINER
   The online spin-off from the Entertainer high street stores; it
   offers much in the way of bargains and this bright and breezy
   site is easy to navigate. You can search by toy, age, price or
   category.

www.newcron.com   UK
   CHARACTER PRODUCTS
   Newcron has taken over the Character Warehouse site to
   produce an online store that offers a wide range of mainstream
   and unusual character products. You can search by character,
   product or price. See also **www.shop4toys.co.uk** which has a
   similar offer.

www.woodentoysonline.co.uk   UK
WOODEN TOYS
A wide range of wooden and innovative toys here covering lots of categories and types, all on a well-categorised and easy-to-use site.

www.krucialkids.com   UK
ALL ABOARD THE KRUCIAL KIDS EXPRESS
This site specialises in developmental toys for children up to eight years old, providing detailed information on the educational value of each of the 200 or so toys. For educational toys see also **www.mulberrybush.co.uk** who specialise in toys for under 12s.

www.outdoortoysdirect.co.uk   UK
LOW PRICES ON OUTDOOR TOYS
Excellent value for money with free delivery, a money back guarantee, plus a wide range of goods. The selection consists of everything from trampolines to swings, slides and play houses. Free delivery on most goods. To complete your outdoor experience you can always pay a visit to **www.kiteshop.co.uk** who offer a wide range of kites and advice from an excellent site.

www.mailorderexpress.com   UK
SHOP IN THE COMFORT OF YOUR HOME
Excellent toy store with games and models too. Shop by brand or by category, with some good prices and special offers. The site design is a little old fashioned but effective nonetheless.

Other sites in this very competitive area that are worth a visit:
www.bearcountryuk.com – wide variety at all prices.
www.drtoy.com – a quirky American site run by someone who has reviewed and rated some 2,000 products for children, includes useful and intelligent 100 best toys of the year awards.
www.huggables.co.uk – specialists in teddies and other cute soft toys.
www.orchardtoys.co.uk – specialists in fun, educational toys.
www.teddybearsearch.com – find the bear of your dreams …
www.theoldtoyshop.com – mainly vintage and collectible toys.
www.totalrobots.com – all sorts of robots, probably one for dads really.
www.toycentre.com – a sparse site with some good prices, most brands represented.

www.toyopia.co.uk – a good toy shop with a sparse design and none the worse for it.

www.toysdirecttoyourdoor.co.uk – good design, specialists in Brio among other things; accompanied by Thomas' music!

www.toywiz.com – an American site where you can get unusual and new toys, even those that are no longer produced; toys are generally cheaper but shipping is costly.

www.tridias.co.uk – good age-ranged site, which means it's easy to find a present to suit.

Children's Clothes and Related Products

www.jojomamanbebe.co.uk   UK

FASHIONABLE MOTHERS AND THEIR CHILDREN

Excellent for everything from maternity wear and designer children's clothes to gifts for newborn babies. Also has sections on toys, maternity products and special offers. All the designs are tested and they aim to be comfortable as well as fashionable.

www.urchin.co.uk   UK

LIVING FOR KIDS

Urchin has a wide range of products and have won awards for their catalogue business. You'll find: cots and beds, bath-time accessories, bikes, clothes, travel goods, toys and things for the independent child who likes to personalise their own room. They boast a sense of style and good design, and they succeed. They also have a bargains section.

www.bloomingmarvellous.co.uk   UK

MATERNITY, NURSERY AND BABY WEAR

Excellent online store with a selection of maternity, baby and nurseryware available to buy, or you can order their catalogue.

www.mothercare.com   UK

MOTHERCARE

An attractive site with a good selection of baby and toddler products, also clothing, entertainment and equipment. It's good value and there are some excellent offers. It's not all about shopping though; there are advice sections on baby care, finance, tips on how to keep kids occupied and more.

www.gltc.co.uk   UK

THE GREAT LITTLE TRADING COMPANY

A good-looking site offering a wide range of child safety

products, furniture and baby equipment, you can search the site by age and by product category.

www.greenbabyco.com   UK

C

FOR GREEN BABIES

A good store where all products are environmentally friendly. There are clothes, nappies, toiletries, furniture, equipment, even laundry products amongst its many sections. For a similar site go to **www.ethosbaby.com** and also the attractive **www.gtexpectations.co.uk**

See also:

www.babiesisland.co.uk – a good selection of products for babies, mums and dads.

www.babycare-direct.co.uk – not the most attractive store but a wide range to choose from and some good offers.

www.babyhut.net – natural products for babies and parents.

www.bibsandstuff.co.uk – great for all those hard-to-get things and equipment generally.

www.cheekyrascals.co.uk – a very good baby equipment store.

www.childhoodinteriors.co.uk – a modern approach to decorating and accessorising your child's room.

www.kiddicare.com – baby accessories and nursery.

www.mamasandpapas.co.uk – good-looking site, you can't buy online but you can order a catalogue.

www.twinkleontheweb.co.uk – specialists in nappies, informative and helpful.

www.twinsthings.co.uk – great if you have … twins.

www.tyrrellkatz.co.uk – excellent but expensive range of clothes and stationery on a good-looking site, you have to fax or phone through orders though.

Things To Do

It has to be said that many of these sites, while good fun, haven't changed that much in years. Perhaps after the initial effort they think that their audience is ever changing, so they don't have to try too hard. Some are too commercial by half and need to tone down the advertising, which in turn would attract more visitors. We have added quite a few more sites this year, especially those that offer some sort of interactivity or virtual world.

www.mamamedia.com   UK
THE PLACE FOR KIDS ON THE NET
This versatile site has everything a child and parent could want,
there is an excellent selection of continually improving interactive
games, puzzles and quizzes, combined with a great deal of wit
and fun. Best of all it encourages children to communicate by
submitting a message and gets them voting on what's important
to them. There's a superb 'Grown-ups' section with information
on getting the best out of the Net with your children.

www.bonus.com   US
THE SUPER SITE FOR KIDS
Excellent graphics and masses of genuinely good games make a
visit to Bonus a treat for all ages. There are quizzes and puzzles,
with sections offering a photo gallery, art resources and
homework help. Access to the web is limited to a protected
environment. Shame about the pop-ups and advertising.

www.show.me.uk   UK
SHOW ME
A lively site specialising in picking out the best of what's going
on in our museums and galleries and representing it online.
There are games, what's on and special features with celebrities.
It's educational without being overtly so and there are special
sections for teachers and parents too.

www.yucky.com   US
THE YUCKIEST SITE ON THE INTERNET
Find out how to turn milk into slime or how much you know
about worms – Yucky lives up to its name. Essentially this is an
excellent, fun site that helps kids learn science and biology.
There are guides for parents on how to get the best out of the
site and links to recommended sites.

www.fffbi.com   US
 THE FIN, FUR AND FEATHER BUREAU OF INVESTIGATION
Outstanding activity site with lots of problem-solving crime
capers and games to play. The emphasis is on teaching children
about other cultures around the world, which it does in a very
entertaining and original fashion.

www.switcheroozoo.com   US
MAKE NEW ANIMALS
Now a commercial affair but you can still make thousands of

combinations of animals, but you need Shockwave and a decent PC for it to work effectively.

www.bigeyedowl.co.uk UK
EARLY YEARS EXPERIENCE
One for parents who want ideas for activities to entertain their preschoolers including how to make playdough. Songs and rhymes, kids' recipes, craft ideas and suppliers of craft equipment.

www.mobile-kids.net US
MOKITOWN
An educational virtual world site sponsored by Daimler Chrysler, it helps children get to grips with road safety. It's a good example of what can be achieved with this sort of technology as it enables kids and parents to sit together and get involved.

www.whyville.net US
ISLAND RACE
One of the best of its type, Whyville is rightly popular; it's bright and breezy and just right for the target 10–16 age range. The idea is to create characters and get involved in various science projects that, although educational, are great fun. For younger children try **www.puzzlepirates.com**, a multi-player, role-playing game with excellent graphics and design.

Other activity sites worth checking out:
http://play.toontown.com/webHome.php – an excellent multi-player game from Disney, suffers from being too commercial though.
http://web.ukonline.co.uk/conker – The Kids Ark – join Captain Zeb gathering material on the world, strange animals, myths and facts – before it all disappears.
www.activityvillage.co.uk – a huge array of activities all designed to keep kids busy.
www.alfy.com – excellent with lots of games and plenty of things to do and see.
www.badgeplanet.co.uk – a great site where you can buy and also design your own badges.
www.coloring.ws – lots of colouring projects to download and print off, but the site is advert laden.
www.cybersmartkids.com.au – a good Australian site with lots of things to do and see.
www.funschool.com – a bit commercial, but there's plenty to do at this American activity come education site.

www.globalgang.org.uk – a Christian Aid sponsored activity and magazine site mainly covering world issues.

www.headbone.com – part of Bonus with chat and games.

www.hotwheels.com – a good-looking, but slow site from a model car maker that has some good features and games. Needs latest Flash Player to work.

www.kiddonet.com – download the interactive play area for games and surfing in a safe environment. Masses to do and good links. Largely aimed at girls.

www.kids.warnerbros.com – a links page to their children's productions. When you consider what they produce, it's a shame they can't do more.

www.kidscastle.si.edu – a pretty average kids' educational magazine site from the Smithsonian Museum. Useful for homework too.

www.kidscom.com – play games, post a message on the message board and write to a pen friend (unfortunately the safe chat lines are still only open during our night-time). Improved but still a bit dull.

www.kidsdomain.com – a family oriented site with masses to download, from colouring books, music demos to homework help games. Split into three age ranges.

www.kidsjokes.co.uk – thousands of jokes and loads of adverts too.

www.kidsreads.com – an American site all about kids' books, with games and quizzes. Good for young Harry Potter fans.

www.lego.co.uk – games, product information, adventures with their leading characters, lots of interactive features make this site something of a gem.

www.lemonadegame.com – how much lemonade can you sell? Learn about market forces in this oddly fascinating game.

www.matmice.com – create your own web site home page and add it to the internet the easy way.

www.missdorothy.com – The good-looking Dot Comic, which has loads of activities and is fun to use. Educational too.

www.neopets.com – look after a multitude of virtual pets, play games and even trade them.

www.netmom.com – a place for mums and kids to hang out in safety.

www.noggin.com – an excellent American activity site for preschool children.

www.projects.ex.ac.uk/bugclub – bugs and creepy crawlies for all ages.

C

Cookery for Kids

www.stickymitts.co.uk   UK
JUNIOR CUISINE
A site devoted to helping children get stuck in to cookery. It
offers a series of courses which introduce the basics of cooking
and also encourages children to have a go. The site itself is a
little dull and often out of date but the content is great. See
also **www.coolmeals.co.uk** which is a brighter affair with the
emphasis on nutrition and food groups. Also the BBC's helpful
suite of pages by Annabel Karmel, **http://www.bbc.co.uk/food/
recipes/mostof_cookingwithchildren1.shtml**

Magic

www.magictricks.co.uk   UK
THE UK'S LEADING ONLINE MAGIC TRICKS STORE
A magic store chock full of tricks, sets and accompanying
equipment. You can send in suggestions for new tricks and even
find a magician. There's also a section on TV magicians and a
bookstore.

See also:
www.magicbypost.com – magic tricks by mail order.
www.magictricks.com – an American site which has lots of info
and links.
www.magicweek.co.uk – well-designed but quite adult.

TV, Book and Character Sites

www.citv.co.uk   UK
CHILDREN'S ITV
Keep up to date with your favourite programmes and talk to the
stars of the shows. There's lots to occupy children here including
chat with fellow fans, play games, find something to do, enter a
competition, e-mail a friend and join the club.

www.nickjr.com   US
THE NICKELODEON CHANNEL
Ideal for under-eights, this has a good selection of recipes, travel
games and quizzes to play either with an adult or solo. For
activities aimed at a wider age range check out **www.nick.co.uk**
where there is chat, gossip, games and plenty of background
info on the shows.

www.sesamestreet.com   UK
THE CHILDREN'S TELEVISION WORKSHOP
Enter Elmo's world which is very colourful, with lots to do. There
are games to play, art and music to create and friends to talk to.
There's plenty for parents too.

www.bbc.co.uk/cbbc   UK
CHILDREN'S BBC
Lots of activities here, you can catch up on the latest news, play
games and find out about the stars of the programmes. There
are also web guide links to other recommended children's sites.
See also **www.bbc.co.uk/cbeebies** which is for the very young
with printable colouring pages, stories and games.

http://news.bbc.co.uk/cbbcnews   UK
NEWSROUND
One of the best bits of CBBC is *Newsround*, here you can get all
the latest news, do quizzes, chat and join their club.

www.disney.com   US
WHERE THE MAGIC LIVES
There are several key sections as listed below, plus other activity
micro sites such as Art and the virtual world of 'Toontown'.

1. Entertainment – details of films, activities and a Disney A–Z.
2. Kids Island – lots of shows and music.
3. Playhouse – games and character sites for younger children.
4. Games – more than anyone can cope with …
5. Character fun – a guide to all Disney characters.
6. Disney Mobile.
7. Destinations – Information on the theme parks.
8. Disney Direct – the Disney store, auctions and other sales
   opportunities.
9. Inside Disney – archives, newsletter and corporate info.

The British version **www.disney.co.uk** is more compact with less
about vacations and more emphasis on activity. Both sites are
commercial and often more about selling Disney than having fun.

www.aardman.com   UK
HOME OF WALLACE AND GROMMIT
This brilliant site takes a while to download but it's worth the
wait. There's news on what the team are up to, links to their
films, e-cards, a shop and an inside story on how it all began.

www.gosh.org UK
HOME OF PETER PAN
A good site from Great Ormond Street Hospital's charity with a
section devoted to Peter Pan – all proceeds from the sale of the
books go to the hospital. There's also lots to do on the site with
competitions, links and information about the hospital itself.

www.guinnessrecords.com UK
GUINNESS WORLD RECORDS
A commercial site that offers much in the way of entertainment
with footage of favourite records and informative sections on key
areas of record breaking such as sport, nature, the material
world and human achievements.

*Here's where the best children's characters from fiction, cartoon and
TV shows hang out:*

Favourites for Younger Children
(and a few older ones)

Andy Pandy – **www.bbc.co.uk/cbeebies/characterpages/
andypandy**
Barbie – **www.barbie.com**
Bill & Ben – **www.bbc.co.uk/cbeebies/characterpages/billandben**
Bob the Builder – **www.bobthebuilder.com**
Boohbahs – **www.boohbah.com**
Fimbles – **www.bbc.co.uk/cbeebies/fimbles**
Ivor the Engine – **www.smallfilms.co.uk/ivor**
Letter Land – **www.letterland.com**
Mr Men – **www.mrmen.com**
Noddy – **www.noddy.com**
Teletubbies – **www.teletubbies.com**
Thomas the Tank Engine – **www.thomasthetankengine.com**
Tweenies – **www.bbc.co.uk/tweenies**

Cartoons and TV

Action Man – **www.actionman.com**
Asterix the Gaul – **www.asterix.tm.fr**
Bagpuss – **www.smallfilms.co.uk/bagpuss**
Batman – **www.batmantas.com** (animated series)
Batman – **www.batmanbeyond.com**
Beyblade – **www.beyblade.com**

Clangers – **www.clivebanks.co.uk/Clangers%20intro.htm**
Danger Mouse – **www.dangermouse.org**
Dragonball Z – **www.dragonballz.com**
James Bond – **http://commanderbond.net**
Mary Kate and Ashley – **www.marykateandashley.com**
Pixar – **www.pixar.com**
Pokemon – **www.pokemon.com**
Spiderman – **www.spiderman.sonypictures.com** or
www.spiderman.com
Thunderbirds – **www.thunderbirdsonline.co.uk**
Yu-Gi-Oh – **www.yugiohkingofgames.com**

Favourite Characters from Children's Books

Alex Rider – **www.alexrider.com**
Angelina Ballerina – **www.angelinaballerina.com**
Animal Ark – **www.animalark.co.uk**
Artemis Fowl – **www.artemisfowl.co.uk**
Beano – **www.beanotown.com**
Eragon – **www.alagaesia.com**
Goosebumps – **www.scholastic.com/goosebumps**
Lemony Snicket – **www.lemonysnicket.com**
Paddington – **www.paddingtonbear.co.uk**
Peter Rabbit – **www.peterrabbit.co.uk**
Roald Dahl – **www.roalddahlclub.com**
Tintin – **www.tintin.com**
Tracey Beaker – **www.bbc.co.uk/cbbc/tracybeaker/**
Winnie the Pooh – **www.just-pooh.com**

*More favourite authors can be found at the following
publishers' sites:*
www.egmont.co.uk – good for younger kids with lots to
download.
www.harpercollinschildrensbooks.co.uk – home of Narnia.
www.kidsatrandomhouse.co.uk – Jacqueline Wilson, Terry
Pratchett, Roald Dahl and the Edge Chronicles.
www.ladybird.co.uk – Ladybird books.
www.puffin.co.uk – find out about the latest books from the
likes of Eoin Colfer, Charlie Higson and more.
www.scholastic.co.uk – lots to see and do here for children and
parents.

Harry Potter

Harry Potter deserves a special mention and with loads of web sites springing up, here are the official and some of the best unofficial ones.

www.jkrowling.com UK

 JK ROWLING

The official site from the author of the Harry Potter books is original in design, cleverly enticing the visitor into exploring the site while guaranteeing they'll have fun. Catch up on the latest rumours and get an insight into what it's like to be the world's best-selling author. You need to switch off your pop-up blocker to use the site.

See also:
http://harrypotter.warnerbros.co.uk – an outstanding site offering the latest news on the films plus downloads and lots of other activities, you can chat, shop for Harry merchandise and play games.
www.bloomsbury.com/harrypotter – find out all about the books, meet JK Rowling and join the Harry Potter club, send a Howler and more.
www.fictionalley.org – a good fan site that encourages Harry fans to have a go at writing and generally releasing their creativity.
www.mugglenet.com – an excellent fan site put together by some teenage fans, it has features on the books and the films plus links, games and the latest news. The Wall of Shame is particularly entertaining.
www.scholastic.com/harrypotter – here's the US publisher's site with wizard trivia, quizzes, screensavers, information about the books and an interview with JK Rowling, all on a fairly boring web site.

Search Engines and Site Directories

www.yahooligans.com US

THE KIDS' ONLINE WEB GUIDE

Probably the most popular site for kids, Yahooligans offers parents safety and kids hours of fun. There are games, articles and features on the 'in' characters, education resources and sections on sport, science, computing and TV. It has an American bias.

For Older Children

The Good Web Site Guide's Top 10s
of the Internet

1. **www.yahooligans.com** – excellent guide to what's on the web
2. **www.fkbko.co.uk** – safe surfing
3. **www.girland.com** – no boys here
4. **www.mykindaplace.com** – very popular site for young teens
5. **www.dubit.co.uk** – needs patience but the 3-D graphics are great
6. **www.mindbodysoul.gov.uk** – health for teens
7. **www.globalgang.org.uk** – see what children around the world are up to
8. **www.teensites.org** – huge directory of sites for teenagers
9. **www.neopets.com** – virtual pets, better than the real thing!
10. **www.jkrowling.co.uk** – the official Harry Potter site

www.ajkids.com   US
> ASK JEEVES FOR KIDS
> A search engine aimed at children, it's simple, safe and is
> excellent for homework enquiries and games.

www.fkbko.co.uk   UK
 FOR KIDS BY KIDS ONLINE
> Part of an EU funded project designed to make surfing the net
> safe for children, it has chat, e-mail, surfing and search facilities
> and the excellent design makes it easy to use too.

> *See also:*
> **www.bbc.co.uk/cbbc/search** – safe and reliable, as expected
> from the BBC.
> **www.familyfriendlysearch.com** – a simple search engine that
> searches several of the major directories' kids' sections.
> **www.infoplease.com** – good for homework.
> **www.kidsfreeware.com** – freeware for kids.
> **www.kidtastic.com/search/websearch/index.html** – safe search
> for kids.

Help for Children

www.childline.org.uk   UK

C

TELEPHONE 0800 111

Probably the best port of call for almost any kind of help and advice. There's masses of child-friendly information on the site with links, true stories, a problem page, competitions and quizzes. If you need to talk, there's always the confidential phone line.

See also:

www.bbc.co.uk/cbbc/yourlife/noproblem – covers bullying, online bullying, divorce, domestic violence, healthy lifestyle. Other issues such as friendship, confidence, jealousy and running away are also tackled here. There is also the useful 'Ask Arron' section where children can talk about their problems with a psychotherapist.

www.nspcc.org.uk/kidszone – information and help on child abuse.

www.rights4me.org.uk – help for children living in care.

www.talktofrank.com – confidential information about drugs.

Christmas

Sites to give some seasonal cheer and also help you prepare for the big day.

www.christmasarchives.com   UK

THE HISTORY OF CHRISTMAS

A curious site written by Christmas historians of noble birth. There is masses of information on Christmas traditions throughout the world, although the site is not easy to navigate. You can buy a traditionally decorated Christmas tree or even one used on a film set, antique decorations and Christmas related books.

www.northpole.com   US

SANTA'S SECRET VILLAGE

A very good activity site for children and adults too, with everything from educational activities to shopping.

www.christmastimeuk.com   UK
CHRISTMAS SHOP
Selling all you could possibly need during the festive season,
this shop has a wide range and an e-mail service if you want
something specific. Delivery charges vary according to what you
buy and where you are. For another site featuring Christmas
related merchandise go to **www.xmastreesdirect.co.uk**

Other Christmassy sites worth checking out:
http://christmas.allrecipes.com – some 1,500 Christmas
recipes and plum puddings.
http://en.wikipedia.org/wiki/Christmas – Wikipedia's entry on
Christmas.
www.buy-christmas-decorations.co.uk – Christmas decorations
and tree lights too.
www.cardsforgoodcauses.org.uk – charity cards.
www.carols.org.uk – a good database of carols but lots of
adverts spoil the site.
www.christmas-carols.net – lyrics for all the best-known carols.
www.christmasdinnercompany.co.uk – everything you need
delivered to your door complete with instructions. Not cheap but
high quality and hassle free.
www.emailsanta.com – too lazy to send a letter? Well, now you
can e-mail Santa.
www.fattypuff.com – a good place to go for Christmas cards.
www.gocrackers.co.uk – not the usual crackers.
www.howstuffworks.com/christmas – all your questions about
the advent season answered including the eternal question 'why
is Christmas sometimes spelled Xmas?'
www.lewisandcooper.co.uk – specialists in hampers and plum
puddings.
www.lights4fun.co.uk – for Christmas lights, no matter how tacky.
www.noradsanta.org – track Santa as he makes his way around
the skies.
www.pinesandneedles.com – buy a tree, get it delivered and, if
you live in London, they'll even decorate it for you.
www.realfooddirect.co.uk – food gifts, hampers, condiments,
soft drinks and Christmas treats.
www.soraiseyourglasses.com – excellent party organising service.
www.teme-mistletoe.co.uk – all you need to know about
mistletoe, order online.
www.thecarvedangel.com – they make great claims for their
Christmas pudding, also supply foodie gifts.
www.thevanillatree.com – folksy Christmas decorations.

www.tobiasandtheangel.com – beautiful handmade Christmas decs for those with a big wallet.
www.whychristmas.com – explains what Christmas is all about with information on traditions and how it's celebrated in other cultures.

Circus Arts

www.circusfriends.co.uk   UK
CIRCUS IN BRITAIN
The place to go it you want to go to the circus, subscribe to their magazine, or find out about circus education programmes. Great for links.

www.oddballs.co.uk   UK
FOR JUGGLERS
For juggling equipment, fire sticks, diabolos, unicycles plus books and videos. The community pages give advice and links to other juggling sites. For a serious approach to the subject and online lessons go to the Internet Juggling database at **www.jugglingdb.com**

Other circus fans and street artists may find these sites helpful:
www.circusnews.com – an American site with loads of information about the circus scene.
www.contortionhomepage.com – for those that want to get into the box.
www.streetentertainers.co.uk – for street entertainers.
www.peopleplayuk.org.uk/guided_tours – brilliant on the history of the circus.
www.trickstutorials.com – a dense site on how to perform acrobatic tricks. Only the most flexible should try.
www.unicycle.org.uk – how to and info for those into unicycles.

Competitions

www.loquax.co.uk   UK

THE UK'S COMPETITION PORTAL
This site doesn't give away prizes but lists the web sites that do. There are hundreds of competitions featured, and if you own a web site they'll even run a competition for you. There are daily updates and special features such as 'Pick of the Prizes' which features the best the web has to offer, with links to the relevant sites.

See also:
www.myoffers.co.uk – a well designed site, with, as the name suggests, lots of offers.
www.theprizefinder.com – a mess of a site which offers a wide range of prizes in lots of categories; you have to register though.

Computers

It's no surprise that the number one place to buy a computer is the Internet. With these sites you won't go far wrong, and it's also worth checking out the price checker sites on page 386 before going shopping and checking the software sites on page 438. Mac users should also check out the section on Apple Macs on page 22.

Information and Reviews

www.itreviews.co.uk   UK
> START HERE TO FIND THE BEST
> IT Reviews gives unbiased reports, not only on computer products, but also on software, games and related books. The site has a good search facility and a quick visit may save you loads of hassle when you come to buy. See also the comprehensive **www.technologyowl.com**

www.pcadvisor.co.uk   UK
> EXPERT ADVICE IN PLAIN ENGLISH
> A derivative from *PC Advisor* magazine, the site offers much in the way of reviews and information on how to find the best PC. It also allows you to pick up advice from experts on technical queries, download programmes and join forum discussions. You have to register, which is free, to gain access to the site.

> *See also:*
> **www.bbcworld.com/clickonline** – the technology pages from the BBC with some entertaining and interesting content.
> **www.byte.com** – one for those who know something about computer technology.
> **www.compshopper.co.uk** – quite techy, but good for reviews and information.
> **www.computerweekly.com** – fairly dull site but informative on all aspects of computing.
> **www.cnet.com** – product reviews aplenty, also has downloads and shopping links.

PC Essentials

The Good Web Site Guide's Top 10s
of the Internet

1. **www.download.com** – all your software needs
2. **www.itreviews.co.uk** – read the reviews before you buy
3. **www.kelkoo.co.uk** – for the best prices
4. **www.isr.net** – all you need to know about internet security
5. **www.pcmech.com** – how it all works, how to repair it
6. **www.tucows.com** – software reviews and downloads
7. **www.compman.co.uk** – good offers on computer manuals
8. **www.handango.com** – the best for PDA software
9. **http://grc.com** – get your PC checked for security with Shield's Up
10. **www.vnunet.com** – UK-oriented technology site

www.streettech.com – opinions and personal reviews with
attitude from several experts.
www.tomshardware.com – a popular, information-heavy but
messy site full of advice and help on the most common
problems and issues facing the computer user.
www.whatpc.co.uk – a good buyer's guide.
www.zdnet.co.uk – very good reviews section at this large and
diverse site.

Information on Repairing and Upgrading Your PC

*The following sites are useful if you want to keep up with the latest
developments, need help when your PC goes wrong or you just need to
learn something.*

www.pcmech.com   US
PC MECHANIC
Plain English explanations of all the bits that make up a
computer, it's easy to follow and use with lots of background
information and support. Excellent.

www.modemhelp.org   CANADA

MODEM PROBLEMS FIXED
Any problems with your modem? Try here, it's very
comprehensive, but then if you have problems with your modem
how are you going to access it? Ask a friend …

C

See also:
www.compinfo.co.uk – a bewildering number of computer
related links all set out in a large directory.
www.driverguide.com – advice on finding and installing the
right drivers for your PC.
www.help.com – part of the high quality CNET site, it has the
most up-to-date information on new products and articles and
advice. It assumes some knowledge and you have to get around
all the adverts and gossip.
www.maximumpc.co.uk – lots of tutorials, useful programs to
download and reviews galore.
www.pcpitstop.com – a host of programs to get your PC
running on top form. They can even test how well your PC is
running and offer advice on how to improve its performance.
www.warrantyex.co.uk – extended warranties the easy way.
www.wired.com – all the latest news and product information.

Stores

It's worth checking out price comparison sites such as
www.kelkoo.co.uk *but these stores specialise in PCs and*
consumables.

www.pcworld.co.uk   UK

THE COMPUTER SUPERSTORE
A very strong offering from one of the leading computer stores
with lots of offers and star buys. They sell a wide range of
electronics from cameras to the expected PCs and peripherals.

www.misco.co.uk   UK

ONE STOP SHOP
Formally Simply.co.uk, this site offers a very wide range of PCs
and related products.

www.dabs.com   UK

1,500,000 CUSTOMERS LATER …
One of the most successful online computer product retailers,
with a very good reputation for service, there are loads of offers

and a wide range of goods including home entertainment, digital photography equipment and mobile phones.

See also:
www.ebuyer.com – good design and some excellent offers.
www.rankhour.com – huge range and competitive.
www.unbeatable.co.uk – very good prices and a wide range.

www.totalpda.co.uk   UK
PERSONAL DIGITAL ASSISTANTS
Good-looking site specialising in PDAs and related products with a wide range and some good bargains. See also **www.expansys.com** who have some very good offers.

PC manufacturers' site addresses:
Apple – **www.apple.com**
Dell – **www.dell.co.uk**
Evesham – **www.evesham.com**
Hewlett Packard – **www.hp.com/uk**
Mesh – **www.meshcomputers.com**
Time – **www.timecomputers.com**
Viglen – **www.viglen.co.uk**

Computer Accessories

www.planetmicro.co.uk   UK
ACCESSORISE YOUR PC
Much in the way of add-ons for PCs and essential equipment that can enable you to get more out of your computer, or keep an old PC going. Good design and some good pricing too.

See also:
www.dreamdirect.co.uk – good-looking site mainly selling software but also with an OK range of PC accessories and equipment.
www.inksaver.com – a program that saves money on printing by allowing you to control the amount of ink your printer uses.
www.keytools.com – a great site devoted to providing equipment that is easy to use.
www.powerdesk.com – a desk with built in PC, excellent space saving idea.
www.tonik.co.uk – excellent computer consumables store with free delivery in the UK.

www.cex.co.uk   UK
COMPUTER EXCHANGE
Computer Exchange buy and sell used electronics, computers
and games. The process is pretty straightforward, so if you have
an old PC give them a call.

C

Consumer Information and Advice

*A new section following requests from readers, these sites help with the
latest consumer law and provide answers or give guidance on what to
do if you've been wronged.*

www.which.co.uk   UK

WHICH? MAGAZINE
Excellent spin off from the magazine with everything from
consumer advice to product reviews. You need to be a member
to get the best out of it.

www.consumerdirect.gov.uk   UK

THE CONSUMER GATEWAY
A consumer advice site run by the government that offers links
and information across all the major areas where issues occur
from cars to shopping to home improvements. A good place to
start if you have issues you feel strongly about.

See also:
www.adviceguide.org.uk – the Citizens Advice Bureau offers a
wide range of tips and advice on the most common problems
and how to solve them, plus how to get in touch if you have
specific issues.
www.bbc.co.uk/watchdog – lots of information on the back
of the TV programme with legal FAQs, example letters for
complaints and specific features.
www.ciao.co.uk – independent product reviews on a wide range
of categories.
www.complaint-letter.co.uk – get your letter written by a
professional, at a price …
www.complaints.com – advice from a good US site.
www.consumerworld.org – a messy American site with a huge
number of useful links.
www.ethicalconsumer.org – a UK-based site devoted to listing
those companies whose environmental and social track records
are less than enviable.

Services

The Good Web Site Guide's Top 10s
of the Internet

1. **www.businesslink.gov.uk** – if you're in business there's no more helpful site
2. **www.uswitch.co.uk** – find the best household deals
3. **www.flickr.com** – easy-to-use photo sharing service
4. **www.nhsdirect.nhs.uk** – if you're feeling unwell go here and get help
5. **www.newsnow.co.uk** – outstanding news feed service
6. **www.which.co.uk** – independent consumer advice
7. **www.skype.com** – free internet telephony
8. **www.consumerdirect.gov.uk** – consumer advice
9. **www.theaa.com** – route planning, finances, motoring and more
10. **http://docs.google.com** – free word and spreadsheet programs

www.howtocomplain.com – find out how to make a complaint at this easy-to-follow site, which even provides specially designed forms to make your complaint even more effective.
www.oft.gov.uk – home of the Office of Fair Trading.
www.tradingstandards.gov.uk – the Trading Standards site offers a wealth of information on safety and legislation for businesses, education establishments and consumers.
www.yell.com/consumer/home.html – a good set of links from Yell.com.

Crime

This section continues to expand. It is intended to be of help to victims of crime or it may even help solve one. Hopefully you won't need it. See also the Legal section on page 300.

www.police.uk   UK

THE POLICE ONLINE
Here you can notify the police of minor crimes and get essential information on the organisation and how it works. There are

sections on specific crimes or appeals, recruitment and information on related organisations. The site is easy to navigate and use.

See also:
www.cia.gov – the Central Intelligence Agency.
www.crb.org.uk – Criminal Records Bureau helps employers with criminal records information amongst other services.
www.fbi.gov – the Federal Bureau of Investigation.
www.interpol.com – the fight against international crime.
www.ipcc.gov.uk – Independent Police Complaints Commission, formerly the Police Complaints Authority.
www.soca.gov.uk – the fight against organised crime.
www.suzylamplugh.org/home/index.shtml – keep yourself safe from crime.

www.cjsonline.org   UK

THE CRIMINAL JUSTICE SYSTEM
A helpful site that tells what happens when someone gets arrested, and provides information about the trial procedure, how a court works and what you need to do if you're a witness. There's a guide to who does what in the legal profession and a section on related links. See also the Crown Prosecution Service at **www.cps.gov.uk** while for more information from the Home Office go to **www.homeoffice.gov.uk**

www.crimestoppers-uk.org   UK
KEEP 'EM PEELED
Information on the Crimestoppers Trust and how you can get involved in their fight against crime with information on the latest campaigns and initiatives, links and, of course, their phone number: 0800 555 111. **www.crimereduction.gov.uk** has been set up by the government to become the number one resource for the crime prevention practitioner and **www.crimeconcern.org.uk** gives advice on helping to reduce crime and also the fear of crime in local communities.

www.neighbourhoodwatch.net   UK
NEIGHBOURHOOD WATCH
A directory of neighbourhood watch schemes by county with advice on preventing crime and how you can set up a neighbourhood watch scheme in your area.

C

www.the-sia.org.uk   UK
PRIVATE SECURITY
The SIA is the managing body for security contractors,
everything from doormen to private investigators. See also
www.theabi.org.uk for the Association of British Investigators
and **www.ipi.org.uk** for the Institute of Professional Investigators
both of which will help you find a private detective should you
need one.

www.iwf.org.uk   UK
INTERNET WATCH FOUNDATION
The IWF works with the police to stamp out the use of
exploitative images of children, obscene and racist content that
is hosted by web sites based in the UK.

www.victimsupport.com   UK
VICTIM SUPPORT
An independent charity that supports the victims of crime
throughout the UK with help and advice. It also advises witnesses
on the justice system and campaigns for equal opportunities. You
can also find out about how you can help or give funds.

www.virtualbumblebee.co.uk   UK
LOST PROPERTY
The place to go if you have lost something. The police use this
site to post details and pictures of lost property in the hope that
someone will claim them.

www.cifas.org.uk   UK
CREDIT CARD FRAUD
Set up by the credit card industry to provide information about
financial fraud in the UK. It's a dry, text-heavy site but they tell
you what to look out for and there's advice on what to do if you
think that it has happened to you.

www.identity-theft.org.uk   UK
KEEP YOURSELF TO YOURSELF
Information about this fast-growing crime: what happens to you,
who can help, how to protect yourself and what is being done to
stop it. For the equivalent US site see **www.consumer.gov/idetheft**

See also:
www.econsumer.gov – the EU's attempt to stop Internet fraud
and set up a process to deal with complaints.

www.fraud.org – find out about how you can be defrauded and how to spot fraud on the Internet.

www.fraudbureau.com – a consumer-oriented scam-listing service, you can search for specific complaints and add your experiences too.

www.privacyrights.org – how to protect your privacy.

www.quatloos.com – a listing of all sorts of scams and fraudulent practices; an entertaining and educational read.

www.scambusters.com – more help on scams and annoyances on the Internet.

www.dumbcriminalacts.com   US

THE STUPIDEST CRIMINALS

Here you can find out about the daftest criminal acts in history and have a good laugh at their expense. Some are truly unbelievable and sadly it does lack a bit of credibility as it doesn't always list the source of the stories. See also **www.dumbcrooks.com** which is a bit low tech but the stories are more detailed.

Cycles and Cycling

See page 506 for cycling holidays and tours and page 454 for information on cycling as a sport.

www.cycleweb.co.uk   UK

THE INTERNET CYCLING CLUB

An attempt to bring together all things cycling. Aimed at a general audience rather than sporting cyclists, it has masses of sections and links on everything from the latest news to clubs, shops and holidays.

See also:

www.bikemagic.com – forums on hot bike topics, reviews of equipment, buying advice, classifieds, the latest news, links and an events calendar.

www.bikeweek.org.uk – find out about Bike Week which is in mid-June.

www.ctc.org.uk – the National Cyclists' Organisation's site offers lots of information on all aspects of the hobby and the benefits associated with getting on your bike.

www.cycling.uk.com – great for cycling links.

www.newtocycling.co.uk – help from Izzy Sez for those who are

new to cycling, with advice and links too.
www.tandem-club.org.uk – a pretty basic site devoted to the world of the tandem with discussion groups, classifieds, buying advice, events and a newsletter.

Buying a Bike

www.bicyclenet.co.uk UK
UNBEATABLE PRICES
Great selection of bikes and accessories, there's also good advice on how to buy the right bike and assembly instructions on all that they sell. Delivery is free for bikes and orders in excess of £50.

See also:
www.cyclestore.co.uk – bikes and gear at discounted prices.
www.cyclestuff.co.uk – a good range of accessories.
www.evanscycles.com – wide range, easy to navigate.
www.pedalon.co.uk – huge range of cycles and accessories.
www.wiggle.co.uk – good name and good shop.

Dance

Here are a few sites for those who dance or think they can.

www.danceart.com US
DANCE!
A slightly messy but enthusiastic site centred on the dance scene, it has lots of links, articles and interviews.

See also:
http://hneeman.oscer.ou.edu/dance_hotlist.html – long url but worth it for a good hot list of dance sites.
www.artslynx.org/dance/companies.htm – exhaustive dance links for all genres.
www.ballet.co.uk – magazine-style site with reviews, interviews, biographies and forums.
www.ballroomdancers.com – excellent and comprehensive offering with video clips.
www.bbc.co.uk/strictlycomedancing – fun stuff about the show, of course, but useful for links to local dance classes and good information to help you distinguish the mambo from the cha cha cha.

www.dancebooks.co.uk – where to go for specialist dance titles; also CDs, DVDs, videos and sheet music.
www.dancescape.com – a good Canadian dance magazine site.
www.dancesport.uk.com – strictly come dancing, the UK ballroom dancing scene covered.
www.dancetv.com – learn to ballroom dance on Dance TV.
www.dancing-times.co.uk – *Dancing Times* and *Dance Today*.
www.folkdancing.org – home of the Folk Dance Association.
www.irishdancing.com – a cheery site from *International Irish Dancing* magazine.
www.istd.org – home of the Imperial Society of Teachers of Dancing.
www.learntodance.co.uk – buy instructional DVDs.
www.rad.org.uk – the Royal Academy of Dance.
www.the-ballet.com – a good e-zine all about ballet.
www.young-dancers.org – dedicated to helping teenagers learn to dance.
www.worldofdanceonline.com – dancing shoes plus tights, bodywear and tutus.

Dating

Using the Net has become an accepted means to meet people, but be careful about how you go about meeting up; many people aren't exactly honest about their details. If in doubt, err on the side of caution. See also the new section on social networking on page 437.

www.onlinedatingmagazine.com US
AN AUTHORITATIVE INSIGHT
An excellent magazine site devoted to all aspects of dating with site reviews, tips, articles and advice. It is well designed and up to date, there are even some cartoons and it's all written in a chirpy style.

See also:
www.dating-agencies-uk.co.uk/dating-tips.htm – good advice all round.
www.topdatingtips.com – attractive site with lots of articles on dating, excellent.
www.wildxangel.com – revamped and still useful with lots of advice about the pitfalls and dating scams.

www.uksingles.co.uk   UK

FOR ALL UK SINGLES
Not just about dating, this site is devoted to helping you get the
most out of life. There are several sections: accommodation,
sport and activities, holidays, help for single parents, and listings
for matchmaking and dating services. All the companies that
advertise in the directories are vetted too.

*Here are some additional sites, there's not much to choose
between them, it's all a matter of taste. All are secure and allow
you to browse and participate in relative safety:*
www.dateline.co.uk – 30 years experience at the dating game
gives Dateline lots of credibility and it's a good site too, easy to
use and reassuring.
www.datingdirect.com – claims to be the UK's largest agency
with over 3 million members, the site is not as sophisticated as
some, though they seem to have lots of success stories.
www.dinnerdates.com – one of the longest established and
most respected dining and social events clubs for unattached
single people in the UK; find out how you can get involved
here.

Disability Help and Information

*In this expanded section you'll find sites that may help if you are
disabled or care for someone with a disability. Sites for specific
conditions are listed on page 240. It's worth checking your local
council's site as they tend to have good local information on the
help that is available in your area.*

Information and Advice

www.direct.gov.uk/DisabledPeople   UK

THE GOVERNMENT'S VIEW
Information and help on rights for the disabled with links
to related departments. They have made this site more
comprehensive and accessible so you shouldn't need to visit
www.dwp.gov.uk/lifeevent/discare for an index of benefits and
services.

www.bcodp.org.uk   UK
THE BRITISH COUNCIL OF DISABLED PEOPLE
An action-oriented site that has information on how the council

Disability Help and Information

The Good Web Site Guide's Top 10s
of the Internet

D

1. **www.dlf.org.uk** – the Disabled Living Foundation with excellent resources
2. **www.disabilityview.co.uk** – very good magazine site
3. **www.disability.gov.uk** – the Government's site with useful links and information
4. **www.disabilitynow.org.uk** – another excellent magazine and portal
5. **www.jobability.com** – find the right job
6. **www.disabledunited.com** – finding friends, chat and dating
7. **www.disabledholidaydirectory.co.uk** – holidays and travel
8. **www.yourable.com** – forums, discussion and lots of links
9. **www.keytools.com** – tools to make life easier
10. **www.abilitynet.org.uk** – how to get the most from your computer

works, useful articles and helpful information. It shows how you can get involved whether you are disabled or not, and most importantly, how you can contribute.

www.disabilityview.co.uk   UK
DISABILITY VIEW
Inspired by the magazine of the same name, this site sets out to be the best source of information for all those who have to cope with a disability, and it largely succeeds. There are loads of links and useful sections such as travel, guides, sports and an events guide.

www.bbc.co.uk/ouch   UK
OUCH! MAGAZINE
Lively e-zine with lots of features and things to do and see, there are regular columnists, blogs and podcasts, as well as links and the latest news. See also **www.disabilityworld.org** and the more radical **www.raggededgemagazine.com**

For more advice check out the following sites:

www.abilitynet.org.uk – excellent regional database offering help whatever your situation.

www.dialuk.info – the Disability Advice Network.

www.disabilitynow.org.uk – great magazine site dealing with issues and offering advice.

www.disabilityresources.org – an American site devoted to resources available on the Internet.

www.makoa.org – another US site, not a good design, but a huge number of links all the same.

www.youreable.com – great for news, features and jobs.

Independent Living

www.dlf.org.uk   UK

THE DISABLED LIVING FOUNDATION
A charity devoted to helping people who need equipment to live life to the full. This excellent site has information on how to choose the best equipment, masses of links to self-help groups, a bookshop, training information and of course a section on how you can contribute.

See section on motability under 'Cars', page 70 as well as:

http://disabledaccessories.com – excellent range and good value make this store stand out.

www.disabledgo.info – a directory of places that have good access and businesses that are sympathetic to disabled people. Pity more towns don't participate.

www.inclusive.co.uk – a plethora of gadgets and useful educational tools to help make life and learning easier.

www.independentliving.co.uk – equipment and advice on making life easier.

www.keepable.co.uk – formerly **motibilitywarehouse.com** – excellent selection of products and a well-designed site.

www.keytools.com – an excellent site from a company specialising in providing computer accessories.

www.motability.co.uk – the scheme that helps you contract hire a car or powered wheelchair or scooter.

www.sunrisemedical.co.uk – a wide range of products. Contact them for your nearest dealer.

www.wheelchair-travel.co.uk – self-drive wheelchairs and cars for hire.

Children

www.ncb.org.uk/cdc   UK

COUNCIL FOR DISABLED CHILDREN
From the National Children's Bureau, this site is basically a
forum devoted to helping parents and children cope with
disability. It's a good starting point if you need information,
but it's not an easy site to navigate so patience is required.

See also:
www.cafamily.org.uk – find advice and support on caring for a
disabled child.
www.childcarelink.gov.uk – excellent government-run children's
information service site.

Students, Education and Sport

www.techdis.ac.uk   UK

HELP FOR STUDENTS WITH A DISABILITY
A site containing masses of help and information designed to
enable disabled students to have the opportunity to learn
effectively. Most of it is free, so an excellent resource.

www.efds.net   UK

ENGLISH FEDERATION OF DISABILITY SPORT
Covers sport for disabled people. It doesn't miss much and
there's an excellent links section which covers many different
types of sport, activity and associations. If you're in Scotland try
www.scottishdisabilitysport.com, in Wales, **www.fdsw.org.uk**
or **www.dsni.co.uk** for Northern Ireland.

See also:
www.abilityinfo.com/index.html – disability information for
students and professionals, it has a good news 'ticker' service too.
www.cforat.org – a charity devoted to helping disabled children
integrate into the school curriculum, now also serving adults
participating in the workplace and in higher education.
www.leeds.ac.uk/disability-studies/archiveuk – an archive of
articles and writings from activists, scholars and those
sympathetic to disability causes.
www.nasen.org.uk – the National Association for Special
Educational Needs.
www.skill.org.uk – who help promote opportunities for post-16
year olds in education.

Jobs

www.jobability.com   UK

> LEADING JOB SITE FOR DISABLED PEOPLE
> Integrated with Totaljobs.com and Leonard Cheshire, this is
> a straightforward site designed to help disabled people find
> employment; it covers the UK by region plus opportunities in the
> rest of the world. There's also advice on careers and how to find
> a job.
>
> *See also:*
> **www.rehab.ie/uk** – training and support to help people with
> disabilities into the workforce.
> **www.remploy.co.uk** – provides employment opportunities for
> disabled people all over the UK and in their own factories.
> **www.shaw-trust.org.uk** – training and work opportunities for
> the disadvantaged.

Rights and Having your Say

www.drc-gb.org   UK

> DISABILITY RIGHTS
> A helpful site offering links and views on rights issues for the
> disabled. The site doesn't always load properly and it's not easy
> to find your way around, but useful nonetheless – at least there's
> a search facility.

www.radar.org.uk   UK

> RADAR
> A campaigning organisation devoted to the social inclusion of
> disabled people. There's lots of information on the campaigns
> and how you can get involved.

www.webequality.org.uk   UK

> DISABILITY EQUALITY TRAINING
> Working with employers to enable disabled people to get
> employed and stay employed. There's masses of practical
> advice and even a quiz to start you off.

www.chooseability.org   US

> CHOOSE ABILITY
> A US-based community site which offers blogging and issues
> forums plus news and articles, it has a great feel and attitude
> although the site itself is a bit clunky.

See also:
www.csci.org.uk – an independent commission devoted to ensuring the rights of those in care. There's also information on what you can do if you are unhappy with the care you are receiving.
www.dpi.org – Disabled People International, promoting disabled people's rights around the world.

For Carers

www.carers.gov.uk   UK
FOR THOSE WHO CARE
A barely useful resource from the government for carers, there are links and details of their policies concerning care.

Social Networking

www.disabledunited.com   UK
 THE MEETING PLACE
A sort of Friends Reunited, but much more as it offers information on travel, links, chat, forums and, lastly, dating.

www.dating4disabled.com   ISRAEL
EMPOWERING DISABLED SINGLES
Provides a dating service as well as a global online community with blogs, forums and chats. Although many participants are from the US and other countries, a significant number are from the UK. For another approach try **www.whispers4u.com**

Travel

www.disabledholidaydirectory.co.uk   UK
HOLIDAY INFORMATION
Very useful directory site devoted to providing holiday information and contacts for disabled people. They have a wide range of holidays and offer sensible advice on how to get the best out of your holiday.

See also:
http://holidayaccessdirect.com – one of the best independent travel companies.
www.abletogo.com – a very wide range of holiday options.
www.access-able.com – poorly designed site but lots of useful information.

www.allgohere.com – a directory of hotels that offer facilities for the disabled.

www.disabilitytravel.com – experienced agent and good if you're confined to a wheelchair.

Do-it-yourself is under the 'Home and DIY' section on page 273.

Dying – Support and Advice

When faced with the death of a loved one, there are a bewildering number of things to be done and decisions to be made at a time of emotional stress and confusion. These sites help you to find your way through this minefield and provide both practical and emotional support.

www.ifishoulddie.co.uk   UK

EVERYTHING YOU NEED TO KNOW
Written in response to the confusion felt following a close death, this site takes you through all that you need to know including all the legalities, organ donation, funeral arrangements, wills, inheritance tax and coping with life-threatening illness and bereavement. There is a helpful section on the various funeral arrangements for the major religions although the site itself is careful not to take a religious stand. If you still need help, join in the forum and there are excellent links for more support.

www.funeralsuk.com   UK

LOCAL DIRECTORIES
Very good listings for everything you need from funeral directors, to printers, to monumental masons and florists. The 'Topics' section also provides help and links to other related services such as repatriation, wills, an online obituary service and even pet funerals.

Other related sites:
www.argonet.co.uk/body – British Organ Donation Society.
www.dignityindying.org.uk formerly **www.ves.org.uk** – Dignity in Dying is the new name of the Voluntary Euthanasia Society with guidelines on writing a living will and news about their campaign.
www.gatesofremembrance.co.uk – a site for online tributes.
www.humanism.org.uk – British Humanist Association, providers of non-religious funeral ceremonies.

www.naturaldeath.org.uk – helps arrange inexpensive, family-run and environmentally-friendly funerals and provides information on burials on private land.

www.the-bereavement-register.com – to remove the names and addresses of people who have died from databases and mailing files.

Legal and Financial Advice

www.hmcourts-service.gov.uk – legal advice and information on probate without recourse to a solicitor.

www.inlandrevenue.gov.uk/leaflets/iht.htm – the Inland Revenue's downloadable leaflets on inheritance tax.

www.lawontheweb.co.uk – jargon-free guide to wills, power of attorney, probate and what happens after a death. Pity about the design.

www.mypersonalfinances.co.uk/life-iht.asp – use the inheritance tax calculator to assess the damage.

www.willaid.org – draw up a will and simultaneously support charity.

Emotional Support

www.crusebereavementcare.org.uk – the leading charity in the UK specialising in bereavement.

www.samm.org.uk – emotional support to those bereaved through murder and manslaughter.

www.tcf.org.uk – support for bereaved parents and their families with local help groups and literature.

www.winstonswish.org.uk – helps bereaved children and young people rebuild their lives after a family death.

Education

Using the Internet for homework or study has become one of its primary uses; these sites will help enormously, especially alongside the reference and encyclopaedia sites listed on page 395. There is also a section aimed at students on page 478 and search engines for children are on page 94.

www.bbc.co.uk/learning   UK

 GET EQUIPPED FOR LIFE
A vast and good-looking site covering lifelong learning from

E

Homework and Learning

The Good Web Site Guide's Top 10s
of the Internet

1. **www.homeworkelephant.co.uk** – masses of help and info, top site
2. **www.kevinsplayroom.co.uk** – award winning and popular site
3. **www.learn.co.uk** – sponsored by the *Guardian*, quality assured
4. **www.schoolsnet.com** – an impressive one stop shop for education
5. **www.schoolzone.co.uk** – a superb education search engine
6. **www.samlearning.com** – tips, past papers even competitions
7. **www.school-portal.co.uk** – create a site for your school
8. **www.s-cool.co.uk** – revision help
9. **www.underfives.co.uk** – a brilliant education site for pre-school kids
10. **www.nc.uk.net** – the home of the National Curriculum

cradle to grave. While they take full advantage of the many educational TV and radio programmes they produce, there is an increasing amount of motivational learning and self help too. The quality is consistently high and the revision sections are excellent.

Free Homework Help (All Ages)

www.homeworkelephant.co.uk   UK

LET THE ELEPHANT HELP
Rightly considered one of the top educational sites with some 5,000 resources and straightforward layout, all aimed at helping children achieve great results. There's help with specific subjects, hints and tips, help for parents and teachers. The agony elephant is great if you get really stuck. It's constantly being updated, so worth checking regularly.

www.kevinsplayroom.co.uk   UK
AWARD-WINNING PORTAL
An excellent site which is put together with the heavy involvement of pupils. It's won numerous awards and is a

favourite among teachers and pupils alike. It has over 2,000 approved sites and they are well categorised and reviewed. There's also a translation service and a links page for teachers.

www.learningalive.co.uk   UK

FOR PRIMARY AND SECONDARY

From one of the larger software providers, the 'Living Library' is a useful resource for homework help for both primary and secondary students; you can either browse by topic or use the search facility. It can also be accessed directly on **www.livinglibrary.co.uk**. The 'Pathways' section provides over 4,000 links to a variety of reference sites. There are loads of resources for teachers too. If you are still short of information, try the children's section of the Internet Public Library at **www.ipl.org/div/kidspace**

www.schoolzone.co.uk   UK

UK'S TOP EDUCATIONAL SEARCH ENGINE

With links to over 41,000 websites, most reviewed by teachers, Schoolzone is an excellent source of information. Use the search facility under 'resources' to find what you are looking for, you'll then find the results summarised and graded. There is free software to download, plus homework help, career advice, teacher support (they do need it apparently) and much more.

www.topmarks.co.uk   UK

EDUCATIONAL PORTAL

Developed by a school teacher, this site steers pupils, parents and teachers to some of the best educational web sites. Search for sites by topic or by age from early years to higher ed.

www.channel4.com/learning   UK

CHANNEL 4 ANSWERS YOUR QUESTIONS

Check out 'Homework High' which is a well presented homework site for 11–16 year olds. It's split into six learning sections: history, geography, science, maths, English and languages. Simply type your question and you'll get answers on that topic.

If you're still at a loss, the following are American question answering sites with a distinct bias towards their system, but useful nonetheless:

www.cln.org/int_expert.html – listing of 'ask an expert' sources listed by subject. Not the best and not all the links work.

www.educationindex.com/education_resources.html – select your subject of interest and they'll give you a good set of links.
www.eduref.org – search under 'educational levels' or 'subjects'. More helpful for teachers than pupils.
www.jiskha.com – maybe the best for youngsters to use, search through old questions and have new ones answered within a couple of days. Also search their links and articles.
www.vrd.org/locator – use the alphabetical listing to find your topic and you'll find a list of relevant sites.

More sources of general homework help:

www.funbrain.com – free source of educational games (US).
www.happychild.org.uk – messy design spoils this site, but look for the box marked 'free educational resources' for some good links.
www.skool.ie – An excellent site covering the Irish curriculum but with lots of free resources, interactive lessons and information. It's well laid out and easy to navigate.
www.sparknotes.com – provide some of their excellent guides free to use online and a helpful forum if you're stuck.
www.thelighthouseforeducation.co.uk – confusing layout, look under 'education web sites' for listings.
www.ukeducationguide.co.uk – good links under 'homework'.

Not for Free

www.brainpop.com – learn through animation, excellent.
www.discoveryschool.com – masses of information and access to the wonderful resources of the Discovery Channel.
www.thebigbus.com – excellent animation and learning-based activities for pre-school and primary children. A trial is available for free.

Pre-school and Infant Education

*Your first point of call is the fab **www.bbc.co.uk/learning**. See also page 86 for activities for children, many of which have educational content.*

www.enchantedlearning.com
FROM APES TO WALES
A messy site aimed at little children, but hunt around the bottom of the page and you'll be rewarded with some excellent resources for young children. Use the search engine to help you

locate activities; don't be put off by the subscription offer, much of the material is available for free.

See also:
www.pbclibrary.org/mousing – a fun way to develop skills with a mouse – the computing kind of course.
www.pre-school.org.uk – home of the Pre-school Learning Alliance.
www.storyplace.org – online stories with associated activities and reading lists.
www.underfives.co.uk – good links and resources for everything educational with lots of suggested activities and downloadable sheets. Great for nursery teachers but useful for parents looking for inspiration too.

Primary

www.parentlink.co.uk   UK
HELPING YOUR CHILD
A site written by teachers aimed at helping parents to help their children by preparing them for the classroom. Very useful although it concentrates on numeracy and literacy. See also **www.parentsintouch.co.uk** which provides comprehensive advice on education and child development; full access costs £5 per year but much is available to non-members.

www.primarygames.com   US
GAME-BASED LEARNING
This site is packed full of educational games, some better than others, but there's loads to do and masses to learn. Check on 'curriculum guide' to find games that match your child's interests or level. **www.funschool.com** is a similar site, while **www.planetpals.com** is an environmentally aware site that encourages children to take care of the earth.

www.bbc.co.uk/schools/revisewise   UK
REVISE KEY STAGE 2 SATS
The BBC's excellent interactive site to support 10- to 11-year olds as they prepare for their Key Stage 2 National Curriculum Tests in English, Maths and Science.

Here are several subscription-only sites which may be of interest; they stand out in terms of quality and content, and they may well be used at your school.

www.atschool.co.uk – strong educational content, but enjoyable for Key Stage 1 and 2. £9.99 for a quarterly subscription.

www.edontheweb.com – written by a teacher, this lively, well-written site is designed to help children pass their SATs. Limited free material, with subscription at £24.99 per year.

www.gridclub.com – excellent use of entertaining educational games to do most of its tutoring but there are links to the more traditional material. KS2, £24.99 per year.

E

Secondary

There are so many brilliant educational support sites that it is impossible to list them all here. Homework help sites are listed above to search for the ones that best suit your needs or use the following to get you started. If you can't find what you are looking for here, don't forget our Reference section, page 395, which is extremely helpful when it comes to homework.

www.coursework.info   UK

UK'S LARGEST ESSAY & COURSEWORK LIBRARY
Thousands of options, but you have to pay £5 per month to access these or submit essays of your own and get three for free.

Also try:
www.123helpme.com – good selection, American, some free, some for purchase.
www.courseworkhelp.co.uk – limited selection, but free.
www.studentcentral.co.uk – same deal as coursework.info.

www.s-cool.co.uk   UK

FOUR STEPS TO REVISION
Well written and presented, this revision site covers GCSEs, AS and A level exams in four steps: principles, a quick learn guide, trial questions and revision summary. There is an interactive careers guide, discussions, a teachers' page and a great magazine with masses of information and advice aimed at young people.

www.studyzones.com   UK

ONLINE TUTORS
Fabulous resource mainly for GCSE and A level students, you can ask a question related to your studies and they'll get back to you within 24 hours. Submit your essays and they'll grade them and comment on how to improve it. You can search through

thousands of archived answers but to have yours answered you'll have to register, but it's free.

Subscription sites:
www.courseshop.co.uk – offers a wide range of courses from GCSE upwards.
www.samlearning.com – brilliant site with mock exams covering every major subject and key stage plus GCSE and A level.

Art

See our section on Art, page 26.

Design and Technology

www.design-technology.info – written by an inspired teacher, covers graphics, resistant materials, industrial production, systems control, textiles and food technology. Excellent.
www.dtonline.org – a bit minimal in presentation but covers electronics, food, mechanics, packaging, pneumatics and manufacturing projects.

English

See also our section on English Usage on page 131.

www.englishbiz.co.uk – excellent help and advice at the biz on how to improve your skills. Includes media studies.
www.englishresources.co.uk – hundreds of free resources available here, it's very useful for revision with a good search engine and sections aimed at each secondary school age range.
www.starfall.com – a US-based phonics site with lots of resources, a hit with the home school fraternity, apparently.

Geography

See also our section on Nature and Environment on page 337.

www.geography.learnontheinternet.co.uk – the place to start, loads of information and activities and the opportunity to ask a geographer if you can't find the help you need.

History

See also our section on History on page 247.

www.learningcurve.gov.uk – covers key stages 2 to 5 using information from the National Archives.

www.schoolhistory.co.uk – excellent site devoted to helping students learn and revise history with quizzes and many free resources. Also has lessons and worksheets for teachers.

www.spartacus.schoolnet.co.uk – masses of information here, organised by topic, so use the search engine to track down information.

Information Technology

www.ictgcse.org.uk – brilliant for GCSE level studies.

www.pctechguide.com – technical information clearly explained.

Languages

See Language section on page 298.

Maths

http://mathforum.org/dr.math – a question and answer service, if your question isn't covered, write to Dr Math direct.

http://mathworld.wolfram.com – an outstanding site devoted to the world of mathematics. It explains the complexities really well and is great for homework. It also has sections on chemistry, physics and astronomy.

http://nrich.maths.org – cheerful site with wide range of activities and problems to enjoy.

www.beam.co.uk – learning maths through game playing, plenty to choose from, covering the very young to teenagers.

www.mathsisfun.com – nicely explained with lots of activities and examples.

www.mymaths.co.uk – lesson format, used in many schools.

www.superkids.com/aweb/tools/math – an American site where you can create your own maths worksheets.

www.tcaep.co.uk/maths/index.htm – comprehensive explanations, also good for Science and Astronomy.

Music

www.essentialsofmusic.com – good overview of classical composers, music and eras with audio clips.
www.musictheory.net – excellent lessons with audio explanations. Staff printing resource is also helpful.
www.revisemusic.org.uk – good revision notes and guides for year 7 through to A level; includes music tech.

Religious Studies

www.reonline.org.uk – good information and a good design makes this a good site for all secondary students and teachers. Provides appropriate links to web resources.

Science

http://lgfl.skoool.co.uk – aimed at 8–14-year olds, there is a wealth of information, simply written with good graphics.
www.biologymad.com – an excellent resource for A level biologists with plenty of information and support resources.
www.exam.net – good site for A level biology, it has lots of interactive features including video clips, but you have to pay.
www.ftexploring.com – quality information with lots of animations.
www.mrothery.co.uk – no frills, A level biology.
ww.sciencemaster.com – great science resource with quality information and links.
www.wpbschoolhouse.btinternet.co.uk – lots of science materials for all secondary levels; particularly good for chemistry A level.
www.zephyrus.co.uk – the advent of whiteboards in the classroom is reflected in this site that brings complete maths and science to the PC. Excellent if you've missed a topic in class, haven't understood it properly, or simply need to revise.

Post-16 and Adult Education

www.learndirect.co.uk   UK
ADULT LEARNING
A government backed site which aims to bring education to everyone whatever their needs. The site explains the background to the initiative plus details of courses and how you can find one that meets your requirements. There's also help for businesses

and a jobs advice section. See also **www.lsc.gov.uk** home of the Learning and Skills Council which provides education for over 16-year olds and **www.lifelonglearning.co.uk** aimed at helping people with their further education ambitions.

www.icslearn.co.uk UK

ONLINE COLLEGE

A great alternative to school or college, enrol in an online course in a wide variety of subjects at GCSE or A level. Alternatively, they offer professional qualifications in such subjects as business, beauty, childminding and IT or certificate courses in a range of 'leisure' subjects, such as gardening and art. Courses vary in fees.

See also:

www.city-and-guilds.co.uk – vocational qualifications with over 500 from which to choose.

www.niace.org.uk – a non-governmental organisation formed to 'support an increase in the total numbers of adults engaged in formal and informal learning in England and Wales; and at the same time to take positive action to improve opportunities and widen access to learning opportunities for those communities under-represented in current provision'.

www.support4learning.org.uk – a wide-ranging resource aimed at helping people support their education needs in a more holistic way.

www.wea.org.uk – the Worker's Educational Association helps provide learning opportunities for everyone but especially those who had missed out or been disadvantaged in some way.

National Curriculum, Government Policy and Support

www.parentscentre.gov.uk UK

HELP YOUR CHILD

For parents who want to be proactive in their child's education, the Government has produced an information packed site to enable you to support your child at home whatever their age and whatever issues you are facing.

www.nc.uk.net UK

NATIONAL CURRICULUM REVEALED

Very detailed explanation of the National Curriculum and prescribed standards.

See also:
www.ace-ed.org.uk – help for parents at the Advisory Centre for Education.
www.dfes.gov.uk – the Department of Education and Skills' site if you want a more overall picture on education.
www.he-special.org.uk – support for people who have children with special educational needs.
www.ofsted.gov.uk – the Office for Standards in Education, check out the standards of your local schools.
www.qca.org.uk – information on the Qualifications and Curriculum Authority.
www.sqa.org.uk – for information on the Scottish education system.

Specialist Education Publishers

Below are listed some of the key education publishers. They often have competitions, online help and free books.

www.activerevision.com – from HarperCollins, at this site you can test yourself to see how likely you are to pass your exams. It then recommends which books would help you to get a pass.
www.cgpbooks.co.uk – a basic online shop with details of their popular study guides, which you can buy online.
www.hoddereducation.co.uk – one of the biggest education publishers offers a fairly staid but useful site. Teachers can order inspection copies of their books.
www.letts-successzone.com – new site from this publisher, it has sections to help with homework plus you can save money on the books.
www.nelsonthornes.co.uk – a typical publishing site with good background on their titles and how to order them. Some books are available as online resources if you register.

Teacher Resources

www.theteachernet.co.uk   UK

ALL A TEACHER NEEDS
An excellent site that pulls together all the education resources that a teacher is likely to need from advice on how to use the Internet to getting a job and, of course, forums; there's even a certificate generator.

See also:
http://edujourney.net – resources, links and ideas for primary teachers.
www.byteachers.org.uk – a collection of useful web sites created by teachers for teachers.
www.darvill.clara.net – online science resources, lots of quizzes.
www.eteach.com – recruitment for teachers.
www.everythingeducation.org – like an education swap shop this site brings education and business together. A great place to find equipment for schools at a decent price.
www.learninginfo.com – excellent site aimed at helping those with learning disabilities.
www.literacymatters.co.uk – a good resource site for teachers on literacy from pre-school to year 7.
www.primaryresources.co.uk – excellent place to go for free lessons, ideas and worksheets.
www.primaryworksheets.co.uk – a straightforward site listing work sheets for primary school teachers.
www.teachingtables.co.uk – work sheet generation and times table help.
www.tes.co.uk – educational resources and news from *The Times Educational Supplement*.

These sites might also be of interest to anyone interested in schools:

www.fundraising.co.uk – helpful ideas.
www.governornet.co.uk – government advice on school governance.
www.ncpta.org.uk – National Association of Parent Teacher Associations.
www.ngc.org.uk – the National Governors' Council.
www.schoolsdirectory.co.uk – good directory of all 33,000 UK schools showing basic information on each school.
www.schoolswebdirectory.co.uk – directory of school websites, see also **www.school-portal.co.uk**

Home Education

It's becoming more common for children to be fully educated at home. Here are a few sites that offer support:

www.heas.org.uk   UK
HOME EDUCATION ADVISORY SERVICE
A good place to start, here you'll find advice and publications
covering the topic, subscription costs £12 per annum.

See also:
www.choiceineducation.org.uk – a magazine devoted to home
education.
www.education-otherwise.org – a site run by a home education
support charity.
www.schoolhouse.org.uk – home education help in Scotland.

Electrical Goods, Gadgets and Appliances

*This section covers stores that sell the usual electrical goods but also
offer a bit more in terms of range, offers or service.*

www.comet.co.uk   UK
ALWAYS LOW PRICES, GUARANTEED
A pretty messy site these days with masses of offers on the front
page, having said that it's a great place to view the widest range
of goods at excellent prices.

www.dixons.co.uk   UK
OFFERS GALORE
The Dixons site has plenty of offers and reflects what you'd
find in their stores very well. It has a similar but slightly wider
product range to Comet, with an additional photographic section.
Delivery costs vary.

www.richersounds.com   UK
LOWEST PRICES GUARANTEED
Despite the fact this site wouldn't win design awards, bargain
hunters will want to include this site on their list. It's similar
to the other electrical goods' retailers but with a leaning
towards music and TVs, with plenty of offers and advice.
There is a search facility and they offer a price challenge
guarantee.

www.maplin.co.uk   UK

ELECTRONICS CATALOGUE

Maplin is well established and it's a bit of an event when the new catalogue is published. Now you can always have access to the latest innovations and basic equipment at this well-put-together site. It features the expected massive range with free delivery for orders over £35.

See also:

www.24-7electrical.co.uk – well designed and looks strong on customer service judging by the number of times they ask you to contact them.

www.be-direct.co.uk – some very good offers and a wide range.

www.clearance-comet.co.uk – electrical giant Comet clears stock through this auction site.

www.discount-appliances.co.uk – excellent range of kitchen appliances but awful site design. Having said that, product pictures are good.

www.electricaldiscountuk.co.uk – a pretty straightforward site with some good offers and a wide range.

www.empiredirect.co.uk – a busy-looking site with lots of offers and a wide range.

www.hughesdirect.co.uk – a solid offer from this well established retailer.

www.rtwodesign.ndirect.co.uk – good-looking site from this kitchen specialist.

www.searchappliance.co.uk – well-illustrated store from another kitchen appliance specialist.

www.we-sell-it.co.uk – is also worth a visit for good prices on kitchen and other domestic appliances.

www.ezee-fix.co.uk formerly www.appliancespares.co.uk   UK

FIX IT YOURSELF

Ezee-Fix has thousands of spare parts for a massive range of products, nearly all illustrated, including fridges, cookers, microwaves, vacuum cleaners, etc. All it needs is online fitting instructions and it would be perfect.

Other places for technology geeks to get their kicks are:

www.gadgetshop.co.uk – offer free delivery on orders over £50 and a free returns policy.

www.firebox.com – for a really wide range of gadgets amongst other boys' toys.

www.simplyradios.com   UK
RADIOS SPECIALIST
An excellent site devoted to radios and the first place to go if
you want something groovy or the latest thing in digital. For
specialists in digital radio go to **www.pure-digital.com**

English Usage

With the success of the book Eats, Shoots and Leaves, *English
grammar, punctuation and usage have come under the spotlight and it
seems there's even more pressure to get it right. If you're not sure
where apostrophes go or what a noun or pronoun is, then these sites
can help. If it is a dictionary you're after, those are found on page 399.*

www.learnenglish.org.uk   UK

LEARNING ENGLISH
An excellent site from the British Council primarily aimed at
those for whom English is a second language but it has a huge
amount of information for students and those who just want to
brush up. Check out the excellent kids' section too.

See also:
www.apostrophe.fsnet.co.uk – learn how to use and misuse
them at the home of the Apostrophe Protection Society.
www.askoxford.com/betterwriting – grammar, spelling, letter
writing and effective communication.
www.cogs.susx.ac.uk/local/doc/punctuation/node00.html – a
guide to punctuation from Sussex University.
www.dailygrammar.com – grammar lessons and quizzes.
www.englishclub.net – learn and teach English with the help of
this comprehensive site; you have to register, but it's free.
www.english-zone.com – an American site and directory
devoted to learning English; it's useful, but you have to register,
around £20 p/a.
www.gramster.com – a free 'light' programme to help with your
grammar; however, the full programme is quite expensive.
www.odps.org/glossword/index.php – the online dictionary of
playground slang.
www.phrases.org.uk – look up the meanings and origins of
thousands of phrases and sayings.
www.plainenglish.co.uk – the Plain English Campaign and their
fight to make everything clear. Check out the free guides, which
are most helpful.

www.soundsofenglish.org – English pronunciation.
www.ucl.ac.uk/internet-grammar – a free online course about English grammar aimed at university undergraduates but useful nonetheless.
www.usingenglish.com – a solid English language learning site.
www.vocabulary.co.il – excellent site for building vocabulary using simple word games such as hangman and wordsearch.
www.whoohoo.co.uk – confused by your English dialects? Here's a translation service!
www.wordspy.com – an excellent place to find new words.
www.worldwidewords.org – an interesting and personal look at English and how it's developing abroad.

E-mail

Here's a selection of the best free e-mail providers. There are hundreds to chose from, but hopefully these sites should help you find the one that's right for you, whether you're after efficiency or a trendy @ moniker.

www.fepg.net   US
FREE E-MAIL PROVIDERS GUIDE
Here's the place to start. It lists over 1,400 providers in 85 countries, including over 40 from the UK, so it's pretty comprehensive. It tends to just list them with a few details but there are recommended sites too. There's also a news section and forums.

http://googlemail.com   US
GOOGLE MAIL
Once you sign up, which is easy, you get access to an e-mail program, which is much like any other online, except there is more than enough storage and you get lots of adverts. You do get quick links to the calendar and other Google services such as spreadsheets, which can be very useful. It also works well with your mobile phone and there appears to be lots of help and support, which is more than can be said for many other services.

www.sneakemail.com   US
TOTAL SPAM CONTROL
Sneak E-mail provides an e-mail protection service whereby you can maintain a level of anonymity, stop spam or unsuitable

e-mails getting to you, avoid unwanted soliciting or prevent others from selling your e-mail address to marketing companies, for example.

www.twigger.co.uk   UK
ANYWHERE IN THE WORLD
An excellent service that enables you to use your chosen e-mail address wherever you may be. One advantage is that you can see attachments before you download them onto your PC. The service is subscription based; unfortunately not all ISPs covered.

www.emailaddresses.com   US
E-MAIL ADDRESS DIRECTORY
A useful directory of e-mail services and programs to help you manage your e-mail and mail to your site if you own one; there are also tips on how to find an e-mail address and a directory of address directories. See also **www.web-email-addresses.com**, a very good directory with site and software reviews.

www.spamcop.com   US
STOP SPAM
Spam is a term used to describe unsolicited commercial e-mail, we all get bombarded by it and at this site you can download a useful little program that will help you minimise it. See also **www.qurb.com** and **http://spamarrest.com** and **www.spaminspector.com**

See also:
http://gmail.google.com – this is Google's e-mail project, it offers lots of memory and flexibility and you can now access via your mobile phone. Make sure you read the small print.
www.cloudmark.com – a highly recommended e-mail security program.
www.didtheyreadit.com – a program that offers an automatic receipt so that you can tell when someone has opened the mail you sent them.
www.hotmail.com – one of the original online e-mail sites from Microsoft and it's still one of the best, but not cool.
www.pocomail.com – a well-recommended-flexible and secure e-mail program.

Ethical and Green Topics

Ethics is a difficult subject but if you are concerned about the effect you are having on the environment, want to live a greener lifestyle and reduce your carbon footprint or are concerned about the origins and manufacture of what you buy, then this listing will help. Some of the sites are already reviewed in other sections of The Good Web Site Guide.

www.alotoforganics.co.uk   UK
  LEAN, GREEN SEARCH MACHINE
  UK search engine for everything organic including facts,
  news, events, gifts, food, alternative therapies, finance and
  shops. For an alternative try **www.greenchoices.org** which is
  comprehensive. For a portal approach, **www.eco-portal.com**
  is a massive site covering all things green.

www.carbonfootprint.com   UK
  WHAT'S YOURS?
  Calculate the amount of carbon pollution you create and find
  out what you can do to minimise it. For alternatives try
  www.mycarbonfootprint.eu, **www.carboncalculator.org** or
  www.carbonneutral.com – all will calculate your CO_2 emissions
  and advise on ways to neutralise your carbon debt.

Animals and Plants

  www.forestry.gov.uk – Forestry Commission has details of its
  work and how you can help sustain Britain's woods and forests.
  www.fsc-uk.org – Forest Stewardship Council UK, an
  international non-governmental organisation promoting the
  responsible management of the world's forests.
  www.ifaw.org – home of the International Fund for Animal
  Welfare.
  www.rspb.org.uk – the Royal Society for the Protection of Birds.
  www.rspca.org.uk – the Royal Society for the Prevention of
  Cruelty to Animals.
  www.traffic.org – a campaigning site working against the illegal
  and sometimes appalling trade in animals throughout the world.
  www.ufaw.org.uk – improving animal welfare using scientific
  knowledge.
  www.wwf.org.uk – WWF site with detailed information for
  conservationists on habitats, areas of global importance,
  endangered wildlife and the latest campaigns.

Earth

The Good Web Site Guide's Top 10s
of the Internet

1. http://earth.google.com – download the Google earth program and amaze yourself
2. www.terraserver.com – buy satellite imagery
3. http://visibleearth.nasa.gov – download superb images from NASA
4. www.geographyiq.com – the online world atlas
5. www.nationmaster.com – more planetary statistics than you'll ever need
6. http://eol.jsc.nasa.gov – astronaut photography of Earth
7. www.fourmilab.ch/earthview – the earth from space
8. www.earthfromtheair.com – aerial photographs
9. www.weatherimages.org – watching the weather
10. www.citypopulation.de – pick a city, learn about it

Energy

www.co2balance.com – information and help on how to lessen your carbon footprint.

www.eaga.co.uk – the Energy Action Grants Agency.

www.energysaving.me.uk – energy saving products.

www.energywatch.org.uk – independent energy watchdog.

www.est.org.uk – home of the Energy Saving Trust.

www.greenelectricity.org – sign up for a greener tariff.

www.nef.org.uk – energy-saving advice from the UK charity for energy efficiency, the National Energy Foundation.

www.ofgem.gov.uk – the UK's electricity and gas regulation body.

www.switchandgive.com – switch suppliers and give the savings to charity.

www.uswitch.com – switch to a green energy supplier.

Environment

http://chooseclimate.org – interactive climate models – scare yourself ...

www.airquality.co.uk – air quality information for the UK.

www.cat.org.uk – Centre for Alternative Technology offering practical solutions to environmental problems.

www.defra.gov.uk – the Department for Environment, Food and Rural Affairs.

www.ecozine.co.uk – a good news site with lots of comment, opinions and links. The design could be more user-friendly though.

www.emagazine.com – the *Environmental Magazine* online.

www.envirolink.org – environmental community site with lots of info and links.

www.environment.about.com – information on environmental issues.

www.environment-agency.gov.uk – the Environment Agency's site offers information on the latest initiatives and news.

www.environmentwebsites.co.uk – a portal for environmental sites.

www.ewg.org – the Environmental Working Group, dedicated to the fight against pollution; US-oriented.

www.foe.co.uk – Friends of the Earth.

www.greenpeace.org – find out about their latest activities and how to get involved.

www.localcooling.com – change the settings of your PC so that it uses less energy.

www.lowimpact.org – Low Impact Living Initiative, a non-profit organisation protecting the global environment.

www.planetdiary.com – monitoring world environmental events.

www.projectearth.com – recognising the damaging effect man has on the environment and pointing the way towards a better future.

www.scorecard.org – the facts on local pollution from this US-oriented but informative site.

www.treehugger.com – outstanding web-based magazine 'dedicated to everything that has a modern aesthetic yet is environmentally responsible'.

www.wen.org.uk – Women's Environmental Network. A campaigning organisation covering environmental and health issues.

www.wri.org – World Resources Institute promoting effective campaigning for a far better world.

Fashion

See also entries under 'Shopping' below.

www.cleanclothes.org – improving conditions for those working in the garment-making industry.
www.ethicalthreads.co.uk – clothing not made in sweatshops.
www.furisdead.com – anti-fur campaigning.
www.iftf.com – the fur trade's organisation for the opposite view.
www.labourbehindthelabel.org – campaigning for workers' rights with a list of good traders and retailers.

Finance

www.abcul.coop – Association of British Credit Unions.
www.co-operativebank.co.uk – banking with a conscience; also **www.smile.co.uk** their online bank.
www.ecology.co.uk – The Ecology Building Society which is a mutual society promoting sustainable housing and communities.
www.eiris.org – The Ethical Investment Research Service offers independent research into corporate behaviour.
www.ethicalinvestment.org.uk – ethical savings.
www.letslinkuk.net – Local Exchange Trading Schemes.
www.switchwithwhich.co.uk – switch bank accounts.
www.triodos.co.uk – Triodos Bank offers environmentally sound savings accounts.
www.uksif.org – UK Social Investment Forum, the UK network for socially responsible investment.

Food

www.ciwf.org.uk – Compassion in World Farming web site, campaigning for farm animal welfare, includes the Eat Less Meat initiative.
www.earthsave.org – promotes vegetarianism by helping you choose the right way to eat.
www.farmersmarkets.net – find your nearest Farmers' Market.
www.foodag.com – food additives.
www.freedomfood.co.uk – RSPCA site on farm animal health.
www.goodnessdirect.co.uk – supermarket with over 4,000 items including good range of grocery, fresh and frozen products.
www.organicdelivery.co.uk – a good organic food retailer – delivers to London only.
www.organicfood.co.uk – news and links on all things organic.

www.soilassociation.org – the Soil Association web site with masses of information on organic food, farming and education resources.

www.sustainweb.org – the Alliance for Better Food and Farming site with lots of information and links on sustainable farming, seasonal food and reducing food miles.

www.swaddles.co.uk – a wide range of organic food including meat.

www.vegansociety.com – The Vegan Society web site.

www.vintageroots.co.uk – excellent for organic wines, spirits and beers.

www.whyorganic.org – a Soil Association site covering a variety of issues about organic versus non-organic produce.

Home and Gardening

www.allotments-uk.com – all you need to know about owning an allotment.

www.communityrepaint.org.uk – a UK network to reuse old paint and redistribute to charities, voluntary organisations and local groups.

www.ecosolutions.co.uk – safe water-based paint and varnish removers.

www.gardenorganic.org.uk formerly **www.hedra.org.uk** – still the leading authority on organic gardening.

www.greenbuildingstore.co.uk – green building products online.

www.greengardener.co.uk – specialists in biological and organic pest control.

www.just-green.com – natural home and garden products, particularly good on natural pest control and gardening backed up with good info.

www.organiccatalogue.com – a comprehensive store related to the HDRA.

www.pan-uk.org – the Pesticide Action Network who are working to eliminate the hazards associated with pesticides.

www.salvo.com – reclaim old furniture.

Miscellaneous

www.downsizer.net – a magazine-style site from an online community consisting of those wishing to live more sustainably.

www.idealswork.com – compare and find out about the ethical track records of major companies.

www.naturaldeath.org.uk – The Natural Death Centre's site, covering woodland burials and green funerals.

www.who.int – the World Health Organisation, the UN specialist agency with comprehensive information on every aspect of health.

www.willaid.org – draw up a will and simultaneously support charity.

Recycling

E

www.cartridges4charity.co.uk – charity recycling inkjet cartridges, toner cartridges and mobile phones.

www.cleanaway.co.uk – recycling specialists.

www.crn.org.uk – the Community Recycling Network.

www.fonebak.com – mobile phone reuse and recycling.

www.freecycle.org – join a local group and give away unwanted items to other members.

www.letsrecycle.com – waste management company directory.

www.oilbankline.org.uk – find your nearest waste oil recycling site.

www.oxfam.org.uk/what_you_can_do/recycle/phones.htm – mobile phone recycling, including school and corporate schemes.

www.paper.org.uk/info/recycling.htm – Confederation of Paper Industries.

www.recoup.org – national charity developing plastics recycling; find a site near your home.

www.save-a-cup.co.uk – join a scheme to recycle cups from vending machines.

www.vao.org.uk – Vision Aid Overseas, international charity which recycles spectacles.

www.wastewatch.org.uk – nationwide organisation promoting action on waste reduction and improved recycling and reuse.

www.webdirectory.com/recycling – general information on recycling.

www.wrap.org.uk – The Waste and Resources Action Programme, creating markets for recycled products.

Shopping

http://alotofshopping.co.uk – guilt free ethical shopping site.

www.afrigoods.org – quality gifts from Africa with profits going to the artists who made them.

www.allthingsgreen.net – huge range of ecofriendly products from UK-based small companies.

www.cardaid.co.uk – charity Christmas cards.

www.crueltyfreeshop.com – a wide range of products on sale all of which are guaranteed not to have involved any animal cruelty or exploitation in their production.

www.ecozone.co.uk – online shopping for environmentally friendly household products.

www.ethicalconsumer.org – *Ethical Consumer Magazine*, ethical information behind the big brand names.

www.ethiscore.org – identify the best products to support and the ones to avoid by following their ethical score.

www.fairdealtrading.com – Fair Deal Trading Partnership for footballs and trainers.

www.fairtrade.org.uk – home of the Fair Trade Foundation, which exists to enable poor artists and workers to get a better deal.

www.getethical.com – who have a wide range of ethically produced and sourced products plus advice, links and a magazine.

www.goodgifts.org – online charitable alternative gifts catalogue.

www.greatgifts.org – World Vision charity website offering alternative, online gifts catalogue.

www.greenshop.co.uk – online shop selling hundreds of environmentally friendly products including paint and household cleaners.

www.naturalcollection.com – comprehensive range of products from clothing to food and cosmetics.

www.onevillage.org – shop specialising in ethnic products and using the Fair Trade system.

www.surefish.co.uk – Christian Aid web site with information on ethical living including shopping, gifts and energy.

www.thegreenshoppingguide.co.uk – green and ethical products and services directory which links to providers' sites.

www.traidcraftshop.co.uk – good selection of crafts, foods and other goods from around the world.

Tourism

See also page 510.

http://travel.guardian.co.uk/tag/green – articles, advice, info from the *Guardian* travel pages.

www.changingworlds.co.uk – worthwhile working holidays.

www.coralcay.org – 'providing resources to help sustain livelihoods and alleviate poverty through the protection, restoration and management of coral reefs and tropical forests'.

www.ecoafrica.com – the wonders of Africa for the ecologically minded.

www.ecoclub.com – a network providing a wealth of information about all aspects of ecotourism.

www.eco-tour.org – Eco Tourism directory.

www.ecotourism.org – the International Ecotourism Society.

www.ecotravel.com – good all-round travel site from US.

www.ecovolunteer.com – if you want to give your services to a specific animal benefit project.

www.responsibletravel.com – eco-friendly and ethically responsible holidays.

www.tourismconcern.org.uk – campaigning for more sensitive tourism and advice on how to be a better tourist.

www.transportdirect.info – find public transport routes and driving instructions between places in the UK. Calculate fuel and emissions costs and more.

Transport

www.carclubs.org.uk – CarPlus charity site looking at responsible car use, car clubs and car sharing.

www.citycarclub.co.uk – formerly Smartmoves, pay for car use by the hour.

www.est.org.uk – the Energy Saving Trust, see under 'transport' for tips on greener driving and alternative transport.

www.eta.co.uk – The Environmental Transport Association.

www.liftshare.com – car sharing web site.

www.sustrans.org.uk – nation-wide charity encouraging alternative methods of transport.

Volunteering

www.btcv.org.uk – The British Trust for Conservation Volunteers, including UK and global projects and Green Gyms.

www.csv.org.uk – Community Service Volunteers, the UK's largest volunteering and training organisation.

Water

www.hippo-the-watersaver.co.uk – water-saving device.

www.ofwat.gov.uk – the government regulator for the water industry.

www.wateraid.org.uk – international non-governmental organisation dedicated to the provision of safe water and sanitation.

www.waterconserve.info – general information on water conservation.

E-zines

E-zines are the magazines of the web and there were masses of them, some with great content and quality writing. They do seem to be in decline, suffering from the popularity of blogging; several of our favourites have met their demise this year. You should be aware that many contain adult or pornographic material.

http://ezinearticles.com   US

FOR WRITERS AND PUBLISHERS
Writers are able to post articles on the site, while publishers in need of content can search the database for ready-to-wear content. Free trial membership.

Some of the Best

www.salon.com   US

 SALON
An outstanding magazine offering a wide range of articles and topics with quality contributors and excellent writing. It's entertaining and witty, covering the latest news and in depth features on current topics.

www.theregister.co.uk   UK

 THE REGISTER
An opinionated and newsy e-zine devoted to the technology and computing worlds – it describes itself as 'biting the hand that feeds'. It's not an easy read but it's very authoritative.

www.theonion.com   US

AMERICA'S FINEST NEWS SOURCE
A great send-up of American tabloid newspapers, this is one of the most visited sites on the Internet and easily one of the funniest.

See also:
www.foocha.com – an 'outspoken entertainment review' covering movies, games, music, books and the media.

ww.urban75.com – boasting 500,000 hits per month, provides a non-mainstream view of life including news on raves, protest, drugs, short stories, photos, analysis and more.

Fashion and Accessories

The big brands have never been cheaper. Selling fashion and designer gear is another success story for the internet as customers flock to the great discounts that are on offer and get access to the latest fashion trends. Many people still prefer to try clothes on before buying but the good sites all offer a convenient returns policy.

Fashion

www.fuk.co.uk   UK
FASHION UK
All you ever need to know about the latest in UK and world fashion, updated daily. There's a good links library, competitions, chat and, of course, shopping. It's all packaged into a really attractive site, which initially looks cluttered but is OK once you get used to it.

www.vogue.co.uk   UK
THE LATEST NEWS FROM BRITISH *VOGUE*
An absolute must for the serious follower of fashion. There's the latest catwalk news and views, Vogue TV for the latest fashion footage and a handy who's who of fashion. You can order a subscription too. For a similar experience try **www.elle.com** or the slightly less fashion-oriented but more fun American **www.cosmomag.com**

www.ftv.com   FRANCE
FASHION TV
The 24-hour fashion station, so popular in gyms and bars, has a good site offering the latest from around the world. Features include video clips, radio interviews with designers plus links, gossip and horoscopes.

www.net-a-porter.com   UK
NET A PORTER
A great-looking site that is easy to use with information on the latest fashions, plus catwalk reports and shopping where you can browse by designer or product type.

www.yoox.com   UK
> TOP DESIGNERS
> A great-looking site with top offers from the top designers. It's
> well laid out and easy to navigate with a refining search facility
> and good returns policy. You can search by designer or category
> and the quality of the photos is good. Offers range from a few
> pounds to massive discounts.

www.haburi.com   UK
> CUT-PRICE DESIGNER CLOTHES FOR MEN AND WOMEN
> Not a big range of clothes but excellent prices. Clear, no-
> nonsense design makes the site easy to use.

www.apc.fr   FRANCE
> FRENCH CHIC FROM APC
> Unusual in style and for something a little different, APC's site
> is worth a visit. Delivery is expensive in line with the clothes,
> which are beautifully designed and well presented. For more of
> the French look go to **www.redoute.co.uk**

www.extremepie.com   UK
> EXTREME FASHION FOR EXTREME SPORTS
> A brand-led selection of clothes from the world of BMX, surf,
> skate and other so-called sports. The site is excellent with clear
> visuals and delivery costs start at £2.95.

www.pop-boutique.com   UK
> BUY SOMETHING THAT'S ALREADY OUT OF DATE!
> A fantastic site devoted to fashion chic from the 60s, 70s and
> 80s, it can be a little slow but worth the wait if you're into the
> period. It also sells accessories and offers a good set of related
> links.

www.badfads.com   US
> IT SHOULD NEVER HAVE HAPPENED ...
> An entertaining site featuring the Bad Fad Museum full of
> clothes, events and collectibles that maybe we'd be better off
> not remembering. The whole is a fun reminiscence of the 70s
> and 80s.

> *Other fashion sites worth a peek:*
> **www.colette.fr** – an eclectic collection of quirky products and
> fashion items, we can't work out if the web site is brilliantly
> designed or just plain annoying.

www.fashionangel.com – excellent directory and portal for fashion-related links.

www.fashionguide.com – US-oriented fashion gossip and tips.

www.fashion.net – a good fashion search engine and directory plus the latest fashion news.

www.fashionplanet.com – New York-oriented fashion magazine and store.

www.firstview.com – be among the first to see the latest from the fashion shows, you have to subscribe though.

www.girlonthestreet.com – home to a New York trend agency with some top tips and a sneak preview on what's coming up.

www.hintmag.com – a well-designed fashion e-zine with regular features, news and links. The photography is especially good.

www.japanesestreets.com – the latest on Japanese street fashion.

www.kitschshop.co.uk – who offer lots beside just clothes.

www.lucire.com – another fashion magazine, this one is well thought of and it covers everything from catwalk style to skincare.

www.monsoon.co.uk – good illustrations and online store.

www.newoxygen.co.uk – nice site, 'activewear' for women, all the big names and reasonable prices.

www.ntgi.net/ICCF&D/textile.htm – an encyclopaedia of textiles and materials used in fashion and tailoring.

www.oasis-stores.com – good-looking site with information on the latest trends, also see the vintage collection not available in many stores.

www.retrorebels.co.uk – quirky and streetwise.

www.toastbypost.co.uk – good mail-order catalogue with the latest designs.

and a few blogs ...

http://stylebubble.typepad.com – a stylish, well-written fashion blog.

www.catwalk-queen.net – entertaining blog that follows the latest fashions and their victims.

www.gofugyourself.com – a very amusing blog devoted to the worst fashions worn by the stars. It introduces the word Fugly, meaning 'frightfully ugly' ... celebrities beware!

Top Designers

www.armaniexchange.com – cheap Armani

www.bensherman.co.uk – Ben Sherman

www.chanel.com – Chanel
www.christian-lacroix.fr – Christian Lacroix
www.dior.com – Dior
www.gucci.com – Gucci
www.hugo.com – Hugo Boss
www.jpgaultier.fr – Jean Paul Gaultier
www.karenmillen.com – Karen Millen
www.kenzo.com – Kenzo
www.paulsmith.co.uk – Paul Smith
www.tedbaker.co.uk – Ted Baker
www.tommy.com – Tommy Hilfiger

General Clothes Stores

www.arcadia.co.uk   UK
THE UK'S LEADING FASHION RETAILER
The Arcadia Group has over 1,200 stores in the UK and the web
sites are accessible, easy to use and offer good value for money.
Each site has its own personality that reflects the high street
store. Delivery charges vary.

www.burton.co.uk – Burton
www.dorothyperkins.co.uk – Dorothy Perkins
www.evans.ltd.uk – Evans
www.missselfridge.co.uk – Miss Selfridge
www.outfitfashion.com – Outfit
www.topman.co.uk – Topman
www.topshop.co.uk – Topshop
www.wallis-fashion.com – Wallis

www.zoom.co.uk   UK
MORE THAN JUST A SHOP
This is an excellent magazine-style site, with lots of features
other than shopping, such as free Internet access and e-mail.
Shopping consists of links to specialist retailers. You can enter
prize draws and there are a number of exclusive offers as well.
Not always the cheapest, but an entertaining shopping site.

Catalogues

www.kaysnet.com   UK
KAYS CATALOGUE
Massive range combined with value for money is the formula for
success with Kays. While they lead with clothes there are plenty

of other sections outside of that: jewellery, home entertainment, toys, etc. They offer free 48-hour delivery.

www.freemans.co.uk   UK
FREE DELIVERY IN THE UK AND GOOD PRICES
A similar site to Kays, not the full catalogue but there's a wide range to choose from, including top brands. They offer free delivery for UK customers. There are also prizes to be won, special features on topical themes and information on how to get the full catalogue. For another version of the same web site see **www.grattan.co.uk** for Grattan's catalogue online.

ww.next.co.uk   UK
THE NEXT DIRECTORY
The online version of the Next catalogue is available including clothes for men, women and children as well as products for the home. Prices are the same as the directory, while you can order the full catalogue for £3.50.

See also:
www.aboundonline.com – a catalogue site with a very good choice, which also offers a style guide and outfit finder service.
www.boden.co.uk – a well presented and efficient offering from one of the big success stories in catalogue selling.
www.cottontraders.co.uk – the site reflects the slightly old-fashioned feel of this company, which some may find comforting. Some good offers too.
www.landsend.com – an amazing amount of choice is available at this well-designed site.
www.littlewoods-online.com – wide selection from across the range.
www.mandmdirect.com – bright and breezy site which has a good layout, plenty of choice and offers.

Specialist Clothes Stores

www.asos.com   UK
CELEBRITY FASHION
Formerly **SeenonScreen.com**, this site no longer features the fashions worn by the stars on telly, instead concentrates on celebrity fashion trends identifying high street look-alike fashion at affordable prices. They claim to be one of the top two visited on-line fashion sites. See also **www.celebfashion.co.uk**

www.enokiworld.com   US
VINTAGE CLOTHES FOR MODERN WOMEN
A nicely designed site with a wide range of vintage clothing.
Prices and delivery costs vary according to what you buy. See
also **www.candysays.co.uk** who offer a wide range of clothes
and accessories plus menswear too.

www.bloomingmarvellous.co.uk   UK
MATERNITY WEAR
The UK's leading store in maternity and babywear has an
attractive site that features a good selection of clothes and
nursery products. There are no discounts on the clothes, but
they do have regular sales with some good bargains.

Underwear and Lingerie

www.figleaves.com   UK
MORE THAN JUST A FIG LEAF
Fig Leaves has become a big Internet success with a huge range
of lingerie from most major designers with plenty of offers and
an easy-to-use site. If it's upmarket or hard to find sizes that
you're after also check out **www.rigbyandpeller.com**

www.amplebosom.com   UK
ITS ALL IN THE NAME
One of the media's favourite Internet success stories, Sally sells
bras for everyone, including large and small sizes, mastectomy,
nursing and maternity bras.

See also:
www.kiniki.com – more men's underwear.
www.knowknockers.co.uk – er … for those with no knockers.
www.lasenza.co.uk – good selection for ladies and reasonable
prices includes glamour, character, nightwear and swimwear.
www.littlewomen.co.uk – solutions for little women.
www.nicolajane.com – good selection of feminine mastectomy
bras and swimwear.
www.pantypostman.co.uk – apparently the average life
expectancy of a pair of panties is 3 months, so here you can set
up a regular subscription to have new pairs posted to you at
regular intervals.
www.victoriassecret.com – for designer style, but beware high
shipping costs.

Shoes

www.shoe-shop.com   UK
> EUROPE'S BIGGEST SHOE SHOP
> A massive selection of shoes and brands to chose from. The
> site is nicely designed with good pictures of the shoes, some of
> which can be seen in 3-D, a facility they are expanding. Delivery
> is included in the price and there's a good returns policy.

> *See also:*
> **http://shoeblogs.com** – get advice from Manolo, entertaining
> blog!
> **www.britfoot.com** – home of the British Footwear Association
> for hard-to-find footwear.
> **www.cosyfeet.com** – a good site devoted to extra roomy
> footwear and socks!
> **www.elephantfeet.com** – stylish shoes in larger sizes.
> **www.faith.co.uk** – a well-reviewed and recommended shoe
> shop aimed at fashion conscious women. It has a good shoe
> comparison feature.
> **www.immortalsole.co.uk** – excellent site devoted to retro
> trainers.
> **www.magnusshoes.com** – another large size specialist, with a
> good site.
> **www.office.co.uk** – neat site design from this High Street
> retailer.
> **www.shoesdirect.co.uk** – straightforward with some good offers.
> **www.shoetailor.com** – a huge range from this popular specialist.
> **www.shoes.co.uk** – a shopping directory devoted to online shoe
> shops.

www.centuryinshoes.com   UK
> SHOE HISTORY
> An interesting and very well-designed site devoted to the
> development of the shoe from 1900 to the present day, each
> shoe and boot is available to view in three dimensions and you
> can get into the detail easily.

Accessories and Jewellery

www.jewellers.net   UK
> THE BIGGEST RANGE ON THE NET
> Excellent range of products, fashion jewellery, gifts, gold and
> silver; the watch section is particularly strong. There is also

information on the history of gems, the manufacturers and brands available. They boast a 30-day no quibble returns policy.

www.watches.co.uk   UK

Retailers of watches for many years; the Swiss Watch Company provides a wide range of upmarket watches, if you can't find the one you want you can contact them for help. For cheaper alternatives try the following sites: **www.easywatch.com**, **www.thewatchhut.co.uk** and also **www.jbwatches.co.uk**

Also check out:

www.designerdivas.co.uk – good designer jewellery for those who are Delightful-Individual-Vivacious-Attractive-Sexy.

www.funkyaccessories.com – a wide choice with shoes, lingerie and some good offers too.

www.ganesha.co.uk – an excellent store featuring Indian products sold and produced on an ethical basis. Limited amount of clothing, but lots of accessories.

www.geraldonline.com – a wide range of jewellery and watches from Gerald Ratner and associates.

www.jewellerycatalogue.co.uk – guaranteed low prices.

www.madaboutjewellery.com – costume jewellery with designer style.

www.newurban.co.uk – hats, gloves, scarves all in the latest styles.

www.timetoindulge.co.uk – a wide range of cheap jewellery.

www.be-a-fashionista.co.uk   UK

DESIGNER BAGS

If you don't want to go to the expense of buying a designer handbag then you can hire one; however at prices starting at £29.99 a month you have to be a real fashionista to want this. For those who just want to buy a bag then choose from any one of the following: **www.blitzbags.co.uk** for designer gear, **www.brandedbags.com** for both designer and the more traditional and **www.ebags.co.uk** for a broad selection.

Finance, Banking and Shares

The Internet is proving to be a real winner when it comes to personal finance, product comparison and home share dealing. With these sites you will get the latest advice and may even make some money.

Money, Money, Money ...

The Good Web Site Guide's Top 10s
of the Internet

1. **www.fsa.gov.uk** – the place to start, the Financial Services Authority
2. **www.find.co.uk** – the biggest and best financial portal site
3. **www.fool.co.uk** – for those who want some fun with their finance
4. **www.bankfacts.org.uk** – all the information on internet banking and more
5. **www.uswitch.co.uk** – switch services here and save money
6. **www.inlandrevenue.gov.uk** – home of the tax man
7. **www.unbiased.co.uk** – go here to find a financial adviser
8. **www.pensionguide.gov.uk** – excellent advice on pensions
9. **www.moneysavingexpert.com** – expert Martin Lewis dispenses financial joy
10. **www.paypal.com** – the secure way to pay for stuff online

General Finance Information Sites, Directories and Mortgages

www.fsa.gov.uk   UK

> FINANCIAL SERVICES AUTHORITY
> The regulating body that you can go to if you need help with your rights or if you want to find out about financial products; it will also help you to verify that the financial institution you're dealing with is legitimate. See also **www.oft.gov.uk** for the Office of Fair Trading and its informative site.

www.financial-ombudsman.org.uk   UK

> FINANCIAL OMBUDSMAN SERVICES
> When you have a complaint about a financial service this is a good point of call for sensible advice and help on how to go about getting a fair hearing.

www.find.co.uk   UK

> INTERNET DIRECTORY FOR FINANCIAL SERVICES
> Access to thousands of financial sites; split into nine sections:

loans, credit cards, insurance, mortgages, investment, banking and savings, life and pensions, advice and information, business services and some hints on best buys. Superb. See also **www.financelink.co.uk**

www.ft.com or www.ftyourmoney.com   UK
FINANCIAL TIMES
FT.com offers up-to-date news and information. The 'Your Money' section is biased towards personal finance. Although it looks daunting, it is easy to use and provides sound, independent advice for everyone.

www.fool.co.uk   US/UK
THE MOTLEY FOOL
Finance with a sense of fun. The Fool is exciting and a real education in shrewdness. It not only takes the mystery out of share dealing but gives great advice on investment and personal finance. You need to register to get the best out of it.

www.thisismoney.com   UK
MONEY NEWS AND ADVICE
Easy-to-use site with reliable 24-hour financial advice from the Daily Mail group. It has loads of information on all aspects of personal finance and is particularly good for comparison tools, especially mortgages, and there's a good 'Ask the Experts' section.

www.iii.co.uk   UK
INTERACTIVE INVESTOR INTERNATIONAL
Now known as Ample, the emphasis is on investment and share dealing with some personal finance thrown in. It retains the interactivity of the original site but with some additional investment information.

www.moneynet.co.uk   UK
IMPARTIAL AND COMPREHENSIVE
Rated as one of the best independent personal finance sites, it covers over 100 mortgage lenders, has a user-friendly search facility plus help with conveyancing and financial calculators. It now also covers banking, refused credit and life insurance.

www.moneychimp.com   US
THE BASICS
If you're baffled by all things financial, here you'll find really simple explanations on most aspects of finance and the

economy. There's a helpful glossary. Be aware that the site is American, so a few of the definitions are slightly different.

For other similar sites go to:

www.advfn.com – a really ugly site but comprehensive, if you can put up with the design.

www.adviceonline.co.uk – independent financial advice on a logically designed site.

www.bbc.co.uk – check out the 'your money guides' under 'business and money', great for keeping up to date with the latest financial news.

www.digitallook.com – one of the leading providers of financial information, excellent site.

www.financialplanning.org.uk – help from the Institute of Financial Planning.

www.financial-planning.uk.com – a wide range of advice available but the site could be more organised and accessible.

www.marketplace.co.uk – 'independent' advisers from Bradford & Bingley help you make the right financial choices from mortgages to investments and pensions.

www.moneymadeclear.fsa.gov.uk – great new look site from the FSA with good financial guides to download and good comparative tools. If you don't know where to start, take their 'financial healthcheck'.

www.moneybrain.co.uk – a slick site offering a wide range of financial products and independent advice.

www.moneyfacts.co.uk – a no-nonsense information site which shows the cheapest and best value financial products with lots of authority, it's also a comparatively fast site and less tricky than some. It also covers annuities and offshore banking.

www.moneysupermarket.com – a very good all-rounder with help in most of the important areas of personal finance; good site layout and lots of practical advice add to the package.

www.unbiased.co.uk   UK

FIND AN INDEPENDENT FINANCIAL ADVISER

A good independent financial adviser is hard to come by if you need one. But here's a good place to start. Just type in your postcode and the services you need and up pops a list of specialists in your area. While at the Personal Finance Society, **www.thepfs.org** you can find out how to get the best financial advice and have a financial health check too.

www.quote-engine.com UK
>BEST VALUE CREDIT
>A guide to help you find the best deals on credit cards and loans. It's easy enough to use and there are online forms as well as links. It also covers insurance and household bills.

Mortgage Specialists

www.charcoalonline.co.uk UK
>JOIN CHARCOAL
>This award winning mortgage adviser owned by Bradford & Bingley offers information on over 800 mortgages. There is also information on life insurance.
>
>*It's worth shopping around, so check out these sites too:*
>**www.mortgageman.co.uk** – aimed at the self-employed or those having difficulty getting a mortgage from the usual lenders, or with CCJs.
>**www.mortgagepoint.co.uk** – geared towards first-time buyers and those with a less than perfect credit history.
>**www.mortgageshop.com** – independent financial advice about which is the best mortgage for you, a somewhat messy site though.
>**www.mortgages-online.co.uk** – good independent source of information.
>**www.yourmortgage.co.uk** – *Your Mortgage* magazine.

Insurance

www.insurancewide.com UK
>HOME OF INSURANCE ON THE WEB
>Claims to have a unique system that gives you personalised comparative quotes from most UK insurance providers. They offer a wide range of insurance policies covering life, travel, motor, home, small business as well as sections for students, young people, women and lifestyle.

www.easycover.com UK
>UK'S BIGGEST INDEPENDENT INSURANCE WEB SITE
>Here you can get a wide range of quotes just by filling in one form. The emphasis is on convenience and speed.

www.warrantydirect.co.uk   UK
EXTENDED WARRANTIES
Here you can get cover for the important things in life: your car,
appliances and your computer.

Other sites worth checking out:
www.confused.com – as seen on TV, a simple comparison site
that doesn't seem at all confusing.
www.eaglestardirect.co.uk – a sparse but useful site from one
of the market leaders.
www.elephant.co.uk – instant quotes on a wide selection of
policies although they mainly specialise in car insurance.
www.inspop.com – choose the specially selected policy and buy
online.
www.insurance.co.uk – another comparison site backed by
Lloyds TSB.
www.morethan.com – hyped with the 'Where's Lucky?' ads, this
site is from Royal Sun Alliance and it's good for quotes in most
areas including pets.
www.quotelinedirect.co.uk – quotes on a wide range of
insurance areas.
www.soreeyes.co.uk – a wide range of policies and options.
www.theaa.com/insurance – AA Insurance covers travel, cars
and home.
www.theidol.com – a wide range of insurance options available
here.
www.ukinsuranceguide.co.uk – a good place to find specialist
insurers.

For advice on insurance or problems with insurance:
www.abi.org.uk – Association of British Insurers, lots of advice
on all aspects of insurance plus industry information.
www.financial-ombudsman.org.uk – help with all aspects of
financial services industry.

Investing and Share Dealing

www.investmentguide.co.uk   UK
FOR THOSE WHO GO IT ALONE
An outstanding site that gives you access to three books from
Harold Baldwin which are regularly updated and contain
high quality information regarding share dealing and other
investments; suitable for beginners or experts. Some information
is by subscription.

See also:

www.aitc.co.uk – an excellent guide and advice site to Investment Trusts.

www.breakingviews.com – a subscription service that has a great reputation within the financial and news industry, keeps you up-to-date with the latest financial news and commentary across the globe.

www.citywire.co.uk – advice and analysis from a well-regarded source, some information is subscription only.

www.h-l.co.uk – a new look, comprehensive site from Hargraves Lansdown providing lots of investment options and advice on where to put your hard-earned cash.

www.investmentuk.org – home of the Investment Management Association where you can find some useful advice and learn how the investment industry is managed and how it works with government.

www.investopedia.com – described as the investment education site, it's packed with information and helps to navigate the investment minefield.

www.londonstockexchange.com – guide to the exchange, how it works plus information on stocks and shares.

www.sharexpress.co.uk

VOTED BEST STOCKBROKER 2003,4,5 & 6
The Halifax share dealing site provides a simple and cost-effective means to play the markets either by managing your own investments or by having the folks at Halifax do it for you. A good beginner's site and charges competitively.

All of the following are good share dealing sites, each with a slightly different focus, just find the one that suits your needs:

www.apcims.co.uk – home of the Association of Private Client Investment Managers and Stockbrokers and a usefully informative site to boot.

www.barclays-stockbrokers.co.uk – good value for smaller share deals and possibly the best for beginners.

www.cmcmarkets.co.uk – learn about spread betting and trade CFDs with live trading sessions and a software walkthough.

www.cofunds.co.uk – have more control over your investments and savings.

www.earningswhispers.com – the latest hot stock picks and earnings news.

www.ethicalinvestment.org.uk – if you want to invest your money in business that has a moral conscience, then here's the site that will lead you in the right direction.

www.etrade.com – a well-designed share trading site.

www.e-traderuk.com – a directory of investment and related financial sites.

www.freequotes.co.uk – an all singing, all dancing site with the latest share information, tips and links to related and important sites.

www.fundsnetwork.co.uk – an online investment superstore with a huge range of options.

www.gni.co.uk – established trading and investment site, good design.

www.hedgeworld.com – a guide to the seemingly complex world of hedge funds.

www.hemscott.com – one of the more comprehensive offerings with good use of other technologies such as SMS.

www.hoovers.com – good for background information; provides comprehensive company, industry and market intelligence on 21 million of the world's top businesses.

www.investorschronicle.co.uk – this established magazine offers a useful site for share information and dealing, especially good for data on medium-sized and large companies.

www.morningstar.co.uk – a very dense site with huge amounts of information, part of its service is to collate and interpret the output of financial journalists, which must be a job in itself.

www.nsandi.com – National Savings and Investments.

www.tdwaterhouse.co.uk – slightly more expensive than Barclays, but still quite good value, well designed with good information to back it all up.

www.trustnet.co.uk – all you need to know about investing in trusts.

Pensions

www.thepensionservice.gov.uk   UK

KNOW YOUR OPTIONS

The Department for Work and Pensions represents the government line on pensions and gives good advice and the latest news. They will also work out the amount of State Pension you will receive. **www.direct.gov.uk/en/MoneyTaxAndBenefits/PensionsAndRetirement** also has comprehensive information and is a good starting point for advice. Still more government advice is available at **www.dwp.gov.uk**

For more information on pensions see:

www.pensionsadvisoryservice.org.uk – the Office of the Pensions Advisory Service offers advice on the whole spectrum of pensions and helps when things go wrong.

www.pensioncalculator.org.uk – a useful and detailed site on calculating your pension.

www.pensionsnetwork.com – good site dedicated to bringing you the best value stakeholder pensions. It's easy to use and comes with a good pensions calculator.

www.sippdeal.co.uk – advice on how to invest your pension in a Self Invested Personal Pension.

www.sipp-provider-group.org.uk – informative site on SIPP.

www.thepensionsregulator.gov.uk – the Occupational Pensions Regulatory Authority ensures pension schemes are run properly.

Banking

*Despite various concerns and scandals surrounding the security of some banking sites, internet banking is here to stay and is a very popular and useful way of keeping track of your finances. Common sense is the key to good security. Never e-mail bank information, card, PIN or account numbers under any circumstances; it's also a good idea not to have the information stored on your PC as there are programs capable of obtaining that information without your knowledge. See our security section on page 423 for more on how you can keep safe but also check out **www.banksafeonline.org.uk** where you'll find a great deal of relevant information and help.*

www.bankfacts.org.uk   UK

BRITISH BANKERS' ASSOCIATION

Answers to the most common questions about banking, advice about Internet banks, the banking code and general information. There's also a facility that helps you resurrect dormant accounts. See also **www.bankingcode.org.uk** where you can find details of the standards of service that all the banks have signed up to. For information on building societies go to the Building Society Association at **www.bsa.org.uk** and also the portal site **www.buildingsocieties.com** which offers a useful regional guide.

Tax

www.inlandrevenue.gov.uk   UK
TALK TO THE TAXMAN
The Inland Revenue has a very informative site where you can
get help on all aspects of tax. You can even submit your tax
return and pay your dues over the Internet and there's a good set
of links to other government departments.

www.tax.org.uk   UK
CHARTERED INSTITUTE OF TAXATION
A great resource, they don't provide information on individual
questions but they can put you in touch with a qualified
adviser. It's a good place to start if you have a problem with
your tax.

www.taxbuddies.com   UK
TAX ADVICE
A pretty comprehensive effort with a huge amount of data,
information and advice on aspects of taxation both personal and
business.

http://listen.to/taxman   UK
THE TAX CALCULATOR
Amazingly fast, just input your gross earnings and your tax and
actual earnings are calculated.

See page 59 for our Business section.

Credit Checking

www.checkmyfile.com   UK
IS YOUR CREDIT GOOD?
For £6.95 you can get a basic online credit rating on yourself, or
if you pay more, they'll send you a more detailed report. Very
useful and informative, they even keep updating your file on a
quarterly basis. You can also work out your likely credit score
using their online calculator for free. They also offer identity
fraud services and will check out car details. Data protection is
guaranteed too.

See also these sites that offer similar information and services:
www.callcredit.co.uk – online consumer credit reference agency
with a variety of services.

www.equifax.co.uk – get a full detailed credit report for £9.95 online. Offers an identity theft alert service too.
www.experian.co.uk – get a credit report sent for £2.

Debt Management

www.citizensadvice.org.uk   UK
CITIZENS ADVICE BUREAU
Often the first port of call for people with debt issues, the site offers useful information and the latest campaigns. There's a search facility to find your nearest office and a link to **www.adviceguide.org.uk** which contains basic advice and information on your rights.

See also:
www.cccs.co.uk – a charity dedicated to helping people get out of debt.
www.creditaction.org.uk – a money education charity, who help out people in debt.
www.debtcounsellors.co.uk – specialists in advising people on what to do if they get into financial difficulty and dealing with creditors.
www.insolvencyhelpline.co.uk – excellent resource for problem solving.
www.nationaldebtline.com – a free debt help service with useful links.
www.payplan.com – a good help site.

Miscellaneous

www.ifs.org.uk   UK
INSTITUTE OF FISCAL STUDIES
Independent analysis of all things financial, especially the tax system; surprisingly interesting but a pretty dull site.

www.paypal.com   UK
SEND AND RECEIVE MONEY ONLINE
A genuinely useful service, especially for small businesses and online auction junkies, it's very easy and straightforward to use; they've extended their service to cover mobiles too. Site owners can find details on how to sign up and links to the related Online Merchant Network. For those who are sceptical about using Paypal, you might want to pay a visit to **http://paypalsucks.com**. See also **www.worldpay.com**

www.moneysavingexpert.com   UK
   SAVE ON EVERYTHING
   Saving money guides to almost everything we pay out on, from
   credit cards to utilities, this is an extremely useful site from TV
   and radio pundit Martin Lewis.

Finding Someone

*Following the success of Friends Reunited, there's been a massive
explosion of sites dedicated to finding old friends and colleagues. Here
we've listed all the best sites, and also the place to go to find a phone
number, contacts for business and the home.*

Directory Sites

www.yell.com   UK
   UK BUSINESS DIRECTORY
   Basically a search engine and directory devoted to businesses.
   The online Yellow Pages is a very handy site to have in your
   favourites list, it's easy to use and you can download the toolbar
   on to your browser to make it even more convenient. You can
   even get your search results shown on a map. See also
   www.bigyellow.com for the US.

www.scoot.co.uk   UK
   THE SIMPLE WAY TO FIND A BUSINESS
   Register, type in the person's name or profession then hit the
   scoot button and the answer comes back in seconds. Oriented
   towards finding businesses but useful nonetheless.

www.thomweb.co.uk   UK
   THE ANSWER COMES OUT OF THE BLUE
   Thomson's offer an impressive site and provide local directories
   online. It's divided up into the following major categories:

1. A business finder – search using a combination of name, type of
   business or region.
2. People finder – track down phone numbers and home or e-mail
   addresses.
3. Comprehensive local information – available on the major cities
   and regions.

www.bt.com/directory-enquiries   UK
BRITISH TELECOM DIRECTORY
The way to cut those bills to directory enquiries. You're given
free access to 10 enquiries per day, but you can have another
200 free searches per month if you register. For a full overview
of BT services including checking up and paying your phone bill
go to **www.bt.com**

See also:
www.anywho.com – straightforward American-oriented search
site with an international section.
www.infospace.com – another good search engine with yellow
(business) and white (people) pages sections, it offers much
more though including a good web directory.
www.royalmail.co.uk – this site offers a useful address and
postcode finder and you can track your recorded deliveries too.
www.ukphonebook.com – simple to use, quick with a no-
nonsense design; also has mapping, a business finder and lots
of adverts.

www.192.com   UK
THE UK'S LARGEST DIRECTORY SERVICE
The Best Portal site of 2005 has plenty available free of charge
such as people and business finders, directories, maps and
route planners. In addition, there are various subscription
options such as access to the electoral role, historical and
current census information and a range of business services.
For a fee, they'll even try to track down individuals you've lost
contact with.

Finding Old Friends

www.friendsreunited.co.uk   UK
THE ONE STOP SITE TO REUNITE
Once the UK's most visited web site, a phenomenal success
story and millions of people have made contact with old friends
using the site; it's got over 14 million of us listed. The read-only
service is free, but access to the full service costs £7.50. For
that you get access to the schools and workplace database and
the ability to contact people through the site. It's very easy to use
and you'll quickly lose yourself. Now offers a genes reunited,
dating and a job search.

See also:
www.disabledunited.com – dedicated to uniting disabled people.
www.friend-ships.com – find that person you met on a cruise.
www.gradfinder.com – good site covering many of the world's schools and universities, but US-orientated.
www.gradumates.co.uk – a free site for UK graduates.
www.scoutsreunited.co.uk – find your old scouting buddies here.

Some similar sites dedicated to re-uniting old service colleagues:
www.armedforcesfriends.co.uk
www.forcesreunited.org.uk
www.servicepals.com

Try also:
www.arielbruce.com – Ariel Bruce is an ex-social worker with a good track record of finding missing people.
www.journalismnet.com/people – a tips sheet that contains links and advice on how to find people.
www.missing-you.net – free message posting designed to help find lost friends thought to be in the UK.
www.peopletracer.co.uk – people traced for a fee.
www.reunite.org – helping families who have suffered the trauma of child abduction.

www.andys-penpals.com   UK
FIND A PENPAL
A site devoted to penpals around the world. It's easy to use and free; there are also links to similar sites and a chat room.

Flowers

Sending Flowers

www.interflora.co.uk   UK
TURNING THOUGHTS INTO FLOWERS
Interflora can send flowers to over 140 countries, many on the same day as the order. They'll have a selection to send for virtually every occasion and they offer a reminder service. The service is excellent, although they are not very up front on delivery costs, which can be high. If you can't get what you

need here then try **www.teleflorist.co.uk** who offer a similar service.

www.flyingflowers.com   UK
EUROPE'S LEADING FLOWERS BY POST COMPANY
Freshly picked flowers flown from Jersey to the UK from £9.99.
They'll also arrange next day delivery in the UK. The site is
simple and there's a reminder service just to make sure you
don't forget anyone.

www.clareflorist.co.uk   UK
STYLISH BOUQUETS AND PRETTY PICTURES
Easy-to-use site with good customer services and free delivery
to UK with surcharge for same day delivery. Cost reflects the
sophistication of the flowers.

*Other florists worth checking out are listed below. It has to be said that
they are all quite similar, but some sell hampers, chocolates and other
gifts too:*

> **www.bloomingbritain.com**
> **www.bunches.co.uk**
> **www.johnlewis.com**
> **www.jwflowers.com**
> **www.marksandspencer.co.uk**
> **www.sayitwith.co.uk**
> **www.serenataflowers.com**

Flower Arranging

www.paula-pryke-flowers.com   UK
LIVE YOUR LIFE IN COLOURS
A bright and well-laid-out site from one of the UK's premium
flower arrangers. There are details of her books and designs,
which you can order.

See also:
www.jane-packer.co.uk – another top celebrity with a site
offering limited information; however, it does come with a
contact e-mail and information on courses.
www.floralartmall.com – check out the free stuff, including
lessons and ideas.
www.nafas.org.uk – informative, if dull, site from the National
Association of Flower Arrangement Societies.

www.silkflowerarranging.com – learn how to arrange silk flowers successfully.

www.thegardener.btinternet.co.uk – details on how to achieve the perfect flower arranger's garden.

Food and Drink

Whether you want to order from the comfort of your own home, indulge yourself, find the latest food news or get a recipe, this collection of sites will fulfil all your foodie desires. It features supermarkets, online magazines and information sites, specialist food retailers, vegetarian and organic stockists, drinks information and suppliers, where to go for kitchen equipment and help in finding the best places when eating out.

Supermarkets and General Food Stores

www.waitrose.com   UK
IF YOU ARE REALLY INTO FOOD
Waitrose is offering a very good, comprehensive and well-designed site that oozes quality, so it's a pleasure to do your grocery shopping online. You can buy wine, gifts, organics and some John Lewis products. In addition it also has all the features you'd expect: articles and recipes in their *Illustrated Food* magazine including information on food-related campaigns and organic issues; an excellent gift shop; plus entertaining, flowers and travel sections and even one on competitions and puzzles, even broadband access.

www.ocado.com   UK
AWARD WINNING
In partnership with Waitrose, Ocado offers a supermarket delivery service dispatched from a central warehouse to the south East, Midlands and North West of England but their range is expanding all the time. This site deserves its success as it's easier to use than most of the other supermarket sites.

www.tesco.co.uk   UK
THE LIFESTYLE SUPERSTORE
This functional site has a comprehensive offering, there's a wide range of goods on offer though, including electrical goods, clothes and books. There's also a section on personal finance, other shops, parenting advice and healthy living. Offers now

Foodies

The Good Web Site Guide's Top 10s
of the Internet

1. **www.epicurious.com** – more recipes that you'll ever need
2. **www.waitrose.com** – excellent for something special and great articles and feature sections too
3. **www.food.gov.uk** – food news and advice from the Food Standards Agency
4. **www.deliaonline.com** – outstanding site from the queen of cookery
5. **www.tudocs.com** – cookery sites rated and listed in this excellent directory
6. **www.3fatchicks.com** – no nonsense healthy eating and diet advice
7. **www.edible.com** – if it moves, it's edible …
8. **www.savoria.co.uk** – the true tastes of Italy
9. **www.cheese.com** – the ultimate site on cheese!
10. **www.vegweb.com** – attractive and very useful vegetarian site

abound with some great savings all aimed at capturing your e-mail address and future custom. As if echoing Tesco's movement away from selling just food, groceries do not seem to be the major function of this site anymore.

www.sainsburys.co.uk   UK
NOT JUST GOOD TASTE
Sainsbury's site has more emphasis on good food, cooking, recommendation and taste, and of course the Nectar loyalty card. The facility to place an advance order at their Calais store, which you can then pick up and pay for in France, will appeal to those who wish to save time on their booze run.

www.asda.co.uk   UK
PERMANENTLY LOW PRICES
There's lots of information about the company and what it stands for plus links to its online shop. There are also sections on financial services, health and offers. Delivery cost alters depending on day and time of delivery.

Supermarkets without internet shopping facilities:
www.iceland.co.uk – the frozen food specialist will deliver from
the store but have ceased their online service.
www.morrisons.co.uk – all you can do online is find out about
their stores, range and offers. A poor show.
www.somerfield.co.uk – the emphasis is on offers but there's
also a recipe finder, wine guide and essential food facts. Check
out whether you're eligible for free delivery, but you can't order
online!

Alternatives to Supermarkets

www.homefarmfoods.com   UK
DELICIOUS FROZEN FOOD DELIVERED FREE
Good selection of frozen foods and huge range of ready meals
with a good use of symbols indicating whether the product is
low fat, microwavable, vegetarian etc. With free delivery, it's
especially good value, and there is no minimum order. See also
www.foodhall.co.uk who have a good selection of specialist
stores to choose from.

www.farmersmarkets.net   UK
NATIONAL ASSOCIATION OF FARMERS' MARKETS
A farmers' market sells locally produced goods. Locate your
nearest market or get advice on how to set one up.

www.freedomfood.co.uk   UK
RSPCA FARM ASSURANCE
Details of a scheme from the RSPCA to improve conditions
for farm animals. The site shows where you can buy these
products, lists producers and has some recipes too. You can
buy freedom food online at **www.farmgatedirect.com**

www.wholefoodsmarket.com/uk   US
WHOLE FOODS
This delicious American natural foods supermarket has crossed
the ocean; find out about their UK stores and explore the site for
their recipes and excellent health information.

The remainder of the Food section is alphabetically arranged by topic.

African Cuisine

www.betumi.com   UK

TRADITIONAL AND CONTEMPORARY
Recipes, information and links on Africa and its food, it also has
some charitable aspects.

See also:
www.afrol.com/Categories/Culture/recipes.htm – West African
recipes.
www.boykie.co.uk/south-african-cuisine.htm – South African
cuisine.
www.congocookbook.com – 150 African recipes and contextual
information as well as a forum.
www.khound.com/topics/africanr.htm – a bit of a mess but a
good overview of African cookery by country and region plus
information on its derivatives too.

Asian and Indian Cookery

www.curryhouse.co.uk   UK

EVERYTHING YOU NEED TO KNOW ABOUT CURRY
Curryholics can get their fill of recipes, recommendations, taste
tests, interviews with famous chefs and a restaurant guide, good
for links too.

See also:
www.curryguidenet.co.uk – a good-looking site with a good
range of recipes and restaurants.
www.currypages.com – an Indian Restaurant guide with good
features.
www.currysauce.com – get all the sauces delivered.
www.gcosta.co.uk/curryclub – join Pat Chapman's famous
curry club, access recipes and buy his range of ingredients.
www.redhotcurry.com/food_and_drink/index.htm – excellent
food and drink section from the well-known British Asian portal.
www.simplyspice.co.uk – buy authentic ingredients, including
spices, oils, pulses and package mixes, at very low prices.

www.straitscafe.com   SINGAPORE

RECIPES FROM SINGAPORE
A straightforward site with lots of recipes not only from
Singapore, but from Southeast and East Asia including Japan
and China, there's also a good set of links and a useful glossary

at the 'pantry'. For Indonesian cooking go to the enjoyable
Henks Hot Kitchen, which can be found at **www.indochef.com**

http://japanesefood.about.com   US
JAPANESE FOOD
From the well respected About.com, their section on Japanese
food is excellent with recipes and background too.

See also:
www.bento.com – a good-looking site with lots of information
on Japanese food and eating out.
www.sushilinks.com – links to all things sushi!
www.yosushi.com – a hi-tech site which features their
restaurants and a sushi ordering service to selected areas.

www.thaicuisine.com   US
RECIPES AND RESTAURANTS
This site offers recipes and ingredient information, though
the restaurant list is only for the US, see also **http://thai-
uk.org/food.html** which has good background information on
Thai food, and **www.importfood.com** who supply Thai foods
and offer up some 145 recipes.

www.chinavoc.com/cuisine/index.asp   US
CHINESE COOKERY
Lots of tips and background information on Chinese cookery
with advice on techniques and recipes. Also **www.chinatown-
online.co.uk** is dedicated to what's going on in London's China
Town; it has an excellent food section.

See also:
www.asianonlinerecipes.com – some 2,000 recipes and useful
for links too.
www.asiarecipe.com – a messy, but well-intentioned site with a
range of recipes and ingredients covering the whole of Asia.

Barbecues

www.barbecuen.com   US
BARBECUES
In the unlikely event that our weather will be good enough to
have a barbecue, then here's a site with all you need to know
on the subject. See also the musically enhanced
www.britishbarbecue.co.uk with 2,000 recipes.

British and Irish Cookery

www.greatbritishkitchen.co.uk UK

BRITISH FOOD TRUST

The Trust is furthering its mission to promote good British food by way of an extensive recipe collection with useful sections on seasonal cooking and information on food traditions, regional cooking, a glossary and a set of links.

See also:

http://pages.eidosnet.co.uk/cookbook/index.html – a tribute to British cooking with some fifty recipes, the site is pretty backward-looking though.

www.godecookery.com/engrec/engrec.html – a curious collection of transcribed 17th-century recipes.

www.recipes4us.co.uk – have over 2,700 recipes although some are international.

www.regionalfoodanddrink.co.uk – a regional guide to the UK's food specialists.

www.rampantscotland.com/recipes UK

A WEE FEAST

A very simple site listing a good selection of traditional Scottish recipes, while **www.scottishrecipes.co.uk** also have a small collection.

www.irishabroad.com/Culture/kitchen IRELAND

A TASTE OF IRELAND

A good selection of Irish recipes plus a forum and articles. It is designed for the US ex-pat audience as is **www.foodireland.com/recipes** with a similar offering and **www.tasteofireland.com** who have more recipes, restaurant reviews.

www.red4.co.uk/recipes.htm UK

WELSH RECIPES

Here are over 120 traditional recipes including lava bread, wines, cawl and Welshcakes. See also **www.hookerycookery.com/welsh-menu.htm** where there's a similar list – and flashing banner ads!

Celebrity Chefs and TV Food Shows

*If you can't find what you're looking for on their dedicated web sites, checkout **www.bbc.co.uk/food** where you'll find a list over 40 TV cooks and presenters. **www.channel4.com/food** is also worth checking out. For high quality sites associated with their programmes:*

www.deliaonline.com   UK
DELIA SMITH

The queen of British cookery has a clean, well-designed site stocked with recipes, which can be accessed by the good search facility. If you join, you get added features such as access to the message-board, competitions and a newsletter. The Cookery School has a good collection of basic 'how tos' and you can find out about joining Delia in Norwich. The shop is a pleasure to browse with sections on gardens, homes and travel as well as the expected cookware and books.

www.jamieoliver.net   UK
WHAT HE'S ABOUT

The official site mainly dedicated to Jamie's diary but there's also advice on school dinners and links to his restaurant, charity and kitchenware. In addition you can buy a limited selection of clothing and other bits and bobs, join in the forums and even see his podcast. The small recipe collection continues to grow and, of course, there's an opportunity to buy the books. See also **www.feedmebetter.co.uk** for Jamie's campaign for better food in schools.

www.nigella.com   UK
DOMESTIC GODDESS

A disappointing offering that promotes her books, her Living Kitchen range and herself. There is a forum for discussion and recipes, although some are from the doyen herself, others are posted by visitors.

www.rickstein.co.uk   UK
PADSTOW, STEIN AND SEAFOOD

Information on Rick, his restaurants and cookery school all wrapped up in a tidy web site. You can also book a table or a room as well as order products from the online deli.

www.uktvfood.co.uk   UK
UK FOOD
Very attractive site from this specialist TV channel with lots of
recipes, tips and features based on their programming.

www.foodtv.com   US
FOOD NETWORK
A rather strange but quite appealing site devoted to American TV
cooks. It has some video footage and a search engine that
covers 20,000 recipes, plus some good articles.

Cheese

www.cheese.com   US
IT'S ALL ABOUT CHEESE!
A huge resource site with information on over 700 types of
cheese. There's advice about the best way to eat cheese, a
vegetarian section, a cheese bookshop and links to other cheese
related sites and online stores. You can even find a suitable
cheese searching by texture, country or type of milk. For more
cheese information try the attractive Cheesenet site at
www.cheesenet.info which has an excellent search facility, or
the American Dairy Association's **www.ilovecheese.com** which
also offers a cheese guide and lots of recipes.

www.cheesemongers.co.uk or
www.paxtonandwhitfield.co.uk   UK
OPULENT SITE FROM UK'S OLDEST CHEESEMONGERS
Paxton and Whitfield, the royal cheesemongers, provide a very
clear and easy-to-use online shop but charge £10.00 to ship
goods. A superb selection of cheese and luxury produce, with
hampers, cheese kitchen, accessories and wine. A pleasure
to browse and it's tempting to buy; you can also join the
Cheese Society. See also the British Cheese Board at
www.britishcheese.com where you can learn about our
cheeses, get some recipes and general cheese propaganda.

www.teddingtoncheese.co.uk   UK
BRITISH AND CONTINENTAL CHEESEMONGERS
Much-acclaimed site offering over 130 types of cheese at
competitive prices. The sections are split by country and there's
a good system for showing whether the cheese is suitable
for vegetarians, pregnant women, etc. There is also an
encyclopaedia, a selection of wine and other produce; you can

even design your own hamper. When buying you can stipulate how much cheese you want in grams (150 minimum), shipping from £8.99 for the UK. At **www.butlerscheeses.co.uk** you'll find excellent farmhouse cheeses.

www.fromages.com   FRANCE
TRADITIONAL FRENCH CHEESE
French cheese available to order and delivered within 24 hours along with wine recommendations and express shipping from France. Delivery is included in the price but if you're worried about cost you probably shouldn't be shopping here.

Chocolate, Confectionery and Cakes

www.hotelchocolat.com   UK
DEDICATED TO GOOD CHOCOLATE
An excellent and well-illustrated site from an experienced retailer, they also offer lots of choice and a wide range of chocolate-related gifts and you can even buy in bulk! There's a really good selection facility and the chocolate tasting club. Delivery to UK included in the price and they will guarantee that it's delivered by a specified date.

www.chocaid.com   UK
HELP THE HUNGRY
A great site where you can give to charity when you buy gourmet chocolates. They have a good selection and you can choose which good cause your donation goes to.

www.thorntons.co.uk   UK
WELCOME TO CHOCOLATE HEAVEN
Thorntons offer a comprehensive and easy-to-use site, with an emphasis on gifts. The range is extensive and they supply worldwide, but delivery isn't cheap. There are product sections for continental, premier, gifts and hampers plus flowers and wine. For handmade chocolates try the tempting selections at **www.handmadechocolates.co.uk**

See also:
www.bettysbypost.co.uk – a wide selection of goodies from this well-known Harrogate confectioner.
www.cadbury.co.uk – where you can learn all about chocolate plus lots of recipes and play games.
www.chocolate.co.uk – home of the Chocolate Society.

www.hersheys.com – tour the famous American factory, good for recipes too.

www.lamaisonduchocolat.co.uk – excellent Parisian chocolate shop with lots of gift options.

www.prestat.co.uk – hand-made chocolates delivered to your door the next day.

www.virtualchocolate.com – where you can send virtual chocolate, read chocolate-inspired stories and poems.

F

www.oldsweetshop.com   UK
SWEETS THE WAY THEY USED TO BE ...
Sweets from an old-fashioned sweet shop, stacked with favourites like Dolly Mixtures, sugared almonds and Parma violets, a visit here is a nostalgia trip as much as anything. Delivery is according to weight. See also **www.sugarboy.co.uk** who offer a wide range of goodies, **www.cybercandy.com** and also **www.aquarterof.com** which is great for old favourites.

www.caketoppers.co.uk   UK
LOOKS GOOD ENOUGH TO EAT
Whether it's a sedate cake for Granny, a Bart Simpson cake for the hooligan in your life, or a cake for that diabetic or celiac aunt, there's a cake here for everyone. They'll even transfer your photos into edible images and place them on a cake. You can request just the cake-top decoration to use on your homemade cake.

www.janeasher.co.uk   UK
JANE ASHER CAKES
A pretty workman-like affair, you can order personalised cakes (London orders only delivered or collected by customer), select from a range of mail-order cakes and you can buy equipment too.

See also:

www.botham.co.uk/cakes.htm – offer a traditional range of iced fruit cakes for delivery world-wide.

www.thecakestore.com – great selection but they only deliver to the London area.

www.clickthecookie.co.uk – wide range of cookies and gift options; particularly useful if you want to send themed fortune cookies or a tube of fortune cookie insults.

www.need-a-cake.co.uk – beautiful range of cakes by post, also have a shop for those wanting to do-it-themselves.

www.squires-shop.com – for sugarcraft paraphernalia.

www.pastrywiz.com   US
PASTRY HEAVEN
A general food site with the emphasis on cakes and pastry of all
sorts; there are plenty of recipes and links to keep cake fans
happy. See also **www.flourbin.co.uk** and get any number of
different types of flour here.

Cookery Courses and Schools

www.cordonbleu.edu – Classic French cookery with schools in
15 countries.
www.deliaonline.com/cookery-school – Delia Smith offers a
range of one day workshops in Norwich. Also online courses.
www.foodofcourse.co.uk – learn to cook in a farmhouse in
Somerset, good range of courses from foundation to chalet
cookery.
www.leiths.com – Leith's School of Food and Wine has an
excellent reputation; courses for amateurs and professionals.
www.manoir.com – Raymond Blanc offers one-, two- and four-
day courses at his wonderful hotel outside Oxford.
www.rickstein.com – The Padstow Seafood School offers one-,
two- and four-day courses on how to cook fish.
www.travel-quest.co.uk/cooking-holidays.htm – specialist travel
company with listings for holiday cookery courses.
www.vegsoc.org/cordonvert – courses for vegetarian cookery.

Diet and Nutrition

www.eatwell.gov.uk   UK
NANNY KNOWS BEST
A well-meaning and informative attempt by the Food Standards
Agency to improve the British diet. There are sections on healthy
diet, ages and stages, health issues, food safety and labelling.

www.3fatchicks.com   US
THE SOURCE FOR DIET SUPPORT
The awesome Three Fat Chicks have produced one of the best
food web sites. It's text heavy but entertaining and informative
about dieting or trying to stay healthy. There are food reviews, a
breakdown of popular diets, low fat and low carb recipes, diet
tips and a 'tool box', which has calorie tables and calculators.
There are also sections on getting started, losing weight, fitness
and a forum. Check out the fast-food guide to get the nutritional
low-down on your fast-food chain favourites.

www.cookinglight.com   US
THE BEST FROM *COOKING LIGHT* MAGAZINE
One of the world's best-selling food magazines, their slow site
offers a huge selection of healthy recipes and step-by-step
guides to cooking. There are also articles on healthy living.

www.weightwatchers.co.uk   UK
WELCOME TO WEIGHTWATCHERS UK
A much improved site with more information on how to lose
weight, keep motivated, keep fit, chat and, of course, where to
find your local group. There's also a shop where you can buy
specially selected foods and related diet products.

http://atkins-uk.com   UK
DR ATKINS
The world's best-selling dietician offers a site that gives the
background to his low-carbohydrate diet and how you can
lose weight and get healthy on it. You can shop for Atkins
supplements and foods. For another approach try **www.low-
carb.com**

www.weightlossresources.co.uk   UK
FAD-FREE TOOLS FOR HEALTHY WEIGHT LOSS
Excellent place to go for information on weight loss and diets;
you can keep a weight loss diary, find out about exercise, get
advice on what to eat and catch up on the latest research. You
can also share your experience with others too, but you have to
register to get the best out of it.

www.hungry-girl.com   US
TIPS & TRICKS FOR HUNGRY CHICKS
A great design combined with useful information all presented in
'bite sized' articles; some is geared towards US readers but it's
still useful and enjoyable to use.

See also:
http://lowfatcooking.about.com – a well-presented and
informative section from the About.com web site.
www.caloriecontrol.org – low fat information from the Calorie
Control Council.
www.caloriecounter.co.uk – a good site with a diet based on
counting calories and exercise.
www.cyberdiet.com – a good all rounder with a wide range of
advice, including specialist diets.

www.dailydiettracker.co.uk – a popular and well-put-together site that enables you to track what you eat and monitor your progress.

www.fatfree.com – almost 5,000 vegetarian recipes, all fat free or very low fat.

www.fatfreekitchen.com – Indian vegetarian, low fat recipes and healthy eating info.

www.foodsubs.com – a useful food thesaurus with the added benefit that it offers up low fat substitutes to fatty foods.

www.freedieting.com – an excellent site on dieting with the major diets reviewed. It comes with useful advice and tools to help you lose weight.

www.lowcarbiseasy.com – recipes and information on low carb and low GI foods, links and a sugar converter.

www.rosemary-conley.co.uk – all about Rosemary and her healthy lifestyle.

www.weightlossresources.co.uk – a good deal of free information on dieting, diets and exercise; you can sign up to their regime too.

Special Dietary Needs

Also refer to the section on Health, page 231.

www.diabeticgourmet.com   UK

DELICIOUS FOR DIABETICS

Lots of recipes and ideas to make food palatable without endangering your blood sugar levels from *Diabetic Gourmet* magazine.

www.bdaweightwise.com   UK

BRITISH DIETETIC ASSOCIATION

Excellent health web site from this association who have produced something that looks sensible and easy to follow. You can follow their tips and get advice from a trained dietician too.

www.nutritionpoint.co.uk   UK

GLUTEN FREE

Their mission is to expand the range of gluten-free products available in Britain. They also provide a helpful checklist indicating which of their products are available on prescription; failing that you can buy goods through a link to an online shop **www.goodnessdirect.co.uk**. For more information try

www.coeliac.co.uk or the US sites www.gfcfdiet.com and
www.celiac.com

www.foodag.com   UK
E-NUMBERS MADE CLEAR
The food additives guide with information on what additives are
bad for you and which are derived from animals. The ingredients
section provides a list of E-numbers in common food groups
indicating the nasties to be avoided.

F

www.foodallergy.org   US
ALLERGY AND ANAPHYLAXIS
A useful site with information and links on food allergies and
their reactions, it's very much oriented to the US so also try
www.anaphylaxis.org.uk which is also very helpful and UK
based.

French Food

http://frenchfood.about.com   US
FRENCH CUISINE
About.com have created a superb resource at this site with a
huge amount of data, articles and recipes. Every aspect of
French cooking seems to be covered from the ingredients to
the shops and presentation.

See also:
www.afrenchkiss.com – make your own gourmet meals with
this fun French recipe-creation program.
www.goodfrance.com – a wide range of French food available to
buy, with good regional sections and hampers too.
www.hertzmann.com/index.php – French recipes from an
obsessive.
www.paniers.com – high-quality French food online, for a price.

Halal

www.halalfoodauthority.co.uk   UK
HALAL FOOD
Information on Halal food and the regulations that surround it; it
explains what Halal means and offers support to suppliers too.
About also provides information on Halal law and food at
www.aboutfood.co.uk/spotlight/halal.html

Holland

www.typicaldutchstuff.com   HOLLAND
DUTCH PRODUCE
A wide range of food available here, though mainly oriented
towards confectionary. Delivery costs vary according to how
heavy the order is. For your Dutch cheese fix go to
www.gestam.com

Hygiene and Food Safety

www.foodsafety.gov/~fsg/fsgadvic.html   UK
FOOD SAFETY
A government site with basic advice on handling foods in all
sorts of situations from product-specific advice to helping those
with special needs; there are also good links to related topics.

See also:
www.food.gov.uk – home of the Food Standards Agency who
have lots of information on what is safe to eat.
www.ourfood.com – an overview of food science and hygiene.

Italian Food

www.mangiarebene.net   UK
EAT WELL
An award-winning site that covers everything to do with Italian
cookery. Its aim is to give a grand tour of Italian cuisine – and it
succeeds, including some 600 recipes in the English language
section, but over 1,600 overall. See also **http://italy1.com/
cuisine** which has good regional cooking and food information
as well as lots of recipes and if that's not enough,
www.italianfoodforever.com. There is also a small but exquisite
collection of recipes from Marcella Hazan at
www.dolcevita.com/cuisine/recipes/recipes.htm

www.ilovepasta.org   US
US NATIONAL PASTA ASSOCIATION
250 recipes, tips, fast meals and healthy options all wrapped
up in a clear and easy-to-use site. There's also information on
the different types of pasta and advice on the right sauces to
go with them.

www.savoria.co.uk UK
>TRUE TASTE OF ITALY
>There will be no problem fulfilling the minimum order of £50 at this wonderful deli full of culinary indulgences. Delivery is free for orders in excess of £100 (ex-VAT). Alternatively, try **www.esperya.com** which sends produce direct from Italy or **www.dolcevita.com/cuisine** where you'll find produce, recipes and a survival kit for Italian cuisine. At **www.nifeislife.com** you'll find a fast delivery service allied to a wide range of Italian products.

www.getoily.com UK
>OLIVE OIL
>All you need to know about olive oil, cooking with it, health benefits and history, oh and you can buy it too, along with a good selection of other Mediterranean products.

www.dominos.co.uk UK
>PIZZA DELIVERY
>Order your pizza online and get it delivered to your home, providing you live near enough to one of their outlets that is. It's a nicely designed site, which also has a few games if you get bored waiting.

Kitchen Equipment

www.lakelandlimited.co.uk UK
>EXCELLENT CUSTOMER SERVICE
>Lakeland pride themselves on service and it shows, they aim to get all orders dispatched in 24 hours and delivery on orders over £45 is free, otherwise they charge £3.50. The product listing for both kitchen and homeware is comprehensive too.

www.urbanbar.com UK
>GLASS AND CLASS
>A very attractive site from this glass specialist, the range isn't large but it's well presented and there are recipes, links and special offers too.

>*See also:*
>**www.alessi.com** – a tour round the kitchen design powerhouse that is Alessi, the best bit is that you can now buy from this site too.
>**www.cucinadirect.com** – a very wide range of kitchen equipment and related products.

www.divertimenti.co.uk – Divertimenti are also worth a look, they go for quality and they are good for gifts.
www.kingsofhagley.co.uk – excellent cookware shop with lots of choice and a personal service.
www.pots-and-pans.co.uk – Scottish company offering kitchen equipment through a good online store; it's good value but delivery charges vary.

Kosher Cookery

www.koshercooking.com   UK
JEWISH CUISINE
Lots of recipes and links covering all forms of kosher cookery and occasions.

www.totallyjewish.com/living/food   UK
J-FOOD
Part of the lively Totally Jewish site, which has a magazine-style approach to modern Jewish cookery, including a message board, restaurant guide, chef's questions and features. For another more personal recipe collection go to **http://screamingmeemies.com/eats**

Luxury Food, Deli and Gift Sites

www.allpresent.com   UK
GIFTS FOR THE DISCERNING
An Amazon-style shop offering gifts in the form of chocolates, drinks and bakery items, such as cakes and biscuits, all beautifully boxed. They also sell flowers and cards; delivery costs vary according to what you buy.

www.fortnumandmason.co.uk   UK
EXQUISITE GIFTS
A wide range of gift chocolates, hampers and more from one of the leading luxury stores. There is a whole section devoted to fine tea including named garden and rare teas plus a wide choice of gourmet ingredients including condiments, wines and spirits.

See also:
www.champershampers.co.uk – family-run hamper business.
www.hamper.com – good design and a wide range of products and you can create your own.

www.harrods.com – not the wide choice that you would expect, but what there is comes with kudos.

www.lewisandcooper.co.uk – they've been producing hampers for many years and here you can create your own or order one of their range.

www.mortimerandbennett.co.uk – London based fine foods retailer with lots of choice and quality too.

www.valvonacrolla-online.co.uk – lots of special food from this Edinburgh retailer.

F

Meat and Fish

For organic suppliers see Vegetarian and Organic below.

www.traditionalbutcher.co.uk   UK
A TRADITIONAL BUTCHER
John Miles is based in Herefordshire and knows a thing or two about meat. You can buy meats and deli products online. There's a good range and delivery is charged at cost. They seem to take a great deal of care on quality.

See also:
http://highlandgame.com – for fresh venison and partridge plus recipes and information.

www.blackface.co.uk – seasonal, regional and traceable; this Scottish site supplies boxes of lamb, mutton, beef, pork, a good selection of game and haggis.

www.buyostrichmeat.co.uk – for ostrich meat and how to cook it.

www.donaldrussell.co.uk – an award-winning butcher who offers a wide range of other produce as well as meats. The site is well illustrated and there are recipes too.

www.richardwoodall.com – if you can't live without Cumberland sausages, then get them here; plenty of cured meats too.

www.swaddles.co.uk – organic butchers, with other produce for sale from a good-looking site.

www.trealyfarm.com – if you like your meat cured, then this online charcuterie is the place to go.

www.simpsons-seafoods.co.uk
WHEN THE BOAT COMES IN
Supplied from Hull Fish Market, this site offers fresh and smoked fish as well as fresh and cooked shellfish. The site is nicely designed with small clear pictures of the fish cuts. Under

'special offers' look out for their mixed fish boxes, which change daily. Order by noon for next day delivery. Try visiting the Sea Fish Industry Authority (**www.seafish.org**) for recipes and more fishy information.

See also:
www.andyrace.co.uk – the peat-smoked salmon comes highly recommended; good for other smoked fish and shellfish as well as other Atlantic fish.
www.fishonline.org – very informative site aimed at helping consumers choose the right fish to eat from a conservation point of view. There's a great purchasing guide and lots of background information on fish farming and how fish are caught.
www.kellyoysters.com – for reputedly excellent oysters.
www.martins-seafresh.co.uk – order your fish fresh from this messy site which also has recipes and helpful information.

Mediterranean Food

www.belazu.com   UK
   CAPTURING THE MED
   This attractive site covers the cuisine of Spain, Italy, Greece and Morocco; there's a shop and a list of recipes too.

Middle Eastern Cookery

www.al-bab.com/arab/food.htm   UK
   MIDDLE EASTERN CUISINE
   An excellent overview of Arab cuisine from Arab Gateway with links to key sites covering all the major styles.

www.arabicslice.com   UK
   STEP-BY-STEP ARABIC CUISINE
   A well-designed and well-written cookery site featuring the best of Arabic food with simple step-by-step recipes, lots of explanation and illustrations.

Miscellaneous Food Sites

www.reluctantgourmet.com   US
   GOURMET COOKING FOR BEGINNERS
   Basically a beginner's cookery book, it's well designed and easy to follow with a glossary, guide to techniques, equipment, tips and recipes.

www.cheftalk.com
UK

THE FOOD LOVER'S LINK TO PROFESSIONAL CHEFS

Excellent site for articles and discussion about food with tips and advice from the top chefs. There's a good links section, recipes and a recommended restaurant guide.

www.expatboxes.com
UK

FOOD PARCELS FOR THOSE LIVING ABROAD

OK so you miss HP sauce, childhood sweet favourites and proper salad cream, relief is at hand here. You can get your rations in the form of specially selected hampers or they will tailor make and shop the high street for you. Delivery costs are high. For the Scottish equivalent try **www.scottishfoodoverseas.com**

www.hardtofindfoods.co.uk
UK

FOR SOMETHING SPECIAL

A great selection of the scarce and unusual from spices to oils to beans. You can learn a lot just by browsing, although that turns out to be an expensive thing to do.

www.edible.com
UK

FOR BBQ WORM CHIPS!

All sorts of insects, unusual meat and bugs you can eat, often mixed with something exotic, the food available here is only for the culinary brave. The site design is excellent though some people might find the intro faintly disturbing … See also the listings at **www.weird-food.com**

Other unusual sites to check out:

www.egullet.com – a messy e-zine devoted to food that has some good articles if you can be bothered to wade through the site.

www.exploratorium.edu/cooking – discover the science of cookery at this site which makes fascinating reading.

www.foodtimeline.org – a timeline marking the history of cookery through the ages, with links and background information.

www.topsecretrecipes.com – discover what really goes into America's big brand-name foods.

Organic

www.organicfood.co.uk   UK
A WORLD OF ORGANIC INFORMATION
A very informative site which gives the latest news on organic
food. There are sections on why you should shop organic,
recommendations on retailers, lifestyle tips, shopping and
chat. There are also links to key related sites. See also
www.accessorganic.com which is great for links and has a
search facility.

See also:
www.abel-cole.co.uk – well respected company that offers
home delivery, there's advice on the site plus recipes and details
on restaurants they supply.
www.crueltyfreeshop.com – the animal-friendly superstore who
sell a wide range of products but a limited amount of foodstuffs.
www.farmaround.co.uk – good London-based supplier.
www.festivalwines.co.uk – organic and ethically produced
wines.
www.goldenvalleyorganics.co.uk – organic meat, nationwide
from Herefordshire.
www.helenbrowningorganics.co.uk – buying advice, recipes
and an online shop from this Wiltshire organic farmer.
www.organic-ally.co.uk – no food here but the place to go for
your napkins and tableware.
www.organicdelivery.co.uk – a good organic food retailer with
some good offers. London delivery only.
www.riverford.co.uk – amazing choice, over 85 types of veg to
choose from.
www.sustainweb.org – a farming site with lots of information
and links on sustainable farming.
www.swaddles.co.uk – a wide range of organic food including
meat.
www.whyorganic.org – a Soil Association site with good
background information, nutritional advice and a good organic
food directory in the 'organic offers' section.

Recipes, General Food Sites and Magazines

www.kitchenlink.com   US
WHAT'S COOKING ON THE NET
A bit clunky to use, but it has so many links to other key foodie
sites and food-related sections that it has to be the place to start

your online food and drink experience. The design can make it irritating to use and it's got a little slow, but persevere and you'll be rewarded with a resource that is difficult to beat.

www.tudocs.com US
THE ULTIMATE DIRECTORY OF COOKING SITES
The main difference with Tudocs is that it grades each cookery site on its site listing. The listing is divided up into 19 sections, such as meat, beverages, low fat and ethnic. British cookery is in the ethnic section. See also **www.cookingindex.com**

http://epicurious.com US
FOR PEOPLE WHO EAT
Owned by Condé Nast, this massive site combines articles from their magazines with information generated by the Epicurious team, the site has been tidied up but there's still plenty of advice with recipes, cooking tips, TV tie-ins, restaurant reviews, live chat, forums, wine and kitchen equipment. It's fast, easy to navigate and international in feel.

www.allrecipes.com US
THE HOME OF GREAT RECIPES
This site gets its own review because it's not overly cluttered, it's just got loads of recipes which can be found easily and each is rated by people who have cooked them.

http://cookbook.rin.ru RUSSIA
COOKERY ART
Really interesting cookery site with all the usual recipe sections but some unusual ones including exotic and erotic!

www.cookingbynumbers.com UK
COOK WITH WHAT YOU HAVE
It's not a new idea to click on a list of ingredients and for a site to come up with a list of recipes, but here it's done particularly well. There's also help for beginners with some excellent step-by-step guides.

Other sites worth checking out are these, all have loads of recipes and it's just a matter of finding one you like:
www.chef2chef.net – outstanding professional cookery portal site with masses of links.
www.cookeryonline.com – very messy design but pretty comprehensive.

www.cyber-kitchen.com – excellent for links and specialised subjects.
www.goodcooking.com – another excellent food site with some good food writing.
www.ichef.com – good search facility, nice design.
www.meals.com – good for meal planning and recipes.
www.mealsforyou.com – recipes for solutions: healthy, tasty, nutritional and so on.
www.netcooks.com – hundreds of recipes submitted by the public.
www.recipes4us.co.uk – over 2,500 British and international recipes.
www.recipezaar.com – the world's smartest cookbook.
www.ucook.com – the ultimate cookery shop with recipes added.
www.yumyum.com – good fun.

www.bl.uk/learning/langlit/booksforcooks/books   UK
HISTORIC BOOKS FOR COOKS
The British Library traces British cooking from medieval times to the 1940s through a series of facsimile extracts from their cookery collection. It would be quite possible to make some of the recipes such as the cheesecakes from the 1600s, but please draw the line at 'Live Birds in a Pie'. Fascinating reading.

Spanish Food

www.spanish-kitchen.co.uk   UK
SPANISH CUISINE
What looks like a thorough walk through of the cuisine with recipes and explanations of what to expect when you go there.

www.tenstartapas.com   UK
TOP TAPAS
An exercise in the creation of the best ever tapas by several of the UK's top chefs. The whole point of it though is actually to get you interested in Sherry of all things. Still the site looks great.

See also:
www.catacurian.com – enjoy Catalan cuisine here.
www.culinaryweeks.com – Spanish food course in hilariously bad English.
www.delicioso.co.uk – excellent Spanish delicatessen.
www.donquijote.org/culture/recipes – some good recipes from this primarily language-learning site.

www.spanishhampers.co.uk – a great selection of Spanish food for sale, recipes are pretty good too.

Spices

www.apinchof.com   US
HERBS AND SPICES
A bit of a mess but it's very informative about a whole range of herbs and spices with articles from chefs and gardeners. It has recipes and lots of links to help you out.

See also:
www.coolchile.co.uk – the place to get the hottest and widest variety of chillies.
www.ringoffire.net – a diverse web ring devoted to all that is hot and spicy.
www.seasonedpioneers.co.uk – recipes and spicy foods from all around the globe. Promises new site with more recipes.
www.spiceadvice.com – useful spice encyclopaedia from this American spice retailer; however, they don't ship outside the US.
www.thespicebazaar.com – a good-looking and well-laid-out UK-based spice store that also sells dried fruits and herbs.

Vegetarian

www.vegsoc.org   UK
THE VEGETARIAN SOCIETY
An informative and attractive site with advice and help on going vegetarian, a business section and recipes; also covers the Cordon Vert cookery school and there's a good education section for teachers and young people.

www.vegweb.com   US
VEGGIES UNITE!
If you're a vegetarian this is a great place, though not a great design. There are hundreds of recipes, plus features, chat and ideas in the VegWeb newsletter.

www.vegansociety.com   UK
AVOIDING THE USE OF ANIMAL PRODUCTS
The official site of the Vegan Society, promotes veganism by providing information, links to other related sites and books. There is a limited selection of goods in the shop, mostly books

and personal items. For a wider shopping experience go to
www.veganstore.co.uk who offer over 800 suitable products.

See also:
www.ciwf.org.uk – campaigning for farm animal welfare and
includes the Eat Less Meat initiative.
www.earthsave.org – a worthy organisation which promotes
vegetarianism by helping you choose the right way to eat.
www.living-foods.com – devoted to the subject of eating only
raw foods.
www.veggieheaven.com – UK restaurant guide for vegetarians
and vegans with nearly 240 listed.

Drink: Non-alcoholic

www.whittard.co.uk   UK
SPECIALITY TEAS DELIVERED WORLD-WIDE
An excellent site dedicated to their selection of teas and coffees;
it's easy to use and they will ship throughout the world. Delivery
varies according to weight for the UK – free if you spend £50 or
more.

See also:
www.anothercoffee.co.uk – coffee making equipment,
accessories common and obscure.
www.coffeegeek.com – an American site covering coffee, it's
very comprehensive.
www.englishteastore.com – a well-designed site and online
shop devoted to all things tea.
www.pgmoment.com – all you need to know about PG tips.
www.realcoffee.co.uk – coffee delivered to your door the day
after roasting from the Roast and Post Coffee company.
www.redmonkeycoffee.com – modern online coffee retailer with
free UK delivery.
www.tea.co.uk – great-looking site from the Tea Council with
lots of facts and reasons given why we should drink more of the
stuff.
www.twinings.com – information on tea and their products too.

Drink: Beer

wwww.camra.org.uk   UK
THE CAMPAIGN FOR REAL ALE STARTS HERE
A comprehensive site that has all the news and views on the

campaign for real ale. Sadly, it only advertises its *Good Beer Guide* and local versions, with only a small section on the best beers. Includes sections on beer in Europe, cider and festivals.

www.realbeer.com   US
THE BEER PORTAL
Over 150,000 pages dedicated to beer, with articles, reviews, links and shopping all wrapped up in a well-designed site.

See also:
www.beerhunter.com – a very good site, home to expert Michael Jackson author of the *World Beer Guide*.
www.beersofeurope.co.uk – a beer store who offer a huge range not just from Europe, but from all over the world.

Drink: Wine and Spirits

There are many web sites selling wine and spirits, the quality of the information in this section is very high. These are some of the best.

www.bbr.co.uk   UK
THE INTERNET WINE SHOP
This attractive and award-winning site offers over 1,000 different wines and spirits at prices from £4 to over £4,500. There is a great deal of information about each wine and advice on the different varieties. You can also buy related products such as cigars. Delivery for orders over £180 is free; otherwise it's £10 for the UK. They will deliver abroad and even store the wine for you.

www.winecellar.co.uk   UK
NOT JUST WINE AND GOOD VALUE
They also sell spirits as well as wine and, while the choice isn't as good as some online wine retailers, Wine Cellar are good value. Use the search facility to find the whole range which isn't obvious from the home page.

www.wine-lovers-page.com   US
ONE OF THE BEST PLACES TO LEARN ABOUT WINE
Highly informative for novices and experts alike, this site has it all. There are categories on learning about wine, reading and buying books and tasting notes for some 80,000 wines. Also within the site there's a glossary, a label decoder, a list of Internet wine shops, wine writers' archive, wine search engine and much more.

Booze

The Good Web Site Guide's Top 10s
of the Internet

1. **www.realbeer.com** – 150,000 pages on beer!
2. **www.bbr.co.uk** – the best wine shop
3. **www.winespectator.com** – the most comprehensive wine site
4. **www.superplonk.com** – Malcolm Gluck's great site
5. **www.idrink.com** – recipes for 5,000 cocktails
6. **www.camra.org.uk** – the Campaign for Real Ale
7. **www.whiskeyweb.com** – a whiskey lover's dream
8. **www.sportspubs.co.uk** – pubs where you can watch sport
9. **www.wine-searcher.com** – the wine lover's search engine
10. **www.wine-pages.com** – UK wine magazine

www.winespectator.com   UK
THE MOST COMPREHENSIVE WINE WEB SITE
From *Wine Spectator* magazine you get a site packed with
information. There's news, features, a wine search facility,
forums, weekly features, a library, the best wineries, wine
auctions and travel. The dining section has a world restaurant
guide, tips on eating out, wine matching and a set of links to
gourmet food.

www.wine-pages.com   UK
A GREAT BRITISH NON-COMMERCIAL WINE SITE
Most independently written wine sites are poor; however, wine
expert Tom Cannavan has put together a strong offering, which
is updated daily. It's well written, informative and links to other
good wine sites and online wine merchants.

www.wineanorak.com   UK
THE WINE ANORAK
For another good British independent wine site, try the Wine
Anorak, it's just a great wine zine, with lots of advice, articles,
issues of the day and general information on wines and regions.

www.jancisrobinson.com   UK
TV WINE EXPERT
Jancis Robinson has a bright site with wine news, tips, features on the latest wines and information on her books and videos.

www.ozclarke.com   UK
OZ ON OZ
Lots about Oz and what he's up to plus information on how to get his books and his pocket wine e-book. There are also recommended wines and merchants of the month, tips on tasting and information on how to access his mobile wine guide for when you're out and about.

www.superplonk.com   UK
MALCOLM GLUCK
Excellent site from Malcolm Gluck, the author of the *Superplonk* books, there are offers and tips on where to buy good-value high quality wines. For full access you have to subscribe.

Other wine sites worth checking out are:
www.booths-wine.co.uk – claims to sell imaginative and distinctive wines. Good for mixed cases of inexpensive wines.
www.cephas.co.uk – superb images of wines and vineyards around the world.
www.internetwineguide.com – a good, if advert laden, all rounder.
www.laithwaites.co.uk – no-nonsense site with lots of offers and a money back guarantee. All wines are illustrated with a picture of the bottle.
www.majestic.co.uk – lots of offers and a well-designed site.
www.vintageroots.co.uk – excellent for organic wines, spirits and beers.
www.wineontheweb.com – good wine magazine with audio features.
www.wine-searcher.com – a wine search engine, type in the wine you want and up pops a selection from various retailers from around the world and UK, all suppliers are vetted for quality and service. Pricey.

www.idrink.com   US
DRINK RECIPES AND COCKTAILS
With over 13,700 drinks recipes you're almost bound to find something to your liking, you have to be a member to get the best out of it though. See also the comprehensive **www.webtender.com**

www.barmeister.com   US

THE ONLINE GUIDE TO DRINKING

Packed with information on everything to do with drink, there are over 2,000 drink recipes available and about 630 drinking games. If you have another, then send it to be featured in the site.

www.whiskyweb.com   UK

A WEE DRAM

A comprehensive site for the whisky lover featuring history, information on how whisky is made, links to all the distilleries by region, a list of events and, of course, a shop (phone for delivery rates according to purchase). For information on the Spayside distilleries and details of their whisky festival go to **www.spiritofspeyside.com**

Eating Out

www.goodguides.com   UK

HOME OF THE GOOD PUB GUIDE

Once you've registered it has an easy-to-use regional guide to the best pubs, which are rated on food, beer, value, good places to stay and good range of wine. You can also get a listing by award winner. The site hosts the Good Guide to Britain, which is a good resource for what's on where. See also **www.greatbeer.co.uk**, one man's passion and guide to over 200 pubs in the UK.

www.dine-online.co.uk   UK

UK-BASED WINING, DINING AND TRAVEL REVIEW

A slightly pretentious, but sincere, attempt at an independent eating out review web site. It has a good and expanding selection of recommended restaurants, covers wine and has some well-written feature articles. It relies heavily on reader recommendation, so there's a good deal of variation in coverage and review quality and some were written some time ago. Not very user friendly, no search by area.

www.theaa.com   UK

AA RESTAURANT SEARCH

Nestled away in the AA site is a little known gem, an excellent regional restaurant guide to the UK. Simply type in the town name or find the location on an interactive map. Each of the 4,000 listed is graded and there are comments on quality of food, facilities, ambience and, of course, how to get there.

www.viamichelin.co.uk   UK
MICHELIN
A site from Michelin with the emphasis on route finding, but
after you register (for free), you get access to a good restaurant
finder and hotel guide.

*Other restaurant review sites worth looking at before you go out
are:*
www.conran.com/eat – a guide to Terence Conran's restaurants
with online booking and some special offers, nice design too.
www.cuisinenet.co.uk – book online at selected restaurants,
nice design.
www.grabameal.co.uk – a pretty comprehensive directory of
takeaways and restaurants in the UK, with some 23,500 listed.
www.local-restaurant.com – good restaurant finder for cities,
not so good for country areas.
www.squaremeal.co.uk – newsy guide to London's restaurants,
it also covers selected ones in the UK.
www.toptable.co.uk – co-ordinates free booking at thousands
of restaurants, bars and party venues in 30 cities in the
UK and popular overseas locations; nice design too.

Free Stuff

*Free stuff is exactly what the term suggests, and these are sites whose
owners have trawled the Net or been offered free services, software,
trial products and so on. It's amazing what you can find.*

www.freeinuk.co.uk   UK
JUST THE UK
Not just free stuff but also excellent Internet offers from British
sites, good design, but not that easy to navigate. The Top Ten
section is great.

*Other sites worth looking into are these listed below, they're all from
the UK.*

www.chooseaprize.com – loads of competitions, try your luck
and collect points.
www.find-a-freebie.co.uk – very well categorised and extensive
selection.
www.freebielist.com – a well-organised listing of web-based
freebies; easy to use and good links.

www.freebiersclub.co.uk – they claim that there's no junk here and members get rewards.
www.freebievillage.co.uk – a forum approach, but freebies expired on some older postings.
www.freestuffjunction.co.uk – loads of offers, top tens are a good starting point.
www.voucherheaven.com – discount vouchers and news on offers.

Here are a couple of US sites, but offers may not apply for the UK.

www.1freestuff.com – one of the oldest and probably best categorised.
www.thefreesite.com – more web stuff, nice layout.

Furniture: see under 'Home and DIY', page 273.

Gambling and Betting Sites

Gambling sites abound on the Internet and they often use some of the most sophisticated marketing techniques to keep you hooked. For example new screens pop up as you click on the close button tempting you with the chance to win millions. All the gaming sites are monitored by gaming commissions but above all be sensible, it's easy to get carried away. As UK based gambling sites are generally better regulated we would recommend you use them, so we have put the country we think they are based in next to the sites listed.

Gambling and Gaming

www.gamble.co.uk   UK
THE GAMBLER'S PORTAL
A good British directory with summary reviews of the various sites it features. Once you find one that appeals, then you can check out a detailed review that helps you get the best out of your chosen site. Lots of good information, advice and tips on betting, horse racing, greyhounds, sports betting as well as casinos, poker, lotteries and bingo.

These are the casinos and gambling sites we liked best:
www.24ktgoldcasino.com – good graphics and fast response times make this great fun, but you need a decent PC to download the software. There are 40 or so games and you can

play either for fun or for money. (MOHAWK TERRIORY OF KAHNWKE, CANADA)

www.32red.com – one of the most popular and best British online casinos, with lots of games and ways to bet ... (UK)

www.888.com – claims to be the world's most popular online casino, great design. (GIBRALTAR)

www.betasyouclick.com – a directory with links to web sites from around the world, which offer, among other things sports books, casinos, poker rooms, lotteries and competitions. (UK)

www.betgambling.net – useful international gambling directory, which also offers forums and guides to the various games and sites. (US)

www.intercasino.co.uk – easy to use and they've over 80 games to choose from. (NETHERLANDS ANTILLES)

www.littlewoodscasino.com – one of the top-rated casino sites. (UK)

www.uk.pogo.com – from EA Games, lots to choose from, lots of prizes to play for. (US)

www.slotland.com – for those who love losing their money in slot machines. (ANJOUAN, COMOROS)

www.williamhillcasino.com – consistently highly rated. (UK)

Betting

www.settle-a-bet.co.uk   UK

BETS EXPLAINED

If you can't tell the difference between a trixie or a yankee and thought spreadbetting was something that went on toast, then this is the site for you. It has (not always simple) explanations of virtually every conceivable type of bet.

www.oddschecker.co.uk   UK

COMPARE THE ODDS

A great way to ensure you get the best deal from the online bookmakers, you just choose the sport and the event, then you get a read-out of the latest odds given by a selection of bookies – you can click on the bookmaker of your choice to place your bet. It's continually being updated; the site's a must for the committed gambler.

www.ukbetting.com   UK

LIVE INTERACTIVE BETTING

Concentrating on sports betting, this is a clear, easy-to-use site; take a guest tour before applying to join. You need to open an account to take part, using your credit or debit card, minimum deposit £10. See also the popular **www.bluesq.com** which also offers a similar but possibly slightly broader service, and special bets on things like soap operas and political elections. Also worth a visit is **www.bet365.co.uk** who cover a wide variety of areas and offer some good deals.

www.mybetting.co.uk   UK

FREE BETTING
My betting works as a collation site for free bets and offers from bookmakers around the Internet. It takes a minute or so to get used to the design but once you're on board it's easy to get yourself a few free bets, albeit at the price of a registration or two.

www.racingpost.co.uk   UK

THE RACING POST
A combination of news, racing and betting on a clear, well-designed site. Also features greyhounds and information on bloodstock.

www.ladbrokes.co.uk   UK

UK'S NUMBER 1 BOOKMAKER
Ladbrokes offer a combination of news, information and sport-related betting with excellent features on racing, golf and the other major sporting events. There's also a casino, lotteries, a specials section where you can bet on politics or big events and, of course, the now ubiquitous poker game.

www.willhill.com   UK

THE MOST RESPECTED NAME IN BOOKMAKING
The best online betting site in terms of speed, layout and design, it has the best event finder, results service and betting calculator. The bet finder service is also very good and quick. All the major sports are featured and there is a specials section for those out-of-the-ordinary flutters. Betting is live as it happens.

See also:
www.bookiealerts.co.uk – a free download, it's essentially a news service geared to betting, useful and you can tailor it to your interests. (UK)
www.paddypower.com – a strong site from Ireland's biggest bookmaker with betting on horses, football and other top sports – even politics. (IRELAND)

www.sportingindex.com – excellent and wide-ranging spread betting site with offers and competitions. (UK)

www.win2win.co.uk – excellent free subscription service for serious race-going gamblers. (UK)

www.totesport.com UK

THE TOTE

The Tote has reinvented itself and become a general betting site with casino and instant reward games. It covers a wide range of sports but is especially strong on horse racing where you'll find lots of useful information to back up your betting decisions.

www.thedogs.co.uk UK

 GONE TO THE DOGS

Everything you need to know about greyhounds and greyhound racing. You can adopt or get advice on buying a dog, find the nearest track, get the latest results and learn how to place bets. You can't gamble from the site but they provide links.

Poker

One of the biggest areas of expansion in online gambling, here are the major sites …

www.partypoker.com – one of the best and most popular poker sites. (GIBRALTAR)

www.pokerroom.com – a good site where you don't necessarily have to download a program to play. (MOHAWK TERRIORY OF KAHNWKE, CANADA)

www.pokerstars.com – the one that seems to breed world champions. (COSTA RICA)

www.williamhillpoker.com – one of the most popular UK-based poker games. (UK)

Miscellaneous

www.national-lottery.co.uk UK

IT COULD BE YOU

Find out about Lotto and even play online, there's info on how to play and results of Euromillions and instant win games too. They also tell you about the good causes that the National Lottery supports. If you want to know whether your premium bonds are worth anything try www.nationalsavings.co.uk (you need your bondholder number handy).

www.highstakes.co.uk UK
HIGH STAKES BOOKSTORE
Books on virtually every aspect of gambling at this minimalist
site. It also offers selected links and you can order online too.

www.gamblersanonymous.org.uk UK
WHEN THE STAKES GET TOO HIGH …
Where to go when it all gets too much, a straightforward site
listing crucial phone numbers and information on how to deal
with the compulsion.

See also:
www.gamanon.org.uk – help and advice for addicted gamblers
and their families.
www.gamcare.org.uk – an authority on the provision of
information on gambling, with advice and practical help in
addressing its social impact.

G

Games

*There's a massive selection of games on the Internet, here are just
some of the very best ones; from board games to quizzes to your
everyday 'shoot 'em up' type. There are more games for Macs listed on
page 24.*

*It's worth remembering that before downloading a game from a site it's
wise to check for viruses. If you've not got anti-virus software on your
PC, then check out our section on virus management on page 424. On
most sites you'll benefit from the speed of a broadband connection,
which is not the assumed norm for gamers.*

***Parents should be aware that some games are quite violent or contain
sexual references, so it's as well to check them out before letting your
child loose on them.***

Finding Games

http://gamespotter.com US
GAMES SEARCH ENGINE
A really handy site where you can get links to virtually every type
of game whether it be a puzzle or action. Alternatively, you can
use the search facility to find something. Each game on the list
is reviewed as well.

Games Magazines and Information

www.gamespy.com   US
GAMING'S HOMEPAGE
Lots here as well as the usual reviews and features. There are
chat and help sections and in the resources section, hundreds of
demos plus free games to play. To maximise the fun, you have to
subscribe. See also **www.gamespot.co.uk** which offers lots of
info as well.

www.gamers.com   US
A MOMENT ENJOYED IS NOT WASTED
A great-looking site with all the features you'd expect from a
games magazine but it has more in the way of downloads and
games to play. There is also a chat section and competitions.

www.gamefaqs.com   US
GAMES FREQUENTLY ASKED QUESTIONS
All information is free and donated, there are FAQs and tip sheets
on any number of games, and it seems to be regularly updated.

http://vgstrategies.about.com   US
ABOUT GAMES
A set of information pages from the excellent About.com with
articles and links covering all the likely strategies needed for
gaming.

www.mpogd.com   US
MULTIPLAYER ONLINE GAMES DIRECTORY
A comprehensive database of popular multi-player games with
details on each game, links and a good search facility. See also
www.onrpg.com

http://games.yahoo.com   US
YAHOO!
This popular search engine has its own games section. Here you
can play against others or yourself online. There's a good
selection, start with their top 20 if you don't know where to begin.
See also Google's selection at **www.google.com/Top/Games**

See also:
http://games.slashdot.org – described as 'News for Nerds' it
looks the part and seems very comprehensive with the latest
games news by format.

www.eurogamer.net – another newsy site, this is better laid out than most but there's still a lot to take in.

www.gamestudies.org – an intellectual and scholarly approach to games with articles and emphasis on the cultural, aesthetic and communicative value of gaming.

www.gaming-age.com – more news and reviews.

www.spong.com – the Internet Video Games Archive has a massive amount of information on games. Their intended objective is to archive every game.

Games to Play

www.boxerjam.com   UK
ONLINE GAMESHOW
Excellent site devoted to giving the user access to original and traditional games played online, for cash and prizes.

www.classicgaming.com   US
GAMING THE WAY YOU REMEMBER IT
Probably one for older gamers but there's some good stuff on here so it's at least worth a look and it's amazing how new some of the games are.

www.gamebrew.com   US
CHOOSE YOUR GAME
Gamebrew specialises in Java games and there are some brilliant ones to download and play here, you choose from twelve categories from puzzles to casino to action.

www.graalonline.com   UK
THE GRAAL KINGDOMS
Set in a mythical realm, this is a good multi-player game with lots of levels and a high degree of interactivity and customisation.

www.worldogl.com   US
ONLINE GAMING LEAGUE
Join a community of gamers who play in leagues for fun and have a zero tolerance policy for cheaters. You can play all the major online games and compete in the leagues and ladders if you like. To quote them: 'What matters is that people are meeting and interacting with other people on the Internet via our services and their game'.

www.planetquake.com   US
THE EPICENTRE OF QUAKE
Quake remains one of the most popular games played on the Internet; we've now arrived at Quake IV. This site gives you all the background and details on the game for singles and multi-players. It's got loads of links and features as well as reviews and a forum.

www.scummvm.org   US
POINT AND CLICK ADVENTURES
Download the program and get access to a number of good games, which were previously unavailable on a PC or Mac.

www.shockwave.com   US
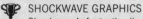 SHOCKWAVE GRAPHICS
Shockwave's fantastic site offers much in the way of high definition games for both action fans and those who prefer to test their minds a bit; the site also offers films and other useful programs. Membership costs a minimum of $5 per month.

www.lysator.liu.se/tolkien-games   SWEDEN
LORD OF THE RINGS
Get immersed in Tolkien's Middle Earth with some 100 games. It's got action games, quizzes and puzzles, strategy games and, of course, role playing games.

www.wireplay.com   US
THE GAMES NETWORK
A good online games resource, the site encourages the players to interact, it has a range of communities and forums and also organises competitions.

www.orisinal.com   US
JUST FOR FUN
A selection of high-quality silly and funny games using a very original and text-free format and design.

www.spaceinvaders.de   GERMANY
SPACE INVADER SHRINE
A fun homage to the original game with history, trivia, tips and of course you can play the game too.

www.popcap.com   US
  100 PERCENT JAVA
  An excellent site with very high-quality games to download onto
  the PC, Mac, Palm or even your mobile; you can also play on
  the web.

www.sodaplay.com   UK
  BUILD YOUR OWN ...
  A really interesting and different gaming experience. Here you
  can design your models and send them to the 'zoo' for display
  and use by others. You can race them and exchange them with
  friends too.

www.stickcricket.com   AUSTRALIA
  IT'S NOT CRICKET!
  Slightly frustrating at first but, once you get the hang of it, it's a
  lot of fun.

Free Games

www.gamehippo.com   US
  OVER 1,000 FREE GAMES
  Enough to keep you occupied for hours with games of every type
  from board to action to puzzles and sports. It's worth checking
  out **www.freeloader.com** which has a more modern selection
  available, but you have to register and jump through a few
  hoops to get them.

  Also worth checking out are the following:
  http://lazylaces.com – a blog from an experienced web developer,
  it's a good place to go if you're looking for more unusual games.
  www.download-game.com – oddly designed offering a large
  number including old favourites.
  www.free-games.com.au – Australian site featuring a good
  selection of games.
  www.freeonlinegames.com – if adverts aren't a problem for you,
  then try this site, which offers many games as well as other time
  wasting features.
  www.millionsofgames.com – a games site with a difference,
  those involved pick the games and share them with fellow site
  members. This means you're not being dictated to by the
  company but with like-minded people who enjoy the same
  games as you ... in theory. There are some 12000 games on
  the site at time of writing.

www.miniclip.com/games/en – hundreds of mini games to choose from, from Sudoku to Clash'n'Slash …

www.protokid.com – from a top clothing manufacturer, you create your Proto Kid (guess what you have to dress them in), then play the games. Cynical exercise from a big company or great fun – not sure …

www.stackopolis.com – a pretty addictive alternative to Sim City, stack blocks to create buildings etc, plus links to similar games.

www.uk.zylom.com – excellent for word games and puzzles, but there is a gambling section too.

www.windowsgames.co.uk – Sean O'Connor's site where there's a small selection of high-quality games to download.

Game Manufacturers and Console Games

http://cube.ign.com   US
GAME CUBE
Dedicated to the format, there are lots of reviews, previews and the latest information on what's coming too.

www.hasbro.com/games   US
HASBRO GAMES
A commercial site from one of the biggest manufacturers with a useful list of what they produce.

www.nintendo.com   US
OFFICIAL NINTENDO
Get the latest news from Nintendo and its spin-offs – Wii, N64, Game Boy and Game Cube. There's also information on the hardware and details of the games, new and old. For a site with wider Nintendo info go to the excellent **www.nintendojo.com**

http://uk.playstation.com   US
OFFICIAL PLAYSTATION SITE
Looks good with games information, information on the hardware, previews, new release details and a special features section with reviews by well-known gamers. There's also a chat section and a shop.

Also check out:
http://wii.com
www.absolute-playstation.com
www.playstation.com
www.psxextreme.com

www.pocketgamer.org   UK
GAMES FOR POCKET PCS
OK so you've bought your handheld PC, you've impressed the
boss, now, what do you really use it for? Oh yes, play games!
There's a great selection here for most different types of operating
systems. If not, then there are links to related sites. Try also
www.handango.com which is not a specialist site, but the games
section has been expanded and the design is much improved.

www.gamespy.com/xbox   US
XBOX
Part of the Gamespy network, this site gives background on
Microsoft's toy, with the latest game news, reviews, demos and
previews too. See also **www.xbox.com** who offer some exclusive
previews and information. There's also **www.majornelson.com**
which is an unofficial, but well put together, blog devoted to the
Xbox.

www.station.sony.com   US
SONY ONLINE GAMES
Sony have put together an exceptional site for online gaming,
and with millions of members, it's one of the most popular. The
site is well designed, easy to use and there are lots of games to
choose from. Providing you can put up with the adverts, it's a
real treat to use.

www.sega-europe.com   EUROPE
SEGA
Get the latest news on the latest games and buy them at the
store. The site is well designed with all the usual features.

Fantasy League and Strategy Games

www.fantasyleague.com   UK
FANTASY FOOTIE
Be a football manager, play for yourself, in a league, or even
organise a game for your workplace or school. Get the latest
team news on your chosen players and how they're doing
against the rest.

www.thedugout.net   UK
CHAMPIONSHIP MANAGER
An excellent site devoted to Football and Championship Manager
and soccer gaming. You can discuss the game, get up to speed

with the latest tactics, get the low-down on the players and generally join in.

www.primagames.com   US

PRIMA

The largest fantasy game publisher offers a site packed with reviews, demos and articles. You can also buy a book on virtually every strategy game. See also **www.strategy-gaming.com** which is pretty comprehensive.

www.gamesworkshop.com   UK

WAR GAMING

A comprehensive offering covering war games including collecting, painting and gaming itself; there are also forums, chat and links to the major games. See also **www.wargames.co.uk** which is pretty comprehensive.

Cheats, Hints and Tips

www.computerandvideogames.com   US

THE CHEAT STATION

Go to the 'cheats' section and type in the game or cheat that you want. There are cheats for thousands of games so you should find what you're looking for.

See also:
http://cheats.freeola.com – UK site with over 74,000 cheats, including PS2.
www.cheatextreme.com – great selection of cheats for most platforms.
www.cheatheaven.com – a one-stop site for cheats in over 2,000 games covering most consoles. Good search facility, but some annoying adverts and pop-ups.
www.lunabean.com – all you need for video games.
www.playstation2-cheats.co.uk – cheats for PS2.

Games Shops

*If you know which game you want, then it's probably better to use a price checker such as Kelkoo (**http://uk.kelkoo.com**) to find the best price on the game. They will put you through to the store offering the best all round deal. If you want to browse, then these are considered the best online stores for a wide range of games:*

www.chipsworld.co.uk – good for Sega and Nintendo.
www.game.co.uk – a good comprehensive offering with daily and weekly offers.
www.gameplay.com – Gameplay is one of the most visited games sites. Once a magazine site, it's now transformed into a well designed store, browsable by platform and good value.
www.play.com – a good selection of games, many at a reduced price and, with free delivery, it's not surprising that it is such a popular site.
www.streetsonline.co.uk – follow the link to 'gamestreet' for one of the top shops on the Internet. Parents will be sorry that the kids' section has gone. Good value too.
www.telegames.co.uk – well-stocked game shop covering all platforms.

Miscellaneous

www.etch-a-sketch.com
UK
REMEMBER ETCH-A-SKETCH?
For those of you who don't remember back that far, Etch-a-Sketch is a rather annoying drawing game. It's been faithfully recreated here and it's still just as difficult to do curves. They do give you a few hints and tips and an art gallery for inspiration, also a few other simple games.

www.hangman.no
NORWAY
HANGMAN
A great hangman game, you can play in many categories. Thankfully you can also turn the music off.

Card and Board Games

www.tradgames.org.uk
UK
TRADITIONAL GAMES
A history and guide to traditional games, including board games, table games, pub games and lawn games too.

www.chess.co.uk
UK
ULTIMATE CHESS
Massive chess site that's got information on the game, news and views, reviews and shopping. There are lots of links to other chess sites and downloads. Also info on backgammon, go, poker and bridge.

See also:
www.bcf.org.uk – for the British Chess Federation.
www.chessclub.com – for the Internet Chess club who had over 2,000 players online when we visited, including 19 grandmasters.

www.bkgm.com
BACKGAMMON
A rather old-fashioned, cluttered site, but there is lots here for the beginner and the more experienced player alike. For a more casino-type approach check out **www.gammonempire.co.uk** where you're given the choice to play for money or just for fun.

www.monopoly.com   US
MONOPOLY
A pretty boring site, it offers a history plus information on where you can buy, along with tips on how to play and how you can get involved in tournaments. See also **www.mymonopoly.com** where you can create your own personalised game to order.

www.thehouseofcards.com   US
LOADS OF CARD GAMES
Huge number of card games to play and download with sections on card tricks, history, links and word games – there's not much missing here. See also **www.pagat.com** for an alternative.

www.solitairegames.com   US
SOLITAIRE
Play online or download a game onto your PC or Mac, there are plenty to choose from and it's quick. There's also a good set of links to other online card games. See also **www.solitaireelaboratory.com** for information on how to get the best out of some favourites such as Microsoft's FreeCell.

http://bridge.ecats.co.uk   UK
BRIDGE RESOURCE
A good place for information on bridge from a software company associated with the game at a high level. See also **www.bridgemagazine.co.uk**

Crosswords, Puzzles and Word Games

www.cluemaster.com   UK
CROSSWORDS AND WORD PUZZLES
A collection of crosswords and word searches. You have to
register to get access to the free puzzles, otherwise it costs
£1.50 to download 50 puzzles.

www.crosswordsite.com   UK
ALL CROSSWORDS
Hundreds to chose from, with the option either to print off or fill
in online. There are four levels of difficulty with the hardest
being quite tough. See also **www.crossword-puzzles.co.uk**

www.fun-with-words.com   US
THE WORDPLAY WEBSITE
Dedicated to amusing English, the Fun with Words site offers
games, puzzles and an insight into the sorts of tricks you can
play with the language.

www.websudoku.com   ISRAEL
SUDOKU
It had to happen, the world couldn't go without an online
Sudoku site for long. In case you have lived in a cave for the
past couple of years and don't know what it's about, here's the
place to start your education with games for players of all levels.
It's a great site for all fans. See also **www.sudoku.com**

*Other crossword and puzzle sites worth checking out are listed
below:*
http://crosswords.about.com – links and tips from this giant
reference site.
www.download.com – the games section here has masses of
choice, some free.
www.lovatts.com.au – plenty to choose from at this Australian
magazine.

Quizzes and General Knowledge

www.thinks.com   UK
FUN AND GAMES FOR PLAYFUL BRAINS
Massive collection of games, puzzles and quizzes with
something for everyone, it's easy to navigate and free.

www.playwithyourmind.com   UK

MIND GAMES AND IQ TESTS

More than 20 mind-stretching games including word, maths, card and logic puzzles; the design isn't great but the games are good.

www.queendom.com   US

SERIOUSLY ENTERTAINING

It's not entirely free but an excellent site for all sorts of brain tingling tests, the major difference is that it also offers personality profiles and psychometric tests which may help you in getting on in your career or just keeping your brain healthy. See also **http://web.tickle.com** (formerly emode.com).

Check out these sites:

www.coolquiz.com – several different types of quiz from sports to movies and quotes. Nice wacky design.

www.funtrivia.com – a massive trivia site with over 650,000 questions.

www.mensa.org.uk – Mensa only admit people who pass their high IQ test – see if you've got what it takes.

www.quiz.co.uk – a couple of hundred questions in several unusual categories including kids, nature, food and sport.

www.quizyourfriends.com – a fun quiz creation site.

www.trivialpursuit.com – A massive disappointment; a purely commercial site geared to selling versions of the official game.

Gardening

There are lots of high-quality British gardening sites, but some sites are based in America, so bear this in mind for tenderness, soil and climate advice. Due to regulations on the importation of seeds and plants, these can't be imported from outside the UK.

www.gardenworld.co.uk   UK

THE UK'S BEST

Described as the UK's best garden centre and horticultural site. It includes a list of over 1,000 garden centres, with addresses, contact numbers and e-mail addresses. Outstanding list of links to other sites on most aspects of gardening; very comprehensive with sections on wildlife, books, holidays, advice, societies and specialists, it now also has the addition of a link to the RHS plant finder service and Latin name converter – excellent.

For Garden Lovers

The Good Web Site Guide's Top 10s
of the Internet

1. **www.rhs.org.uk** – home of the Royal Horticultural Society
2. **www.gardenworld.co.uk** – for a garden centre near you
3. **www.crocus.co.uk** – the best gardening shop
4. **www.hdra.org.uk** – the authority on organic gardening
5. **www.carryongardening.org.uk** – gardening chat
6. **www.bbc.co.uk/gardening** – great stuff from the Beeb
7. **www.ngs.org.uk** – home of the excellent National Garden Scheme
8. **www.chilternseeds.co.uk** – masses of seeds, order online
9. **www.nhm.ac.uk/science/projects/fff** – our wild flora and fauna
10. **www.allotments-uk.com** – all you need to know about your allotment

G

www.gardenweb.com   UK

GARDEN QUESTIONS ANSWERED

Probably the best site for lively gardening debate; it's enjoyable, international, comprehensive and has a nice tone. There is a blog, several discussion forums on various gardening topics, garden advice, plant dictionary and competitions. Using the forums is easy and fun, and you're sure to find the answer to almost any gardening question.

www.kew.org.uk   UK

ROYAL BOTANIC GARDENS

Kew's mission is to increase knowledge about plants and conserve them for future generations. This site gives plenty of information about their work, the collections, features and events. There are also details of the facilities at the gardens, conservation, educational material and lots of links to related sites.

www.rhs.org.uk   UK

ROYAL HORTICULTURAL SOCIETY

An excellent site from the RHS which features a plant-finder service covering some 70,000 plant types, a garden finder and an event finder. There's also advice and information about the RHS, an opportunity to buy advance tickets to their shows and the opportunity to buy from their garden gift collection.

Other gardening advice and information sites well worth trying are:
www.carryongardening.org.uk – award-winning site with all the usual features plus some celebrity input. Good for links and the idea exchange feature.
www.gardenforum.co.uk – outstanding gardening forum site, good if you're a novice to using forums and chat sites.
www.gardenguides.com – a useful American resource site with loads of information on every aspect of gardening. It has lots of tips, handy guides, and a free online newsletter.
www.gardenlinks.co.uk – 'hand-reviewed' links to gardening sites in over 40 categories, a good place to start searching for something specific.
www.gonegardening.com – nice design, wide-ranging magazine and shop.

Allotment Gardening

www.allotments-uk.com   UK
ALLOTMENT ADVICE
Lots of links, advice and tips, plus a forum to discuss all your allotment problems. See also **www.nsalg.org.uk**, home to the National Society of Allotment Gardeners, which isn't a great site it has to be said.

Gardening Stores

www.greenfingers.com   UK
COMPREHENSIVE GARDENING
A gardening superstore with many categories and some good offers. There's also plenty in the way of advice and tips, plus an ask the gardener facility.

www.crocus.co.uk   UK
GARDENERS BY NATURE
A good-looking site full of ideas enhanced by excellent photographs, there are some good articles and features, but it's basically a gorgeous shop with thousands of plants and products to choose from and some good offers. Delivery to England and Southern Scotland starts at £5.95 (£1 for seeds). If you live

elsewhere you need to contact them to see if delivery is possible for a surcharge.

Other gardening shops worth checking out are:
www.blooms-online.com – once this site stood out from the crowd, but many features have gone and now it is just a good online shop for plants with some general information and details about their shops.
www.burncoose.co.uk – nice design, searchable plant catalogue with some good offers.
www.gardentrading.co.uk – less about gardening more about accessorising your patch.
www.glut.co.uk – the Gluttonous Gardener provides unusual presents for every gardener.
www.rkalliston.co.uk – excellent for gardening accessories and gifts.
www.wheelie-bin-art.co.uk – decorate your wheelie bin so it adds colour to your garden.
www.wyevale.co.uk – from one of the UK's largest garden centre chains, a good site offering advice and plenty of choice in their shop.

Garden Design

www.thegardenplanner.co.uk   UK
THE GARDENER'S DIRECTORY
Everything you need to plan your perfect garden, this excellent directory is the place to start.

See also:
http://gardendesign-uk.com – a good directory of garden designers.
www.bali.co.uk – the home of the British Association of Landscape Industries, here you can find a company qualified to do the work you want.
www.englishgardeningschool.co.uk – gardening courses from the Chelsea Physic Garden.
www.gardendesigner.com – a serious American site with in-depth advice.
www.sgd.org.uk – Society of Garden Designers to find a landscape gardener.
www.the-landscape-design-site.com – excellent DIY advice and information on garden design from this American designer.

Organic and Environmentally Friendly Gardening

www.hdra.org.uk UK

HENRY DOUBLEDAY RESEARCH ASSOCIATION
The leading authority on organic gardening. Their site offers a superb resource if you're into gardening the natural way. It's particularly good if you're growing vegetables and includes fact sheets and details on why you should garden organically.

See also entries on page 138:
www.greengardener.co.uk – specialists in biological and organic pest control and wormeries.
www.just-green.com – natural pest control with advice and products.
www.organiccatalogue.com – a comprehensive store related to the HDRA.
www.pan-uk.org – the Pesticide Action Network who are working to eliminate the hazards associated with pesticides.
www.recyclenow.com – the best ways to recycle your rubbish.
www.soilassociation.org – for advice on growing organic food plus the latest news on their campaigns.

British Wildflowers and Plants

www.nhm.ac.uk/science/projects/fff UK

FLORA AND FAUNA
Using the postcode search, find out which plants are native to your area, where to get seeds and then how to look after them once they're in your garden. Sponsored by the Natural History Museum. Visit **www.floralocale.org** for information on sustainable planting as well as a list of approved suppliers.

www.british-trees.com UK
FORESTRY AND CONSERVATION
Comprehensive information on British trees plus a good set of links and a list of books and magazines. For more information on how to care for trees go to **www.trees.org.uk**

www.wildflowers.co.uk UK
BRITISH WILDFLOWERS
An online store specialising in British wildflowers with advice on how to grow them; there's also a search engine where you can

find the plants you need using common or Latin names. If you
want a wildlife-friendly garden try **www.wildlifegardening.co.uk**
which is a basic but informative site.

www.wigglywiggler.co.uk   UK
TOUCHY FEELY WILDLIFE

Small business champions Wiggly Wigglers have an online shop
specialising in wildlife products for the garden. If you want to
attract wildlife, you can find a home for them here, you can
stock your pond and buy plants and composters. They also sell
seasonal English-grown flowers. Sign up to the podcast or visit
the blog for regular updates on what they're up to down there on
the farm. For another personal approach visit Jenny's garden at
www.wildlife-gardening.co.uk

See also:

www.meadowmania.co.uk – another specialist but also offers
bulbs and plug plants.
www.wildseeds.co.uk – specialist suppliers of wild seeds and
grasses.

Specific Plants, Societies and Specialists

www.alpinegardensociety.net   UK
ALPINES

An informative site on Alpines with articles from the society
magazine, seed exchange, newsletter and shop. You can also
find out about their tours to the best Alpine territories.

www. www.discoveringannuals.com   UK
ANNUALS GALORE

Based on the successful book, this site offers information on
hardy annuals, half-hardy annuals, biennials and seed-raised
bedding plants of all kinds. There's an A–Z listing on the plants
and it tells you where you can buy them.

www.thecgs.org.uk   UK
COTTAGE GARDEN SOCIETY

The place to go if you want the picture-perfect cottage garden.
The site is quite basic but there's plenty of information to get you
started plus a seed exchange service via their magazine.

www.hardy-plant.org.uk UK
HARDY PLANT SOCIETY
A society devoted to conserving the older, rare and unusual garden plants. There's information about how you can get involved, where their fairs are, plus a seed list and limited plant information.

www.herbnet.com US
GROWING AND COOKING HERBS
An American network specialising in herbs, with links to specialists, and to trade and information sites. It can be hard work to negotiate, but there's no doubting the quality of the content – although the quality of the music is up for debate. See also **www.herbsociety.co.uk** which isn't a great site but does contain some useful info.

www.nccpg.com UK
CONSERVING PLANTS AND GARDENS
The National Council for the Conservation of Plants and Gardens is responsible for maintaining the national plant collections of which there are over 600. Here you can find out about the NCCPG's conservation work and plant database and how you can get involved.

www.rareplants.co.uk UK
RARE PLANT NURSERY
A site developed by a specialist nursery, which is well illustrated, and pretty comprehensive, it offers information on the plants and can supply plants world-wide.

www.rosarian.com UK
ROSES
If you love roses or just need information on them, drop in here for a good, long browse. See also **www.davidaustinroses.com** the outstanding rose specialist and also the Royal National Rose Society at **www.rnrs.org**

www.treesbypost.co.uk UK
MAIL ORDER TREES
A wide variety of trees and shrubs delivered to your door from this specialist grower.

www.vegetable-gardening-club.com UK
GROWING VEG

Lots of advice and help on growing most types of vegetables, with links and information on what tools to use; for seeds try **www.vegetableseedwarehouse.com** who offer a wide choice.

www.windowbox.com US
CONTAINER GARDENING

A really good American site which is well worth a look if you're into container gardening in any form. It's well laid out and very well written with great ideas for unusual plant combinations. Worth a long browse.

Other specialists worth checking out:
http://lockyerfuchsias.co.uk – good mail-order service from this Bristol-based company, supplying fuchsias.
www.brogdale.org – basically all you need to know about fruit grown in the UK.
www.citruscentre.co.uk – the place to go for your lemons, limes and more.
www.junglegardens.co.uk – a delicious display of exotic plants to lust over. Especially useful for selecting conservatory plants.
www.orchid.org.uk – home of the North of England Orchid Society with a well-illustrated site.
www.orchids.uk.com – attractive site and home of specialist grower Burham Nurseries and you can buy orchids online.
www.topiary.org.uk – dull site from the Topiary Association.
www.frostatmidnight.co.uk – informative site about Topiary but could do with some illustrations.

Seed Specialists

www.chilternseeds.co.uk UK

SEED SPECIALIST

Choose from over 5,000 different types of seeds with many unusual plants including organically grown seeds. Very easy to find the right plant, excellent.

See also:
www.suttons-seeds.co.uk – comprehensive offering with a money back guarantee and an easy-to-use site.
www.thompson-morgan.com – huge range, good advice and good value too.

Gardening Peripherals and Equipment

www.lawnmowersdirect.co.uk   UK
: BUY A LAWNMOWER ONLINE
A retailer specialising in mowers and other power tools. You can browse the site by make and it's quick and easy to use, if a little basic.

www.lightingforgardens.co.uk   UK
: LIGHT UP YOUR GARDEN
A specialist that offers advice, ideas and a wide range of products to light up your garden, all on a nicely designed site.

www.agriframes.co.uk   UK
: GARDEN STRUCTURES
An improved site, from probably the UK's leading supplier, which now shows off their wide range of non-plant garden products to good effect. There's everything here from pergolas, fruit cages, watering cans and tools, plus information on their made-to-order service too.

www.simplygardeningtools.co.uk   UK
: GARDEN TOOLS
A messy, bright site offering a wide range of tools and equipment and free delivery in the UK, plus a money back guarantee. See also **www.fredshed.co.uk** for reviews of the best products.

www.garden-sheds-online.co.uk   UK
: SHEDS!
A company that is passionate about sheds. There is information to help you pick the right one and a good selection to choose from. For the lighter side of life in garden sheds, you should check out the bizarre but excellent **www.readersheds.co.uk**

www.watergardening-direct.co.uk   UK
: WATER GARDENING PRODUCTS
Not a great web site, but it all works and there is a good range. You can order online and ask for advice too.

See also:
http://home-garden.ebay.co.uk – it's amazing what you can find at eBay.

www.gardengames.co.uk – specialists in giant garden games.
www.philipmorris.uk.com – very good equipment shop.

TV Tie-ins and Celebrities

www.bbc.co.uk/gardening   UK
GARDENING AT THE BEEB
A set of web pages from the BBC site which offer a great
gardening magazine, featuring celebrities but mixed with
helpful advice and sections such as design inspiration, plant
profiles, ask the expert and today in your garden. You can
sign up for their free newsletter.

www.barnsdalegardens.co.uk   UK
GEOFF HAMILTON'S GARDEN
To many people the real home of *Gardener's World*, this site tells
you all about Barnsdale and has features about the garden,
Geoff and his work. There's also an online store selling a limited
range of products and a good set of gardening site links.

www.alantitchmarsh.com   UK
ALAN TITCHMARSH
Part of the Expert Gardener site with competitions, biographical
details, sponsored events and some gardening details.

Other important and well-known gardeners:
www.bethchatto.co.uk – find out about her garden and shop for
plants too.
www.gertrudejekyll.co.uk – devoted to the work of this
amazing woman.
www.perennial.org.uk – home of the Gardeners Royal
Benevolent Society.

Visiting Gardens and Garden History

www.gardenvisit.com   UK
GARDENS TO VISIT AND ENJOY
With over 2,000 gardens listed world-wide, this site offers
information on all of them and each is rated for design, planting
and scenic interest with Sissinghurst scoring top marks. There's
also information on the history of gardening, tours and hotels
with good gardens. We found some of the information is a little
out of date.

See also:

http://hcs.osu.edu/history – from Ohio State University, the history of horticulture through biographies of the most famous gardeners.

www.edenproject.com – for the grandest garden scheme of them all.

www.gardenhistorysociety.org – an overview of what the society is about and information on what they're up to, but little in the way of history bar a few articles.

www.greatbritishgardens.co.uk – good regional reference and guide that includes biographies of great British garden designers.

www.museumgardenhistory.org – based in Lambeth, this site offers details of the museum and the famous Tradescant family.

www.nationaltrust.org.uk – offering information on their gardens and places of interest.

www.ngs.org.uk   UK
NATIONAL GARDEN SCHEME
This is basically the famous yellow book converted into a web site with details on over 3,300 gardens to visit for charity and the work they undertake with the money they earn from your support. See also **www.gardensofscotland.org** which operates a similar scheme.

Gardeners with Special Needs

www.thrive.org.uk   UK
NATIONAL HORTICULTURAL CHARITY
This charity exists to provide expert advice on gardening for people with disabilities and older people who want to continue gardening with restricted mobility. The site gives information on how the charity works and links to related sites. See also **www.gardenforever.com** who offer lots in the way of horticultural therapy.

Gay and Lesbian

www.rainbownetwork.com   UK
 LESBIAN & GAY LIFESTYLE
A very well thought out magazine-style web site catering for all aspects of gay and lesbian life. It primarily covers news, fashion, entertainment and health, but there's a travel agency as well. There are also forums and chat sections, classified ads as well as profiles on well-known personalities.

www.gayindex.co.uk   UK

   GAY BRITAIN NETWORK
   A well-designed and extensive index of gay sites categorised by
   region, type and orientation. Covers everything from health, chat,
   adult sites, business, travel and shopping. If you can't find what
   you are looking for you could also try **www.queery.com** or the
   American **www.gayscape.com**

For other good gay/lesbian sites try:
www.aegis.com – an excellent site giving the latest information
on combating AIDS and HIV.
www.civilpartnerships.org.uk – all you need to know about Civil
Partnerships.
www.gaybritain.co.uk – excellent graphics, a gay portal site.
www.gaylifeuk.com – well-rounded magazine site with support
and advice sections.
www.gaytravel.co.uk – gay travel guide, UK-oriented but with
some good world-wide information.
www.glinn.com – the gay gateway to the web.
www.lesbianuk.co.uk – a good information site.
www.outintheuk.com – an excellent gay community site.
www.pinkparents.org.uk – advice site for gay, lesbian and
bisexual parents.
www.pinkproducts.co.uk – an excellent site devoted to gay &
lesbian weddings.
www.pinkuk.com – another community site with local
information.
www.planetout.com – a good all-round magazine site.
www.stonewall.org.uk – campaigning for justice and equality for
gay and lesbian people. Good section on parenting issues.
www.uk.gay.com – British and Irish pages from the big
American magazine site.

Genealogy

With more interest generated by the BBC's series Who Do You Think
You Are? *and the release of yet more census data, there has been a
big upsurge in interest in tracing your family tree. Here are the best
sites to help you in your quest. It's a shame that many of the sites are
aimed at getting you to part with your money rather than genuinely
helping you to find what you want. Others are so poorly designed that,
despite their willingness to help, we couldn't put them in the book.*

Family Tree

The Good Web Site Guide's Top 10s
of the Internet

1. **www.ancestry.co.uk** – searching for your ancestors
2. **www.nationalarchives.gov.uk/familyhistory** – UK archives and census data
3. **www.originsnetwork.com** – specialising in UK and Irish research
4. **www.familyhistory.com** – US records
5. **www.bmdindex.co.uk** – Birth, Marriage and Death certificates
6. **www.thegenealogist.co.uk** – good genealogy subscription portal site
7. **www.britishdataarchive.co.uk** – the census on CD
8. **www.spatial-literacy.org** – how surnames spread over time
9. **www.genuki.org.uk** – genealogy first timers start here
10. **www.cyndislist.com** – more genealogy sites than you can shake a stick at

www.sog.org.uk UK

THE SOCIETY OF GENEALOGISTS
This is the first place to go when you're thinking about researching your family tree. It won't win awards for web design, but it contains basic information and there is an excellent set of links you can use to start you off.

www.cyndislist.com US

CYNDI'S LIST
A comprehensive listing site where you'll find over 26,000 links in 150 categories to help with your family history research.

www.nationalarchives.gov.uk/familyhistory UK

NATIONAL ARCHIVES
An excellent site from what used to be the Public Record Office. The site is easy to use and the information is concisely presented and easy to access. It has all the census data and lots of advice on how best to use it. For the 1901 census go to **www.1901census.nationalarchives.gov.uk** where you can search the database for free but for detailed information you

have to pay using a rather odd system. Mapping is also available to help with place names or boundary changes. See also **www.familyrecords.gov.uk** which is a consortium of various libraries and archives. It is excellent for tracing your family tree and the links selection is excellent.

www.bbc.co.uk/history/familyhistory   UK
WHO DO YOU THINK YOU ARE?
Loads of fascinating material on how to find out more about your family's history, plus articles on other people's journeys of self discovery. There is also an excellent set of links.

www.scotlandspeople.gov.uk   UK
SCOTLAND
Excellent place to start your quest if you're ancestors were Scots. See also **www.tartans.com** which is a great resource.

www.origins.net   UK
DEFINITIVE DATABASES
This site has information provided from the Society of Genealogists' records from Scotland going back to 1553 and from England going back to 1568, and unlike many other sites in this area, it's also well designed and easy to use. There are also search tips, access to discussion groups and a new section devoted to Ireland.

www.genuki.org.uk   UK
VIRTUAL LIBRARY OF GENEALOGICAL INFORMATION
An excellent British-oriented site with a huge range of links to help you find your ancestors. There is help for those starting out, news, bulletin boards, FAQs on genealogy and a regional search map of the UK and Ireland.

www.ukfamilyhistory.co.uk   UK

ST CATHS
St Catherine's House has been at the forefront of family tree research for some time now and remains a great place to start your search. It offers a full service but without a lot of the hassles that you get through some of the more commercial sites.

www.1837online.com   UK
THE KEY TO FAMILY HISTORY
Probably the best of the commercial genealogy sites, it's well designed and relatively free of all the clutter that besets many

other pay sites. The resources are excellent although the census data seems limited.

Other useful sites that may help in your family research:

www.achievements.co.uk – a research outfit that have a track record working with TV companies, but who will also give you a quote to research your family tree.

www.ancestral-research.com – one of the better value research companies for those who are unable to do the work themselves.

www.ancestry.co.uk – UK spin-off from the successful US-based site of the same name (see review below). Invaluable resource as it hosts the six British census from 1841–1891.

www.a2a.org.uk – a site that catalogues available archives in the UK; it gives a good description of what each one contains and access details.

www.britishorigins.com – information from an excellent database for people tracking their Welsh and English relatives, some free access, but the full service costs.

www.familysearch.org – The Church of Jesus Christ of the Latter-day Saints' excellent research site with good step-by-step information.

www.genealogypro.com – a very comprehensive genealogists and genealogy services directory.

www.genealogysupplies.com – a shop specialising in genealogy software.

www.genesreunited.co.uk – from the Friends Reunited camp, here you can build your family tree online and share it with your family. There are plenty of resources available to help you too.

www.genfair.com – a bookshop specialising in family history books.

www.historicaldirectories.org – a searchable collection of digitally reproduced directories for England and Wales from 1750 to 1919.

www.ihgs.ac.uk – the Institute of Heraldic and Genealogical Studies offer information on heraldry and help to research your family background.

www.landsearch.me.uk – find out who owned what property … for a price.

www.morrigan.com – specialists in Irish genealogy.

www.nla.gov.au/oz/genelist.html – a good starting point for Australians.

www.one-name.org – the place to go if you're only interested in researching one surname.

www.spatial-literacy.org – a really interesting site where you can track over time, the movement and distribution of surnames in the UK.

www.thegenealogist.co.uk – this spin off from the *Genealogist* magazine claims to have the most complete birth, marriage and death records. It's a shame that the site, along with its many spin-off sites, is so poorly designed.

www.ukbmd.org.uk – links to over 400 sites containing local information on births, deaths and marriages.

American Genealogy Sites

Genealogy is a big deal in the US; here are some of the best and most useful.

www.accessgenealogy.com   US
GENEALOGY WEB PORTAL
A massive number of links and access to web rings from a number of different countries give this site 'must check out' status. It is biased towards an American audience but it's very useful nonetheless. See also another portal site
www.genealogyportal.com

www.ancestry.com   US
NO 1 SOURCE FOR FAMILY HISTORY
This US-oriented site has 1 billion names and access to 3,000 databases. It's especially good if you're searching for someone in the US or Canada. It offers some information for free, but for real detail you have to join. How much you pay to find out about your ancestors depends on what you wish to know. Linked to this is the chat site **www.familyhistory.com** where you can visit surname discussion groups.

www.surnameweb.org   US
ORIGINS OF SURNAMES
A great place to start your search for your family origins. On top of the information about your surname, there are thousands of links and they claim 2 billion searchable records.

See also:
www.ellisislandrecords.org – records of all who entered the US via Ellis Island.
www.genforum.com – a huge number of forums devoted to specific family names.

www.gengateway.com – claims to have the number one family-tree-making software, excellent for links.
www.rootsweb.com – genealogy software.

Google

The world's most visited web site deserves a section to itself, basically because few people use it to its full potential. Here's a run-down of the things you can do and find by going beyond the search engine.

Alerts – get reminded about anything any time.
Answers – ask any question; get an answer … for a price.
Blog search – allows you to find blogs that interest you.
Book search – one of the best and most controversial aspects of Google is the ability to search the text of thousands of books. Google and the book industry are in a heated debate about exactly how much of the book should be available to view.
Calendar – organise yourself and share with friends and colleagues.
Directory – a good site directory, categorised by topic.
Docs & Spreadsheets – here are free, working programs that replicate online those that we are familiar with (Excel and Word). Excellent service.
Earth – view satellite imagery of the whole planet, very detailed in some cases.
Froogle – one of the best places to find the cheapest online prices – for everything from toasters to jets … well, model ones anyway.
Groups – Google Groups allow people with a shared interest to use the site to host discussions on a myriad of topics. These are all fully searchable too.
Image Search – click on the 'Images' button and type in your request and up pop hundreds of related images. Typing in *Good Web Site Guide* produced a number of cover images of this book both past and present, thankfully though no images of the author!
Labs – (**http://labs.google.com/**) here you can try out some of the exciting things that Google are developing.
Local – a very fast way to find a local service, check out a location and get route planning too. It includes mapping and satellite images and a hybrid of the two as well if that's what you'd like.

Mail – the free e-mail program, which is OK

Maps – fairly detailed maps and a lot easier to use than many specialist sites.

Mobile – a version for mobile users who like to browse on the move. There's also an SMS version for those who want information in the form of a text message.

News – allows you to search some 4,500 news sources, while using the 'Alerts' service allows you to keep up to date with the latest news on any topic of your choice.

Scholar – allows you to search 'scholarly' papers, although in practice the term is loosely applied.

Special searches – here there are some topic-related searches which may be helpful, the most popular probably being the Google Apple Mac one. There's also a University search facility.

Video search – upload videos, vote for the ones you like.

Web search features – where you'll find a number of helpful search tools and services. For example, an excellent calculation tool, local search, a feature that enables you to see a site as it was when it was first indexed by Google, a spell checker and a translation service.

You can also download the toolbar and a pack which includes many free and useful programs. In addition, there are several services and programs that are associated or owned by Google featured on the site …

Blogger – a very easy-to-use blogging tool.

Code – an area for site and program developers.

Desktop – a downloadable program that can be used to search your computer.

Picasa – find, share and edit your photos.

Talk – free instant messaging and phone calls to other Google Talk users.

Translation – free translation service, good for small blocks of text.

This review scratches the surface of what Google is about and what it is developing. Some think it's becoming too powerful and all encompassing but often it's hard to see a better alternative. For Google's rivals see the section on Search Engines on page 419.

Government

The UK government is in the process of reducing the number of official sites down from almost a thousand to around twenty six, this may result in some inaccuracies.

www.direct.gov.uk   UK

THE ENTRY POINT FOR GOVERNMENT INFORMATION
A massive portal for public service information. You can browse information by going 'straight to' a subject section or by audience group under 'people'. Alternatively, you can use links to find information on government services online, local councils, statistics, public records and jobs. The newsroom service gives the latest headlines on the public sector.

www.parliament.uk   UK

UK PARLIAMENT
A good site giving information on how Parliament works, what's on in the House of Commons, Hansard and a directory of MPs and Peers, should you want to write, as well as links and a glossary.

Other key links:
www.cabinetoffice.gov.uk – how the Civil Service supports the government.
www.clicktso.com – The Stationery Office bookstore.
www.electoralcommission.org.uk – managing and modernising the electoral process in the UK.
www.localegov.gov.uk – Communities and Local Government site with information on their remit, their team and associated agencies.
www.number10.gov.uk – send an e-mail to the Prime Minister, sign a petition, or learn about the history of No.10 Downing Street.
www.parliamentlive.tv – the workings of Parliament broadcast live. Comes with a calendar of events too.
www.royal.gov.uk – for the monarchy.
www.scottish.parliament.uk – for Scottish issues. To watch live broadcasts of the parliament in action go to **www.holyrood.tv**
www.theyworkforyou.com – find out about your MP's voting history and how often he turns up in Parliament.
www.wales.gov.uk – The National Assembly for Wales.

The Major Political Parties

www.conservatives.com – Conservative party.
www.greenparty.org.uk – Green Party.
www.labour.org.uk – Labour party.
www.libdems.org.uk – Liberal Democrats.

International Government and Political Bodies

http://europa.eu.int – the European Union.
www.commissionforafrica.org – working to make Africa a better place.
www.congress.org – an excellent overview of the US Congress and how it works.
www.europarl.eu.int – how the European Parliament works and **www.europarl.org.uk** for info on your MEP.
www.politicsonline.com – a messy and dense site with an overview of US politics.
www.un.org – United Nations.

Activist and Monitoring

For a satirical approach to politics see under Humour, page 288.

www.epolitix.com – an excellent political news site with lots of links and the latest policy announcements.
www.fistfulofeuros.net – a blog site devoted to the goings on in the Eurozone, with lots of contributions and some good writing too.
www.hrc.org – home of the Human Rights Campaign.
www.hrw.org – Human Rights Watch identifies corrupt governments and provides information on where they are going wrong.
www.liberty-human-rights.org.uk – Liberty, protecting human rights and civil liberties.
www.spinwatch.org – an excellent guide to the murky world of spin and corporate garbage.
www.ukpol.co.uk – a good fortnightly political magazine.
www.writetothem.com – the easy way to contact your MP or MEP, there's background information on them too.
www.yougov.com – get involved in polling and take part.

Encouraging the Young

www.citizen.org.uk and **www.citizenshipfoundation.org.uk** –
both promoting greater participation in democracy and active
citizenship. Good educational resources.

www.explore.parliament.uk – the UK Parliament's education
site aimed at school-age children. It offers lots of information and
a tour.

www.votesat16.org.uk – a campaigning site aimed at getting
16-year-olds the vote.

www.ukyp.org.uk – home of the Youth Parliament, a
campaigning organisation aimed at 11–18-year-olds.

G

Greetings Cards

*What used to be free on the Internet is now largely charged for, and
most of the e-card sites now follow the trend, which wouldn't be so bad
except that you often have to search through a lot of rubbish to get to
the good ones ...*

www.bluemountain.com   US
E-CARDS
Blue Mountain has thousands of cards for every occasion; it's
easy to use but you have to subscribe to get the best designs.
There are all sorts of extras you can build in like photos, music,
cartoons and even voice messages.

See also:
http://cards.webshots.com – good for photographic.
www.bigfoto.com – collection of beautiful photos to customise
and send.
www.egreetings.com – big range, busy design that gets on your
nerves after a while.
www.greeting-cards.com – massive range and geared to the
American market, not all free, masses of adverts.
www.jimpix.co.uk – excellent site for unusual and free e-cards,
everything from interactive flash cards to ones with an anti-war
message.
www.regards.com – nice design and the best bit is that it's free!
www.ukfuncardsforyou.com – thousands of cards and promises
no spyware, adware or registration.
www.web-greeting-cards.com – massive selection and well
categorised too.

www.fattypuff.com   UK
REAL CARDS

One of the better online card shops, they have a wide range and you can personalise them too.

See also:

www.getcards.co.uk – wide range, personalising service.
www.greencardcompany.co.uk – Christmas cards on recycled paper, can provide bespoke designs.
www.kisskisscards.com – lots of choice and gifts too.
www.moonpig.com – one of the best and you can upload photos and create your own cards too.
www.sharpcards.info/sk – good design and easy to use.
www.worldwidecards.com – personalised cards.

H

www.charitycards.co.uk   UK
 CONTRIBUTIONS TO CHARITY

Buy your cards here and give money to charity, this is traditionally a Christmas thing but Charitycards have turned it into an all-year round possibility. They will also design and Greetings Cards personalise Christmas cards. There are discounts available and free postage if you buy in quantity, and they also sell stamps. See also **www.cardsforgoodcauses.org.uk** who have a good range and choice.

www.what2write.co.uk   UK
WHAT TO WRITE

A fairly cheesy site that offers suggestions for those situations where you can't think what to write in your card, you can also make suggested entries and send e-cards too.

Health and Fitness

Here are some of the key sites for getting good health advice featuring online doctors, fitness centres, nutrition and sites that try to combine all three. As with all health sites, there is no substitute for the real thing and if you are ill, your main port of call must be your doctor. Dietary advice sites are listed on page 175, specialist sites aimed at men on page 305 and for women on page 576. The advice for parents, page 361 and teens, page 485 may also be useful. For opticians see page 356.

Health

The Good Web Site Guide's Top 10s
of the Internet

1. **www.nhsdirect.nhs.uk** – the first place to go for advice on your ailments
2. **www.embarrassingproblems.com** – for all those difficult issues
3. **www.patient.co.uk** – excellent health portal
4. **www.mayohealth.org** – medical information and health tools
5. **www.dipex.org** – exchange experiences on health issues
6. **www.stjohnsupplies.co.uk** – for everything First Aid
7. **www.allcures.com** – excellent online pharmacy
8. **www.netfit.co.uk** – how to get fit
9. **www.self-help.org.uk** – where to help yourself
10. **www.healthfinder.com** – online check up and health library

General Health

www.nhsdirect.nhs.uk   UK

NHS ADVICE ONLINE
NHS Direct is a telephone advice service and this is the Internet spin-off, it comprises of an excellent guide to common ailments with the emphasis on treating them at home and a superb selection of NHS-approved links covering specific illnesses or parts of the body. There's also health information and an A–Z guide to the NHS.

www.drfoster.co.uk   UK

KNOWLEDGE IS POWER
Provides information about health services including help finding a consultant and hospital (NHS and private), plus waiting list times and performance data. There's an A–Z of conditions, a hospital survey and you can fill in your health profile to find out what conditions people matching your profile are admitted for. Also gives information on complementary therapists.

www.healthline.com   US
> CONNECT TO BETTER HEALTH
> Award-winning, health-oriented portal site with a difference,
> joining allows you to create your own personal health site
> dedicated to your own needs.

www.nelh.nhs.uk   UK

> NATIONAL ELECTRONIC LIBRARY FOR HEALTH
> This program is working with NHS Libraries to develop a digital
> library for NHS staff, patients and the public; it is an outstanding
> resource already and can only get better. It should be the first
> port of call when researching.

> *See also:*
> **www.avma.org.uk** – an organisation working for better safety for
> patients. If something goes wrong then this site is worth a visit.
> **www.doh.gov.uk** – for the Department of Health's informative
> site.
> **www.helpthehospices.org.uk** – information on how you can
> support hospices and where to find one.
> **www.npsa.nhs.uk** – the NHS Patient Safety Agency.
> **www.nice.org.uk** – the National Institute of Clinical Excellence
> provides 'robust and reliable guidance on current health best
> practice'.
> **www.patients-association.org.uk** – an organisation
> campaigning for patients' rights.

H

www.self-help.org.uk   UK

> THE SELF-HELP DATABASE
> A portal site devoted to providing a searchable database of
> self help and patient organisations in the UK. There are
> currently over 1,000 on file. You could also check out
> **www.ukselfhelp.info** for links.

www.dipex.org   UK

> PATIENT EXPERIENCES
> An award-winning site devoted to showing you a wide variety of
> personal experiences of illness, which covers over 100 from
> cancers to mental health. The idea is to use Internet technology
> to share information and experiences and to help fellow sufferers
> get through their illness.

www.patient.co.uk UK

FINDING INFORMATION FROM UK SOURCES
This excellent site has been put together by two GPs. It's
essentially a collection of links to other health sites, but from
here you can find a web site on health-related topics with a UK
bias. You can search alphabetically or browse within the site. All
the recommended sites are reviewed by a GP for suitability and
quality before being placed on the list.

For a second opinion you could visit **www.surgerydoor.co.uk**
which is more magazine-like in style with up-to-the-minute
news stories. It's comprehensive and has an online shop. Also
try the well-designed **www.netdoctor.co.uk** who describe
themselves as the 'UK's independent health web site' and offer a
similar service and encyclopedia.

www.embarrassingproblems.co.uk UK

FIRST STEP
An award-winning and much-recommended site that works well;
it's what the Internet should be about really, although it has
become rather advert-laden. The site helps you deal with health
problems that are difficult to discuss with anyone; it's easy to
use and comprehensive. Younger people and teenagers should
also check out **www.coolnurse.com** which is an excellent
American site with similar attributes.

www.drkoop.com US

THE BEST PRESCRIPTION IS KNOWLEDGE
Don't let the silly name put you off, Dr C Everett Koop is a former
US Surgeon General and is acknowledged as one of the best
online doctors. The goal is to empower you to take care of your
own health through better knowledge. The site is very
comprehensive covering every major health topic and is aimed
at all, including both young and old; loads of ads though.

www.mayohealth.org US

RELIABLE INFORMATION FOR A HEALTHY LIFE
The Mayo Clinic has an excellent web site where you can look
up a symptom, condition or what to do in an emergency. You
can go on to learn about your illness and its management, look
up the full fact sheet on prescribed drugs, collect information on
healthy living, or ask a specialist for advice. There are also risk
calculators and self assessments to help you understand your
risk of poor health.

www.cellscience.com UK

MEDICAL DICTIONARY

The dictionary covers Aids, HIV, cancer, cystic fibrosis and diabetes. It's easy to use and contains listings for links, hospitals and charities as well as other essential information.

www.quackwatch.com US

HEALTH FRAUD, QUACKERY AND INTELLIGENT DECISIONS

Exposes fraudulent cures and old wives tales, then provides information on where to get the right treatment. It makes fascinating reading and includes exposés on everything from acupuncture to weight loss. Use the search engine or just browse through the site; many of the articles leave you amazed at the fraudulent nature of some medical claims. See also the National Council Against Health Fraud at **www.ncahf.org**. For a very scary experience visit the Museum of Questionable Medical Devices at **www.mtn.org/quack**

www.kidshealth.org US

 KIDS' HEALTH

An engaging American site with three areas, one for parents, one for kids and one for teenagers with each having their content adjusted and focused accordingly. The kids' section is particularly effective with even quite complex illnesses and personal issues explained well. See also **www.coolnurse.com**

www.stjohnsupplies.co.uk UK

FIRST AID AND MORE

Here at the St John's Ambulance Brigade shop you can buy several first aid kits and all the health and safety equipment you're ever likely to need. For information on the Brigade, volunteering or taking one of their courses go to **www.sja.org.uk**

For more health information:

http://medlineplus.gov – a health information centre from the US National Library of Medicine.

www.24dr.com – a site from a UK doctor, lots of help with self diagnosis and what appears to be a good medical encyclopaedia.

www.bbc.co.uk/health – good all rounder covering lots of topics, good links.

www.e-med.co.uk – wherever you go your doctor is the strap line for this site; it costs £20 to join then £15 per consultation.

www.gmc-uk.org – home of the General Medical Council, the place to go if you have a problem with a doctor.
www.healthcyclopedia.com – a straightforward health portal with comprehensive coverage by topic.
www.medterms.com – a straightforward glossary of medical terms.
www.merck.com/mmhe/index.html – excellent health encyclopedia.
www.studenthealth.co.uk – written by doctors, sensible and funny with some good competitions.

Private Health

www.privatehealth.co.uk   UK
MAKE THE RIGHT CHOICE
An excellent and comprehensive portal site devoted to all things related to private health.

See also:
www.axappphealthcare.co.uk – health insurance specialist.
www.bupa.co.uk – health fact-sheets, special offers on health cover, health tips and competitions are all on offer at this well designed site. You can also find your nearest BUPA hospital and instructions on referral.

Medical Tourism

www.medicaltourist.co.uk   UK
MEDITOURISTS ...
An interesting twist on the issue of hospital waiting lists, here you can find out how to have your operation abroad and even combine it with a holiday. See also **www.treatmentabroad.net**

Medicine and Pharmacy

www.allcures.com   UK
UK'S ONLINE PHARMACY
After a fairly lengthy but secure registration process you can shop from this site which has all the big brands and a wide range of products and offers. There are also sections on conditions and by gender as well as product.

See also:
www.boots.com – for prescriptions go to the 'pharmacy', which

takes a bit of hunting down, then use the free postal delivery service. There's also an A–Z of common conditions and info on embarrassing problems.

www.drugscope.org.uk – how to get information on drugs.

www.mhra.gov.uk – the government department that deals with safety in medicines.

www.mypharmacy.co.uk – good basic health site from a real pharmacist, with a shop stocking a relatively wide range of products.

www.pharmacy2u.co.uk – who have lots of offers and cover lots of health areas, even a section on embarrassing problems. Prescription service available.

www.rxlist.com – detailed information on drugs and their effects.

H

Fitness and Exercise

www.netfit.co.uk   UK

DEFINITIVE GUIDE TO HEALTH AND FITNESS

Devoted to promoting the benefits of regular exercise with a dedicated team who put a great deal of effort into the site. You can gauge your fitness plus there's information on some 1,500 exercises, tips on eating and dieting, nutrition advice and links to useful (mainly sport) sites. If you don't like going it alone, they will even try to link you up with a training partner in your area. For those hooked on the idea, there's a subscription-based membership scheme which promises to sculpt your body into shape.

www.fitnessonline.com   US

PROVIDING PERSONAL SUPPORT

This good-looking site is from an American magazine group. It takes a holistic view of health offering advice on exercise, nutrition and health products. In reality what you get is a succession of articles from their magazines, all are very informative but getting the right information can be time consuming.

The following sites also offer good advice and information:
www.exercise.co.uk – a good health equipment store with information on exercise and choosing the right equipment.

www.fitnesspeak.co.uk – the best prices for gym equipment but hard on the eyes.

www.nrpt.co.uk – find a personal trainer at the National Register of Personal Trainers.

www.thefitmap.com – a portal site for the UK's health and fitness clubs, find your nearest one.

Alternative Medicine and Therapies

www.altmedicine.com   US

ALTERNATIVE HEALTH NEWS

Keep up to date with the latest therapies and trends with articles and features from some of the key figures in the world of alternative medicine. The site is supplemented by an excellent medical search engine, an overview of the major philosophies and associated healing techniques plus a good set of related links.

www.therapy-world.co.uk   UK

THERAPY WORLD MAGAZINE

A well-put-together magazine covering many different types of therapies with a good overview of all of them and some interesting articles.

www.medical-acupuncture.co.uk   UK

ACUPUNCTURE

A good-looking site with information from the British Medical Acupuncture Society on the nature of acupuncture and where to find a practitioner in your area. There are also good links and information on courses. See also **www.acupuncture.org.uk** and also **http://accupuncture.com**

www.drlockie.com   US

 HOMEOPATHY MADE EASY

An interesting, clear and simple site that offers sensible advice at all levels. Click on any of the medicine jars to get to the relevant sections on everything from basic information, products and links.

www.thinknatural.com   UK

THINK NATURALLY

A nicely designed site with a mass of information on every aspect of natural health including a comprehensive shop with loads of special offers and a very wide range of products.

See also:
http://nccam.nih.gov – home of the US National Center for Complementary and Alternative Medicine, it's a good place for research.

www.alternativemedicines.co.uk – use the ailment search to find the right alternative products.

www.bbc.co.uk/health/healthy_living/complementary_medicine/ – excellent pages from the BBC.

www.drweil.com – the vitamin guru has a site that offers much in advice and his own brand of balanced living.

www.eoco.org.uk – the Essential Oil Company for aromatherapy.

www.holisticshop.co.uk – for everything from books to Buddhism.

www.homeopathyhome.com – slightly confusing to use but comprehensive.

www.homeopathy-soh.org – home of the Society of Homeopaths.

www.interconnections.co.uk – a confusing portal but there is information on living holistically somewhere in there …

www.internethealthlibrary.com – a good directory for alternative health sites.

H

Yoga

www.yogauk.com   UK

YOGA

Welcome to the yoga village where you can get information on yoga in the UK, subscribe to their magazine, or browse the links section, which has a comprehensive list of stores.

www.abc-of-yoga.com   US

ASANAS, PRANAYAMAS AND CHAKRAS

The background information on this site is excellent with information on the history, yogic styles, mediation and health benefits. The best bit though is the comprehensive list of exercises (asanas) with clear photographs or illustrations to back up the instructions.

See also:

www.ashtanga.com – ashtanga yoga explained.

www.bwy.org.uk – the British Wheel of Yoga.

www.iyengaryoga.org.uk – all about Iyengar yoga techniques.

www.mydailyyoga.com – simple yoga exercises.

www.yogatherapy.org – using yoga to cure.

Sites Catering for a Specific Condition or Disease

*Here is a list of the key sites relating to specific diseases and ailments. We have not attempted to review them, but if you know of a site we've missed and would like it included in the next edition of this book please e-mail us at **goodwebsiteguide@hotmail.com**. There is a separate section on cancer which follows our list. For sites relating to children see the section on parental concern on page 367.*

Acne

www.acne-advice.com
www.acne.org
www.m2w3.com/acne

AIDS and HIV

www.avert.org
www.hivstopswithme.org
www.tht.org.uk

Alcohol and Drug Abuse

www.al-anon-alateen.org
www.alcoholconcern.org.uk
www.alcoholics-anonymous.org
www.streetdrugs.org

Allergies

www.allergy.co.uk
www.allergyuk.org **formerly** www.allergyfoundation.com

Alzheimer and Dementia

www.alzheimers.org.uk
www.dementia.ion.ucl.ac.uk

Anxiety

www.anxieties.com
www.healthanxiety.com
www.anxietynetwork.com

Arthritis

www.aboutarthritis.com
www.arc.org.uk

Asthma

www.asthma.org.uk

Autism

www.nas.org.uk

Back and Spinal Problems

www.backpain.org
www.chiropractic-uk.co.uk
www.spinalnet.co.uk

Blindness

www.rnib.org.uk
www.sense.org.uk

Bowels and Bladder

www.continence-foundation.org.uk
www.digestivedisorders.org.uk
www.ibsnetwork.org.uk
www.incontact.org

Brain Disease and Injury

www.bbsf.org.uk
www.headway.org.uk

Breast Cancer

See Cancer, page 246.

Bullying

www.bullying.co.uk

Cancer

See page 246.

Cerebral Palsy

www.scope.org.uk

Chiropody

www.drfoot.co.uk
www.feetforlife.org

Crohns Disease and Colitis

www.crohns.org.uk
www.nacc.org.uk

Deafness

www.britishdeafassociation.org.uk
www.rnid.org.uk
www.thehearingaidcouncil.org.uk

Death and Suicide

www.med.uio.no/iasp
www.naturaldeath.org.uk
www.suicide-helplines.org
www.uk-sobs.org.uk

Dental

www.bda-dentistry.org.uk
www.dentalwisdom.com
www.gdc-uk.org

Depression

http://www.depressionalliance.org

Dermatology

> **www.dermatology.co.uk**
> **www.skincarecampaign.org**

Diabetics

> **www.diabetes-insight.info**
> **www.diabetes.org.uk**

Digestion

> **www.digestivecare.co.uk**

Donation

> **www.blood.co.uk**
> **www.nibts.org** – blood and bone marrow donation
> **www.scotblood.co.uk**
> **www.uktransplant.org.uk** – organ donation
> **www.welsh-blood.org.uk**

Drugs

> **www.acde.org**
> **www.drugs.gov.uk**
> **www.release.org.uk**

Eating Disorders

> **www.edauk.com**

Eczema

> **www.eczema.org**

Epilepsy

> **www.epilepsynse.org.uk**
> **www.epilepsy.org.uk**

Eyes

> **www.moorfields.org.uk**

Fertility

www.infertilitynetworkuk.com
www.ifconline.org

Fibromyalgia

www.ukfibromyalgia.com

Gambling

www.gamblersanonymous.org.uk

Heart

www.bhf.org.uk
www.heartuk.org.uk
www.invisionguide.com/heart
www.riskscore.org.uk

High Blood Pressure

www.hbpf.org.uk

Kidney Problems

www.kidney.org.uk

Liver Problems

www.britishlivertrust.org.uk

Lupus

www.lupusuk.com

Meningitis

www.meningitis-trust.org

Mental Health

www.mentalhealth.com
www.mind.org.uk

www.nshn.co.uk
www.rcpsych.ac.uk
www.youngminds.org.uk

Migraine

www.migraine.org.uk
www.migrainetrust.org

Multiple Sclerosis

www.mssociety.org.uk

Older People

www.elderabuse.org.uk
www.helptheaged.org.uk

Osteopathy

www.osteopathy.org.uk

Pain Management

www.pain-talk.co.uk

Plastic Surgery

www.baaps.org.uk

Psoriasis

www.psoriasis-association.org.uk

Repetitive Strain Injury

www.rsi.org.uk

Sexually Transmitted Diseases (STDS)

www.playingsafely.co.uk

Smoking

www.ash.org.uk
www.givingupsmoking.co.uk
www.quit.org.uk

Social, Personal and Emotional Support

www.samaritans.co.uk
www.shyness.com

Spina Bifida

www.asbah.org

Stress

www.isma.org.uk
www.stressrelease.com

Stroke

www.differentstrokes.co.uk
www.stroke.org.uk

Cancer

www.cancerhelp.org.uk   UK
CANCER RESEARCH
An overview of what causes cancer, its treatments and the
latest news. You can also find out how to donate and details
of ongoing clinical trials. See also the sister site at
www.cancerresearchuk.org which has more information.

See also:
www.bcc-uk.org – the Breast Cancer Campaign.
www.bowelcancer.org – a good overview with advice on
prevention and what to do if you have the symptoms.
www.breakthroughgenerations.org.uk – details of a major study
on breast cancer.
www.breastcancercare.org.uk – very informative on breast
cancer.
www.cancer.gov – excellent site from the US health
department.

www.cancerfacts.com – detailed information on most forms of
cancer.

www.goingfora.com – excellent site covering what happens in
oncology and radiology.

www.leukaemiacare.org.uk – useful support for sufferers of the
blood cancers including leukaemias, Hodgkin's and other
lymphomas.

History and Biography

*The Internet is proving to be a great storehouse, not only for the latest
news but also for cataloguing historical events in an entertaining and
informative way, here are some of the best sites. We make no apology
for listing quite a few links to Wikipedia, in our research it came up
time and again as the best source for information and history on
specific subjects.*

General History

www.historyworld.net   UK

 HISTORY WORLD
An outstanding site containing timelines, articles, quizzes
and tours all designed to educate and bring history to life
in an engaging and stimulating way, and it's successful.
The OCEAN historical index which was once part of this
site has gone it alone and now contains more than 35,000
precise links to external sites. It can be found at
www.oceanindex.net

www.historytoday.com   UK
WORLD'S LEADING HISTORY MAGAZINE
Contains some excellent articles from the magazine, the
'classroom' offers a range of study guides, a timeline and
historical dictionary. There are a range of interactive features
making it a cut above most magazine-derived sites.

www.bl.uk   UK
THE BRITISH LIBRARY
An overview of who they are and what they provide, on the site
you can get information about the library and see some of their
key treasures such as the Magna Carta. Access the 'Turning the
Pages' project where you can virtually 'turn' the pages of
digitised manuscripts. There are many available including

History

The Good Web Site Guide's Top 10s
of the Internet

1. **www.ancientcivilisations.co.uk** – stunning site from the British Museum
2. **www.thehistorychannel.com** – great use of interactive features
3. **www.visionofbritain.org.uk** – detailed local information about Britain
4. **www.netserf.org** – excellent resource about Mediaeval times
5. **www.biography.com** – 25,000 people listed
6. **www.newsplayer.com** – relive the drama
7. **www.nationalarchives.gov.uk** – tracing history with Britain's national archives
8. **www.thebanmappingproject.com** – outstanding site on ancient Egypt
9. **www.bbc.co.uk/history** – another great site from the Beeb
10. **www.besthistorysites.net** – comprehensive index of history sites

Leonardo's notebook, a charming Jane Austin text and the Lindisfarne Gospels, and still more are planned.

www.nationalarchives.gov.uk   UK
DOWNLOAD YOUR HISTORY
From the Public Record Office, the history section has workshops for students, sections for researching and exhibitions. You can also pre-order documents for your visit to the centre in Kew. See also **www.learningcurve.gov.uk** where teachers, parents and students can see how best to use the resources available.

www.nationsencyclopedia.com   US
THE ENCYCLOPAEDIA OF NATIONS
From the United Nations, this site gives basic information on 190 listed countries plus an overview of their history and culture.

www.pbs.org/commandingheights   US
GLOBAL ECONOMY
An outstanding site devoted to the explanation of how the global economy works, great for students of politics and history alike. The broadband version of this site is exceptional but some of the information is a couple of years old.

www.historyforkids.org   US
HISTORY WRITTEN FOR CHILDREN
A good attempt to explain history to children with the emphasis on ancient times. There are sections on Islam, India and the major early European cultures. Unfortunately, the site is laden with adverts, so keep your pop-up blocker on.

H

For more general history sites try these:
http://en.wikipedia.org/wiki/History – Wikipedia's useful starting point.
http://timelines.ws – more history timelines than you can shake a stick at.
www.about.com/education – a good set of educational history pages.
www.besthistorysites.net – an attempt to list the best history sites by category; it has a strong US bias.
www.eyewitnesstohistory.com – containing a large catalogue of historical recollections both ancient and modern, takes the 'history through the eyes of those who lived it' approach.
www.fordham.edu/halsall – a messy site presenting copies of history source books that are freely available for use.
www.historyhouse.com – excellent for history trivia, irreverence and odd facts.
www.historylearningsite.co.uk – great for school, it covers Key Stage 3 and upwards.
www.historymole.com – historical timelines – good, but the number of queries you can run is limited.
www.historyofnations.net – this site offers a potted history on virtually every country in the world.
www.spartacus.schoolnet.co.uk – a useful history encyclopaedia.
www.thehistorynet.com – a good resource from a US magazine site.

Listed here is a selection of specific sites or pages from larger university sites that cover specific periods in time, events or regions. They may not win design awards but the information that they contain is usually

*comprehensive or sufficient to get you started and direct you to
sources of further information.*

UK History

www.bbc.co.uk/history   UK
HISTORY INTERACTIVE
Part of the outstanding BBC site, here you can find sections
covering all the important bits of British history. The site uses
technology well and there are some good articles too. It also
shows what's on TV and radio that's history related.
www.uktv.co.uk/uktvHistory is also useful.

www.visionofbritain.org.uk   UK
BETWEEN 1801 AND 2001
A well designed and truly informative site which, using maps
and statistics, tracks the development of Britain through 200
years. Just type in your postcode and you get access to lots
of background information on your area such as industry,
population, work and poverty. Excellent for schools and for
those interested in local history.

See also:
**http://eudocs.lib.byu.edu/index.php/History_of_the_United_Ki
ngdom:_Primary_Documents** – documents.
http://hds.essex.ac.uk/gbh.asp – the Great Britain Historical
Database has masses of statistics from the 19th and 20th
centuries.
www.bbc.co.uk/wales/history – BBC Wales has an excellent
section on Welsh history.
www.britannia.com – an American site devoted to travel. It
contains a British history section that offers a good overview of
the subject.
www.britarch.ac.uk – a portal for British archaeology.
www.british-history.ac.uk – very useful and unfussy site from
the Institute of Historical Research.
www.british-history.co.uk – a site offering sections on Roman
Britain, 100 Years War, Wars of the Roses, English Civil War,
Napoleonic Wars and the Second World War plus access to the
British History Webring.
www.britainunlimited.com – biographies of 250 people who
shaped Britain.
www.britains-smallwars.com – detailed site on all of Britain's
conflicts since 1945.

www.electricscotland.com/history – a good place to start researching Scottish history.

www.history.uk.com – excellent directory and portal featuring some 28,000 sites.

www.historyofengland.net – a bitty site that covers English history.

www.iwm.org.uk – home of the Imperial War Museum with an impressive site.

www.livinghistory.co.uk – effectively a portal site for those who love to re-enact history.

www.movinghere.org.uk – a history of migration to England.

www.nidex.com/history.htm – an overview of Northern Ireland's complex history with links.

www.number10.gov.uk/output/page123.asp – British prime ministers in history.

www.questia.com/library/history/european-history/great-britain – free books to download on British history from Questia.

www.scottishhistory.com – Scottish history portal.

www.wewerethere.mod.uk – the Ministry of Defence's internet version of the 'We Were There' exhibition. Covers the period from the British Empire to the present day. Interesting read.

Royalty

www.royal.gov.uk   UK

THE BRITISH MONARCHY
A comprehensive and entertaining site with a very good overview of the history of the British monarchy, though for information on other royal families see the rather messy **www.royalty.nu**

Middle Ages and Before

www.netserf.org   US

MEDIAEVAL LIFE
Excellent and well-categorised portal site covering every conceivable aspect of life in the Middle Ages.

See also:
http://the-orb.net – covering European history in mediaeval times.
www.darkagestrust.org.uk – an attempt to recreate England as it was 1,000 years ago.
www.learner.org/exhibits/middleages – a good educational resource.

www.mnh.si.edu/vikings – an exhibition about Viking voyages from the Smithsonian.
www.pbs.org/wgbh/nova/vikings – good interactive overview on Viking life.
www.postroman.info – a good overview of early mediaeval Britain.
www.regia.org – Anglo-Saxons, Vikings and Normans.
www.suttonhoo.org – information on the ship burial.
www.vikingsword.com – a sword expert's view, not only of Viking weaponry but also of swords generally, good links section.

www.essentialnormanconquest.com   UK
THE NORMANS
A good-looking site from Osprey Publishing, which features a 1066 timeline, and blow-by-blow account of the conquest. It's got some good maps and a quiz too.

See also:
http://en.wikipedia.org/wiki/Norman_Conquest – Wikipedia's overview.
www.bayeuxtapestry.org.uk – a scene-by-scene explanation of the Bayeux Tapestry.
www.domesdaybook.co.uk – introduction and overview of the famous account commissioned by William the Conqueror.

The Tudors to the Georges

www.warsoftheroses.com   UK
WARS OF THE ROSES
Excellent site covering the period 1450 to 1490 with all its turmoil and politics, it also has a good timeline and links.

www.tudorhistory.org   UK
TUDOR FAMILY TREE
A basic but informative site with a who's who of Tudor times with background information on what it was like to live then.

See also:
http://elizabethan.org – the Renaissance and the Elizabethan era was an amazing time and, while this site doesn't cover it that well, it does have a good links section.
http://tudors.crispen.org – a good period-by-period overview, with music if so desired …

www.elizabethi.org – a biographical site with a good deal of background on Elizabethan life as well as biographical details.
www.tudorgroup.co.uk – re-enacting Tudor and Elizabethan times.

www.pepysdiary.com   UK
DIARY OF SAMUEL PEPYS

Put together by an aficionado of Pepys, this is updated daily with an entry from the diaries on the day he wrote them over 340 years ago. Apart from the fascinating social history, there's lots of annotation, explanation and cross referencing too, as well as audio readings, which all help you to picture the scene.

See also:

www.17thcenturynet.net – a list of links, articles and web pages on the 17th century.
www.17thc.us – a site devoted to 17th century America with a particular focus on witch trials ...
www.gunpowder-plot.org – interesting site devoted to the happenings that surround the Gun Powder Plot of 1605.

www.olivercromwell.org   UK
OLIVER CROMWELL

A detailed biography of the man and his times, there's background on the civil wars and a guide to places linked with him that you can visit.

See also:

http://en.wikipedia.org/wiki/Charles_I_of_England – Wikipedia's excellent section on Charles I.
www.british-civil-wars.co.uk – a detailed review of the wars and why they happened, backed up with biographies and links.
www.ecwsa.org – the English Civil War Society of America with a good site with lots of detail, articles and links.
www.open2.net/civilwar – detailed information on the English Civil War.

www.georgianindex.net   UK
ALL THINGS GEORGIAN

A scrappy site but one with a wide range of information on Georgian times, what it was like to live then and what events took place.

See also:
www.fashion-era.com/regency_fashion.htm – regency fashion.
www.pemberley.com – excellent site on Jane Austen but with
plenty of background on the Regency era.

The Victorians and Empire

www.victorianweb.org   UK
VICTORIANS EXPLAINED
Background on events, social and political history, biographies
and even entertainment, it's all here.

See also:
http://victorianresearch.org – a scholarly site but with excellent
material.
www.hiddenlives.org.uk – essentially a graphic account of the
lives of the children looked after by the Waifs and Strays Society
but it's also an incredibly interesting insight into Victorian
Britain.
www.victorians.org.uk – for information on the daily lives of the
Victorians.
www.victorianstation.com – everything from architecture to
shopping.

www.britishempire.co.uk   UK
THE BRITISH EMPIRE
A thorough walk through the Empire with articles, maps and
sections on science, arts and military power that round
everything off. It also has a useful timeline, just to put everything
in context.

See also:
http://regiments.org – an overview of the land forces who
served the Empire and Commonwealth.
www.empiremuseum.co.uk – home of the excellent Empire
Museum which is based in Bristol.

The 20th Century

*There doesn't seem to be one really good site dedicated to 20th-
century history, although many of the larger history sites do major on
this time period. Those listed below do a great job in bringing history to
life, whilst informing us about the historical details.*

For timelines and links try these sites ...
http://history1900s.about.com/library/weekly/aa110900a.htm
– good timeline and links.
www.britannia.com/history/h90.html – a good index of events
in the 20th century.
www.britishpathe.com – Pathe films covered most of the major
events of the century and you can buy and see clips here.

1900–1910

**http://en.wikipedia.org/wiki/Edward_VII_of_the_United_Kingd
om** – biography of Edward VII.
http://firstflight.open.ac.uk – descriptive site on the Wright
Brothers and the first flight.
www.anglo-boer.co.za – describing the Boer Wars.

1911–1920

www.greatwar.co.uk – a well-laid-out site on the 1914–18 war.
www.bbc.co.uk/history/british/easterrising – excellent site from
the BBC on the Dublin Easter rising.
www.armenian-genocide.org – read about this horrendous
event which will gain more interest with Turkey joining the EU.
www.marxists.org/history/ussr/index.htm – excellent site on
early Soviet history and the 1917 Russian revolution. For Stalin
try **www.stel.ru/stalin** – devoted to Stalin.

1921–1930

http://kclibrary.nhmccd.edu/decade20.html – US-oriented
overview of the decade.
www.1920-30.com – excellent site devoted to almost every
aspect of the decade.
**www.kidsnewsroom.org/elmer/infoCentral/frameset/decade/19
20.htm** – a light overview of the Twenties.
www.stock-market-crash.net/1929.htm – detailed information
on the crash and its effects.

1931–1940

http://en.wikipedia.org/wiki/Great_Depression – the Great
Depression.
http://en.wikipedia.org/wiki/Spanish_Civil_War – an
exceptional Wiki on the Spanish Civil War.

www.achome.co.uk/artdeco/index.php?page=links – more Art Deco links than you'll ever need.

www.amatecon.com/greatdepression.html – a poor site but the content is good, it covers the great depression, mainly from a US point of view but covers its wider effects too.

www.geocities.com/flapper_culture – some good content and links on the Jazz Age.

www.historyplace.com/worldwar2/riseofhitler/index.htm – the rise of Adolf Hitler.

1941–1950

http://en.wikipedia.org/wiki/Indian_Independence_Movement – Independence for India and Pakistan.

http://history1900s.about.com/library/holocaust/blholocaust.htm – links page for research into the Holocaust.

www.1940.co.uk – remembering the 40s, a nice site and shop.

www.secondworldwar.co.uk – site devoted to chronicling WW2.

www.war-experience.org – experiences of those who took part in WW2.

1951–1960

http://news.bbc.co.uk/1/hi/world/middle_east/5199392.stm – BBC's excellent resources covering the Suez Crisis.

http://news.bbc.co.uk/onthisday/hi/dates/stories/june/2/newsid_2654000/2654501.stm – coronation of Elizabeth II.

www.korean-war.com – informative site on the Korean War.

www.fiftiesweb.com – entertaining overview of the decade's events and culture.

www.bergen.org/AAST/Projects/ColdWar/index2.html – a chilling reminder of what it was like to live through the Cold War.

www.nationalcoldwarexhibition.org.uk – excellent site aimed at giving an idea of what living through the Cold War was really like, and it works … Good audio guides to download help set the tone as well as the evocative intro, which is one of the best we've come across.

www.thespacerace.com – see how it all started.

1961–1970

www.apartheidmuseum.org – an outstanding site on Apartheid.

www.bbhq.com/sixties.htm – a very ugly site but lots of info on the 60s.

www.backdate.co.uk – an entertainment site devoted to the 60s and 70s.
www.mcps.k12.md.us/curriculum/socialstd/African_Am_book marks.html – links covering the Civil Rights Movement.
www.sixties.net – a bright and breezy stroll through the 60s.
www.vietnampix.com – excellent site on the Vietnam War but for detail go to **www.vietnamwar.com**

1971–1980

http://en.wikipedia.org/wiki/1973_oil_crisis – the first major Oil Crisis.
www.bbc.co.uk/history/recent/troubles – detailed overview of the recent history in Northern Ireland.
www.edwebproject.org/sideshow – a moving site devoted to remembering the holocaust caused by the Khmer Rouge.
www.infoplease.com/ipa/A0005252.html – a good timeline for the decade.
www.watergate.info – detailed site on the Watergate scandal and its after-effects.

1981–1990

http://news.bbc.co.uk/hi/english/static/in_depth/uk/2002/falkla nds – Falklands War.
http://news.bbc.co.uk/onthisday/hi/dates/stories/july/29/newsi d_2494000/2494949.stm – Charles and Diana marry.
www.margaretthatcher.org – Margaret Thatcher's official site.
www.fsmitha.com/h2/ch33.htm – Glasnost and Perestroika explained.

1991–2000

http://en.wikipedia.org/wiki/Gulf_War – Wikipedia comes up trumps again with comprehensive coverage of the Gulf War.
http://newarkwww.rutgers.edu/guides/glo-sov.html – informative round-up on the collapse of the Soviet Union.
www.bbc.co.uk/cult/ilove/years/90sindex.shtml – the BBC's 90s.

European History

www.hartford-hwp.com/archives/60   UK

EUROPE AS A WHOLE

A directory of links and articles covering the whole of Europe
and its history; the selection can be a bit disparate, but there is a
search facility on the main site. See also Wikipedia's pages
which are a great starting point at **http://en.wikipedia.org/
wiki/History_of_Europe**. It is particularly strong in areas not
well covered by other encyclopaedias such as the Balkans and
the cold war.

France

http://chnm.gmu.edu/revolution – the French Revolution
explored, this site offers a huge amount of information.
http://en.wikipedia.org/wiki/History_of_France – an alternative
overview.
www.napoleonguide.com – an outstanding site on Napoleon
and his times, with lots of background information and links to
related subjects.
www.napoleonic-literature.com – a site about Napoleon and
the effect he had on Europe, with background on the battles and
his writing.
www.rinfret.com/frhistory.html – a good overview from ancient
to modern.

Germany

www.barnsdle.demon.co.uk/hist/weilin.html – the Weimar
Republic and more.
www.rootsweb.com/~deubadnw/history/maps/maps.htm –
maps showing the changing face of Germany and Prussia over
the centuries.
www.tatsachen-ueber-deutschland.de/en/geschichte.html – a
chronological set of links and articles covering German history
from ancient times.

Greece

www.ancientgreece.com – an excellent site devoted to all
aspects of Ancient Greece.
www.mythweb.com – all the Greek myths illustrated in a fun
and entertaining way.

Holland, Belgium and Benelux

http://en.wikipedia.org/wiki/History_of_Belgium – as is so often the case, there's nothing really to beat Wikipedia's section on Belgium, see also **http://en.wikipedia.org/wiki/Benelux**
http://www.minbuza.nl/history/en/home – an excellent chronological site.

Ireland

www.irelandstory.com – from prehistory to the latest Anglo-Irish agreement.
www.ucc.ie/celt – excellent resource on Irish historical events, literature and politics too.

Italy

www.arcaini.com/italy/italyhistory/ItalyHistory.html – a good chronological history of Italy from pre-history to the 20th century.
www.roman-empire.net – excellent site covering all aspects of the Roman Empire with a good kids' section.

Russia

www.alexanderpalace.org – a history of the Romanov family.
www.barnsdle.demon.co.uk/russ/rusrev.html – an interesting site covering the events surrounding the Russian Revolution.

Scandinavia

http://virtual.finland.fi – virtual Finland with a good overview.
http://woldhagen.org/woldhagen/norway/Nor_hist.htm – Norway's story.
www.lib.byu.edu/estu/wess/scan/hist.html – the Scandinavian studies web for links and documents.
www.pip.dknet.dk/~pip261/denmark.html – Denmark's history.
www.royalty.nu/Europe/Scandinavia – Scandinavian royalty.
www.sverigeturism.se/smorgasbord/smorgasbord/society/history – a short history of Sweden.

Spain

www.sispain.org/english/history – a chronology of Spanish history with links.
www.users.dircon.co.uk/~warden/scw/scwindex.htm – the Spanish Civil War.

Turkey

http://vlib.iue.it/history/asia/Turkey/index.html – a virtual history of Turkey with links.
www.theottomans.org/english/index.asp – a good site on the Ottomans and their achievements.

H

World History

Ancient History

www.ancientsites.com   US
ANCIENT SITES
Seven key times and sites are featured and you must subscribe to get the best out of it. The whole thing is a little long winded although worth the faffing around as you get access to lots of background information and social history. You can also chat to fellow members.

www.ancientcivilisations.co.uk   UK
INTERACTIVE HISTORY
An outstanding site design from the British Museum. You choose a theme from the map: cities, religion, buildings, technology, writing or trade; this provides you with a short overview plus a timeline which you can stop at any point to get the information you need. If you want real detail, then go to a specialist site; however, this site provides sufficient information to start you off.

www.anthro.net   US
ANTHROPOLOGY
Masses of links in this well-categorised site which covers everything from Ancient Egypt to Ethnomathmatics!

Other ancient history directories:
http://ancienthistory.about.com – well-categorised links section with relevant articles from About.com.

www.fordham.edu/halsall/ancient/asbook03.html – the ancient history source book has many links covering all important areas and regions.

Africa

www.thebanmappingproject.com   US
> THEBES AND THE VALLEY OF THE KINGS
> A great and genuinely interesting site devoted to life in ancient Thebes in what is now Egypt, with over 200 interactive maps, narrative tours and 3-D features. Excellent.

www.homestead.com/wysinger/ancientafrica.html   US
> ANCIENT AFRICA'S BLACK KINGDOMS
> A thorough overview of the continent's civilisations with links and pictures. While the design isn't great, it is well worth a visit by any student wanting to know about Africa's ancient history.

> *See also:*
> **http://library.stanford.edu/africa/history/hisking.html** – links for loads of articles on African history, especially south of the Sahara.
> **http://royalafricansociety.org** – the Royal African Society. Promotes the continent and its many causes, useful for links and current affairs.
> **http://web.cocc.edu/cagatucci/classes/hum211/timelines/htimeline.htm** – a timeline of African history.
> **www.africainformation.net** – a useful site with plenty of links to help when researching African history.
> **www.columbia.edu/cu/lweb/indiv/africa/cuvl** – Columbia University's comprehensive African studies pages.
> **www.eternalegypt.org** – excellent and accessible site covering 5,000 years of Egyptian history with lots of interaction and information too.
> **www.fordham.edu/halsall/africa/africasbook.html** – excellent database of sources and links covering African history from the Ancient Egyptians to Nelson Mandela.
> **www.newton.cam.ac.uk/egypt** – the excellent Egyptology resource.

Asia

http://coombs.anu.edu.au/   AUSTRALIA
WWWVL-AsianStudies.html
ASIAN STUDIES
Basically a selection of links that cover the whole of Asia by
country, region and centre.

See also:
http://afe.easia.columbia.edu/mongols – a comprehensive site
covering the Mongol empire and its history.
http://depts.washington.edu/chinaciv – lots of information on
China with an excellent timeline.
http://en.wikipedia.org/wiki/Cultural_Revolution – Wikipedia
has an excellent set of pages on the Cultural Revolution.
http://goasia.about.com/ – Asian history links and articles from
About.com.
**http://newton.uor.edu/Departments&Programs/AsianStudiesDe
pt/japan-history.html** – Japanese history covered, good links
page.
http://sun.sino.uni-heidelberg.de/igcs – some 1700 links on
China.
www.1421.tv – interesting site from people who have proved
that the Chinese discovered and mapped the world before the
Europeans.
www.angkor-planet.com/UK-hase.html – an odd site but it does
have a graphic overview of South East Asian history.
www.asianinfo.org/asianinfo/korea/history.htm – an outline of
Korean history.
www.fordham.edu/halsall/india/indiasbook.html – excellent
overview of India's history.
www.gimonca.com/sejarah/sejarah.shtml – a timeline of
Indonesian history.
www.infolanka.com/org/srilanka/hist.html – history of Sri
Lanka.

Australasia and Oceania

www.academicinfo.net/histaus.html   AUSTRALIA
AUSTRALIA
A pretty good directory of sites relating to Australian history
ancient and modern. There's an explanation and review of each
site featured.

See also:
http://en.wikipedia.org/wiki/History_of_Oceania – good as a starting point for research.
www.awm.gov.au – Australian war memorials.
www.enzed.com/hist.html – useful overview of New Zealand's past.
www.hartford-hwp.com/archives/24/index-f.html – A history of Polynesia and Oceania.

Latin America

http://users.snowcrest.net/jmike/latin.html   US
LATIN AMERICAN LINKS
An outstanding collection of links, categorised by country and region covering Latin and South America and also the Caribbean.

www.ancientmexico.com   US
ANCIENT MEXICO
A beautifully illustrated site covering ancient Mexico and the Mayan and Aztec empires; there are also similar sister sites on Chile and Peru.

Middle East

www.albany.edu/history/middle-east   US
HISTORY IN THE NEWS
A very good resource site with lots of documents, articles and links plus a chronology and social background on the Middle East and its tormented past.

See also:
http://aina.org/aol – all about the Assyrians.
www.al-bab.com/arab/history.htm – a good overview of Arab history with links and articles.
www.arab.net – this site offers a short history on most Arab countries.
www.cnn.com/SPECIALS/2003/mideast – great and detailed site from CNN.
www.fordham.edu/halsall/ancient/asbook05.html – all you need on ancient Persia.
www.mesopotamia.co.uk – excellent site from the British Museum.
www.prc.org.uk/palestine%2048/history.html – an account of Palestinian history.

www.dinur.org/1.html?rsID=219   US
JEWISH HISTORY RESEARCH CENTRE
This site is a little difficult to navigate and use but it does offer
some 6,000 links which are well categorised, it covers biblical
history too. See also **www.cjh.org**, the Center for Jewish History:
well illustrated with a US bias.

http://yadvashem.org   ISRAEL
THE HOLOCAUST
A moving and well-put-together site from the Holocaust Martyrs
and Heroes Remembrance Society. There are thousands of
photographs and accounts, all of which make a visit here pretty
moving, to say the least.

H

North America

http://americanhistory.about.com   US
ABOUT AMERICA
Just about all you'll be needing on American history from the
ever excellent About.com; it's well categorised with links and
related articles too.

See also:
http://americanhistory.si.edu – National Museum of American
History.
www.loc.gov/index.html – excellent collection of articles, micro-
sites and links from the American Library of Congress.
www.brightmoments.com/blackhistory – excellent African
American history site.
www.canadahistory.com – a good place to start.
www.historybuff.com – entertaining site that uses old
newspaper coverage to illustrate aspects of US history.
www.historyplace.com – good for articles, features and links.
www.ourdocuments.gov – excellent and advanced site showing
the 100 most important documents in US history.
www.lib.washington.edu/subject/History/tm/native.html –
Native American history.
www.remembersegregation.org – very effective site
remembering the effects of institutionalised racism.
www.timearchive.com – *Time* magazine's archive is excellent
but you have to subscribe.
www.u-s-history.com – an academic approach.
www.ushistory.org – a history of the US with an amusing touch
of bias …

Biography

www.biography.com US

FIND OUT ABOUT ANYONE WHO WAS ANYONE

Over 25,000 biographical references and some 4,000 videos make this site a good option if you need to find out about someone in a hurry, however it is commercial and has developed a big US bias.

See also:

http://almaz.com/nobel/nobel.html – a fascinating site about the people who have won the Nobel prize.

www.britainunlimited.com – biographies of 250 people who shaped Britain.

www.royalty.nu – the world of royalty: historical and recent.

www.rulers.org – an amazing database providing a list of the rulers of every country going back to 1700.

www.s9.com/biography – a biographical dictionary covering the lives of over 33,000 people!

www.sbrowning.com – create your own biographical timelines at this innovative site, which also links to Google and Wikipedia.

www.who2.com – a good biography portal site that covers celebrities as well as the historically famous.

www.whosaliveandwhosdead.com – basically a list of celebrities cross-referenced by what they did. It shows who's alive, who died and when. Morbidly fascinating.

www.whoyoushouldknow.com – in an attempt to educate Americans about the world, this blog features a new world leader every weekday. It's turned out to be an educationally useful and informative site.

Visual History

www.newsplayer.com UK

RELIVE THE LAST CENTURY

Relive the events of the past hundred years; witness them at first hand as they happened. A truly superb site with real newsreel footage worth the £4 annual subscription fee. See also the BBC's excellent site **www.bbc.co.uk/onthisday** where you can see what happened on a particular day in history. Strongly biased to the 20th century with film clips and eye witness reports.

www.history.com   US

THE HISTORY CHANNEL
Excellent for history buffs, revision or just a good read, the
History Channel provides a site that is packed with information.
Search by key word or timeline, by date and by subject, get
biographical information or speeches. It's fast and easy to get
carried away once you start your search.

www.francisfrith.com   UK
HISTORY IN PHOTOGRAPHS
This remarkable archive was started in 1860 and there are over
365,000 photographs featuring some 7,000 cities, towns and
villages. The site is very well designed with a good search
facility. You can buy from a growing selection of gifts, photos,
maps and now aerial shots too; different sizes are available and
it's pretty good value too. See also **www.photolondon.org.uk**
where you'll find an excellent photo archive of the capital.

www.old-maps.co.uk   UK
OLD MAPS
Access to mapping as it was between 1846 and 1899, just type
in your town and you get a view of what it looked like in those
times. The quality is variable but it's fun to try and spot the
changes. See also **www.alangodfreymaps.co.uk**

www.museumofcostume.co.uk   UK
COSTUME THROUGH THE AGES
Excellent site showing how the design of costume has changed
through the ages. There's a virtual tour and links to other
museums based in Bath.

See also:
www.costumegallery.com – portal site containing over 10,000
web pages.
www.fashion-era.com – a wealth of information and
illustrations.
www.siue.edu/COSTUMES/history.html – plates from history of
costume published from 1861–1880.

Other History-related Sites

www.findagrave.com   US
FIND A GRAVE!
Find graves of the rich and famous or a long-lost relative, either
way there's a database of over 3 million to search. It really only
covers the US and is laden with ads.

www.the-reenactor.co.uk   UK
TAKE PART IN A BATTLE
OK so you feel the urge to play at being a Viking for the day, well
here's where to start. The site lists some 90 societies to join and
play a part in. It is divided into sections according to time period
and you can find out where re-enactments are taking place, plus
the latest news.

www.uchronia.net   US
ALTERNATIVE HISTORIES
A bibliography and review site featuring almost 2,500 books
that in some way or another scope out alternative histories. It
makes interesting reading – the 'what if' scenario fascinates
most historians after all.

www.nwhp.org   US
NATIONAL WOMEN'S HISTORY PROJECT
An educational site devoted to highlighting and celebrating the
achievements of women through history.

Hobbies and Crafts

www.yahoo.co.uk/recreation/hobbies   UK
IF YOU CAN'T FIND YOUR HOBBY THEN LOOK HERE
Hundreds of links for almost every conceivable pastime from
amateur radio to urban exploration, it's part of the Yahoo service
(see page 420) and there's a UK section too.

See also:
http://jobsinart.com/encyclopedia/List_of_hobbies – a list of
hobbies and links.
www.about.com/hobbies – a similarly large list but with an
American bias.
www.allcrafts.net – a wide-ranging directory covering all the
major crafts and many minor ones. Very good links pages.

www.diynetwork.com/diy/crafts – links, projects and programs from the Craft Channel.

http://craftster.org   US
NO TEA COZIES WITHOUT IRONY
A forum site from craft enthusiasts, who share their opinions and projects, and very entertaining it is too. See also the equally quirky **http://cutoutandkeep.net** which has photo tutorials, blogs and even podcasts.

www.etsy.com   US
HANDMADE MARKET PLACE
A well designed site intended to be a store for craftspeople, it's pretty wide ranging, though all prices are in dollars and some sellers may not export outside the US. See also the beautifully designed **www.wemake.co.uk** who sell a variety of handmade goods, you can buy project leaflets for some them, if you want to make them yourself.

Craft Supplies

www.save-on-crafts.com   US
SAVINGS EVERYWHERE YOU LOOK
An excellent craft supply and interiors store covering an extensive range of crafts and merchandise. It's well worth a browse and good for the unusual, but shipping is expensive.

www.artdiscount.co.uk   UK
WHY PAY MORE?
A good value art store with a wide range on offer, with a price guarantee and free delivery (when you spend a certain amount) you should be a happy customer.

www.hobbycraft.co.uk   UK
ARTS AND CRAFTS SUPERSTORE
A nice retro feel to this site with a wide selection of inspirational ideas and information on what they sell and where their shops are, sadly you can't buy online.

See also:
http://crafts.ebay.co.uk – it's amazing what you can get on eBay.
www.cass-arts.co.uk – nice looking site but you can no longer buy online, there is a shop listing though.

For a Beautiful Mind

The Good Web Site Guide's Top 10s
of the Internet

1. **www.queendom.com** – test yourself, beat the experts
2. **www.bbc.co.uk** – knowledge, community and TV
3. **www.howstuffworks.com** – so that's how they do it
4. **www.newsnow.co.uk** – keep ahead
5. **www.yahoo.co.uk/recreation/hobbies** – find a hobby
6. **www.thefitmap.com** – get healthy to get brainy
7. **www.wikipedia.org** – look it up, make a contribution
8. **www.24hourmuseum.org.uk** – get cultural
9. **www.bodyandsoulholidays.com** – rest your mind and body
10. **www.readinggroups.co.uk** – join a reading group

H

www.pictureframes.co.uk – show off your masterpiece to best effect.

Sewing, Knitting and Fabrics

www.sewandso.co.uk   UK
> SHOP AT THE SPECIALISTS
> This site offers a huge range of kits and patterns for cross-stitch,
> needlepoint and embroidery. In addition, there's an equally large
> range of needles and threads, some 20,000 products in all.
> There are some good offers and delivery cost is calculated by
> weight. It's also worth checking out the specialist pages at
> About.com **http://sewing.about.com** and if you're a quilter
> seeking inspiration visit **www.fatquartershop.com**

http://isew.co.uk   UK
> SEWING TECHNIQUES
> Excellent site if you need advice with sections on techniques,
> tips, designer features and events. Projects also feature strongly
> and a section on what you can make for kids too. See also
> **www.sewessential.co.uk** and **www.sewing.org**

www.whaleys-bradford.ltd.uk   UK

FANTASTIC FABRICS

Whether you're looking for a simple cotton lawn, a shot taffeta, or fabrics for the theatre, Whaley's have it all – and they will send you up to 10 samples free of charge. There is a useful A–Z of fabrics and a good search facility.

http://getknitted.com   UK

PATTERNS AND YARNS

The best of many stores selling a wide range of patterns and products, see also **www.laughinghens.com** who have a great range of yarns and **www.texere.co.uk** and **www.purlescence. com**

www.kleins.co.uk   UK

HABADASHERY

A great place to go for all those trimmings, accessories and fastenings, while at **www.littlebeader.com** not surprisingly you can find lots of beads.

Wood Working Projects

www.woodworking.co.uk   UK

WORKING WITH WOOD

A good amateur site offering loads of information about all aspects of woodworking. There's a gallery of work from featured craftsmen plus advice for beginners. For a comprehensive offering with advice sections, projects and even a tool guide try **www.finewoodworking.com**

http://buildeazy.com   US

PROJECT PLANS

A huge selection of plans, mainly easy-to-follow projects including some for kids, some you can even get a video to show you how.

www.jigboxx.com   CANADA

JIGSAWS

Excellent for jigsaw enthusiasts, there's a wide range, a search facility, plus loyalty scheme and you can be kept abreast of the latest designs too. Delivery charges vary.

Coins and Stamps

www.royalmint.com   UK

THE VALUE OF MONEY
The Royal Mint's web site is informative, providing a history of
the Mint, the coins themselves, plus details on the coins they've
issued. You can buy from the site and delivery is free.

See also:
http://acoins.com/index.html – US coins and much more from
the Austin Coin Collecting Society.
www.coinclub.com – good for information and links.
www.coinlink.com – a good directory devoted to all things
numismatic.
www.tclayton.demon.co.uk/coins.html – Tony Clayton's
informative home page on coins.
www.tokenpublishing.com – owners of *Coin News*.

H

www.stanleygibbons.com   UK
STAMPS ETC.
The best prices and a user-friendly site for philatelists. You can
buy a whole collection or sell them your own. Their catalogue is
available online and you can take part in auctions.

See also:
www.corbitts.com – auctioneers for stamps, coins, notes and
medals.
www.duncannon.co.uk – for accessories and albums.
www.postcard.co.uk – home of the Postcard Traders
Association.
www.robinhood-stamp.co.uk – for good prices and range.
www.stamp.co.uk – excellent resource for all stamp collectors.
www.stampsatauction.com – a good auction site devoted to
stamps.
www.ukphilately.org.uk/abps – information on exhibitions and
events at the Association of British Philatelic Societies.

Model-making

www.themodelmakersresource.co.uk   UK
MODEL-MAKING MATERIALS
A wide range of tools, materials, kits and other modelling
essentials here, plus lots of information and links; some good
prices too.

www.towerhobbies.com   US
> EXCITING WORLD OF RADIO-CONTROLLED MODELLING
> An excellent, clearly laid out site offering a vast range of radio
> controlled models along with thousands of accessories and
> parts. The international delivery charge depends on the size of
> the order.
>
> *See also:*
> **www.ehobbies.com** – large US retailer with an international
> division where you'll find a wide range of models, kits and radio-
> controlled cars.
> **www.fusionhobbies.com** – for cars and tanks.
> **www.otherlandtoys.co.uk** – radio-controlled gifts and gadgets too.

H

www.brmodelling.com   UK
> *BRITISH RAILWAY MODELLING*
> A high-quality magazine site devoted to model railways, it
> includes a virtual model set for you to play with and articles on
> specific types of trains and railways. There's also a forum where
> you can chat to fellow enthusiasts.
>
> *See also:*
> **http://uk.games-workshop.com** – for Warhammer and *Lord of
> the Rings* models with hints on painting and model-making.
> **www.corgi.co.uk** – home of the leading model car maker.
> **www.toysoldier.freeuk.com** – informative site devoted to toy
> soldiers.
> **www.ukmodelshops.co.uk** – a directory, mainly railways
> oriented.
> **www.wingsandwheels.co.uk** – model aircraft specialists.

www.ontracks.co.uk   UK
> MODEL AND HOBBY SUPERSTORE
> They sell over 35,000 models and hobby items, but it's tricky
> to find what you want as the site is a bit messy with lots of
> annoying graphics. Having said that there are some good special
> offers and delivery prices are reasonable.

Other Hobbies

www.horology.com   UK
> THE INDEX
> The complete exploration of time, this is essentially a set of links
> for the committed horologist. It's pretty comprehensive, so if your

hobby is tinkering about with clocks and watches, then this is a must.

www.thesunneversets.talktalk.net/calligraphy/index.htm   UK
CALLIGRAPHY
A good introduction into calligraphy with lots of advice and help as well as links to related sites. See also **www.calligraphy.co.uk** who also have lots of links.

Home and Do-It-Yourself

The web doesn't seem a natural home for do-it-yourself, but there are some really useful sites, some great offers on tools and equipment and plenty of sensible advice.

H

Superstores

www.diy.com   UK
THE DIY SUPERSTORE
B&Q has a bright and busy site with lots of advice, inspiration, tips and information on projects for the home and garden. It also has an excellent searchable product database. There are also plenty of offers and the store has a good selection of products covering all the major DIY areas. Delivery costs vary according to how much you buy and how fast you want it. Returns can be made to the stores. You need to be able to accept cookies before the site can operate effectively or before you place an order.

www.wickes.co.uk   UK
DIY SPECIALISTS
Good ideas, inspiration and help are the key themes for this site; it's easy to use and genuinely helpful with well laid out project details. You can visit their showrooms for product information and download leaflets on a wide variety of domestic jobs. There's a handy calculator section where you can work out how many tiles or rolls of wallpaper you may need.

www.focusdiy.co.uk   UK
FOCUS DO-IT-ALL
A functional site, which attempts to put over lots of ideas and Home and DIY inspiration, it also carries a wide range of

products at good prices. Delivery is £4.99 on most items and you can return unwanted goods to your nearest store.

www.homebase.co.uk   UK
NEW-LOOK HOMEBASE
The site does not sell paint, wallpaper or small items such as garden trowels, which you might expect in their stores. Instead, they concentrate on an extensive range of household, gardening and DIY equipment, furniture, sheds and conservatories. Other featured items such as kitchens and bathroom ranges are only available in store – which is slightly confusing. There are also a few guides available to help you plan and execute you DIY project.

Other DIY stores worth checking out are:
www.buildbase.co.uk – good site for the professional.
www.decoratingdirect.co.uk – functional and easy-to-use site that concentrates on home décor products at excellent prices.
www.jewson.co.uk – Jewson's site is more corporate than anything but it does have a small section on each part of the house and how they can help.

Buying Tools and Equipment

www.screwfix.com   UK
PRODUCTS FOR ALL DIY NEEDS
Rightly considered to be one of the best online stores, Screwfix offer excellent value for money with wholesale prices on a massive range of DIY products.

www.draper.co.uk   UK
QUALITY SINCE 1919
An attractive site that is easy to use, the only downside being that you have to have the latest downloads for it to work effectively. If you're a regular visitor and know the stock number of the item you want there's a good fast-track service too.

www.diytools.co.uk   UK
MORE TOOLS
Another well-designed and extensive tool store with a huge range of products and a well-categorised search engine. Also check out **www.blackanddecker.co.uk** who have lots of advice on how to use power tools correctly, and also the slow but thorough **www.worldofpower.co.uk** who also supply garden equipment, plus quad bikes and other motorised toys.

Tool Hire

www.hss.co.uk   UK
>WHERE YOU CAN HIRE ALMOST ANYTHING
>A useful site where you can organise the rental of a huge range
>of tools and equipment, it's great for those one-off jobs.

Trade Information

www.fmb.org.uk   UK

>THE FEDERATION OF MASTER BUILDERS
>Get advice on avoiding cowboys and on getting the best out of a
>builder. There's information and articles on most aspects of
>home maintenance, plus hints on finding reputable help. For the
>FMB's straightforward search facility, **www.findabuilder.co.uk**
>will find a local builder in seconds.

www.trustmark.org.uk   UK
>TRUSTY BUILDERS
>A Government-backed initiative to help consumers find
>reputable firms to do repair, maintenance and improvement
>work in the home or garden. The site links to approved scheme
>operators. There is also advice on what to do if things do go
>wrong.
>
>*See also:*
>**www.buildersguild.co.uk** – who also offer much in the way of
>information.
>**www.findabuilder.co.uk** – a trade organisation that will help you
>find a builder in your area.
>**www.homepro.com** – well designed site with a good search
>facility, each tradesperson is rated and you can check on their
>ratings too. Best of the bunch.
>**www.ratedtradesmen.com** – excellent design and, with some
>50,000 tradesmen to choose from, this site looks the business,
>but it asks for plenty of personal information before giving up
>search results.

Advice and DIY Encyclopaedias

www.hometips.com   US
>EXPERT ADVICE FOR YOUR HOME
>American the advice may be, but there is plenty here for every
>homeowner. The site is well laid out and the advice good.

Alternatives are **www.naturalhandyman.com** which is fun, or the extensive **www.doityourself.com** which is very detailed.

www.diyfixit.co.uk UK

ONLINE DIY ENCYCLOPAEDIA
Get help with most DIY jobs using the search engine or browse by room or job type. The information is good especially now they've added more illustrations.

See also:
www.diydata.com – not fully comprehensive but one of the better DIY encyclopaedias.
www.diydoctor.org.uk – ask a professional for advice, excellent links pages.
www.diyfaq.org.uk – practical information from this UK-based forum site.
www.diynot.com – encyclopaedia, forum, adverts but the best bit is the growing Wiki section with contributions from experts and amateurs alike.
www.finddiy.co.uk – a list of DIY sites and store.
www.freddyfixit.co.za – DIY help from South Africa.
www.homedoctor.net – an American site with lots of homey tips.
www.practicaldiy.com – loads of helpful articles categorised on a project-by-project basis.
www.ultimatehandyman.co.uk – a thousand pages of hints and tips, even a humour section.

Building and Home Improvements

For further information and advice on finding and using an architect, refer to the section on Architecture, page 25.

www.ebuild.co.uk UK

BUILD YOUR OWN HOUSE
All the information and contacts you need if you're thinking of buying that plot of land and getting stuck in. There's also a continually updated list of what plots of land are available and where.

The following sites will also prove useful if you're out to build your own:
www.aecb.net – the Association for Environmentally Conscious Building has a helpful site with the relevant information.

H

www.bricksandbrass.co.uk – the place to go if you have a period home to renovate.

www.builditthisway.co.uk – a good overview from a retired builder on what it takes to build your own house.

www.bwpda.co.uk – home of the British Wood Preserving and Damp Proofing Association, with a 'find a contractor' service.

www.homebuilding.co.uk – a spin off from a magazine, lots of resources and information.

www.planningportal.gov.uk – a huge and very useful resource about planning regulations, with advice and a guide to the process.

www.plotfinder.net – find a spot to build your dream home, but you have to subscribe.

www.selfbuildit.co.uk – help for first timers.

Salvage

www.salvo.co.uk   UK

SALVAGE AND RECLAMATION
Salvo provides information on where to get salvaged and reclaimed architectural and garden antiques. The site is comprehensive and easy to use with interesting information such as what buildings are due to be demolished and when, so you can be ready and waiting.

Conservatories

www.conservatoriesonline.co.uk   UK

ALL YOU NEED TO KNOW ABOUT CONSERVATORIES
A good portal site which offers links and advice on conservatories, sunrooms, garden rooms and solariums. There's a buyer's guide plus information on materials, styles, even on pools and orangeries.

See also:
www.advisoryservice.co.uk – home of the Conservatory and Windows Advisory Service, a good place to go for getting advice on the right sort of materials to use.

www.conservatories-direct.co.uk – a good, comprehensive site from this specialist.

www.diy-conservatories-uk.co.uk – all you need if you want to erect your own.

Plumbing, Bathroom and Kitchen

www.plumbworld.co.uk   UK
AN ONLINE PLUMBING SHOP

A clean, well organised site catering for all your bathroom and kitchen needs plus a good selection of plumbing tools and paraphernalia at competitive prices. They have improved the ordering and delivery information available on the site too. See also **www.plumbase.co.uk**

www.bathroomexpress.co.uk   UK
BETTER BATHROOMS

A wide range of bathrooms and accessories are available at decent prices, with some interesting luxury items such as après-shower driers and some unique toilet seats. See also **www.brighterbathrooms.com**

www.alarisavenue.co.uk   UK

KITCHENS AND CANE

A beautifully designed store that offers much in the way of inspiration and quality products for the kitchen.

See also:

www.bathrooms.com – huge portal for bathroom needs and, if you need a plumber, try the directory of plumbers.
www.fixatoilet.com – could be invaluable!
www.ksa.co.uk – advice on planning kitchens, bathrooms and bedrooms with a handy facility to find a design specialist.
www.plbg.com – plumbing forums galore with access to loads of advice.
www.iphe.org.uk – home of the Institute of Plumbing with a member directory and their code of practice.
www.plumbingpages.com – excellent source for information on plumbing projects.
www.tapsshop.co.uk – useful if you need taps.
www.victoriaplumb.com – well designed site with lots of choice.

www.toppstiles.co.uk   UK
TILES

You can't get tiles delivered but there's a shop-finder service and details of available ranges including floor tiles.

See also:

www.digitile.co.uk – find out about how to get custom-made tiles.

www.green-bottle.co.uk – recycling glass into usable products such as tiles.

www.taylortiles.co.uk – a wide range and sample ordering service.

www.tiles.org.uk – home to the Tile Association and full of good advice.

Doors

www.handlesdirect.co.uk UK
HANDLES GALORE

A functional site where you can buy, well, handles. It's also got a selection of locks, switches and sockets that match certain handles. The emphasis is on contemporary style, and there's a good advice section which shows you how to fit them. See also **www.diytools.co.uk** who offer a wide range including security products in their 'knobs and knockers' section.

www.doorsdirect.co.uk UK
DOORS AND HANDLES

Features replacement doors for kitchens and bathrooms, you can order made-to-measure or standard and there's a selection of fittings as well.

www.locksmiths.co.uk UK
FINDING A LOCKSMITH

A useful site where you can get help to find a locksmith in your area and some advice on home security.

Paint and Wallpaper

www.decoratingdirect.co.uk UK
 DECORATING MATERIALS

A really well-designed store offering a very wide range of decorating products, it's fast, simple to use and it will save a trip to one of those huge DIY stores, or is it just me that hates them? Check out the refund policy before you buy though.

www.dulux.co.uk UK
DULUX

A good-looking, interesting but slow site from Dulux, with a 'mouse painter' that you can use to redecorate a number of preselected rooms; there's also product information, and top tips on painting techniques. You can't buy from the site although

there is a list of stockists. Crown has a similar but less
interactive site that can be found at **www.crownpaint.co.uk**

www.farrow-ball.co.uk   UK
TRADITIONAL PAINT AND PAPER
Excellently designed web site featuring details on how their paint
and paper is manufactured – something they obviously take
pride in. You can also order from the site or request samples.
See also **www.firedearth.com** for more traditional high quality
paints, tiles and inspiration.

www.paintquality.co.uk   UK
PAINT QUALITY INSTITUTE
A very attractive site from a company that specialises in testing
paints. There's information on choosing the right type of paint
with decorating tips, a calculator and glossary.

www.sanderson-online.co.uk   UK
CLASSIC, CONTEMPORARY AND TRADITIONAL STYLE
Find out about the company, its heritage and what designs
they have – new and old. You can also order a brochure and
visit the Morris & Co pages where they have all the favourite
designs. For more information on William Morris try visiting
www.morrissociety.org

www.wallpaperdirect.co.uk   UK
BUY WALLPAPER
A good store offering a wide range of wallpapers, sampling
service, advice and free delivery if you order more than
£150 worth. For stickers and stencils check out **http://
interactivewallpaper.co.uk** and also **www.stencils4u.com**

www.communityrepaint.org.uk   UK
REUSING OLD PAINT
A very useful service. The site highlights a number of schemes
across the country that take reusable paint and redistribute it to
those who can't afford to buy their own.

www.photo-furnishings.com   UK
YOUR PHOTOS ON YOUR FURNISHINGS
Outstanding use of web design to sell a novel service, here they
will put your photos onto soft furnishings or wallpapers. You
have to apply for prices. See also **www.artmeetsmatter.com**
who offer all sorts of products.

Lighting

www.lightsaver.co.uk   UK
SAVE ON LIGHTING

With lots of savings and a wide range to choose from this site is worth a visit, it's not the epitome of great web design but it's effective nonetheless. You should also check out **www.thelightingsuperstore.co.uk** and **www.simply-lighting.co.uk** who both offer good alternatives.

Inspiration, Design and Interiors

www.design-gap.co.uk   UK

DESIGNER DIRECTORY

A directory of UK-based designers and manufacturers with some 300 pages to browse through. They are arranged alphabetically by first name or company name as well as by category. The illustrations are excellent. See also **www.designdirectory.co.uk** which is a listing of design consultants.

See also:
http://myinteriordecorator.com – advice from a professional interior designer with good articles. The links are to American stores, unfortunately.
www.bida.org – home of the British Interior Design Association.
www.tribu-design.com/en – an encyclopaedia of 20th century design and decorative arts.

www.bhglive.com   UK
BETTER HOMES AND GARDENS

There's more to this than DIY, but superb graphics and videos give this site the edge. There's lots of help on design and decorating and the encyclopaedia under 'home improvement' is excellent. It's American, so some information isn't applicable to the UK.

www.fengshuitips.co.uk   UK
FENG SHUI YOUR HOME

Understand the natural forces and apply these tips to enhance and attract good health, wealth and happiness … though they don't tell you how to stop the family leaving their shoes by the door! If you want to buy some accessories **www.fengshuiweb. co.uk** has a selection of fountains, crystals and other such items.

Stores for Design

www.habitat.net UK
HABITAT STORES
An information-only site with lots of details on their product
range. It's all wrapped up in a funky design, which is a little
jerky with a normal modem and needs the latest version of Flash
to work. You can't order online although you can check store
availability. See also the US store **www.crateandbarrel.com** who
offer similar products but shipping is very expensive.

www.ikea.com UK

IKEA STYLE
You can't buy from the site (they're running a trial at time of
writing) but you can check whether a store has the item you
want to buy in stock before you go (it would be great if more
stores did this). Otherwise the site is more the usual store fare
with plenty of ideas, articles and product lists.

See also:
http://sawitfirst.co.uk – excellent shop featuring contemporary
designer furniture and home accessories.
www.afternoah.com – great for the unusual and the eclectic.
www.bluedeco.com – a selection of designer products for the
home, from furniture to ceramics, with free delivery to the UK.
Unfortunately, returns have to go to Luxembourg.
www.grahamandgreen.co.uk – stunning selection of homeware
and interiors.
www.interiorinternet.co.uk – a well-illustrated and unusual
selection of designer furniture.
www.next.co.uk – a good selection of Next homeware as well as
the usual products on a fairly impractical site.
www.pier.co.uk – a very good offering from the Pier. Eclectic
and always interesting, there's a wide range to choose from.
www.pussyhomeboutique.co.uk – an eccentric and slightly
kitsch range of products, furniture, home accessories and wall
panels.
www.scarlettwillow.co.uk – gorgeous placemats and tableware.
www.skandium.com – get the Scandinavian look.
www.thelinenworks.com – beautifully made and designed
homeware.

Soft Furnishing

www.simplyfurnishings.com UK

SOFT FURNISHING
All you need to know about making and buying soft furnishing
with plenty of advice for all levels and a good store directory.

See also:
www.bemz.com – give your sofa a second chance! Excellent for
soft furnishings.
www.clarissahulse.com – gorgeous leafy designs on soft
furnishings, and wallpaper too.
www.crowsonfabrics.com – nice products but no online
ordering.
www.monkwell.com – beautiful ranges but you can't buy online.

Furniture

www.mfi.co.uk UK

MFI HOMEWORKS
MFI offer a nicely designed site with all the best aspects of
online shopping and a wide range of surprisingly good furniture
for home and office available for order online or via a hotline.
Delivery is included in the price.

www.furniture123.co.uk UK

SMART PLACE TO BUY FURNITURE
This company has a well laid out web site offering a good range
of furniture, many offers, tips and free delivery.

www.heals.co.uk UK

STYLISH CONTEMPORARY DESIGN
Heals has a beautifully designed web site which gives
information about the store and inspiration for the home.
There's an online store which stocks primarily gifts and home
accessories, but there's a special services section where you
can get information on furniture and interior design.

www.conran.com UK

TERENCE CONRAN STYLE
As well as information on all his restaurants, this site has an
online shopping facility that allows you to buy Conran-designed
accessories as well as stuff for the home including a good range
of furniture and kitchen products.

www.ancestralcollections.co.uk   UK

REPRODUCTIONS FROM THE BEST HOMES

A web site that has developed well with a wide range of high quality beds and furniture on an attractive site with good pictures and descriptions of the products. They've expanded into gifts too and offer good value for money.

www.dwell.co.uk   UK

CONTEMPORARY FURNITURE

Nice site design for designer furniture with a wide range and some good prices too.

Other furniture retailers and sites that may be worth a virtual visit are:

www.bfm.org.uk – a useful directory of British furniture makers.

www.connectedlines.com/styleguide – a basic guide to furniture styles.

www.davidlinley.com – posh contemporary classics.

www.furniturebusters.com – a wide range and masses of offers too.

www.mufti.co.uk – more posh, beautifully designed furniture.

www.new-heights.co.uk – simple, stylish solid wood.

www.pinesolutions.co.uk – a very well-designed furniture store, they also sell sofas and oak furniture.

www.sofaweb.co.uk – good value sofa and sofa bed shop.

www.sofaworkshopdirect.co.uk – well designed with quality photos of the sofas and what looks like a good online service.

www.thebedshed.net – the jaw-droppingly bad jingle has now gone, leaving a decent product range and store directory.

www.frn.org.uk   UK

FURNITURE REUSE NETWORK

Instead of throwing your furniture away find out how it can be reused to good effect. See also **www.reelfurniture.co.uk** to find furniture made from reused materials.

TV and Celebrity Designers

www.llb.co.uk   UK

LAURENCE LLEWELYN-BOWEN

Join the fan club, view Laurence's designs from greeting cards to cutlery to wallpaper, then find out how to buy them. There's lots here, even competitions. See also **www.bbc.co.uk/homes** with lots of ideas and helpful hints, in particular, go to 'Changing Rooms' which has top tips, articles and biographies.

www.ukstyle.tv/homesandproperty   UK

UK STYLE TV

A bright and breezy site packed with ideas from the TV shows and features on the various projects and aspects of the home. There's an 'ask the expert' section and a guide full of practical ideas and tips too.

www.channel4.com/4homes   UK

GRAND DESIGNERS

Nicely designed site from Channel 4, with helpful guides and an excellent style section. Help and advice is on hand from their resident guru.

www.bbc.co.uk/homes   UK

NEW IDEAS

Loads of inspiration here, the period style guides are particularly helpful, with links to their main programmes and celebrities.

Miscellaneous

www.howtocleananything.com   CANADA

STAIN REMOVAL PAR EXCELLENCE

A group of cleaners have got together to produce a site that contains over 1,000 cleaning tips for outside or inside the house or the car – except for curry!

www.thistothat.com   US

GLUE

A site that helps you work out which is the right glue to use. Just input the two things you want to glue together and the site makes a recommendation … what could be easier!

Humour

The Internet has become home to an amazing array of funny sites. Here's just a few of the best. You should be aware that most aren't suitable for children.

Funny, Adult and Entertaining

The Good Web Site Guide's Top 10s
of the Internet

1. **www.snopes2.com** – urban legends, all true of course
2. **www.comedy-zone.net** – the place to start, loadsalinks
3. **www.b3ta.com** – great for the gross
4. **www.joecartoon.com** – freaky entertainment
5. **www.emotioneric.com** – pick an emotion and Eric will act it for you
6. **www.theonion.com** – irony from the USA
7. **www.funnymail.com** – more jokes than you can shake a stick at
8. **www.boreme.com** – adult entertainment
9. **www.davesdaily.com** – unusual stories from around the world
10. **www.engrish.com** – excellent selection of Asian English

Jokes, Links and Directories

www.comedy-zone.net   UK

COMPLETE COMEDY GUIDE
Excellent and wide-ranging comedy site with lots of links and
competitions, alongside quotes, jokes, chat and humorous news.

For other comedy portals and loads of jokes go to:
http://uk.dir.yahoo.com/entertainment/humour – Yahoo's
excellent listing devoted to humour and bizarre sites.
www.bored.com – a great directory of humour sites, loads of
ads though.
www.comedycentral.com/jokes/index.jhtml – typical jokes
directory but these are rated tame, racy etc …
www.funnybone.com – huge database with lots of rude jokes.
www.humorlinks.com – massive portal for all things funny.
www.jokecenter.com – hundreds of jokes, vote for your
favourites.
www.kidsjokes.co.uk – 12,000+ jokes, great for the family.
www.sarcasmsociety.com – learn how to be sarcastic at this
sarcastic site.

Multi-media

www.youtube.com UK

 BROADCAST YOURSELF
One of the most celebrated websites ever offers you the chance
to put your own videos on the 'net, but whether it continues to
be as popular now it's owned by Google remains to be seen.
Lots of adult content, unofficial clips, whole TV series – there's
a staggering amount to choose from and there's an excellent
search facility.

www.funny-downloads.com US

THE BEST IN MULTI-MEDIA HUMOUR
What used to be Olley's Place has transformed into a
subscription-only site costing $15 for lifetime membership. For
that you get access to a superb selection of funny video clips
and comedy downloads, there is some free content though and
you should be aware that most of it is adult oriented.

*Other sites offering video clips, e-mails and generally daft adult-
oriented entertainment:*
**http://uk.entertainment.yahoo.com/office-attachments/
index.html** – Yahoo's excellent Office Attachments page.
www.b3ta.com – a particularly silly and very popular e-zine
with a reputation for originality when it comes to creative uses of
Photoshop.
www.boreme.com – excellent collection of video clips.
www.britpod.com – alternative talk radio, available as podcasts.
www.cyberparodies.com – a mixed bag of song parodies … too
many 'smileys'.
www.ebaumsworld.com – good but a pain to use.
www.jengajam.com – a daily listing of photos, games, trivia and
videos.

Stand-up Comedy

www.chortle.co.uk UK

GUIDE TO LIVE COMEDY IN THE UK
Chortle provides a complete service, listing who's on, where and
when – also whether they're any good or not. There's also a
comics' A–Z so that you can find your favourites and get reviews
on how they're performing, or not, as the case may be. See also
www.jongleurs.co.uk whose entertaining site has audio clips
and details of what's on and when at their clubs.

Comedy Magazines and Satirical Sites

www.theonion.com   US
AMERICA'S FINEST NEWS SOURCE
A great send-up of American tabloid newspapers, this is one
of the most visited sites on the Internet and easily one of the
funniest. See also **www.thespoof.com**, a great spoof news site.

www.private-eye.co.uk   UK
PRIVATE EYE
A pretty average effort really considering the wealth of material
that must be available, there are a few of the best cartoons and
features, but it's only updated every couple of weeks or so.

www.freakingnews.com   US
PHOTOSHOP CONTESTS
Playing with Photoshop to make new pictures is the hobby of
many, but here you can enter your masterpiece of deception in
competitions. See also **www.howstrange.com**

www.whitehouse.org   US
THE WHITE HOUSE
A great micky-take on the US presidency, very clever and vicious
too. **www.deadbrain.co.uk** has a similar feel and approach but
is mocking British politicians and celebs.

www.punch.co.uk   UK
PUNCH MAGAZINE
A new look and more commercial approach from *Punch* with
plenty of cartoons and some of the best of *Punch* available to
browse and buy.

www.viz.co.uk   UK
NOT FOR CHILDREN
A very good reflection of what you get in the real thing with lots
of games and downloads, you can even contribute to Roger's
Profanisaurus.

http://community.sparknotes.com/sparktests/index.epl   US
TAKE THE SPARK TESTS
The Spark is actually a spin-off from the Spark notes revision
guides. Its best feature, and the reason why millions visit, is the
tests. From the popular personality test, through bitch and
bastard tests to the wealth test, all are good for a laugh and, of

course, very accurate. Dare you take the 'death test' or the 'unintelligence test' though?

www.nicecupofteaandasitdown.com   UK
TAKE A BREAK
Put your feet up and while away some time here, review your favourite biscuit or not … take your time … make tea … lovely.

TV Comedy

www.bbc.co.uk/comedy   UK
BBC COMEDY
An outstanding site with a comedy guide and lots to see and do. There are features on each major programme and even a comedy blog, also links to associated sites, clips to watch and radio features to download.

www.comedycentral.com   US
THE HOME OF *SOUTH PARK* AND MORE
Great for *South Park* and selected American TV shows, but also with clips and background information and stand-up comedy too.

www.thesimpsons.com   US
HOME OF *THE SIMPSONS*
The official site with biographies, background, quizzes and more, plus the ever-present merchandise store. If you are a real fan then go to the *Simpsons* archive at **www.snpp.com**

See also:
www.britishcomedy.org.uk – a poor site but good background on some classic radio comedy.
www.britishcomedyhelpdesk.moonfruit.com – any questions about British and TV comedy, ask the helpdesk …
www.phill.co.uk – a comprehensive directory of TV comedy.
www.rickygervais.com – home site of the popular comedian.

Urban Legends, the Unlikely and the Unloved

www.snopes2.com   US
URBAN LEGENDS
An outstanding collection of all those stories and myths that have that edge of unlikely truth about them. Well categorised and with a good search facility, it's easy to find your favourites.

See also **http://urbanlegends.about.com** which is full of unlikely but true stories.

www.darwinawards.com   US
FATAL MISADVENTURES
The Darwin Awards have been going several years now and their site is packed with stories, urban legends and personal accounts of those who have 'improved our gene pool by removing themselves from it in really stupid ways'.

www.halfbakery.com   US
INVENTIONS OR NOT
A fun catalogue of useless inventions and ideas, some real, most not; it's very silly really and it's a shame that there are not more illustrations.

www.idler.co.uk/crap   UK
OUR CRAP TOWNS
The site that spawned a best-selling book. Here's an eclectic collection of towns in the UK and US that have been awarded the status of being crap, most for no apparent reason. Irreverent and pretty funny, there are some very angry people out there.

www.iusedtobelieve.com   US
CHILDHOOD BELIEFS
A catalogue of childhood misconceptions and beliefs, you can rate them and even add your own. It's the sort of site that makes you smile and you can't help joining in.

www.museumofhoaxes.com   UK
HOAXES
The world's greatest hoaxes and April Fools are catalogued here. It makes entertaining browsing and is sometimes unbelievable.

Cartoons
www.bcdb.com   US
THE BIG CARTOON DATABASE
A catalogue covering all the major producers of cartoons, the main characters and of course the cartoon series themselves. It has an American bias but it's pretty comprehensive and you can rate your favourites too.

www.weebls-stuff.com   UK
WEEBLS
An award-winning site and one of our favourites. It's home to the Weebl and Bob cartoons as well as many other cartoons and includes the unforgettable tune that is 'Everyone loves Magical Trevor'.

www.joecartoon.com   US
FREAKY CARTOONS
Follow the gruesome, messy adventures of Joe, download the cartoons and send them to your friends and buy the T-shirt – he's a legend after all. Superb animation and very funny, but you need patience for the downloads and the adverts.

www.emilystrange.com   US
ENTER THE WORLD OF EMILY STRANGE
Another animated site with outstanding illustrations that's worth a visit just to look at the design, if nothing else. Emily is a popular icon with teenagers and here you can participate in her freaky adventures.

See also:
www.cartoonbank.com – outstanding New Yorker cartoons for sale in various formats and guises.
www.cartoonstock.com – a database of over 70,000 cartoons.
www.nonstick.com – home of Warner Brothers cartoons with some available to download, plus links and background information on those involved.
www.tomandjerryonline.com – all you need to know about the awesome Tom & Jerry.
www.unitedmedia.com/comics/peanuts – home of Charlie Brown and Peanuts.

www.super-jam.com   UK
YOU BE THE DANCING QUEEN …
Pick a digital photo of yourself or your friend, crop and download, pick a body and start dancin' …

Miscellaneous and Just Weird

www.weirdwebbed.com   US
WEIRD
A good directory of the weirdest web sites, you can subscribe to and search the archives for the best.

www.strangereports.com US
PRANKS ONLINE
Play pranks on your friends using the service available here,
with trick web sites and fake news reports it's almost
irresistible, but beware their revenge … See also
www.computerpranks.com and also **www.prank.org**, both of
which contain classics.

http://officeolympics.net US
THE OFFICE OLYMPICS
OK so it's a slow day at the office, you've got nothing to do, well
you could follow the example set here and set up your own
Office Olympics … with events such as cubicle hurdles and
chair hop, you can't go wrong. See also **www.bullshitbingo.
co.uk** where you can create your own bingo cards featuring
the latest office slang and buzzwords.

www.freakydreams.com US
DREAM INTERPRETED
You just type in the description of your dream and an 'accurate'
interpretation pops up in seconds.

www.staregame.com US
HE WHO BLINKS …
Pick your character, press play and the first to blink loses …

www.20q.net US
TWENTY QUESTIONS
Pick something and the site will guess what it is within twenty
questions, it's amazingly accurate and very time consuming as
you try to beat it without cheating.

www.smalltime.com/dictator UK
GUESS THE DICTATOR
You think of a dictator or TV sit-com character, answer the
questions put to you and the site will guess who you are
thinking of … it's spookily accurate.

www.uebersetzung.at/twister AUSTRIA
TONGUE TWISTERS
An international collection of tongue twisters, over 2,000 in 107
languages when we last visited, nearly 400 in English – 'Can
you can a can as a canner can can a can?' as they say.

www.optillusions.com   US
OPTICAL ILLUSIONS
A good selection of optical illusions to download, plus links to
other similar and funny sites. The visit is completely spoiled by
the large amount of adverts both pop-ups and banners.

www.emotioneric.com   US
EMOTIONAL ERIC
A cult site in the US. Eric will act out any emotion in any
situation, you just have to place your request.

www.snapbubbles.com   US
VIRTUAL BUBBLE WRAP
How comforting, when you have the urge to pop and there's no
bubble wrap to hand, just come here for the nearest substitute.

www.engrish.com   US
MISTAKEN ENGLISH
This site started off as a list of humorous mistakes that the
Japanese made with English; it's now expanded slightly to take
in other cultures and it's very funny. See also **www.rahoi.com/
2006/03/may-i-take-your-order.php**

www.thetoastshop.co.uk   UK
IT'S ALL ABOUT TOAST
One of the best fake commercial web sites lovingly put together.
See also **http://isolatr.com/** and **www.petroldirect.com**

www.pickthehottie.com   US
PICK THE HOTTIE!
Probably the best of many sites where people post photos of
themselves and their friends (or enemies), the idea being that
you vote for the hottest-looking people and the ugliest too.

*While we're on the subject of the unattractive, check out these
sites listed below ...*
www.badfads.com – home of the Bad Fads Museum, fashion
victims galore.
www.mulletmadness.com – in celebration of the haircut and
culture.
www.uglydress.com – Bridesmaids' dresses from hell, dare you
to look at this without putting your hand over your mouth.
www.uglyfootballers.com – yes, we well remember them ...

Internet Service Provision

*There are so many Internet Service Providers (ISPs) that it would
be impossible to review them all and it's moving so fast that any
information soon becomes outdated. However, help is at hand and
here are some sites that will help you chose the right one for you.
See also our section on Broadband on page 58.*

www.ispreview.co.uk   UK

INTERNET NEWS
Find out what's really going on at this impressive site – they are
especially good at exposing the worst performers. There's plenty
in the way of news, offers and a top 10 ISP list.

See also:
www.cisas.org.uk – home of the Communications and Internet
Services Adjudication Scheme, which aims to solve disputes
between ISPs and customers.
www.ispa.org.uk – Internet Service Providers Association with
an informative site.
www.net4now.com – a newsy site that provides a directory of
Internet Service Providers offering news and advice on the best
ones
www.thelist.com – the ISP providers guide from the US.

Jobs and Careers

*There are several hundred sites offering jobs or careers advice but
it's largely a matter of luck if you come across a job you like. Still, it
enables you to cover plenty of ground in a short space of time without
trawling the newspapers. These sites offer the most options and best
advice.*

Career Guidance
www.careers-gateway.co.uk   UK
THE CAREERS GATEWAY
Great advice and lots of information, for example, how to launch
a proper career, evaluate your options and read articles to help
you decide what you can do with your life. There's a virtual
career show, quizzes designed to help and advice for HR
professionals too as well as an excellent links section.

www.connexions-direct.com   UK
INFORMATION FOR YOUNG PEOPLE
The section on careers is a very useful resource for young
people, the emphasis is on helping you to make the right career
choice.

www.careersolutions.co.uk   UK
HELP TO GO FORWARD
A good place to start if you're not sure what you want to do next
with your career, don't know where to start or you've been made
redundant. Using the site enables you to narrow your options
and clarify things. The list of links is logically laid out and very
helpful.

www.jobseekersadvice.com   UK
FREE ADVICE
A wide-ranging site offering help with all aspects of job hunting
and career development; a good first port of call. There are forums
and useful articles on many of the key issues facing job seekers.

Job Finders

www.transdata-inter.co.uk/jobs-agencies   UK
DIRECTORY OF JOB SITES
Don't let the long URL put you off, this is an excellent place to
start on your search. The Directory lists all the major online
employment agencies and ranks them by the average number of
vacancies, the regions they cover, whether they help create and
store CVs and what industries they represent. Clicking on the
name takes you right to the site you need.

www.jobs.co.uk   UK
JOB SEARCH ENGINE
With this facility you can search all the major job sites in one go,
it's easy to use and quite accurate providing you have a defined
job title. They also offer all the usual features such as CV help
and advice. See also **www.jobsearch.co.uk** with over 30,000
jobs on offer.

www.gisajob.co.uk   UK
SEARCH FOR YOUR NEXT JOB HERE
The largest of the UK online job sites with over 28,000
vacancies. You can search by description or sector or get advice
on your career. It's good for non-senior executive types.

www.workthing.com UK

IT'S A WORK THING

One of the best-looking job sites with a reputation to match, this site must be one of the first to visit when job hunting across a wide range of industries. Registered users can set up an e-mail alert when a job matching their search criteria appears. There is also help for businesses trying to improve their people skills and recruitment. There is also advice on training and personal development too.

www.monster.co.uk UK

GLOBAL JOBS

With thousands of jobs available in 26 countries, there are plenty to choose from. The site is well designed and easy to use with the usual help features. At the time of writing there were over 70,000 UK jobs listed in over 20 categories.

www.stepstone.co.uk UK

EUROPEAN INTERNET RECRUITMENT

Regarded as one of the best, Stepstone has a huge number of European and international vacancies. It's quick, easy to use and offers lots of time-saving cross-referencing features. You can also register your CV. For other overseas jobs see **www.overseasjobs.com**

Other job finder and career sites worth checking out:
www.careerbuilder.com – find the right career, lots of advice and jobs, although the best thing is downloadable program that shows how you may look over time if you stay in the wrong job.
www.charityjob.co.uk – excellent site servicing the charity industry.
www.deskdemon.com – jobs and resources for secretarial and support staff.
www.doctorjob.com – graduates only need apply.
www.fish4.co.uk/iad/jobs – part of the excellent Fish4 suite of sites, here you'll find plenty of jobs from several major agencies and big recruiters.
www.jobserve.co.uk – a well-categorised job search engine covering the major industries, good design.
www.jobsite.co.uk – award winning site listing some 40,000 jobs; offers some good career advice too.
www.reed.co.uk – some 300,000+ vacancies from a wide range of categories.

www.thegumtree.com – jobs in London.
www.totaljobs.co.uk – 100,000+ jobs listed in a wide range of sectors.

These government-run sites might also be useful:
http://jobseekers.direct.gov.uk – jobs, training and voluntary work.
www.apprenticeships.org.uk – find out about how to start off with an apprenticeship.
www.dfes.gov.uk – the Dept of Education has lots of helpful advice.
www.direct.gov.uk/en/Employment/index.htm – the government's pages on employment.
www.jobcentreplus.gov.uk – information about job centres and how to go about finding a job.
www.volunteering.org.uk – volunteer for something, it looks good on the CV.

Other Careers and Related Sites

www.i-resign.com/uk   UK
THE INS AND OUTS OF RESIGNATION
Pay a visit before you send the letter, it offers a great deal of advice both legal and sensible. The best section contains the funniest selection of resignation letters anywhere. There are also jobs on offer, links to job finder sites and a career guide service. For a helpful site on employment law go to **www.emplaw.co.uk** which does a thorough job.

www.homeworking.com   UK
WORKING FROM HOME
A site full of advice and information for anyone considering or actually working from home. There are links and directories as well as forum pages where you can share experiences with other home workers. For more advice on home working try **www.startups.co.uk/aERh62A.html**

www.eoc.org.uk   UK
EQUAL OPPORTUNITIES COMMISSION
A very informative site and it's where to go if you think you are being discriminated against.

www.adastra-cm.com   UK
CAREERS ADVICE
An excellent site from a career management consultancy with
some really sound careers advice within their newsletters, which
is written in a very accessible style.

www.alec.co.uk   UK
CV WRITING
A site that charges for advice on how to prepare yourself
for interviews and how to write and use your CV, see also
www.cvspecial.co.uk, **www.cvtips.com**, **www.bradleycvs.co.uk**
and **www.ineedacv.co.uk**

Online Practice Tests

www.queendom.com   UK
SERIOUSLY ENTERTAINING
Apart from the fun tests there's a serious side to this site that
allows you to take the sort of tests you're likely to face when
applying for a job. See also **www.psychometric-success.com**
and also **www.psychometricadvantage.co.uk**

Language: Learning and Translation

*In this new section you'll find a selection of sites that will help you learn
a language, whether it's in depth or for a short trip. There's also help if
you just want some text translated.*

www.ilovelanguages.com   US
LANGUAGE LINKS
A directory of language-learning sites; it's US oriented but a good
place to start. The list is pretty comprehensive, featuring some
2,400 sites.

www.bbc.co.uk/languages   UK
LEARN WITH THE BBC
Featuring the BBC's extensive list of language courses, it covers
all the major European languages plus Chinese and Japanese.
There are lots of features and the site is well integrated with the
books and TV programmes.

See also:

http://learningchineseonline.net – the place to start if you want to learn Chinese.

www.elanguage.com – language-learning software to buy.

www.ethnologue.com – excellent resource regarding the history of the 6,900 known languages of the world.

www.eurocosm.com – excellent free resources for the major European languages and cultures.

www.ielanguages.com – basic tutorials for nine European languages.

www.indianlanguages.com – a good introduction to Indian languages.

www.languageguide.org – tries to pull together language resources using volunteers; it is a bit of a mess but you may find something useful.

www.learn-japanese.info – basic course in Japanese for English speakers.

www.linguascope.com – interactive language-learning resources, unfortunately not free.

www.nationalarchives.gov.uk/latin/beginners – a guide to Latin for beginners.

www.parlo.com – learn about the culture as well as the language; again fee-paying courses.

www.usingenglish.com – excellent range of resources for English as a second language for students and teachers.

Translation Services

Listed below are a few sites that are helpful if you just want to translate a short piece of text.

http://babelfish.altavista.com/tr – one of the originals, easy to use and good for the major European and Far Eastern languages.

http://dictionaries.travlang.com – some 35 language dictionaries to choose from.

www.foreignword.com – lots of links and dictionaries, good for the less widely used languages.

www.freetranslation.com – very good for short phrases, also offers professional services.

www.langtolang.com – more links, services, e-books and software to download.

www.smartphrase.com – a helpful online phrase book.

Sign Language

Not all language can be heard ...

> **www.british-sign.co.uk** – a sign dictionary, help and discussion forums.
> **www.britishsignlanguage.com** – a visual dictionary.
> **www.handspeak.com** – good site on international sign language.
> **www.learnbsl.org** – excellent and well-designed virtual guide to British Sign Language.

Legal Advice and the Law

We all need help with certain key events in life: marriages, moving house, making a will or getting a divorce. Maybe you need advice on lesser issues like boundary disputes or problems with services or property? Here are several good sites that could really make a difference. There's more on divorce and separation in the section on problem relationships, page 365.

www.advicenow.org.uk   UK

INDEPENDENT LAW AND RIGHTS ADVICE
A great site designed to keep up with and explain the law in layman's terms. It's well designed and information is easy to find; it also offers links to the relevant site if required. Excellent.

www.compactlaw.co.uk   UK

LEGAL INFORMATION FOR THE UK
An extremely informative and useful site that covers many aspects of the law in a clear and concise style, there are usable documents – you can download some free, others to buy, case histories, news, tips and plenty of fact-sheets.

www.uklegal.com   UK

LEGAL RESOURCES AT YOUR FINGERTIPS
This site offers a superb selection of links to everything from private investigators to barristers to legal equipment suppliers plus the ability to download a wide variety of legal forms.

www.family-solicitors.co.uk   UK

FAMILY LAW REFERENCE
Excellent resource for everyday legal issues covering everything

from wills to neighbourhood disputes. Great for links too with an excellent search facility for finding a family law solicitor near you. See also **www.solicitors-online.com** for the Law Society's advice on lawyers. Another site that will help you find a lawyer is the well-put-together **www.lawyerlocator.co.uk**

www.desktoplawyer.net UK
THE UK'S FIRST ONLINE LAWYER
This site is quite straightforward if you know what you need and have read through the instructions carefully. First you register, then download the software (Rapidocs) enabling you to compile the document you need. The legal documents you create will cost from £2.99 upwards depending on complexity. The range of documents available is huge and there are more being added.

www.legalservices.gov.uk UK
GOVERNMENT ADVICE
The replacement for legal aid, this is the official line on legal matters with guidance on how to access legal assistance, where to get information and news on latest changes to the Community Legal Service and Criminal Defence Service. It could be a lot more user friendly. For Scottish legal aid go to **www.slab.org.uk**

See also:
http://library.kent.ac.uk/library/lawlinks/gateways.htm – a useful portal containing categorised links.
http://nchacti01.uuhost.uk.uu.net/carelaw – an explanatory law site aimed at young people.
www.childrenslegalcentre.com – accessible site on how the law works for young people and how to protect their rights.
www.clsdirect.org.uk – free legal advice from the Community Legal Service.
www.hmcourts-service.gov.uk – information on how the court service works.
www.divorce-online.co.uk – fast-track divorces and good advice.
www.eisil.org – an amazing resource covering aspects of international law, everything from the charter of the UN to laws governing the recovery of astronauts from international waters!
www.findlaw.com – an American law portal.
www.freelawyer.co.uk – a London-based legal services shop.
www.infolaw.co.uk – a legal document search engine and document resource.
www.justcite.com – a legal document search engine.

www.lawassure.co.uk – subscribe to personal legal advice and related services.

www.lawpack.co.uk – legal book specialist.

www.lawscot.org.uk – the Law Society of Scotland.

www.lawsociety.org.uk – the Law Society of England and Wales.

www.lawsoc-ni.org – the Law Society of Northern Ireland.

www.legalpulse.com – well-designed site along the lines of Desktop Lawyer.

www.legalshop.co.uk – affordable solutions to your legal problems; a good site, with a business section too.

www.multikulti.org.uk – legal documents and other helpful information for new citizens and minorities available in many languages.

www.oldbaileyonline.org – interesting site offering up the proceedings of the Old Bailey from 1674 to 1834.

www.sweetandmaxwell.co.uk – specialist legal publisher.

www.dumblaws.com   US

L

THE DAFTEST, STUPIDEST LAWS

Did you realise that in England placing a postage stamp that bears the Queen's head upside down is considered treasonable, or that in Kentucky it's illegal to fish with a bow and arrow? These are just a couple of the many dumb laws that you can find on this very entertaining site. It's now been expanded to include dumbest criminals, dumbest warnings and place names.

Linux

Linux is a free operating system that competes with Windows; it has a reputation for stability and is gaining popularity. Here are some informative sites to help you.

www.linuxlinks.com   US

LINUX DIRECTORY

A Yahoo style directory with thousands of links, forums and articles. It's well categorised and a good place to start.

See also:

www.linux.com – authoritative site with good tutorials.

www.linux.ie – helpful site if you're a beginner.

www.linux.org – a Linux community site, good once you've learnt a bit.

www.redhat.com – a company with its own version of Linux, lots of support.

www.ubuntu.com – a very well regarded version of Linux.

Magazines and Subscriptions

Where to buy and subscribe to your favourite magazines, see also our News section, page 351.

www.newsstand.co.uk   UK
A GIFT THAT LASTS ALL YEAR
A wide range of titles that are available by subscription, on a well categorised site. It has a strong British bias, a pity there are not more overseas and foreign language magazines available.

www.zinio.com   US
DIGITAL MAGAZINES
You have to download the bespoke viewer and subscribe, but here are a large selection of magazines for you to read on your PC – UK editions of some magazines now available. The quality is good and it allows you to turn the pages realistically; however, it's best viewed on a wide-screen PC.

See also:
www.actualidad.com – newspapers of the world and links to their sites.
www.magazinecity.com – large selection of subscriptions, you pay in dollars.
www.magazinesubscriptions.com – subscriptions from one of the biggest magazine publishers, IPC.
www.subscription.co.uk – a good range of UK magazine subscriptions.
www.whsmith.co.uk – some good offers on subscriptions which are available to UK addresses only, back issues available.

Men

Here are a few sites especially for blokes, lads and real men. For more information on fatherhood, check out the section on Parenting, page 361.

For Men

The Good Web Site Guide's Top 10s
of the Internet

1. **www.sharpman.com** – odd but essential advice on staying sharp
2. **www.menshealth.co.uk** – excellent magazine site
3. **www.firebox.com** – the place to find 'boys' toys'
4. **www.fathersdirect.com** – advice and support
5. **www.kiniki.com** – the best underwear
6. **www.clareflorist.co.uk** – because you're bound to need a florist at some stage
7. **www.realbeer.com** – 150,000 pages devoted to beer … perfect
8. **www.hard2buy4.co.uk** – when you need help buying a gift
9. **www.askmen.com** – a great e-zine full of information
10. **www.blokesonly.co.uk** – a shopping sanctuary

M

Magazine Sites

www.fhm.co.uk   UK

FHM MAGAZINE

A good reflection of the real thing, with sections on everything
from serious news to the lighter side, with the usual blokey
features, it's slow and suffers from lots of advertising though.

www.gqmagazine.co.uk   UK

GENTLEMEN'S QUARTERLY

A stylish site, which gives a flavour of the real magazine, it contains
a few stories, competitions, fashion tips and the odd feature.

www.sharpman.com   UK

SHARP!

While a little odd, it's good fun and there's some useful advice.
Split into seven key sections: dating, with tips on conversation
and repartee; toys, from fitness gadgets to snowboards; work,
getting the best out of the Internet; travel, staying sharp abroad;
grooming, looking the part; toys – the best advice on
windsurfing; tips (a new section), a motley selection of articles
on how to make yourself even sharper.

See also:
www.askmen.com – a very good American men's magazine covering almost every topic you're likely to need.
www.dullmen.com – the dullest web site from the National Council for Dull Men, very funny too.
www.modernman.com – nicely designed men's magazine site from the US with loads of interesting articles and features.
www.nutz.co.uk – a portal site featuring men's interests; some adult content.

Health

www.menshealth.co.uk   UK

MEN'S HEALTH MAGAZINE
Lots of advice on keeping fit, healthy and fashionable too. There's also an excellent section on the number one topic – sex, plus others on wealth, health, sport and a shop that sells subscriptions and recommends the latest gear.

www.menshealthforum.org.uk   UK
HEALTH MATTERS
An excellent all-rounder revealing the truth behind the state of men's health and lots of discussion about specific and general health issues facing men today – good for links too.

Other men's health sites:
www.dipex.org – excellent cancer help site.
www.orchid-cancer.org.uk – promotes the awareness of testicular and prostate cancer.
www.sda.uk.net – The Sexual Dysfunction Association.

Fatherhood

www.fathersdirect.com   UK
A MAGAZINE FOR FATHERS
Once an e-zine written by fathers for fathers, this domain has been taken over by the National Information Centre on Fatherhood. It's loaded with advice and support for dads trying to fit in both work and kids. There's information on policy and practice as well as on issues such as parenting, domestic violence, child protection, young offenders and separated families, with special sections for African Caribbean and Muslim fathers.

www.fathers-4-justice.org   UK
FIGHTING FOR ABSENT FATHERS' RIGHTS
Learn more about their well-publicised campaign for truth,
justice and equality in family law. Here you can join the
movement, find out about forthcoming events and buy the
T-shirt.

See also:
www.coeffic.demon.co.uk – father's rights and other male
discrimination issues on a word-heavy but consequently
informative site.
www.fathers.com – an American magazine-style approach to
fatherhood.
www.fnf.org.uk – Families Need Fathers campaigning for the
child's right to access two parents.
www.parents4protest.co.uk – ugly but useful with lots of sad
stories, anger and frustration. Great links.

Shopping

www.firebox.com   UK
WHERE MEN BUY STUFF
An online shop aimed totally at boy's toys, with its own bachelor
pad containing all you need for the lifestyle. There are masses of
games, videos, toys and, of course, the latest gadgets. Delivery
costs vary. See also **www.boysstuff.co.uk** – worth a visit if you
can't find what you want at Firebox. If you want to be the first
and the one with the most talked about gadgets then go to
www.coolest-gadgets.com

www.mankindonline.co.uk   UK
MALE GROOMING
An above-average shop devoted to male grooming products and
gifts, it also offers advice on things like skincare and has a
newsletter you can subscribe to. Delivery is free on orders
over £70. See also **www.maleorder.co.uk**

www.condomsdirect.co.uk   UK
CONDOMS UK
Many different types of condoms are available to buy, and you
get free delivery if you spend more than £10 – there's even a
price promise and the assurance of a fast and discreet service.
It's also worth checking out **www.condomania.com**

Motorcycles

See also the section on Cars on page 62 as many sites cover both forms of motoring.

www.bmf.co.uk   UK
> BRITISH MOTORCYCLISTS' FEDERATION
> At this site you can join the BMF, get involved with their activities or just use the site for information. You can also get club information and e-mail them on any issues. For the international governing body go to **www.fim.ch/en**

www.motorcycle.co.uk   UK
> THE UK'S MOTORCYCLE DIRECTORY
> Essentially a list of links by brand, dealer, importer, classics, gear, books and auctions. **www.moto-directory.com** is a similar American site with listings in 24 categories.

www.motorworld.com   US
> ALL YOU NEED TO KNOW ABOUT MOTORCYCLES
> Good coverage of both machines and events with multimedia features. Although the site is American there's good British coverage.

M

www.customlids.co.uk   UK
> WHERE TO GET YOUR GEAR
> A smart looking site housing a good shop and information dedicated to motorcycles, clothing and accessories. Also worth a visit is **www.fowlers.co.uk** who offer a wide range of clothing.

> *See also:*
> **www.autotrader.co.uk/BIKES/bikes.jsp** – a section of *Auto Trader* magazine, *Bike Trader* has a huge number of bikes for sale and is a good place to put your bike up for sale too.
> **www.bikenet.com** – home of the Big Bike Book – parts, gear and accessories.
> **www.classic-motorbikes.com** – great if you want to purchase a classic bike.
> **www.hondahornet.co.uk** – a good-looking specialist site.
> **www.mag-uk.org** – home of the Motorcycle Action Group dedicated to campaigning on behalf of motorcyclists in the UK.
> **www.mcia.co.uk** – home of the Motorcycle Industry Association, this site offers a fair amount of information for all levels.

www.motorbikes.be/en – a Belgian site which offers the technical specs of some 6,000 motorbikes.

www.motorcycleshow.co.uk – details of the motorcycle show.

www.scootering.com – home of *Scootering* magazine.

www.twistngo.com – *TAG Magazine* for scooter fans. See 'What Scooter' section to help make your choice.

www.umgweb.com – owned by the auctioneer e-Bay, here you can find used motorcycles for sale.

Movies

All you need to know about films and film stars including where to go to get the best deals on DVDs and videos. For information on the stars also check out the Celebrities section on page 75.

News and Information

http://uk.imdb.com US

INTERNET MOVIE DATABASE

The best and most organised movie database on the Internet. It's very easy to use and every film buff's dream with lots of features and recommendations, plus games, quizzes, chat and movie news. Another good database site is **www.allmovie.com** which has a really good search engine.

www.aintitcoolnews.com US

AIN'T IT JUST COOL

A renowned review site that is very entertaining and likeable, albeit a bit messy. Harry Knowles's movie reviews are by far the best bit of the site, although they can go on a bit. You can search the archive for a particular review or contribute a bit of juicy gossip by e-mailing Harry direct.

See also:

www.firstshowing.net – a collaborative site aimed at connecting Hollywood with its audience, there are plenty of reviews and content, it's well worth a visit for any film buff.

www.metacritic.com – a site that compiles reviews from around the world, and gives the reviewed movies a score based on them. Also covers games, music and books.

www.mrqe.com – the Movie Review Query Engine. Just enter the film title, and reviews from magazines from all round the world pop up.

M

www.mymovies.net – a portal, shop, news and e-zine all wrapped up in an average site. Having said that there's a lot here so patience is rewarded, but you have to subscribe to get the best out of it.

www.rottentomatoes.com – a comprehensive review site and store.

Film Magazine Sites

www.empireonline.co.uk   UK

THE UK'S NUMBER ONE
An epic of a site with masses of information and background on the latest movies and the stars. There are two main review sections, one dedicated to the cinema and one entitled, 'At home' for DVD and soundtrack and book reviews. You can also see trailers of new films, see pictures of the stars and production stills in the gallery and subscribe to the magazine.

www.insidefilm.com   US

FILM FESTIVAL DIRECTORY
Comprehensive news on the film festival with a calendar and features on awards.

M

www.eonline.com   US

E IS FOR ENTERTAINMENT
This is one of the most visited and vivid entertainment news sites, it has a reputation for being first with the latest gossip and movie news. It's vibrant, well designed and has a tongue-in-cheek style which is endearing; some of the reporters do prattle on though.

www.variety.com   US

VARIETY MAGAZINE
The online version of the show business stalwart magazine has an excellent and entertaining site with all the hot topics, news and background information you'd expect plus biographies and international film news. You have to subscribe to get access to many of the sections.

www.brightlightsfilm.com   US

FILM JOURNAL
A diverse and well written e-zine devoted to film that covers a wide variety of topics and film styles. It can be quite eccentric, which adds to the appeal, and some of the content is pretty odd, but it's essential reading for film buffs.

For more gossip see:
www.boxofficemojo.com – excellent US film news and box office information site.
www.cinematical.com – Hollywood news and gossip, well categorised too.
www.ew.com – *Entertainments Weekly* has a really attractive site with lots of features.
www.hollywood.com – over one million pages of gossip, news, trailers and multi-media library.
www.hollywoodreporter.com – all the latest gossip and you can subscribe to the magazine.
www.obsessedwithfilm.com – an above average movie blog with reviews, news and discussion.
www.teenhollywood.com – aimed at teenagers, following the top teens in Hollywood.
www.themovieblog.com – the official home of correct movie opinions, apparently.

Bollywood

www.bollywoodworld.com   INDIA

THE BOLLYWOOD PORTAL
If it's Bollywood, then it's covered on this site. There are the movie reviews you'd expect plus lots of news, what's hot and what's not, pictures of the stars and much more. There is a music channel, radio, blogs and chat.

See also:
www.bollywhat.com – here you can find a good beginner's guide.
www.planetbollywood.com – odd design but loads of information, gossip and awards.

Awards and Industry

www.oscars.com   US

THE ACADEMY AWARDS
Stylish and as tastelessly glitzy as you'd imagine it should be, this is the official tie-in site for the Oscars. There's an archive and even some games to play. See also **http://oscartorrents.com** where you can download the film (usually from another site and possibly illegally) and then vote for yourself. For the Golden Globes go to **www.thegoldenglobes.com** and for a celebration of the worst Hollywood has to offer, the Razzies, go to **www.razzies.com**

www.bafta.org   UK

BRITISH ACADEMY OF FILM & TELEVISION ARTS
A site giving all the information you need on the BAFTAs, their
history and how it all works.

www.bfi.org.uk   UK
BRITISH FILM INSTITUTE
A top site from the BFI packed with information on how the film
industry works with archive material, links and how to make
movies. Refreshing that there's not much mention of Hollywood!
For the American Film Institute go to **www.afi.com** where you'll
find an excellent site, plus the Australian Film Institute has an
informative site at **www.afi.org.au**

British Movie Industry

www.britmovie.co.uk   UK

DEDICATED TO BRITISH CINEMA
A site devoted to the history of British cinema and its wider
contribution to film-making in general. There's a great deal
of information, links and background and it's all well cross-
referenced. There is now a search facility on the site, which we
called for in previous editions, and the site seems to be more
regularly updated than of old.

See also:
www.britishfilm.org.uk – excellent set of articles on the history
of British cinema.
www.britishhorrorfilms.co.uk – a very entertaining romp
through the history of British horror films, with lots of detail!
www.britshorts.com – short British and European films.

Independent Film-making

www.indiewire.com   UK
INDEPENDENT CINEMA
An enthralling site covering independent cinema, the films,
people and gossip. It stands out as a site that genuinely feels
like it's contributing positively to an industry. See also
www.exposure.co.uk who cover the low budget end of
film-making.

www.kamera.co.uk   UK
ART HOUSE & INDEPENDENT REVIEWS
A well-written review site covering the world of art house and
independent cinema. It also has a good book review section and
interviews with important actors and directors. There's also a
directory and forums where you can put your views.

See also:
http://shootingpeople.org – a community site aimed at the
independent film maker, with lots of advice and help.
www.bifa.org.uk – British Independent Film awards.
www.raindancefilmfestival.org – a high profile sponsor of
independent films, with a useful site and e-zine.

Specialist Film Sites

www.bmonster.com   US
COOLEST CULT MOVIES
A highly entertaining site devoted to B movies, oddities and
actors that aren't quite top drawer. It's well categorised and
obviously a labour of love for its contributors. See also
www.badmovieplanet.com

See also:
http://commanderbond.net – the place to go for all Bond fans.
www.americanwest.com/films/films.htm – good for links to all
things Western.
www.b-westerns.com – The Old Corral, a directory devoted
mainly to Westerns.
www.classichorrorfilms.com – not a great site but it's got all
you need on the subject.
www.classicmoviemusicals.com – a well-categorised but
slightly dull site covering musicals.
www.earlycinema.com – excellent site on the first decade of
cinema with timeline, biographical details and information on
the technology they used.
www.horror.net – a database of some 3,200 horror-related sites.
www.moderntimes.com – movie classics.
www.movie-locations.com – a guide to the world's movie locations.
www.mysterynet.com/movies – the top movies reviewed with
links to other related genres.
www.notstarring.com – excellent movie trivia site focusing on
those roles that stars turned down, got dropped from or just
didn't get.

www.paulkerensa.com/movietimeline – an historical timeline of everything that happened in the Movies and when.

www.scifispace.com – excellent fan site with lots of detail and links.

www.sciflicks.com – a comprehensive site covering the Sci Fi genre.

www.scriptfly.com – buy movie scripts, thousands to choose from.

www.silentsaregolden.com – a great place to start if you want to find out about silent movies.

Cinemas

Listed below are the major cinema companies and their sites – although it is hard to keep up with their mergers:

www.cinemas-online.co.uk – a portal site with links to all the country's cinemas.

www.cineworld.co.uk – straightforward and easy-to-use guide. You can't book on line but they promise a new site soon.

www.odeon.co.uk – book online at this attractive site.

www.showcasecinemas.co.uk – lots here to see and do.

www.myvue.com – Vue, the company formed from the amalgamation of Warner Village Cinemas and SBC International Cinemas, has a cleanly designed site with hidden extras.

M

Movie Humour

http://rinkworks.com/movieaminute   US

DON'T HAVE TIME TO WATCH IT ALL?
Summaries of the top movies for those who either can't be bothered to watch them or just want to pretend they did, either way it's really funny.

www.moviecliches.com   US

THE MOVIE CLICHÉ LIST
Clichés listed by topic from aeroplanes to wood, there's something for everyone here …

See also:

www.badmovieplanet.com – a collection of the worst films ever made.

www.continuitycorner.com – the place to go if you're a born nitpicker, it has hundreds of movie mistakes and believe it not one person has submitted over 120 of them.

www.nitpickers.com – more pettiness.
www.razzies.com – awards for the worst movies.
www.thestinkers.com – more awards for bad films.

Film Companies

Some of the best web sites are those that promote a particular film. Here is a list of the major film producers and their web sites, all of which are good and have links to the latest releases. Most have clips, downloads, screensavers and lots of advertising.

http://spielbergfilms.com
www.disney.com
www.dreamworks.com
www.foxmovies.com
www.miramax.com
www.paramount.com
www.sonypictures.com
www.uip.com
www.universalpictures.com
www.warnerbros.com

Downloading Movies

There's no doubt that downloading films and TV shows is the big thing in digital. As technology moves on, the facility to carry large movie files such as MP4 will get ever easier. Once downloaded you can burn your own DVDs too.

BitTorrent

This is a technology that allows for the downloading of large amounts of data using a speedier, more user-friendly technology than has previously been available. Staggering to believe, but BitTorrent has been taken up at such a rate that it's apparently been responsible for over a third of all internet traffic in the past year, some estimates put it at 50%.

This is changing the way that ISPs allocate their data flow and makes possible the transfer of extremely large files by taking small bits of the required file, not from just one computer, but all the other computers that have downloaded the relevant BitTorrent program and have the file that you have requested. This group of computers is called a 'swarm' and the transfer of data using this method is called a 'torrent' and it means download speeds can be some twenty times faster than normal.

Check out the following …

http://bitlord.com – a slick torrent program with the promise of no spyware.

http://en.wikipedia.org/wiki/Bittorrent – from the ever helpful Wikipedia a guide to BitTorrent and the terminology.

http://jabberwalker.com.ar – a torrent search engine.

http://utorrent.com – a simple torrent client but it seems to be incompatible with a lot of standard software so check out the FAQs before using.

www.bittorrent.com – the original site and program.

Interestingly, the film industry has embraced the technology and unlike the music industry seems to welcome peer-to-peer (P2P) file sharing. The BBC has started to make available some programs as downloads and it's just a matter of time before other channels follow suit. With the latest technology you'll need a broadband connection. Here are a few sites that are leading the way (be warned that some carry adult-oriented material and illegal content, which should be protected by copyright).

http://filmdownloads.aol.co.uk – AOL with some of the first proper blockbusters available.

www.cinemanow.com – the world's largest legal video download store, apparently; whatever, the quality is great.

www.ezmovies.net – a good subscription service specialising in movies.

www.freemovienow.com – not much free but one of the better designs and lots of choice.

www.moviedownloadworld.com – a selection of some 15,000 movies.

www.sharedmovies.com – the one with possibly the most content.

www.ultimatemoviedownload.com – a popular file-sharing program with lots of content; costs vary according to what you buy.

www.xvidmovies.com – a well-used service using the MP4 format.

Buying and Renting Movies

*It's probably best to start with visiting a price checker site first such as **www.kelkoo.com** (see page 386) but these are the best of the movie online stores.*

www.sendit.com   UK

THE UK'S BIGGEST VIDEO STORE

The biggest online video and DVD retailer, it is very good value, boasts free delivery and has a reputation for excellent customer service. If you want to shop around try **www.blockbuster.com** who have a less packed site and offers on a wide variety of films.

www.lovefilm.com   UK

RENT A DVD

Rent as many DVDs as you want with packages starting from £9.99 per month. Pick the title of your choice and it's dispatched the same day, you then return it seven days later in the pre-paid envelope and they immediately dispatch the next DVD on your list. The range offered is excellent covering over 65,000 titles in twenty genres plus new releases coming soon and a good search facility too. For alternative contractual arrangements based on £1.99 per DVD hired, go to **https://dvd.easycinema.com**

See also:

http://svp.co.uk – internet retailers of blank CS/DVD media. Sells computer accessories too.

http://uk-dvd-rentals.co.uk – reviews the DVD online rental services helping you to select the best for your needs.

www.dvdpopcorn.com – a good-looking UK-based DVD shop with some good offers, and prices include postage and packing.

www.dvdreview.com – great for news and reviews.

www.dvdtimes.co.uk – DVD and cinema news and reviews.

www.movieprofiler.com – get film recommendations based on the emotional input you give; once done you can buy from Amazon … of course, your mood might have changed by the time you actually get the DVD.

www.mymovies.net – a good review and film store with a movie club.

www.play.com – a very strong selection of DVDs and CDs too with some good offers.

www.xiddi.com   UK

DVD SHARE AND SWAP

A good alternative to DVD rental, here you build up credits (Xids) that enable you to select from a good range of films and popular titles, you only really pay for the postage.

Memorabilia

www.vinmag.com   UK

POSTERS, CARDS AND T-SHIRTS

Vintage magazines, stand-up cut-outs, posters, T-shirts and
magazine covers complete the picture from this established
dealer.

www.propstore.co.uk   UK

PROPS FOR SALE

An extensive selection of props and replicas await you here with
everything from snow globes to clothing. Each piece is unique
and has been bought from the relevant film company and the
provenance is provided.

See also:
www.efilmposters.com – who sell posters from a good British
site.
www.memomine.com – for Hollywood memorabilia.
www.moviemarket.co.uk – posters, framed prints and
memorabilia delivered to your door.
www.ricksmovie.com – some 14,000 posters and related items.
www.vinylandfilmposters.co.uk – film and music related
posters.

Music

*Most people with a computer know about downloading music and
much has been written about the effect that downloading free music
has had on the music industry, mainly at the expense of musicians
losing income. Some suggest that it's damaging to the industry by
taking away their livelihoods, while others say it stimulates sales by
enabling potential customers to sample music they wouldn't have
heard otherwise.*

*Whatever the stance, some of the sites listed are really different file
sharing programs that allow users to exchange files easily whether it is
music or not. It's best to read up on the subject (see the section on
BitTorrent on page 314) before downloading any of the programs, but
once you're up to speed it couldn't be easier.*

*Some of these sites are also prone to change, as regulations are
introduced to block their activities, it's also quite difficult to establish*

Podcasting

The Good Web Site Guide's Top 10s
of the Internet

1. **www.podcastalley.com** – the podcast portal
2. **www.podcast.net** – the podcast directory
3. **http://en.wikipedia.org/wiki/Podcast** – Wikipedia explains it all
4. **www.podcastingnews.com** – all the latest and best podcasts
5. **www.ipodhacks.com** – for the technically minded
6. **www.bbc.co.uk/radio** – listen again, download your favourite radio programme
7. **http://encyclopodia.sourceforge.net/en/index.html** – get Wikipedia on your iPod
8. **www.guardian.co.uk/rickygervais** – the world's most popular podcast
9. **www.podcastbunker.com** – quality not quantity, excellent selection
10. **www.podcastpickle.com** – podcasts and vidcasts too

their origin in some cases. The legal constraints that surround music file sharing are unclear but it's fair to say that in many cases copyright laws are broken. If you're not sure about using them, then I suggest you go to the pay sites.

In America, some of the big music companies have prosecuted people who have downloaded music without paying, so be cautious. Having said all that, there are high-quality sites that allow you to sample music, offer legitimate free tracks and charge reasonable prices for the music – it's often still cheaper than buying a CD.

Please be aware that some may contain adult material including pornography (music files aren't the only things traded) and many carry some sort of spyware so that they can adapt to your tastes and advertise accordingly. See our security section on page 423 if you want to get rid of spyware. There are compatibility issues too, for example a track downloaded from Napster won't work on an iPod, as they use different software. There are two reasons for this, the first is about securing the track so that the artist gets paid and copyright is

maintained, the second is about keeping you loyal to the product.
Again it's best to read up on the subject before you buy.

iTunes, Audio Players and Download Sites

These are the most popular digital audio players, all offer a basic free
version with a full featured version to buy and download. With these
you can download music, rip and burn CDs and get access to radio
stations. Some offer movies and video playback too. We'll start with the
gadget that has dominated music downloading over the past few years,
the iPod. If you own a digital player that is not an iPod, then it probably
comes with its own software or is affiliated with one of these programs.
For information on Podcasting, see page 385.

www.apple.com/uk/itunes   UK
    UK IPOD
    If you have an iPod here's where to start, the iTunes program
    can be used with a PC or Mac and it's very easy to select, buy
    and download your music choice. They offer possibly the largest
    quality selection of music and audio products including over
    1,000 music videos available to download.

http://tunetuzer.com   UK
    NOT ALL DOWNLOADS ARE EQUAL
    Check out which music download stores offer the best value for
    money and quality at this informative service.

    See also:
    www.dailytunes.com – linked to iTunes, it gives
    recommendations and rediscovers long-lost songs.
    www.ipodhacks.com – all the iPod tips and tricks.
    www.ipodlounge.com – excellent site devoted to all things iPod.

www.musicmatch.com   US
    MUSIC MATCH PLAYER
    Award-winning, good-looking and popular audio player with lots
    of functions and access to a catalogue of some 800,000 songs,
    competitively priced.

www.real.com   US
    REAL PLAYER
    A popular and versatile audio and video player; the free version
    is probably good enough for most users, the radio features are
    great too.

www.winamp.com   US
WINAMP PLAYER
The Winamp player is better looking than most and easy to use,
but the free version isn't as good as some of the other free
players. Having said that, the Pro version, which costs, is
excellent. There's also plenty of stuff to download on the site.

*Here's a list of sites that enable you to download a wide variety of
music and audio files, although I suggest you start your search at
www.100topmp3sites.com. Some of these sites come with their own
downloading formats and players, which may mean they can't play
some other formats.*

http://magnatune.com – from record label Magnatune, you can
get a decent sample of their artists' tracks before you buy.
http://music.yahoo.com – high-quality offering from Yahoo with
lots of features, the emphasis is on popular music and the latest
releases.
www.artistdirect.com – download music direct from the artist
who made it.
www.bleep.com – award-winning site with a good selection of
the usual artists and tracks with the addition of 'some obscure
gems that have passed under the radar'.
www.dmusic.com – independent digital music site with
subscription fee.
www.eclassical.com – many free classical greats and many
more to buy.
www.emusic.com – offers exclusive DJ mixes, live performances
and prides itself on quality alternative music, over one million
MP3s to choose from. One of the most highly rated.
www.napster.co.uk – attractive and easy to use, it also claims to
have one million tracks available. Prices start at £9.95 per
month. Doesn't support Mac.
www.peoplesound.com – an attempt to sell the work of
unsigned artists by promoting them alongside established artists,
some surprisingly good stuff here and much of it is free.
www.pro-music.org – a useful information site on the music
industry and legitimate music downloading.
www.tescodownloads.com – very popular site, good value
downloads from Tesco.
www.wippit.com – good looking, wide range of downloads and
pretty good value too.

File-sharing Programs and Free Downloading

With the advent of BitTorrent (see page 314) it will be interesting to see how many of these survive.

www.zeropaid.com   US
FILE-SHARING PORTAL
A site that lists all the many file-sharing sites, it seems very comprehensive but is not that easy to navigate as the text is quite dense.

http://opennap.sourceforge.net   US
CONNECTING PEOPLE
A variant of the original Napster program, this is freeware and you can select some of the many specialist and general servers which hold music, then use the program to search them for the music you like.

www.imesh.com   ISRAEL
SHARE THE PASSION
No central servers here, you join the network and as a member you can use the search facility to find music or files available from other members. Supposed to be spyware free but you have to subscribe to get the best stuff.

M

www.kazaa.com   US
NUMBER 1
Kazaa rapidly became probably the most popular music download site in 2003. It has lots of features, it's easy to use and, unlike some of its competitors, attractive to look at. It comes with virus protection too, although some files we downloaded came with spyware attached. It works in a similar way to iMesh. Note, this program was illegal in Australia at the time of writing.

www.limewire.com   US
THE FASTEST
With over 100 million versions of Lime Wire downloaded, it has to be regarded as one of the most successful file sharing programs of all. The latest version is clear and very easy to use, it is apparently free of spyware and other nasties.

www.shareaza.com   US
HIGHLY RATED
One of the best P2P file management programs, it's very flexible
and can easily be customised, it seems destined for great things.

www.xolox.nl   HOLLAND
SHARE AND DISCOVER
An excellent program which allows you to search for files and
music across many of the established networks featured above.
It's very easy to use and there's a parental control option.

www.riaa.org   US
RECORDING INDUSTRY ASSOCIATION OF AMERICA
Get the latest information on their attempts to stop music piracy,
the legal issues plus their awards and industry statistics. See
also the site for Electronic Frontier Foundation **www.eff.org** who
campaign on legal issues surrounding digital media.

www.goaudio.co.uk   UK
DIGITAL PLAYERS
A specialist retailer devoted to digital players with some
competitive prices on iPods and other makes such as Creative
and Rio.

www.last.fm   GERMANY/US
WORLD'S LARGEST SOCIAL MUSIC PLATFORM
Exploiting music technology to create a vibrant music
community. Here you can share your musical taste with friends,
create a personalized radio feed, download free music and
extend your musical knowledge. Great site, hope the recent
purchase by CBS doesn't spoil things.

Buying CDs and Other Audio Products

*It's as well to start by checking prices of CDs through price comparison
sites such as those listed on page 386. These will take you to the store
offering the best combination of price and postage. All the stores listed
below offer good value plus a bit extra.*

www.hmv.co.uk   UK
HIS MASTER'S VOICE ONLINE
Excellent features and offers on the latest downloads, CDs and
videos. There are sections on most aspects of music as well as
video, DVD and games with a good search facility. Free UK delivery.

www.buy.com US

OUTSTANDING VALUE

An American site for good deals on downloads. If you want a
physical CD, then you could do well to visit
www.musiczone.co.uk

www.cduniverse.com US

WIDE RANGE AND GREAT OFFERS

There is a massive range to choose from and some good
discounts; delivery normally takes only five days. You can also
buy games, DVDs and videos. Excellent, but can be quite slow,
and delivery is very expensive.

www.minidisco.com US

HOME OF THE MINIDISC

Amazingly the minidisc is alive and well here with some good
offers on the players and information on the latest developments.
Delivery to Europe takes about a week, costs vary. See also
www.minidisc.org which is a messy site but contains everything
you need to know about minidiscs.

For more great offers on music try these sites:
www.101cd.com – renowned for offering good value.
www.amazon.co.uk – as good as you'd expect from Amazon.
www.andante.com – excellent classical e-zine and online store.
www.recordstore.co.uk – choose from thousands of vinyl
records, CDs, T-shirts, record bags and assorted DJ gear.
www.timelesstracks.com – devoted to the music of the 50s,
60s, 70s and 80s with some excellent prices on CDs.
www.towerrecords.co.uk – wide variety and some good offers –
better service than you get from the real store. US-based site so
beware of delivery charges.

www.htfr.co.uk UK

HARD TO FIND RECORDS

Although they specialise in new and deleted house, garage,
techno, electro, disco, funk, soul and hip-hop vinyl, they will
try and find any record previously released. They also offer a
complete service to all budding and serious DJs.

See also:
www.eil.com – who specialise in rare and collectible CDs and vinyl.
www.funkishere.com – rare funk and jazz funk.
www.recordfinders.com – a US-based vinyl specialist.

Bands, Groups and Stars

http://ubl.artistdirect.com   US

THE ULTIMATE BAND LIST
It is the place for mountains of information on groups or singers.
It has a brilliant search facility, and you can buy and download
from the site as well, although the prices are not as good as
elsewhere. For a similar, but better organised site try
www.allmusic.com where you can also get excellent
information and videos.

www.onehitwondercentral.com   US

A CATALOGUE OF ONE HIT WONDERS
US-oriented information site on those who only triumphed once,
never to be seen again. It's arranged by decade and you get
some interesting titbits in the artist profiles.

www.musicbrigade.com   US

WATCH YOUR FAVOURITE ARTIST
An excellent site where you can download your favourite
music videos; when we visited they had more than 20,000.
Subscription prices vary and it doesn't work with those who
have Macs, iPods or Firefox.

For Aspiring Bands

www.taxi.com   US

FOR UNSIGNED BANDS
Looking to get a music contract for your band? You should start
here, there's loads of information, contacts and links that will
help you on the rocky road to success and stardom – well that's
the theory anyway!

*For more places to find something new and get help if you're in
a band, see also:*
www.audiogalaxy.com – for sampling new and some existing
bands.
www.bpi.co.uk – the British Phonographic Industry and what
they do.
www.hitsquad.com – a well-categorised portal site aimed
primarily at musicians.
www.myspace.com – the music section at the hugely popular
social networking site has become the place to promote new
bands.

www.totalband.com – an excellent web resource for bands and musicians who want to set up their own web site.

www.joescafe.com/bands   UK
BAND NAMES
So you can't think of a name for your band? Here is the 'Bando-matic' which will offer all sorts of never before used band names in seconds. This time we got 'The Roger Box'. They've branched into song titles too, but we can't imagine 'My Big New Pants' making the top 20!

Music TV, Awards and Magazine Sites

www.bbc.co.uk/totp   UK
TOP OF THE POPS
Despite It's demise on mainstream TV Top of the Pops still survives, the sites are different, with the principle site being a magazine featuring the current charts with loads of good features and articles as well as competitions, trivia and lots of information. For those with longer memories try **www.bbc.co.uk/totp2** for golden oldies, 23,000 artists' biographies, and 1 million sound clips and loads of general interest content.

M

http://uk.fmagazine.com   UK
F MAGAZINE
This one is for broadband users only. The look is stunning and it's a pleasure to use. The content is pretty good too; it's aimed at the UK market and covers the new bands and artists with interviews and videos as well as articles.

www.grammy.com   US
THE GRAMMY AWARDS
An overview of the awards, who won what and when, and then where to buy their music. For the Brit awards go to **www.brits.co.uk** where you'll find a similar site.

www.mtv.co.uk   UK
MUSIC TELEVISION
MTV offers loads of info on events, shows and the artists as well as background on the presenters and creative bits like movie and music video clips. Great design.

Music

The Good Web Site Guide's Top 10s
of the Internet

1. **www.apple.com/itunes** – great design, songs from 79p
2. **www.kazaa.com** – possibly illegal but for free downloads none better
3. **www.cd-wow.com** – for those who still buy CDs, here's the best for value
4. **www.htfr.co.uk** – hard to find records has been a saviour to many
5. **http://ubl.artistdirect.com** – info on virtually anyone who has recorded a song
6. **www.clickmusic.co.uk** – all you need to know on the subject
7. **www.lyrics.com** – stop the arguments, the lyrics to hundreds of songs
8. **www.ticketmaster.co.uk** – for your concert tickets
9. **www.sunhawk.com** – the place to download sheet music
10. **www.mediauk.com/directory** – more radio stations than you'll ever need

M

www.nme.com   UK

NEW MUSICAL EXPRESS
If you're a rock fan then this is where it's at. There's all the usual information, it's well laid out and easy to access. The archived articles are its greatest asset, featuring 150,000 artists and every article, feature and review they've ever published plus full UK discographies, pictures, e-cards, ring tones and links to the best web sites.

www.q4music.com   UK
Q MAGAZINE
A music magazine site that reflects its parent magazine extremely well, with many of the features and all the authority that goes with it.

www.popworld.com   UK
WHERE POP COMES FIRST
Reinvented site, but it still retains the attitude and the gossip, not as much fun and more commercial than it was though.

www.rollingstone.com
UK
ROLLING STONE MAGAZINE
The archetypal music magazine has an excellent site with all the features you'd expect to see including reviews, photos, articles on the bands, downloads, links and games.

www.thebox.co.uk
UK
SMASH HITS YOU CONTROL
Similar to many sites but with added features such as the ability for you to select a tune to be played on their TV channel and you can influence their overall selection by voting for your favourite songs. You need to be a member to get the most out of it.

www.vh1.com
UK
MUSIC CHANNEL
VH1 is a music channel and here's the associated web site which is packed with information, interactive features, preview videos and downloads.

Sites for Specific Types of Music

Blues

www.bluesworld.com
US
HOMAGE TO THE BLUES
If you're into the blues then this is your kind of site. There are interviews, memorabilia, 78 auctions, bibliographies, discographies and lists of links to other blues sites. You can order CDs via affiliated retailers and if the mood takes you, order a guitar too. See also the blog **www.bluesmusicnow.com** and also the magazine site **www.bluesmatters.com**

Classical and Opera

www.gramophone.co.uk
UK

GRAMOPHONE MAGAZINE
An outstanding site with features, reviews, competitions, shop and concert listings; there's also an awards section plus the editor's choice with the top recommendations.

www.operabase.com/en
US
OPERA BASE
This site offers opera listings, information on festivals and provides background to the history of opera. For the Opera

magazine site go to **www.opera.co.uk** which offers articles and links.

Other key classical music sites:
www.andante.com – excellent classical e-zine and online store.
www.aria-database.com – information on over 1,000 arias.
www.branarecords.com – restores and publishes recordings from neglected artists.
www.choralnet.org – excellent site devoted to choral music.
www.classical.com – portal site with links, information and downloads.
www.classical.net – great for information and links.
www.eclassical.com – download MP3s, many are free.
www.eno.org – the English National Opera.
www.mdcmusic.co.uk – good offers on CDs.
www.royaloperahouse.org – book online, see where your seat is and get the latest news.
www.wno.org.uk – Welsh National Opera.

Country

www.thatscountry.com　　　　　　　　　　　　　CANADA
COUNTRY MUSIC SCENE
A good overview of country music with offers and links as well as information on the artists and bands. For a similar offering go to **www.gactv.com**

See also:
www.acountry.com – excellent US-based news site.
www.countrymusic.org.uk – a naff but informative site that covers the UK scene.
www.cmaworld.com – home of the Country Music Association.
www.countrystarsonline.com – find the link to your favourite country stars.
www.roughstock.com – all-round magazine site, live radio and recommended for its excellent history of country.

Dance and Beat

www.anthems.com　　　　　　　　　　　　　　　UK

DANCE, HOUSE AND GARAGE
Great design combined with brilliant content, there's everything here for dance fans – news, information and samples of the

latest mixes or, if you're feeling rich, you can buy them too, although you'll probably find them cheaper elsewhere.

See also:
www.artofthemix.org – playlists, create your own or use someone else's.
www.beatport.com – digital download dance and beat specialist, great design.
www.garagemusic.co.uk – reviews and samples plus the latest on the UK scene, annoying adverts though and adult content.
www.juno.co.uk – good dance music store with a wide range.

Disco

www.disco-disco.com   US
DISCO FEVER
A great site devoted to all things Disco. It's quite comprehensive but it's also worth checking out **www.discomusic.com** which has lots of downloads and also **www.radiowdrc.com** for the World Disco Community.

Folk

www.folkmusic.net   UK
FOLK ON THE WEB
A straightforward site from *Living Traditions* magazine, a collection of articles, features, reviews and news.

See also:
www.folking.com – a good all-round site with news, downloads and shopping.
www.folkmusic.org – links and information.
www.thetraditionbearers.com – a project aimed at keeping alive our traditional songs.

Hip Hop and Rap

www.sohh.com   US
SITE OF HIP HOP
Voted the best of its kind by *Rolling Stone*, this site offers all you'd expect in terms of news, reviews, forums, interviews and samples. It also has links to shops and other related sites.

See also:
www.britishhiphop.co.uk – the story of British hip hop and artist listing and discography.
www.hiphopville.com – where to go for all the gear.
www.rapdict.org – the Rap Dictionary helping you through hip hop slang.
www.rapstation.com – a temperamental site but one that really delivers in terms of information and news.

Indie

www.playlouder.com UK
INDIE MUSIC
Great graphics and excellent design make Playlouder stand out from the crowd; it covers the indie music scene in depth with all the usual features, but with a bit more style. See also **www.drownedinsound.com** which is a very good e-zine devoted to the scene and **www.pennyblackmusic.co.uk** for more articles.

Jazz

M

www.jazzonln.com US
JAZZ ONLINE
Reviews, links, artist interviews and a guide to the different types of jazz are all features here. You can download videos too, although you need 'Quicktime' to view them.

See also:
www.allaboutjazz.com – well organised, slightly dull but very comprehensive.
www.jazzcorner.com – a beautifully designed jazz magazine site and directory.
www.jazzimprov.com – an e-zine about jazz improvisation.
www.jazzreview.com – lots of reviews and discussion plus a photography section and downloads.

Karaoke

www.streamkaraoke.com US
SING ALONG
Over 20,000 tunes to download but you have to subscribe, which costs from $4 a month depending on which package you take. See also the British **www.singtotheworld.com**

Pop

www.popjustice.com   UK
> POP MUSIC
> Opinionated, a bit pompous but very well informed, Pop Justice
> gives you the insider's guide to pop music. See also **www.pop-music.com** and **www.bbc.co.uk/music/pop**

Reggae

www.reggaetrain.com   US
> REGGAE TRAIN A COME
> An excellent and comprehensive portal site devoted to all things
> reggae, with several hundred links.
>
> *See also:*
> **www.niceup.com** – comprehensive reggae archive site with a
> massive database and links.
> **www.reggaefusion.com** – a huge site devoted to Jamaican music.
> **www.reggaereview.com** – a monthly web magazine from
> California.
> **www.reggaetimes.com** – a good site connected with *Reggae
> Times*, lots of reviews and links.

M

Rock and Heavy Metal

www.rocksite.com   US
> INFORMATION THAT ROCKS
> Devoted to rock music, there are band listings, tour news,
> reviews plus links and a musicians directory. All this wrapped up
> in an appropriately designed site.
>
> *For more try:*
> **www.heavy-metalinks.com** – horrible-looking site but it does
> have all the links you'll need.
> **www.history-of-rock.com** – a good overview of the roots of rock
> and roll.
> **www.live4metal.com** – good e-zine with reviews, interviews
> and tour news amongst other things.
> **www.rockhall.com** – the Rock and Roll Hall of Fame has an
> outstanding site dedicated to celebrating only the best.
> **www.rocklist.net** – a compilation of lists from the major music
> magazines categorised by year, from the 50s to date, with links
> to the relevant sites.

www.rocknrollzone.com – a good, colourful portal and news site.

World Music

www.fly.co.uk   UK
GLOBAL MUSIC CULTURE
An excellent e-zine devoted to world music, with sections by continent including features and links and a search facility.

See also:
www.africanmusic.org – the African Music Encyclopaedia.
www.frootsmag.com – a highly rated e-zine.
www.worldmusiccentral.org – excellent portal and information site.

Music Information

www.clickmusic.co.uk   UK

EVERYTHING YOU NEED TO KNOW ABOUT MUSIC
This is great for all music fans. It's newsy and has quick access to details on any particular band, with tickets, downloads, gigs and gossip. Shopping is straightforward: just click on the store or use the search engine to find something specific.

www.musicsearch.com   US
THE INTERNET'S MUSIC SEARCH ENGINE
Musicsearch is a directory site with thousands of links to reviewed music sites, the search facility has improved and you can offer up sites to be included. See also **www.musites.com** which is a little inconsistent but occasionally very good.

www.bl.uk/collections/sound-archive/cat.html   UK
BRITISH LIBRARY SOUND ARCHIVE
This catalogue contains over 3.5 million entries; there are only a few sounds you can listen to online, but more are being put on the site. You can find out how to get a listening appointment and order copies of the sounds, music or oral recordings. For more sound effects check out **www.sounddogs.com**

See also:
www.gracenote.com – what looks like a corporate site also holds the CD database. Click on the CDDC tab and you get

access to an excellent search facility which also offers relevant links to bands and labels.

www.thisdayinmusic.com – what happened on a particular day plus quizzes and information on music history, although you have to join to make the most of it.

www.useyourears.co.uk – unusual site providing an extensive music portal, everything from instrumental help to recording studios.

Learning Music

Long-winded though the site URL is, it's worth paying a visit to **www.si.umich.edu/chico/instrument/** *where you can find a music encyclopaedia in which you can sample the sound of many instruments.*

www.youthmusic.org.uk   UK
MUSIC SUPPORT

Youth Music is a charity that aims to provide music learning and opportunities to hear live, high quality music to those who may not have the means to hear it or see it performed. They have several interesting projects and you can learn about how to get involved here.

See also:

www.abachamusic.com.au – who offer a fun approach to music theory.

www.bbc.co.uk/music/learning – help from the Beeb.

www.bbc.co.uk/music/parents – learn hope to motivate your child with music.

www.playmusic.org – great for kids to learn about the orchestra with audio clips to hear the sounds produced by the different instruments.

www.musictheory.net – good, free music theory lessons.

Sites for Specific Instruments
General

www.backstreet.co.uk – equipment hire and shop from this London-based studio.

www.electricbluesclub.co.uk – hours of fun digging around on this site, with links and online lessons for a range of instruments plus masses of info on a variety of styles not just blues.

www.harmony-central.com – all sorts of instruments reviewed and rated.

www.music4worship.co.uk – a music store covering a wide range of musical instruments.

www.musicianshop.com – another musical instrument store, especially good for guitarists.

www.starland.co.uk – musical instruments by mail order, some good offers too.

www.yamaha-europe.com – information on their full range of instruments, including digital pianos and a range of music technology gear plus info on their music schools and teaching system.

Electronic

http://nmc.uoregon.edu/emi – great introduction to electronic music and instruments.

www.etcetera.co.uk – download all the latest sampling and music creation software here.

www.kvr-vst.com – technical site with downloads and reviews of the latest hardware and software.

www.synthzone.com – excellent source for articles, links and reviews for all things to do with electronic music making.

Guitar

www.accessrock.com – free interactive web site for aspiring rock guitarists, great range of lessons.

www.guitarsite.com – masses of information.

www.guitarstrings.co.uk – a guitar specialist shop.

www.ultimate-guitar.com – brilliant guitar site with news, reviews, lessons (including complex effects) but maybe best of all, over one thousand tabs.

Keyboard

http://learnpianoonline.com/login.html – some free lessons.

www.pianonanny.com – complete piano course.

www.pianoshop.co.uk – masses of links, pianos for sale and information on learning.

Percussion

www.drummersweb.com – drummer's delight.
www.giggear.co.uk – a well-stocked shop for all the band's needs.
www.rhythmweb.com – the place to go for all things percussive.

Strings

www.violin-world.com – complete resource for all string instruments.

Wind and Brass

www.brass-forum.co.uk – serving the Brass community!
www.phys.unsw.edu.au/jw/woodwind.html – a look at how woodwind instruments work.
www.saxophone.org – great for info and links.
www.wfg.sneezy.org – woodwind.

Sheet Music

www.freehandmusic.com   US
DOWNLOAD SHEET MUSIC
Well-designed site where you can download music from a wide variety of styles including pop, Christian, country, Broadway, jazz and classical; you have to pay but there are some freebies.

See also:
www.musicroom.com – a huge range and free postage in the UK, excellent site.
www.sheetmusicarchive.net – specialising in classical music.
www.sheetmusicplus.com – US-oriented but a wide range and some new stuff.

Lyrics and Songs

www.lyrics.com   US
THE WORDS TO HUNDREDS OF SONGS
There are songs from hundreds of bands and artists including Oasis, Madonna, Britney Spears and Queen. You'll have to ignore the directory section that makes up most of the page, there's an A–Z listing at the bottom. Hopefully they'll redesign soon.

Other good lyric sites:
http://home.iae.nl/users/kdv/en/ring.htm – a web ring for lyrics.
www.azlyrics.com – over 50,000 lyrics.
www.britishacademy.com – support and advice for songwriters.
www.letssingit.com – big archive plus karaoke!
www.songfacts.com – information, background and trivia about thousands of songs.

www.kissthisguy.com   US
MISHEARD LYRICS
Mr Misheard lists all those lyrics that you thought were being sung but in reality you were just not quite listening properly. This time we liked the Red Hot Chili Peppers' lyric 'Can't stop the spirits when they need you' misheard as 'Can't stop the ferrets when they need food', but there are hundreds more.

Concerts, Clubs and Tickets

www.bigmouth.co.uk   UK
UK'S MOST COMPREHENSIVE GIG GUIDE
UK based, with lots of links to band sites, news, events listing and information on what's up and coming. Great search facilities and the ability to buy tickets make this a really useful site for gig lovers everywhere. It's geared to rock and pop though.

www.ticketmaster.co.uk   UK

TICKETS FOR EVERYTHING
Book tickets for just about anything and you can run searches by venue, city or date. The site is split into five key sections:

Theatre – theatre, drama and musical
Performing arts – comedy, classical and opera
Music – gigs, jazz, clubs, rock and pop
Attraction – shows, anything from Disney on Ice to air shows to museums
Sports – tickets for virtually every sporting occasion

See also **www.seetickets.com**

www.efestivals.co.uk   UK
FESTIVALS
Excellent place to review and preview festivals, there are photo galleries and you can buy online too.

www.uk-clubbing-directory.co.uk   UK

Find out about your local hot spots, link through to their site and
buy tickets. You'll also get the low-down on events, holidays and
international music festivals. See also **www.uk-cl.co.uk** which is
great for links.

Nature and the Environment

*The Internet offers charities and organisations a chance to highlight
their work in a way that is much more creative than ever before, it also
offers the chance for us to get in-depth information on those species
and issues that interest us.*

Wildlife and Environmental Organisations

www.panda.org   UK

WWF

The official site for WWF with information on projects designed
to save the world's endangered species by protecting their
environment. You can find out about how to support their work,
how to get involved, the latest news, information on the key
projects and some great photos. There is also some good kids'
and educational material embedded in the news section. An
American organisation called the National Wildlife Fund has a
similar excellent site at **www.nwf.org**

www.foe.co.uk   UK

FRIENDS OF THE EARTH

Not as worthy as you might imagine, this site offers a stack of
information on food, pollution, green power, protecting wildlife in
your area and the latest campaign news.

www.envirolink.org   US

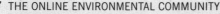
THE ONLINE ENVIRONMENTAL COMMUNITY

A huge site focused on personal involvement in environment
issues. There are several well-categorised sections including:
organisations, educational resources, jobs, governmental
resources, actions you can take to help and environment links.
There is also a good search facility on environment-related
topics.

www.environment-agency.gov.uk   UK
THE GOVERNMENT'S RESPONSE
The Environment Agency's site offers information on the latest
initiatives and research. It also has sections on air quality,
conservation, flooding, waste and navigation. There is help on
how to improve the environment plus contact details regarding
any issues you have.

www.planetdiary.com   US
WHAT'S REALLY HAPPENING ON THE PLANET
Every week Planetdiary monitors and records world events
in geological, astronomical, meteorological, biological and
environmental terms and relays them back via this web site. It's
done by showing an icon on a map of the world, which you then
click on to find out more. Although very informative, a visit can
leave you a little depressed.

www.biodiversityhotspots.org   US
 CONSERVATION INTERNATIONAL
A pleasure to visit, this site is a great example of how the Internet
can be used to inform us about what is going on in the world.
It highlights 34 places in the world where wildlife and the
environment are in a particularly perilous state. Click on the
interactive map and you get taken to a beautifully produced micro
site with as much information as you need on each place. It shows
how you can help and you can sign up for the newsletter too.

http://earthobservatory.nasa.gov   US
 THE EARTH FROM ABOVE
Really outstanding photography and detailed information on the
environment presented in an interesting and thought-provoking
way. Owned by NASA, the site offers sections on the
atmosphere, land and air as well as the latest news stories.

www.projectearth.com   US
NAVIGATING TOWARDS A BETTER ENVIRONMENT
Outstanding site devoted to recognising the damaging effect man
has on the environment and pointing the way towards a better
future.

http://earth.google.com   US
GOOGLE EARTH
Download the program and you get access to an amazing array
of geographical and mapping tools. It's addictive stuff with

incredible detail and in 3-D too. The Mac version is now available and there are more sophisticated versions for those who want to pay.

http://tolweb.org/tree/phylogeny.html   US

MAPPING THE TREE OF LIFE
A good attempt to show the animal kingdom graphically, its goal is 'to contain a page with pictures, text, and other information for every species and for each group of organisms, living or extinct'. Like Wikipedia it's put together by hundreds of enthusiasts and experts.

For more or specialised information on ecology, nature and the environment try these sites:

http://wcs.org – home of New York's Wildlife Conservation Society who have a very informative site.

www.ace.mmu.ac.uk/eae – most of your questions answered here at the excellent Encyclopaedia of Atmospheric Environment.

www.airquality.co.uk – a site devoted to monitoring the air quality around the UK.

www.cat.org.uk – a messy site from the Centre for Alternative Technology, but contains good information.

www.defra.gov.uk – the Department for Environment, Food and Rural Affairs has a newsy site that offers lots of information and does it pretty well when you consider the size of their brief.

www.environmentwebsites.co.uk – a portal for environmental sites.

www.ewg.org – an excellent and detailed site from the Environmental Working Group, dedicated to the fight against pollution – warning, contains some scary information.

www.genewatch.org – an organisation devoted to monitoring the development and effect of GM plants and other uses of gene modification and testing.

www.greenpeace.org – find out about their latest activities and how to get involved.

www.grist.org – an e-zine devoted to nature and the environment. It's well written and in places pretty funny. You can have your say in the forums and catch up with the latest news.

www.ifaw.org – home of the excellent International Fund for Animal Welfare.

www.jncc.gov.uk – find out what advice the government is receiving from the Joint Nature Conservation Committee. Very detailed and technical reports available, which may be of use to campaigners.

N

www.nhpa.co.uk – staggeringly beautiful nature photography from a commercial site; although you have to pay for images it at least reminds us what it's all about.

www.nationalgeographic.com/animals – excellent site with details of their travels and photos, it's a shame that the '.co.uk' site is no more than an advert for their TV channel as there are many aspects of the US site that could be replicated in the UK one.

www.scorecard.org – the facts on local pollution; US-orientated, but an informative site.

www.traffic.org – a campaigning site working against the illegal and sometimes appalling trade in animals throughout the world.

www.ufaw.org.uk – improving animal welfare using scientific knowledge.

www.wri.org – World Resources Institute promoting effective campaigning for a far better world.

Climate Change

The hot topic of the moment, here are some sites that provide the scientific evidence to enable you to make up your own mind.

www.bbc.co.uk/climate – excellent overview.

www.campaignncc.org – join the Campaign against Climate Change and become an activist.

www.climatecrisis.net – the companion site to Al Gore's film *The Inconvenient Truth* has downloads, information and advice on what you can do to make a difference.

www.climatehotmap.org – a map showing temperature fluctuations and other indicators of climate change.

www.epa.gov/climatechange – pages from the US Environmental Protection Agency, providing good, detailed information with a US emphasis – is anyone out there listening? Excellent references for further reading.

www.exploratorium.edu/climate – excellent interactive museum site with lots of graphs and maps and information about the research.

www.globalgiving.com/climatechange.html – give to projects that help slow the rate of climate change.

www.guardian.co.uk/climatechange – extensive collection of relevant articles and comment covering the political response as well as the scientific view. The Special Reports are excellent.

www.royalsoc.ac.uk/landing.asp?id=1278 – scholarly articles and opinion.

www.thec-changetrust.org – a charity that enables you to off-set your carbon emissions by planting trees in British woodlands.

Eco Help

www.coralcay.org   UK

HOW YOU CAN JOIN IN
In Coral Cay's words its aim is 'providing resources to help sustain livelihoods and alleviate poverty through the protection, restoration and management of coral reefs and tropical forests'. Sign up for an expedition or a science project in Malaysia or the Philippines.

See also:
www.ecoclub.com – a network providing a wealth of information about all aspects of ecotourism.
www.eco-portal.com – a messy but huge database and links site.
www.ecotourism.org – American site with useful links.
www.ecovolunteer.com – if you want to give your services to a specific animal benefit project.
www.environmentjob.co.uk – jobs and volunteer work in the environment industry.

N

Natural Phenomena and Geology

http://library.thinkquest.org/C003603   US

FORCES OF NATURE
An amazing site that covers all the known natural disasters, giving background information, simulations and multimedia explanations with experiments for you to try at home.

www.em-dat.net   US

EMERGENCY DISASTERS DATABASE
Browse through the dispassionate facts covering disasters both man-made and natural, you can search by country, region and type of disaster. Fascinating and disturbing, believe it or not, there's a running commentary called 'disasters of the week'.

See also:
http://gldss7.cr.usgs.gov – the Earthquake Hazards Program has plenty of information on earthquakes. In fact it's amazing how many there are.

http://serc.carleton.edu/NAGTWorkshops/visualization/ collections/tsunami.html – an amazing site devoted to tsunami of December 2004 with excellent animation.

http://volcano.und.nodak.edu – all you need to know about volcanoes, the site is poor but the photos are spectacular.

www.discoveringfossils.co.uk – excellent guide to the UK's geology and where to go fossil hunting.

www.exploratorium.edu – Museum of Science, Art and Human Perception has an excellent site particularly on seismic science.

www.fema.gov/kids – Federal Emergency Management Association site aimed at young kids.

www.geographyiq.com – comprehensive geography site.

www.geology.com – an American site covering the whole subject.

www.naturalhazards.org – interesting site with basic information on natural phenomena and links.

www.phenomena.org.uk – a very British view of natural phenomena and the more enjoyable for it.

www.rockwatch.org.uk – an ebullient site aimed at bringing geology to life for young people.

www.tsunami.org – the Pacific Tsunami Museum with stories, photos and links.

www.ukfossils.co.uk – excellent and informative site on where to find fossils in the UK, includes information on geology too.

Dinosaurs

The definitive, glossy site on dinosaurs has yet to appear, but combined, the following have stacks of information and pictures. See also the sites on geology above, particularly those relating to fossils.

http://internt.nhm.ac.uk/jdsml/nature-online/   UK
dino-directory

NATURAL HISTORY MUSEUM
They could start by getting a better address, as this is a good starting point for information on dinosaur classification with timelines and geographic distribution. It's low tech with line drawings; they direct you to Wikipedia for more detailed information on species.

See also:
http://dino.lm.com – development of this site has stalled, but the image gallery is impressive and worth visiting.

www.bbc.co.uk/sn/prehistoric_life – excellent site with lots of features.

www.dinodata.net – easy to use and information-packed, you have to register and wait for full access.

www.dinosauria.com – masses of information and articles for the serious-minded adult and child.

www.search4dinosaurs.com – links to dinosaur artwork categorised by type.

www.strangescience.net – an interesting site showing how scientists have developed the latest theories about dinosaurs and made mistakes along the way.

www.prehistoricplanet.com – under development with interactive images, news and features. Promises much, watch this space.

www.ucmp.berkeley.edu/diapsids/dinolinks.html – horrid URL but phenomenal list of dino-related web links.

Nature Information and Media

www.nhm.ac.uk   UK

 THE NATURAL HISTORY MUSEUM
A superb user-friendly web site that covers everything from ants to eclipses. You can get the latest news, check out exhibitions, take a tour, browse the Dinosaur database or explore the wildlife garden. There are details on the collections, galleries, educational resources and contacts for answers to specific questions. See also the Smithsonian National Museum of Natural History, which also has a great site at **www.mnh.si.edu**

www.bbc.co.uk/nature   UK
WILDLIFE EXPOSED
A brilliant nature offering from the BBC with sections on key wildlife programmes and animal groups. The information is good and enhanced by video clips.

Other nature sites worth checking out are …
www.enature.com – an American magazine site with a huge amount of information and features on all aspects of nature.
www.naturephotographers.net – a magazine devoted to wildlife photography with a great selection of shots and advice.
www.virtualparks.org – just stunning photography from the parks of Canada and the US.

N

Rainforest and Plant Conservation

www.rainforest-alliance.org   UK
RAINFOREST INFORMATION
Excellent for information and links to related sites, with lots of
news and background on major rainforest projects. A good place
to start any research.

See also:
http://ths.sps.lane.edu/biomes/rain3/rain3.html – a long URL
but worth a visit for the information it contains. It also offers
possibly the worst combination of background and text colours
we've seen so be prepared!
www.greenpeace.org.uk/forests – a campaigning site from
Greenpeace aimed at exposing the tragic loss of rain forests
throughout the globe.
www.plantlife.org.uk – devoted to saving wild habitats and
conserving botanically important sites.
www.rainforestconcern.org – home of a charity which aims to
protect the world's rainforests. The site gives an overview of the
problems faced and details on how you can help.
www.rainforestlive.org.uk – a UK education site, it could do
with an update, but there is some good stuff here.
www.rainforestweb.org – a comprehensive portal devoted to all
things to do with rainforests.
www.rbgkew.org.uk/conservation – the conservation schemes
from the Royal Botanical Gardens at Kew.

British Nature

www.naturenet.net   UK

UK COUNTRYSIDE, NATURE AND CONSERVATION
Ignore the rather twee graphics and you'll find a great deal of
information about nature in the UK. Their interests include:
countryside law, upkeep of nature reserves, voluntary work,
education and environmental news. There is also a useful guide
to planning regulations. You can also search the site for specifics
and there is a good set of links to related sites.

www.uksafari.com   UK
BRITAIN'S WILDLIFE
A good overview of the UK's wild animals with a section on each
and tips on wildlife gardening, a photo gallery and lots of additional
stuff like film clips, facts and figures and information on nature sites.

www.naturescalendar.org.uk UK

UK PHENOLOGY NETWORK

Phenology is the study of nature through recurring natural phenomena; this site aims to catalogue all that's relevant to the UK. It has several excellent sections, in particular the children's and the one devoted to mapping, where you can create your own records.

www.wildlifebritain.com UK

ONLINE GUIDE

A 'growing' guide to the UK's wildlife. Comprehensive and with some good articles addressing the latest debates.

See also:

www.bbc.co.uk/nature/animals/wildbritain/springwatch – join Bill Oddie's Springwatch initiative, which involves recording the advent of spring in your locality. There's Autumnwatch too now.

www.british-trees.com – information on native trees with good links.

www.englishnature.org.uk – supply maps, photos and information on all our nature reserves and explains why reserves are so important – all on an excellent site.

www.forestry.gov.uk – Forestry Commission has details of its work and how you can help sustain our woods and forests.

www.habitas.org.uk – Ulster Museum has a huge resource on the flora and fauna of Northern Ireland.

www.snh.org.uk – excellent site on Scotland's nature and heritage.

www.swt.org.uk – home of the Scottish Wildlife Trust.

www.treecouncil.org.uk – inspiring a love of trees, it comes with a section on some of our favourite trees.

www.wildlifetrusts.org – one of our most wide-ranging nature charities, highlighting the work of the 47 Wildlife Trusts and 2,500 nature reserves around the UK.

www.woodland-trust.org.uk – dedicated to protecting our woodland heritage.

General and Endangered Animals

www.arkive.org UK

RAISING AWARENESS OF ENDANGERED SPECIES

Sponsored by the Wildscreen Trust this site's aim is to catalogue and picture all the world's endangered species and has a separate section for the UK. Each animal and plant has a page devoted to it giving details on how and where it lives, including pictures and movie clips. You can help by donating pictures and film.

For further ecological sites devoted to endangered species try:
www.animalaid.org.uk – join a campaign to stop exploitation of animals.
www.endangeredspecie.com – American site with lots of good photography and background on the causes of species decline.
www.rarespecies.org – an organisation that devises conservation strategies, very interesting to find out how it's done.
www.redlist.org – the Red List of critically endangered and threatened species.

And a few more animal related sites:
http://digimorph.org – a collection of x-ray and computer generated photos of many animals including dinosaurs, fascinating stuff.
http://netvet.wustl.edu/e-zoo.htm – a fun portal site devoted to the animal kingdom, good for research and homework.
www.wildlifesearch.com – links to sites on almost every animal.

Evolution

www.pbs.org/kcet/shapeoflife   US
THE RISE OF THE ANIMAL KINGDOM
The site is based on the content of the PBS series *The Shape of Life*, which shows how science has enabled man to trace his history back to the sponge. Fascinating and with excellent photographs.

See also:
http://evolution.berkeley.edu – take Evolution 101 for a general overview, then there is masses of further information.
www.talkorigins.org – An award-winning Usenet newsgroup devoted to the creation vs evolution debate.

Apes and Early Humans

www.becominghuman.org   US
HUMAN ORIGINS
A superb site detailing the progress of human evolution, showing our development in an interactive and enthralling way. Beautifully illustrated throughout; however, it can be a little slow, so best seen by broadband users.

For other sites that feature our evolution and our nearest relatives try:

www.archaeologyinfo.com/evolution.htm – good site on human evolution, the Hall of Skulls is great for showing our development through time.

www.chimps-inc.org – a non-profit organisation devoted to chimpanzees.

www.gorilla.org – home of the Gorilla Foundation and Koko.

www.greatapeproject.org – campaigning on rights for apes.

www.janegoodall.org – very well-put-together site featuring the work of this pioneer with biographical details and information on chimpanzees and how you can help preserve them.

www.unep.org/grasp – the Great Apes Survival Project aims to help preserve the species, specifically orangutans, bonobos, gorillas and chimpanzees.

African Wildlife and the Big Cats

www.africam.com   SOUTH AFRICA

 ALWAYS LIVE, ALWAYS WILD

Web cameras have come a long way and this is one of the best uses of them. There are strategically placed cameras at water holes and parks around Africa and other of the world's wildlife areas, and you can tap in for a look at any time. You have to register to get the best out of it, but even a quick visit is rewarding.

See also:

http://elephant.elehost.com – an excellent elephant-only portal site.

www.5tigers.org – excellent site on tigers and how we can help to save the remaining five species.

www.cheetahspot.com – all you need to know about the cheetah.

www.greatcatadventures.com – an overview of the big cats from a US nature centre.

www.lioncrusher.com – all large carnivores and a good picture archive.

www.wildwatch.com – nice site from a eco-tourism company with good information on animals and eye-witness accounts of interesting sitings. Also information on sustainable development for people too.

Bears

www.bears.org   US
BEAR BELIEFS
An overview of the major species of bears with lots of
background, photos, myths and also detailed information on
their habits and lifestyles.

See also:
http://nationalzoo.si.edu/Animals/GiantPandas – excellent site
on pandas from the Smithsonian.
www.polarbearsinternational.org – the web's most complete
polar bear site! Lots of info and photos too.

Birds

www.birds.com   US
ALL ABOUT BIRDS
An online directory and guide to birds covering both wild and
pets. It's biased towards America but otherwise excellent, except
that it's a bit too commercial.

See also:
www.birdguides.com – informative site with free videos and a
specialist store.
www.birdlinks.co.uk – some 500 bird-related links.
www.birdsofbritain.co.uk – a strong monthly web magazine for
British bird watchers.
www.bto.org – tracking birds and their behaviour.
www.ornithology.com – a good, if serious, site dedicated to wild
birds.
www.rspb.org.uk – the Royal Society for the Protection of Birds
have a nice site detailing what they do, and how you can help.

Insects

www.bugbios.com   US

BUGS AND INSECTS
A beautifully designed site exposing insects as miracles of
nature, with amazing macro-photography, information and links.
See also **www.virtualinsectary.com** which contains some great
photography. A visit to **www.buglife.org.uk**, home of the
Invertebrate Conservation Trust is also very informative.

http://butterflywebsite.com US

BUTTERFLYING
Not that great design-wise but an interesting site on butterflies.
Although it's biased towards the US, it does have sections that
cover Britain and it also has a very good links section. For
another excellent site devoted to British butterflies go to
www.butterfly-conservation.org who hold information on all
resident and migrating butterflies and moths found in the UK.

Marine

www.wdcs.org UK

WHALE AND DOLPHIN SOCIETY
All the latest news and developments in the fight to save whales
and dolphins. There's also information on them, how and where
they live, a 'Sightings and Strandings' section and details of how
to book a whale-watching holiday.

www.marlin.ac.uk UK

MARINE LIFE INFORMATION
Fabulous resource that will stop you going into the sea forever,
just look at the sea slug pictures. There's lots of serious
information about species, habitat, biological traits, marine
environmental data plus an excellent learning zone for children.

See also:
www.flmnh.ufl.edu/fish – the University of Florida's Department
of Ichthyology has a good site where you can find an overview of
all things fishy plus links and a good selection of photographs.
www.seasky.org – one man's love affair with the sea and space.
In the sea half you'll find some excellent sections on such things
as coral reef and ocean exploration.
www.seawatchfoundation.org.uk – here you can learn more
about cetaceans, and their sightings around the UK.

Reptiles

www.herpconbio.org US

HERPETOLOGICAL CONSERVATION
Serious site on how to look after reptiles and related species in
the wild. Its not well designed but the links pages are good and
there are some high quality articles too.

See also

http://reptilis.net/wordpress – a messy but information rich blog.
http://www.whozoo.org/herps/herpphylogeny.html – the reptile family tree.
www.chelonia.org – conservation of turtles and tortoises.
www.crocodilian.com – all you need to know about crocs and their relatives.

Zoos and Safari Parks

www.safaripark.co.uk   UK
SAFARI ONLINE
A detailed site on the UK's safari parks including opening times, animal information and facts on endangered species.

www.sandiegozoo.org   US
SAN DIEGO ZOO
Probably the best zoo site. You can get conservation information, check out the latest arrivals and browse their excellent photo gallery. The highlights are definitely the zoo cams featuring pandas, elephants, apes and polar bears (remember the 8-hour time difference).

http://library.thinkquest.org/11922/index.htm   US
VIRTUAL ZOO
Visit the African wildlife section, followed by cats corner, monkey island or ocean life and more. Information is given on all these animals and lots of lovely pictures; plus the animals remain in the wild.

Other good zoo sites:
www.bristolzoo.co.uk – good looking and fun for kids.
www.dublinzoo.ie – slow but good content.
www.londonzoo.co.uk – excellent and comprehensive zoo site, also covers Whipsnade Wildlife Park.
www.marwell.org.uk – masses to see and do.
www.mbayaq.org – beautiful site from Monterey Bay Aquarium with web cams, online field guide and info on ocean research projects.

www.bornfree.co.uk   UK
ZOO CHECK
Zoo Check is a charity whose mission is to promote Born Free's core belief that wildlife belongs in the wild. They expose the

suffering of captive wild animals and investigate neglect and cruelty. They want tighter legislation and the phasing out of all traditional zoos. If you want to know more then this is where to go.

News and the Media

The standard of web sites in this sector is usually very high, making it difficult to pick out one or two winners, just find one which appeals to you and you won't go far wrong. Nowadays it's easy to create your own news feeds, in this section we show you how.

World News

www.sky.com/skynews   UK

WITNESS THE EVENT
Sky News has fast developed a reputation for excellence and that is reflected in their web site. It has a well-rounded news service with good coverage across the world as well as the UK. You can view news clips, listen to news items or just browse the site. There are special sections on sport, business, technology and even a few games.

www.bbc.co.uk/news   UK
FROM THE BBC
As you'd expect, the BBC site is excellent – similar to Sky but without the adverts. You can also get the news in several languages and tune into the World Service or any of their radio stations.

www.channel4.com/news   UK
AWARD-WINNING NEWS
High quality journalism reflects the independent and serious nature of their news coverage. There are some interesting links and a forum – you can even register to receive 'Snowtext' from Jon Snow himself.

www.itn.co.uk   UK
INDEPENDENT TELEVISION NEWS
As well as links to independent TV, ITN houses the world's largest TV-based video archive and is also home to the ITN stills collection. It's not cheap (video starts at £100 and stills at £25 for a one-off use) and is aimed at the professional market, but

N

there is some amazing stuff here and much you can watch on the site for free.

www.cnn.com
US

THE AMERICAN VIEW
CNN is superb on detail and breaking news with masses of background information on each story. It has plenty of feature pieces too. However, it is biased towards the American audience, for a similar service try **www.abcnews.com**

www.newsnow.co.uk
UK

NEWS NOW!
A superb news-gathering and information service that you can tailor to your needs and interests. The layout is confusing at first but it allows you to flick between latest headlines from 3,000 leading news sources without visiting each site separately, you can then read their choice of stories in full on the publishers' web sites. It's updated every five minutes!

www.ananova.co.uk
UK

NEWS ON THE MOVE
Ananova has been changed a few times and in the latest guise you get a well-put-together site that is much clearer than some. They've also teamed up with Orange to produce a mobile text messaging news service.

http://v.moreover.com
US

DYNAMIC CONTENT
With real-time news and rumour reporting, Moreover has become the news site of choice for many business people and journalists as it enables them to target the type of news and information they are looking for, saving time and effort all round. You need to subscribe to gain access.

http://english.aljazeera.net
UAE

AL JAZEERA
The English version of the well-known Arab news agency. It's very good for world events and as you'd expect outstanding when it comes to gaining an insight into the Arab world. See also **www.arabnews.com** the Arab English language daily.

http://news.google.com   US
GOOGLE NEWS
Google's news service gleans and sorts information from over
4,500 sources. It's fast and the results are bang on.

Other news sites worth a visit are:
www.anorak.co.uk – humorous newspaper reviews.
www.copydesk.co.uk – a very good blog site devoted to news
and popular culture, it's great for news links too.
www.economist.co.uk – business, world events and in-depth
reports.
www.findarticles.com – an article search engine from
LookSmart with access to some 900 publications.
www.irishnews.com – a competent site from *Irish News*.
www.newseum.org – an attempt to archive US newspapers.
www.nuzgeeks.com – excellent links.
www.positivenews.org.uk – for a positive spin on the news.
www.private-eye.co.uk – some of the best features from the
mag, but not much news if truth be told.
www.publist.com – a news search engine covering over
150,000 titles world-wide.
www.reuters.co.uk – strong site from this world-renowned news
agency. Those with broadband can benefit from their excellent
TV news feeds.
www.salon.com – pithy commentary from this well respected
site, with regular features and some excellent articles.
www.theregister.co.uk – for technology news.
www.time.com – an excellent site from *Time* magazine.
www.topix.net – a news collation site which is exceptional for
American news.
www.worldflash.com – download a news ticker and get the
latest news as it happens.
www.worldnews.com – comprehensive doesn't do this site
justice, it's excellent regionally too, although there is a US bias.

Events and Future News

www.worldflash.com   US
NOW FOR THE REAL NEWS
One of the most visited sites on the web. It's a pain to use, but
the gossip and tips about upcoming features in the papers make
it worthwhile. One of its best features is its superb set of links to
other news sources.

www.foreignreport.com   UK

PREDICT THE FUTURE

Owned by Janes, the Foreign Report team attempt to pick out trends and happenings that might lead to bigger international news events. Browsing through their track record shows they're pretty good at it too.

Newspapers Online

www.telegraph.co.uk   UK

THE *TELEGRAPH*

The *Telegraph* has the best site for news and layout with all its sections mirrored very effectively on the site.

Other major newspapers with sites worth a visit include:
www.dailymail.co.uk – some good articles and features that reflect the ethos of the newspaper pretty accurately.
www.guardian.co.uk – clean site with lots of added features and guides.
www.independent.co.uk – good online debate as well as news.
www.thesun.co.uk – very good representation of the paper with all you'd expect.
www.timesonline.co.uk – no surprises here.

www.fish4news.co.uk   UK

LOCAL NEWS MADE EASY

An outstanding web site, just type in your postcode and back will come a collated local 'newspaper' with regional news headlines, sport and links to the source paper sites and small ads. Also see **www.newspapersoc.org.uk** and go to the 'newspaper' to find your local paper.

www.thepaperboy.com   AUSTRALIA

Can't be bothered to sift through the papers for information? The paperboy will do it for you using a good search facility. You can sign up for RSS and listen to radio news via the site too.

RSS – Creating your Own News Feed

RSS or Really Simple Syndication is one of the latest Internet toys and it enables you to create your own news feeds or newspaper, tailoring them to your tastes. You can even share them with friends and family. First you download your 'aggregator' program (see below for the list) then look out for sites that offer a feed; they usually have an RSS or

XML sign at the bottom of the page or an orange button. Most major sites have them, while some programs and sites allow you to set up your own.

http://uk.my.yahoo.com   UK
MY YAHOO
Probably the simplest way to construct your own news feed, sign up then follow the well-written instructions. It's pretty easy to maintain; however, you are limited in terms of look and design.

www.feeddemon.com   US
FEED DEMON
Considered to be one of the best RSS newsreader programs, it's certainly very straightforward and easy to set up. It costs $29.95, although you can download a trial version. Everything is explained and for those new to this technology, it's probably the best on the market.

See also:
www.bloglines.com – excellent for creating your own news blog.
www.feedster.com – free and it's relatively easy to set up, although you'll ideally need to know your news feed URLs first.
www.jetbrains.com – home of the Omega Reader, which is highly rated for its ability to find things fast.
www.newsgator.com – synchronise your news gathering with Outlook.
www.newzcrawler.com – hot on Feed Demon's tail as one of the best RSS services. It has the advantage of looking like a familiar e-mail program.
www.sharpreader.net – excellent if you want your news organised by topic.
www.syndic8.com – another news feed and directory site.

www.daypop.com   US
THE NEWS SEARCH ENGINE
Day Pop searches the latest news events using as its source news sites and weblogs. It's continually updating, taking news from the top sites every three hours. We found it variable but it's a lot more selective than Google, for example. It's at its best when a hot new story appears and doubtless it will improve over time.

Online Storage

The internet is become a vast depository for information and if you have huge amounts of data, music and photos clogging up your computer, then you could do worse than visit one of these sites where you can store your files ... usually for a price.

www.xdrive.com   US

5 GIGABYTES FOR FREE
Owned by AOL, XDrive is probably the leader in this field. It's very well laid out, easy to use, secure and comes with free software that enables you to transfer and manage files very easily. How long it remains free we can't say but if you're an AOL user, it's especially useful.

See also:
http://openomy.com – 1GB of storage, free ... for now.
www.allmydata.com – not sure about this one, but there is free space available providing you agree to share some of your PC space, which sort of defeats the object. There are paid for packages up to 100GB though.
www.box.net – basic, good-looking and simple to use – costs start at $4.99 per month for 1GB of storage.
www.ibackup.com – well regarded with lots of extra features and the ability to schedule your transfers if needed; $9.99 per month for 5GB.
www.mediamax.com – 25GB free of charge but there are restrictions and any deviation means charges.

Opticians

Buying glasses and contact lenses online isn't as daft as you'd think, there are great savings to be had ...

www.glassesdirect.co.uk   UK

FROM £15
A well-designed site with sections on standard, rimless, semi-rimless and bendable glasses. There's also advice on how to interpret your prescription and what sort of frame would suit. You can order trial glasses to see if the frames fit comfortably too.

See also:

www.allaboutvision.com – US site providing all you need to know about eyes and vision.

www.antiquespectacles.co.uk – maybe you'd rather go for an antique pair?

www.boots.co.uk/bootsopticians – advice-laden section, you can book an appointment for an eye test.

www.glassesonspec.co.uk – upload a photo and try on virtual glasses until you find a pair that suits you.

www.optical.org – home of the regulatory body for opticians in the UK.

www.postoptics.co.uk – eye-care products and contact lenses by post.

www.privatehealth.co.uk/hospitaltreatment/find-a-treatment/laser-eye-surgery – the low down on laser eye surgery.

www.specs2go.co.uk – good range and money back guarantee.

www.specsavers.co.uk – see their whole range of frames and contact lenses; book an appointment.

www.thecontactlensshop.com – aim to supply the cheapest contact lenses in the UK. Free delivery.

Organiser and Diary

O

www.opendiary.com   UK

THE ONLINE DIARY FOR THE WORLD

Your own personal organiser and diary, easy to use, genuinely helpful and totally anonymous. Simply register and away you go but follow the rules faithfully or you get deleted. Use it as you would any diary, go public or just browse other entries. Also check out the calendar being developed by Google.

See also:

http://uk.calendar.yahoo.com – Yahoo has an excellent, free and easy-to-use calendar facility.

http://voo2do.com – prioritise your tasks the easy way.

www.backpackit.com – organise yourself and your friends with this wide-ranging service.

www.calendars.net – create your own calendar here, especially good for web masters.

www.calendarzone.com – information on calendars, categorised by subject from astrology to the religious.

www.datereminder.co.uk – never forget a birthday or anniversary again, just load them in here and you'll get reminded near the time.
www.filofax.co.uk – if you can't live without the real thing.
www.livejournal.com – download your own journal and customise it to suit.
www.supercalendar.com – good for groups and businesses as well as individuals but it costs around £12 per annum.
www.tadalist.com – simple, sharable to-do lists.
www.yourorganiser.com.au – good-looking site, easy to use with a personal or group organiser facility.

Over 50s

If you're over 50 then you're part of the fastest growing group of Internet users, and some sites have cottoned on to the fact with specific content just for you.

Links

www.50connect.co.uk   UK

LIVE LIFE TO THE FULL
A very strong portal site with masses of information and links covering a wide range of topics. It's incredibly useful; however, there are plenty of annoying adverts to go with it.

See also:
www.age-net.co.uk – another portal site but one that takes a magazine-style approach.
www.laterlife.com – a comprehensive site with lots of links and advice in many categories.
www.lifes4living.co.uk – an upbeat site dedicated to chat and links, some good offers too.
www.seniority.co.uk – a very comprehensive offering covering all you are likely to need with advice and links. Not exactly the most inspiring design though.
www.silversurfers.net – not the easiest site to get to grips with but it has a huge number of links in over 50 categories.
www.silversurfersday.org – find out about this annual event.

Magazines, Fun and Advice

www.saga.co.uk   UK

THE SAGA GROUP
While this is a commercial organisation aimed at the over 50s, it offers much in the way of advice, help and information in key areas such as health, travel and money; plus the magazine is excellent.

See also:
http://notdeadyet.co.uk – for blogs, rants, classified and chat.
www.theoldie.co.uk – *The Oldie* magazine, which is great fun.
www.togs.org – where devoted fans of Terry Wogan meet.
www.over50s.com – a well-designed magazine-style site, good information and financial advice.

Information and Help

www.over50.gov.uk   UK

ARE YOU OVER 50?
A useful and informative site from the government devoted to helping older people by offering practical help. You'll find many links to government departments and voluntary organisations, plus help guides to download.

www.helptheaged.org.uk   UK

HELP THE AGED
Find out how you can get involved in their work, what they do plus the latest news. You can also go to the online shop and buy all sorts of useful gadgets to make life easier.

www.grandparents-association.org.uk   UK

THE GRANDPARENTS' ASSOCIATION
Offers a newsletter, factsheets, advice and support for grandparents who are caring for their grandchildren as well as those who have lost touch with theirs.

See also:
www.csv-rsvp.org.uk – home of the Retired and Senior Volunteer Programme.
www.experiencecorps.co.uk – voluntary work and a positive use of your experience.
www.hmrc.gov.uk/pensioners/index.htm – income tax details for pensioners.

www.housingcare.org – information on housing options for older people, their relatives and carers.

www.info4pensioners.gov.uk – the government's guide to pensioners' entitlements.

www.age-exchange.org.uk   UK

MAKE YOUR MEMORIES MATTER

Share your experiences and pass them on. Age Exchange aims to 'improve the quality of life for older people by emphasising the value of their memories to old and young, through pioneering artistic, educational, and welfare activities', they are also active in improving care for older people. This site gives details of how you can join in.

Activism

www.ageconcern.co.uk   UK

WORKING FOR ALL OLDER PEOPLE

Learn how to get involved with helping older people, get information and practical advice on all aspects of getting old. You can also make a donation and join one of the many campaigns they are running.

See also

www.agepositive.gov.uk – a government site with information on the latest anti-ageism legislation.

www.caredirections.co.uk – excellent site devoted to rights with the emphasis on care.

www.cspa.co.uk – a campaigning group devoted to getting better pensions, improved NHS facilities, care for the elderly and an end to age discrimination.

www.entitledto.co.uk – work out which benefits you are entitled to claim.

www.natpencon.org.uk – home of the National Pensioners Convention.

www.wiseowls.co.uk – dedicated to tackling ageism, while providing a good community site.

Lifelong Learning

www.hairnet.org   UK

TECHNOLOGY EXPLAINED

So you've bought the PC and now you need to know how to work it properly? Hairnet, which in 2006 changed its name to

Digital Unite, explains all through a series of forums and specific courses designed to help you get the most from technology. See also **www.seniornet.org** which is a pretty boring but comprehensive guide.

www.u3a.org.uk
UK

LIFELONG LEARNING

An organisation working to improve the lives of older people through the concept of life-long learning and learning for the pleasure of it. The site offers details of the subjects covered and how to contact the relevant groups.

Travel

www.saga.co.uk/travel
UK

HOLIDAYS FOR THE OVER 50S

A superbly illustrated and rich site from Saga who've been specialising in holidays for older people for many years. Here you'll find everything from top-quality cruises to weekend breaks.

See also:

http://retiredbackpackers.com – for the older than average back packer ...

www.classicski.co.uk – a skiing operator specialising in mature skiers whether they be beginners or experienced.

www.eldertreks.com – a good site from a specialist in adventure travel for the over 50s.

www.responsibletravel.com – have an excellent range of environmentally sensitive holidays for over 50s in their 'activities' listing.

www.travel55.co.uk – a great database of travel sites specialising in travel for older people.

Parenting

As a source of advice, the Internet has proved its worth, and especially so for parents. As well as information, there are useful sites that filter out the worst of the web and give advice on specific problems. Some of the education web sites, page 117, also have useful resources for parents as do the health sites, page 231. For shopping, see the children's section on page 82 and the general shopping section, starting on page 428. In addition, there is loads of

For Parents

The Good Web Site Guide's Top 10s
of the Internet

1. **www.raisingkids.co.uk** – detailed encyclopedia on bringing up kids
2. **www.babyworld.co.uk** – information and community services
3. **www.babycentre.co.uk** – all the top topics covered
4. **www.parentalk.co.uk** – excellent magazine site
5. **www.nctpregnancyandbabycare.com** – National Childbirth Trust
6. **www.kidshealth.org** – health advice for kids and parents
7. **www.bestbear.co.uk** – childcare help and advice
8. **www.babygoes2.com** – travelling with kids
9. **www.nhsdirect.nhs.uk** – help with ailments
10. **www.miriamstoppard.com** – advice from the leading guru

useful stuff for parents in the travel section on pages 499 and 553 about taking children on holiday and activities to do with the children in the UK.

Advice and Information

www.babyworld.co.uk   UK
BE PART OF IT

Babyworld is an online magazine that covers all aspects of parenthood. There's excellent advice on how to choose the right products for your baby and for the pregnancy itself. The layout is good and it's easy to find information.

www.babycentre.co.uk   UK
A HANDS-ON GUIDE

A superb site with a massive amount of information and links to all aspects of pregnancy, childbirth and early parenthood. The content is provided by experts and you can tailor-make your profile so that you get the right information for you. There's also a series of buying guides to help you make the right decision on baby shopping.

www.babyzone.com
US

THE NORTH AMERICAN WAY

From the massive American site on parenting, here you get a week-by-week account of pregnancy, information on birth and early childhood. The links are very good and there's plenty of information on offer to parents. For more of the same see **www.ivillage.co.uk** which is also well designed and interactive.

www.raisingkids.co.uk
UK

 FROM BIRTH TO …

An information-laden site devoted to helping parents get through the minefield of child raising with sections on every life stage, it's particularly good on parenting teens. You can also ask an expert, and, amongst many sections, there's advice on travel, education and safety.

www.netmums.com
UK

LOCAL INFORMATION

A very useful support site for mums that provides localised information about what's going on and what help is available.

www.ukparents.co.uk
UK

YOUR PARENTING LIFELINE

Chat, experiences, stories and straightforward advice make this site worth a visit – there are competitions, links and plenty of opportunities for interaction.

www.all4kidsuk.com
UK

IF YOU'RE LOOKING FOR SOMETHING TO DO

This aims to be a comprehensive directory covering all your parental needs from activities to schools. It's got an easy-to-use search engine, where you can search by county if you need to.

www.miriamstoppard.com
UK

MIRIAM STOPPARD LIFETIME

An excellent web site from the best-selling author with lots of advice on being a parent, how to cope with pregnancy and keeping yourself and your family healthy. New information is continually being added, so it's very up to date and will become a great resource for parents.

www.parentalk.co.uk
UK

THE SENSIBLE APPROACH

Interesting articles and sensible advice characterise this site.

P

There is a helpful section for working parents and one for employers plus a good links section for expert advice on a wide range of topics. If the advice here isn't enough, you can buy their books or take the course. For another good site with the same aims try **www.parentlineplus.org.uk**

www.parentcentre.gov.uk   UK
THE LOW-DOWN ON EDUCATION
The Parent Centre is for all parents and carers who want to help their child or children to learn. It really covers everything from choosing a school or nursery to detailed information on what a child should learn. It also provides information about the rights and responsibilities of parents in a wider sense, advice and links.

www.babydirectory.com   UK
A–Z OF BEING A PARENT
The Baby Directory catalogue is relevant to most parts of the UK. It lists local facilities plus amenities that care for and occupy your child. The quality of information varies by area though.

www.tommys.org   UK
PREMATURITY, MISCARRIAGE AND STILLBIRTH
Information on getting through some of the tragedies that occur in pregnancy plus details on how you can help.

Other useful sites:
www.allkids.co.uk – a well-categorised portal site covering all things for children including a good shopping directory.
www.arc-uk.org – a charity that helps with antenatal results and the choices that surround them when an abnormality is found.
www.baaf.org.uk – British Association for Adoption and Fostering is a good place to start for anyone thinking of either; plenty of information and great links.
www.babyandkids.co.uk – an American-style advice site aimed at the UK.
www.babynames.com – over 6,500 names to choose from plus other services and lots of adverts!
www.ecobabybasics.com – good site for products and information on environmentally friendly baby products. See also **www.greenbaby.co.uk**
www.ncb.org.uk – home of the National Children's Bureau who provide support for children's charities and organisations.
www.nct.org.uk– a well-designed and informative site from the NCT covering the first year or so.

www.parenting.org.uk – home of Positive Parenting, an organisation that arranges workshops for parents; lots of information on the site too.

www.parentingteens.com – although some of the advice smacks of hometown righteousness, this is a huge and valuable resource for parents of troubled teens, as well as those who just want to get it right.

www.parenthood.com – lots of advice from this US-oriented site.

www.pinkparents.org.uk – support site for lesbian, gay and bisexual parents and parents-to-be and their children. You need to subscribe to get access to all areas.

Family Relationships

Sites of particular interest to fathers are found on page 305 and mothers on page 573.

www.ondivorce.co.uk   UK

MANAGING DIVORCE AND SEPARATION
The first place to go when faced with divorce or separation. There is sound financial, legal, practical and emotional support and excellent links. See also **www.family-solicitors.co.uk**

www.itsnotyourfault.org   UK

SUPPORT FOR CHILDREN AND PARENTS
A useful site with sections for parents, teens and children that attempts to take some of the anguish and guilt out of divorce and separation. See also page 96 and for legal advice, page 300.

www.gingerbread.org.uk   UK

SUPPORT FOR LONE-PARENT FAMILIES
Gingerbread is an established charity run by lone parents with the aim of providing support to lone parents. The site is fun to use and well designed, and is one of the few web sites that is available in several languages. For more advice on being a single parent see **www.oneparentfamilies.org.uk** who have a useful 'helpline' information search facility.

See also:
http://britishdna.co.uk – paternity testing.
www.baaf.org.uk – British Association for Adoption and Fostering work with children separated from their birth families and their carers.

www.blendedfamilybliss.com – offers US-style practical and sympathetic advice.

www.home-start.org.uk – the leading family support charity.

www.napac.org.uk – National Association for People Abused in Childhood.

www.ncds.org.uk – National Council for the Divorced and Separated, information on their network of local clubs.

www.nfm.org.uk – offers mediation services for those facing separation and divorce. Aims to help find solutions to problems before resorting to court.

www.relate.org.uk – relationship counselling for couples or families, face-to-face, online or by phone.

www.reunite.org – a charity specialising in international child abduction provides an impressive site with loads of information.

www.stepfamilies.co.uk – chat with other step-parents, read articles, submit poetry all on an informal, upbeat site.

www.thestepfamilycoach.com – help for newly formed families.

Childcare

www.bestbear.co.uk   UK
MARY POPPINS ONLINE

Select your postcode and they will provide you with a list of reputable childcare agencies or nurseries in your area. There are also homepages for parents, carers and agencies all with information and ideas. There is also a parents' forum. See also **www.sitters.co.uk**

www.childcarelink.gov.uk   UK
SURESTART

Surestart is part of the government's childcare programme and the web site is designed to provide information about childcare options in a given locality. Search by postcode or town name. It also has a good links section.

www.daycaretrust.org.uk   UK
CHILDCARE ADVICE

Daycare Trust is a national childcare charity which works to promote high-quality, affordable childcare for all. This site is designed to give you all the information you need on arranging care for your child; there are sections on finance and news, and you can become a member.

Dealing With Areas of Parental Concern

General

www.childline.org.uk UK
A CHILD'S-EYE VIEW
There's a huge amount of advice on a wide range of issues from
bullying, domestic violence, dealing with death, racism and
exam stress. The advice is aimed at youngsters, but it is worth
parents looking at that advice too.

www.nchafc.org.uk UK
NATIONAL CHILD HELP
A charity aimed at helping children and parents across a wide
range of subjects, issues and problems. A good place to start
getting help.

Alcohol

See the section on drugs and alcohol on page 369.

Allergies

www.anaphylaxis.org.uk UK
ALLERGY AND ANAPHYLAXIS
A useful site with information on food allergies and their
reactions with good alerts and advice for schools and young
adults. Also try the helpful American site **www.anaphylaxis.com**.
For info on E-numbers go to **www.foodag.com**

Bereavement

www.childbereavement.org.uk UK
CHILD BEREAVEMENT TRUST
Support for those who have suffered the loss of a loved one.
There is a section dedicated to families and one for young
people. The Cruse Bereavement Centre also has a site aimed at
young people at **www.rd4u.org.uk**

Bullying

www.bullying.co.uk UK
HOW TO COPE WITH BULLYING
Advice for everyone on how to deal with a bully; there are

sections on tips for dealing with them, school projects, problem pages and links to related sites. Another good site to try is **www.kidscape.org.uk**

Child Protection

www.teachernet.gov.uk/wholeschool/ familyandcommunity/childprotection   UK
KEEP THEM SAFE
Although primarily aimed at teachers, this site gives the low-down on child protection law and policy. For the Government's integrated agenda for the well-being of every child go to **www.everychildmatters.gov.uk**. Should you need advice of reporting a case of child abuse, The Citizen's Advice Bureau has a factsheet at **www.adviceguide.org.uk/ nm/f_child_abuse.pdf**

Childhood Diabetes

http://ndep.nih.gov/diabetes/youth/youth.htm   US
RESOURSES FOR CHILDREN AND PARENTS
A range of downloadable factsheets from the US Department of Health on dealing with diabetes in children, some aimed at parents, others written for children. See also **www.childrenwithdiabetes.com/kids** where children can find a diabetic pen pal and read about the experiences of others, the main section of this site is full of information and support too.

Computers and the Internet

www.netnanny.com   US
INTERNET FILTERING SOFTWARE
ContentWatch filters out unwanted web sites, images and words enabling parents to manage the content that comes into their homes. You can download a free trial from the site. For a free alternative, try **www.naomifilter.org**, a very good internet filtering program aimed at protecting families with children from unwanted nasties.

www.getnetwise.org   US
An industry initiative to 'ensure that internet users have safe, constructive, and educational or entertaining online experiences'. They provide excellent advice for anyone, but their advice for children and parents is particularly helpful. Their quick tips

provide an ideal starting point when discussing safety issues and terms of access with children and teens.

See also:
http://tcs.cybertipline.com – home of the 'Don't believe the type' campaign with advice on how to spot dodgy characters online.
www.iwf.org.uk – the Internet Watch Foundation who combat child online abuse.
www.kidsmart.org.uk – aimed at schools, this is a good course on how to stay safe on the net.
www.missingkids.com/adcouncil – advice to parents on how to spot internet exploitation.
www.netsmartz.org – good advice for staying safe online.
www.parentscentre.gov.uk/usingcomputersandtheinternet – a government site used to promote the benefits of the Internet as an educational tool to parents. Excellent for links.
www.safekids.com – a basic site that is a useful place to go for links and resources if you're worried about your children coming across something unsuitable on the Net.

Disability and Rare Disorders
www.cafamily.org.uk   UK
SUPPORT FOR FAMILIES
A charity that provides support and advice to parents of children with a medical problem or disability. They have information on over 1,000 rare syndromes and can often put families in touch with others facing similar problems. See also the Council for Disabled Children at **www.ncb.org.uk/cdc**

Drugs and Alcohol
www.theantidrug.com   US
TRUTH: THE ANTIDRUG
An outstanding site devoted to the fight against drugs with help for parents and children alike. There's plenty of advice, articles and general information and it's all written in an accessible style, and in several languages.

www.talktofrank.com   UK
TALK TO FRANK
The NHS's drug site has non-judgemental, factual information on all the major recreational drugs with useful information on

what to do in an emergency – or call The National Drugs Helpline 0800 776600. **www.hit.org.uk** or **www.drugscope.org.uk** are good alternatives.

Dyslexia/Dyspraxia

www.bdadyslexia.org.uk   UK
BRITISH DYSLEXIA ASSOCIATION
A good starting point for anyone who thinks that their child might be dyslexic. There is masses of information on dyslexia, choosing a school, a list of local Dyslexia Associations where you can get assessment and teaching, articles on the latest research and educational materials for sale. There is also information on adult dyslexia. For similar material visit **www.dyslexiaaction.org.uk** who also offer testing and teaching through their centres. If you're thinking of opting out and taking the home education route go to **www.dyslexics.org.uk**

www.dyspraxiafoundation.org.uk   UK
DYSPRAXIA EXPLAINED
Information and practical help aimed at anyone who is coping with a dyspraxic child including how to find your local support group and up-to-date research news.

Eating Disorders

www.edauk.com   UK
EATING DISORDERS ASSOCIATION
If you think you have a problem with eating then at this site you can get advice and information. It doesn't replace going to the doctor but it's a place to start. There are helplines – youth is 0845634 7650, others 0845634 1414.

Health

See the section on Health Advice, page 232, and Women's Health on page 576.

www.kidshealth.org/teen   US
IT'S GOT IT COVERED
An excellent American site divided into three sections: parents, kids and teens. It is really comprehensive and a good place to go if you want information about an illness, developmental concern of just some advice. The teen section is particularly good,

especially on food and its relationship to health. Another
excellent site can be found at **www.childrenfirst.nhs.uk**

Law

www.childrenslegalcentre.com UK
FREE LEGAL HELP
A charity that provides free and confidential legal advice and an
information service, which covers all aspects of the law affecting
children and young people. They can help provide advocates in
disputes with the Local Education Authority and campaigns for
children's rights in the UK and overseas. To keep in touch with
policy changes relating to children and young people go to
www.childpolicy.org.uk

Missing Children

www.missingkids.co.uk UK
UK'S MISSING CHILDREN
This site is dedicated to reuniting children with their families.
The details of those missing are based on police and home office
data. You can search by town or date and there's also a section
on those who've got back together.

Also try:
www.fredi.org/anglais/indexen.htm – a French charity devoted
to helping and preventing child abuse and abduction.
www.missingpersons.org – the missing persons helpline 0500
700700.
www.ncmec.org – the National Center for Missing Children, an
American site with a great deal of information.
www.salvationarmy.org.uk – look under 'quick links' for their
family tracing service.

Racism

www.britkid.org UK
DEALING WITH RACISM
A game that shows how different ethnic groups live in the Britain
of today, full of interesting facts and information. There's a
serious side, which has background information on dealing with
racism, information on different races and their religious beliefs.
See also the football-related **www.kickitout.co.uk** which is also
very useful.

Safety

www.childalert.co.uk   UK
CHILD SAFETY
This is about bringing up children in a safe environment;
there are tips, product reviews and a shop, stories, links and
masses of advice and information. Except for the shop, the
site is well designed and it's easy to find things. See also
www.yoursafechild.com

www.childcarseats.org.uk   UK
CAR SAFETY
All you need to know about buying, fitting and using child car
seats.

Sex

*The following sites provide accessible, factual information. The sections
on health, page 231, men, page 305, teens, page 485, and women,
page 576, may also provide relevant information.*

www.playingsafely.co.uk   UK
HERE TO ANSWER YOUR QUESTIONS
Great site that has lots of information on sex as well as games
and links to related sites. The emphasis is on safe sex and
AIDS prevention. See also the Terence Higgins Trust at
www.tht.org.uk. This is the leading AIDS charity.

www.likeitis.org.uk   UK
TELLING IT LIKE IT IS
A really outstanding site from the Marie Stopes Institute giving
good, straight information on all the major issues around sex
and puberty that face teenagers today. The 'Cool or Fool' quiz is
excellent and there's a 'Dear Doctor …' facility too.

www.fpa.org.uk   UK
FAMILY PLANNING ASSOCIATION
Straightforward and informative, you can find out where to get
help and there's a good list of web links too. See also the British
Pregnancy Advisory service at **www.bpas.org**

Speech

www.speechteach.co.uk UK
SPEECH THERAPY
Information, help and advice on what to do if your child has
speech problems or communication difficulties. The site aims to
provide a learning resource for parents and teachers alike.

Stem Cells

www.virginhealthbank.com UK
TO STORE OR NOT TO STORE
An overview of the issues regarding stem cell storage, which
Virgin now offer – at a cost, as do **www.smartcells.com**,
www.futurehealth.co.uk and **www.cells4life.co.uk** – take
your pick. For a scientific overview visit The Royal Society's
investigation of the issues at **www.royalsoc.ac.uk/
landing.asp?id=1202** where in addition to the science and
ethics, there are links to government policy statements and
other related sites.

Stress and Mental Health

www.youngminds.org.uk UK
FOR CHILDREN'S MENTAL HEALTH
There is a wealth of information at the 'info centre' on all aspects
of mental health and related topics. You can also order their
publications and join their campaign for better services and
understanding.

www.isma.org.uk/exams.htm UK
EXAM STRESS
Top tips on coping with exams from the International Stress
Management Association.

Party Organising

In this section you'll find all you need to organise the perfect party.

www.partydomain.co.uk UK
PARTY PARTY!!
Probably the best of the party shop sites with a wide range of
fancy dress gear, lots of themed party ideas and options plus a

party calendar. Shopping is secure with lots of delivery options.

See also:
www.charliecrow.co.uk – a wide range of fancy dress costumes primarily for kids' parties.
www.evite.com – where you can create your own invitations.
www.fancydress.com – masses of fancy dress costumes.
www.justforfun.co.uk – a good selection of party products here.
www.kids-party.com – a great resource, find out all you need to hold a kids' party in your area.
www.partypieces.co.uk – very experienced party suppliers with a wide range of products.
www.printed4u.co.uk – party invitations printed.

Pets

Here's a selection of web sites devoted to pets: shop and information sites, and specialists too.

www.mypetstop.com   UK
MULTINATIONAL PETS
Apparently the only multilingual web site about pets. It's superb for information and health advice as well as links too. It has sections devoted to each type of pet and animal, and each is pretty comprehensive.

For other good online pet information, services and stores visit:
www.allaboutpets.org.uk – excellent advice and care site from the Blue Cross charity.
www.animalpure.co.uk – an attractive store selling a good range of natural, healthy and eco-friendly dog and cat accessories.
www.lostpets.co.uk – an informative site on what to do if you lose your pet includes a lost pet finder service.
www.newpet.com – advice and help for those who are thinking about getting a pet for the first time.
www.petpals.com – at-home pet-care services.
www.petplanet.co.uk – good for the shop and up-to-the-minute news.
www.petsathome.com – a fairly basic site from this pet retailer.
www.petsmiles.com – a good directory site featuring some 55,000 companies.

www.ukpets.co.uk – a directory of pet shops and suppliers, plus advice and a magazine devoted to pets.

Pet Insurance

www.pethealthcare.co.uk   UK

PET INSURANCE

This is a good place to start looking for insurance to cover your vet's bill. It also has lots of good advice on how to look after pets and what to do when you first get a pet.

See also:

www.animalfriends.co.uk – an insurance company that devotes all profits to animal charities.

www.petplan.co.uk – one of the largest pet insurers.

Travel

www.pethealthcare.co.uk   UK

UK HOLIDAYS WITH PETS

This site is devoted to finding holiday accommodation where your pets are always welcome – simply arranged by region, easy. There's also a bookshop and a good set of links.

See also:

www.defra.gov.uk/animalh/quarantine/index.htm – animal quarantine and advice on overseas travel.

www.preferredplaces.co.uk – a holiday specialist with a good 'pets welcome' section.

Animal Charities

www.rspca.org.uk   UK

THE RSPCA

News (some of which can be quite disturbing) and information on the work of the charity plus animal facts and details on how you can help. There's also a good kids' section. It's a good site but a bit tightly packed.

Other charity sites:

www.aht.org.uk – applying clinical and research techniques to help animals.

www.animalrescue.org.uk – fight animal pain and suffering.

P

www.animalrescuers.co.uk – a directory of centres and people who will help distressed animals.
www.animalsanctuaries.co.uk – index of charities and animal rescue centres.
www.bluecross.org.uk – excellent site with information, help and advice.
www.pdsa.org.uk – People's Dispensary for Sick Animals has a good-looking site with details on how to look after pets and how you can help.

www.giveusahome.co.uk   UK
RE-HOMING A PET
A nice idea, a web site devoted to helping you save animals that need to be re-homed; it's got a large amount of information by region on shelters, vets and the animals themselves as well as entertainment for kids.

TV-related

www.channel4.com/petrescue   UK
PET RESCUE
Details of the programme plus information and links on animal charities and sites, there are also stories, games and chat. See also the excellent BBC web pages on pets which can be found at **www.bbc.co.uk/nature/animals/pets**

Sites for Different Species

Birds

www.avianweb.com   US
FOR BIRD ENTHUSIASTS
A massive site devoted to birds, it's especially good for information on parrots. There are sections on species, health and equipment as well as advice on looking after birds.

See also:
www.birdcare.co.uk – lots of articles and advice on avian health.
www.birdfood.co.uk – neat site from a bird food manufacturer.
www.boglinmarsh.com – racing pigeons.
www.parrot-rescue.co.uk – excellent site devoted to rescuing and looking after birds that have out-grown their owners or need help.

www.rspb.org.uk – mainly wild birds but some good advice.
www.theaviary.com – oddly designed American site but one
with lots of information and links.

Cats

www.cats.org.uk   UK
HOME OF CAT PROTECTION
A well-designed and informative site, with advice on caring, re-
homing, news and general advice, and an archive of cat photos
with competitions for the best. The online shop offers delivery in
the UK but charges vary.

See also:
www.catoutofthebag.com – a wide range of cat-related products
from a good-looking site. It also includes things like homewares
and gifts.
www.crazyforkitties.com – nice site devoted to all things cat
and kitty.
www.fabcats.org – a charity devoted to cat care.
www.freddie-street.com – fantastic and funny: the story of the
Freddie Street cats. There's some good information in there too.
www.i-love-cats.com – a directory of cat sites.
www.moggies.co.uk – home of the Online Cat Guide, not an
easy site to use, but it has exceptional links to pet sites.

Dogs

P

www.thekennelclub.org.uk   UK
DOGS OFFICIAL
The place to go for the official line on dogs and breeding with
information on Crufts and links to related web sites, plus shop
and tips on looking after your pooch.

www.dogs.co.uk   UK
COMPLETE DOGS
A comprehensive if slightly unattractive site that seems to have
all bases covered when it comes to dogs – although it's mainly a
good shop. There are also forums and links.

See also:
www.bugsie.co.uk – yes, it's a mobile dog washing service!
www.canismajor.com/dog – an American magazine site.
www.chazhound.com – for information, fun and games.

www.doglost.co.uk – the place to go if your dog is missing; if you still need help, try **www.lost-doggies.com**

www.dogmadshop.com – good-looking doggie-oriented shop with lots of interesting products for you and your pooch.

www.dogpatch.org – a directory and search engine devoted to dogs.

www.dogster.com – yes, you can set up a web site devoted to your dog alone …

www.i-love-dogs.com – a directory of web sites devoted to dogs.

www.loveyourdog.com – a children's guide to caring for dogs.

www.ncdl.org.uk   UK

THE DOG'S TRUST
Excellent web site featuring the charitable works of the Dog's Trust (formerly the National Canine Defence League), the largest charity of its type. Get advice on how to adopt a dog, tips on looking after one and download doggie wallpaper. For Battersea Dogs Home go to **www.dogshome.org** who have a well-designed site.

Fish

www.ornamentalfish.org   UK

ORNAMENTAL AQUATIC TRADE ASSOCIATION
An excellent site beautifully designed and well executed. Although much of it is aimed at the trade and commercial side, there is a great deal of information for the hobbyist about looking after and buying fish.

See also:
www.aquariacentral.com – a huge site with masses of information on every aspect of looking after fish.
www.fishdoc.co.uk – excellent site of fish illnesses and ailments.
www.fishlinkcentral.com – a good directory site for information on fish.

Horses

www.equiworld.net   UK

GLOBAL EQUINE INFORMATION
Not the most helpful design but a directory, magazine and advice centre in one, with incredible detail plus some fun stuff too including video and audio interviews and footage, holidays and the latest news. The shop consists of links to specialist traders.

See also:
www.equine-world.co.uk – lots here too, including classified ads, shopping and links.
www.horseadvice.com – a health-oriented site that supplies a huge amount of information.
www.horses-and-horse-information.com/horsehealth.shtml – health information from a large American site.

Rabbits and Rodents

http://www.rabbit.org   US
HOUSE RABBIT SOCIETY
It's all here, from feeding, breeding, behaviour, health advice and even info on house-training your rabbit. Has a nice kids' section and plenty of cute pictures.

See also:
www.caviesgalore.com – information, forums, games and names.
www.cavycapers.com – a guinea pig haven on the web! A nice site too.
www.gerbils.co.uk – home of the National Gerbil Society.
www.rabbitwelfare.co.uk – lots of chat, advice and links from the Rabbit Welfare Association.
www.webcom.com/lstead/rodents/rodents.html – good information on caring for rodents and some interesting material on genetics. Shame there are no pictures.

Other Pets

http://exoticpets.about.com – comprehensive information and news stories.
www.ameyzoo.co.uk – a specialist exotic pet shop with fact sheets on how to look after them properly.
www.easyexotics.co.uk – attractive site covering exotic plants as well as pets, it aims to take the mystery out of looking after them; sections on tarantulas and arrow frogs.
www.exoticpetvet.net – advice from specialist vets.
www.kingsnake.com – an American community site devoted to snakes.
www.petreptiles.com – comprehensive pet reptile information.
www.ukreptiles.com – an OK directory site for reptile enthusiasts, good for links.

Photography

www.photographyworld.co.uk
COMMUNITY OF PHOTOGRAPHERS

A good portal site with links to all aspects of photography, there's information on everything from models to lessons. For more links and research try **www.photolinks.net** which is pretty comprehensive.

www.rps.org
THE ROYAL PHOTOGRAPHIC SOCIETY

An improved site dedicated to the works of the RPS. There are details on the latest exhibitions and the collection, you can become a member and get the latest news about the world of photography.

www.nationalmediamuseum.org.uk
NATIONAL MEDIA MUSEUM

Details of this Bradford museum via a high-tech web site: opening times and directions, what's on, education resources and a very good museum guide.

www.eastmanhouse.org
THE INTERNATIONAL MUSEUM OF PHOTOGRAPHY

George Eastman founded Kodak and this New York-based museum too. This site is comprehensive and amongst other things, you can learn about the history of photography, visit the photographic and film galleries, or obtain technical information. Become a member and you're entitled to benefits such as free admission and copies of their *Image* magazine.

www.nationalgeographic.com/photography
NATIONAL GEOGRAPHIC MAGAZINE

Synonymous with great photography, this excellent site offers much more. There are sections on travel, history, maps, news, education, and for kids. In the photography guide pick up tips and techniques, follow their photographers' various locations, read superb articles and accompanying shots in the 'Visions Galleries'. Good links to other photographic sites.

www.life.com/Life
LIFE MAGAZINE

Life magazine is wonderfully nostalgic and still going strong.

There are several sections, features with great photos, excellent articles, and an option to subscribe; however, they could do much more and it's a little frustrating to use.

See also:
www.iphotocentral.com – a dealer in old photographs.
www.lensartistuk.com – excellent showcase for some leading photographers to sell and display their work. Lots of framing options makes this site stand out.
www.photographymuseum.com – odd site from the American Museum of Photography.
www.photolinks.com – a comprehensive but slightly messy links directory.
www.photonet.org.uk – home of London's Photographers' Gallery, find out what's on and buy prints.
www.rleggat.com/photohistory – the history of early photography.

www.bipp.com   UK
BRITISH INSTITUTE OF PROFESSIONAL PHOTOGRAPHY
The place to go if you want to hire a professional photographer, there are some 3,500 on its books. It also offers advice to students and others interested in a career in photography.

Great Photographers

www.masters-of-photography.com   US

ONLINE GALLERIES
A simple site with a superb array of galleries devoted to the real masters of the art of photography – you can spend hours browsing here.

See also:
www.anseladams.com – a great place to buy Ansel Adams photos.
www.davidbaileyphotography.com – the official site with some great shots to view.
www.npg.org.uk – National Portrait Gallery offer up interviews, biographies and the work of some of the great photographers.
www.rleggat.com/photohistory – a fairly basic site but one that has biographical details of all the key photographers and milestones.
www.r-cube.co.uk/fox-talbot – the Fox Talbot Museum.
www.staleywise.com – excellent gallery, very strong on Norman Parkinson.

www.temple.edu/photo/photographers – excellent site with essays on all the great photographers and their work.

Photo Libraries

www.bapla.org   UK
PICTURE LIBRARIES
Home of the British Association of Picture Libraries and although it's basically an industry site it has lots of information and links to all the major libraries in the UK.

See also:
www.corbis.com – one of the biggest libraries, much of which is free.
www.francisfrith.co.uk – great archive, quality local prints and maps too.
www.freefoto.com – who say they offer the largest free image database.
www.freeimages.co.uk – 2,500 free quality pictures.
www.gettyimages.com – the leading commercial library with lots of royalty-free images to download.
www.loc.gov/rr/print/catalog.html – the US Library of Congress has many free historical photographs.
www.vam.ac.uk/collections/photography/index.html – excellent selection from the V&A.
www.webshots.com – which is great for wallpaper and screensavers.

P

Photographic Advice

www.bjphoto.co.uk   UK
THE BRITISH JOURNAL OF PHOTOGRAPHY
An online magazine with loads of material on photography. Access their archive or visit picture galleries that contain work from contemporary photographers, find out about careers in photography and where to buy the best photographic gear.

www.betterphoto.com   UK

TAKE BETTER PICTURES
A very well-laid-out and comprehensive advice site for new and experienced photographers with a buyer's guide plus introductions to and overviews of traditional and digital photography.

See also:

www.88.com/exposure – a temperamental site but one that offers up a great deal of information both for beginners and the well versed.

www.photo.net – an American site with lots of advice and reviews.

www.photographyblog.com – a lively and personal blog created by a professional photographer.

www.photozone.de – a brave attempt at providing a rounded community site covering most aspects of photography with reviews and technical help.

www.shortcourses.com – all you need to know about digital photography.

Photography Stores and Equipment Reviews

www.jessops.com   UK
TAKE ADVICE, TAKE GREAT PICTURES
Jessops are the largest photographic retailer in the UK and they offer advice on most aspects of photography plus courses and free software for their digital printing service. They do give you an opportunity to go shopping for your camera and accessories.

See also:

http://photography.ebay.co.uk – eBay's comprehensive photo equipment auction section.

www.bestcameras.co.uk – good range and a clutter-free site. Recommended.

www.cameras2u.com – this store has a wide range, good prices and you can download their helpful guides too.

www.dcresource.com – information and reviews on digital cameras.

www.digitaltruth.com – unusual design, but very comprehensive equipment shop and portal site.

www.dpreview.com – digital photography cameras and equipment reviewed.

www.ffordes.com – a good site offering used equipment alongside the new.

www.photoglossy.com – specialists in paper, material and printing accessories.

Photo Storage, Development and Sharing

See also the section on Online Storage on page 356.

www.flickr.com

CANADA

PHOTO COMMUNITY
A fast-growing membership and an indication of what will be
the way forward for sharing photos with friends, family and
colleagues. It's very easy to set up with the best feature being
the facility to tag your photos with key words making it easier
to search and share your collection. It's also got good security
should you only want to share your album with a few people.

www.fotopages.com
US

PHOTO BLOG
Here you can set up your own photo blog, which you can share
with friends and family. It's pretty easy to get going and it's really
effective, you can archive material, add captions, text and even
links.

http://picasa.google.com
US

ORGANISE YOUR PHOTOS
Picasa is one of Google's many projects, download it and you
can organise your photos and, more to the point, quickly find
them when you need to. See also **www.hello.com** which is
another program that works a little like an instant messenger
service but for photos. If you discuss photos with friends or as
part of your business, it's a good way to see them at the same
time. Mac users should check out **www.apple.com/dotmac/**

See also
www.beanpix.com – aside from offering the usual storage and
online album facilities, Beanpix also enables you to market and
sell your own photos.
www.bootsdigitalphotocentre.com – photo sharing and an
online developing service from Boots.
www.kodakgallery.co.uk – excellent site from Kodak.
www.my-expressions.com – expose yourself with this photo
blogging service.
www.photobox.co.uk – great design, probably the best for digital
photo storage.
www.ringo.com – simple to use photo sharing site, has the
popular vote.
www.snapfish.co.uk – a site that offers good value prints from
digital shots as well as a sharing facility.

Miscellaneous Photography Sites

www.getmapping.com   UK
AERIAL PHOTOGRAPHS
Just type in your postcode and get a picture of your home taken
from above on a sunny day last year. There are lots of cost
options and you can also get a map to go with it.

www.panoramas.dk   DENMARK
PANORAMIC PHOTOGRAPHY
A great use of the Quicktime program, thousands of sites and
movies all devoted to or celebrating panoramic photography.

www.playingwithtime.org   US
TIME-LAPSE PHOTOGRAPHY
This site is part of a larger photographic project, here you can
see incredible movies filmed with time-lapse photography.
Excellent.

See also:
www.darknessandlight.co.uk – atmospheric prints from this
Cambridge-based photographer.
www.pimpampum.net/bubblr – a fun site where you can create
comic strips from photos uploaded from Flickr and your own
Mac or PC.

Podcasting

P

*Driven by the popularity of the iPod, creating downloadable broadcasts
is one of the fastest growing and most popular pastimes on the
Internet. Here are the major sites where you can get help, download
for free or just learn how it's done. See also Radio on page 392.*

*www.podcast.net is the best podcast directory, while a good podcast
portal is to be found at www.podcastalley.com. Both are useful starting
points. A good audio/video search engine can be found at the Singing
Fish http://search.singingfish.com*

*If you're new to podcasting visit http://en.wikipedia.org/wiki/Podcast
where Wikipedia explains it all; however, if you want to get Wikipedia on
your iPod, then go to http://encyclopodia.sourceforge.net/en/index.html*

For podcast content try ...

www.bbc.co.uk/radio – listen again, download your favourite radio programme.

www.guardian.co.uk/podcasts – the latest from *The Guardian*.

www.loudish.com – a podcast service aimed at businesses.

www.podcastblaster.com – the easy way to create podcasts, apparently.

www.podcastbunker.com – quality not quantity, excellent selection.

www.podcastingnews.com – all the latest and best podcasts.

www.podcastpickle.com – podcasts and vidcasts too.

www.podcastplatform.com – 'podcasting easified' with information, how-to, software, directories and links.

Price Checkers

Here's a good place to start any online shopping trip – a price comparison site. There are many price checker sites; however, the sites listed here allow you to check the prices for online stores across a much wider range of merchandise than the usual books, music and film.

It should be said that some fail to take into account the cost of sending the products. For example, the last edition of this book was listed by one supplier at a sale price of £1, but they charged over £4 to send it! However, it was listed by the price checker as the cheapest option.

www.kelkoo.co.uk   UK

 COMPARE PRICES BEFORE YOU BUY
Kelkoo is probably the best price-checking site with 20 categories in their shop directory including books, wine, white goods, even cars and utility bills – they have links with eBay. There are plenty of bargains to be had, in fact they keep popping up on every page.

www.checkaprice.com   UK

CONSTANTLY CHECKING PRICES
Compare prices across a huge range of products, from the usual books to cars, holidays, mortgages and electrical goods. If it can't do it for you, it patches you through to a site that can.

Other good sites:
www.buy.co.uk – excellent for home utilities, insurance, credit cards as well as broadband and mobile phones.

To Pick Up a Bargain

The Good Web Site Guide's Top 10s
of the Internet

1. **www.ebay.co.uk** – bid for a bargain
2. **www.kelkoo.co.uk** – compare prices
3. **http://froogle.google.co.uk** – search for the product, find the best price
4. **www.pricechecker.co.uk** – get a great deal on thousands of products
5. **www.freeinuk.co.uk** – your guide to everything free
6. **www.which.co.uk** – it may be cheap but is it reliable?
7. **www.thesimplesaver.com** – the simple way to save money
8. **www.gooddealdirectory.co.uk** – the best brand names for the best prices
9. **www.abebooks.com** – the cheapest place to buy a book
10. **www.unbiased.co.uk** – sort your finances out, then shop!

www.dealtime.co.uk – easy-to-use directory and price checker covering a wide range of goods.
www.froogle.co.uk – Google's price checker service.
www.pricechecker.co.uk – a straightforward site which also covers flights and telephone tariffs.
www.priceguideuk.com – a good UK-oriented service.
www.pricerunner.com – a good all-rounder with a news section giving the latest information on deals and technology updates.
www.pricescan.com – all the usual, plus watches, jewellery, sports goods and office equipment – good store finder.
www.price-search.net – mainly computers and gadgets.
www.pricewatch.co.uk – the full range of consumables.
www.unravelit.com – unravel your troubles and get the best deal here. Good for utilities and finances.

Property

Every estate agent worth their salt has got a web site, and in theory finding the house of your dreams has never been easier. These sites

have been designed to help you through the minefield. For advice on
building your own house go to page 276 in the Home section.

www.upmystreet.com
UK

FIND OUT ABOUT WHERE YOU WANT TO GO
Type in the postcode and up pops almost every statistic you
need to know about the area in question. Spooky, but
fascinating, it's a good guide featuring not only house prices, but
also schools, the local MP, local authority information, crime and
links to local services and trades people. It also has a classified
section and puts you in touch with the nearest items to your
area. See also **www.hometrack.co.uk** which is a subscription
service but offers a huge amount of data about house prices and
the area.

www.landreg.gov.uk
UK
LAND REGISTRY
A new look for this site which provides information on house and
land prices by region, details on how to register land and your
rights. You can also make inquiries about a property's history.

www.conveyancing-cms.co.uk
UK
CONVEYANCING MARKETING SERVICE
Conveyancing is a bit of a minefield if you're new to it, but
this site aims to help with advice and competitive quotes.
www.theclc.gov.uk is the home to the Council for Licensed
Conveyancers, which lists them and offers advice on how to
choose one. See also **www.easier2move.com** which is nicely
designed and very informative.

www.checkmymove.com
UK
PROPERTY SALE TRACKER
Check on the progress of your house move by using this handy
tracking service. The only downside is that it depends on your
solicitor and estate agent signing up to the service, which they
are charged for. It will be interesting to see how this idea
progresses.

www.home-repo.org
UK
HOME REPOSSESSION
A very useful and informative site that blows the lid off the
goings on behind what happens when a house is repossessed
and what you should do if you find yourself in arrears. It's
assertive and entertaining too.

For more properties and help with moving home try these sites. Some are just for buyers, but many have homes to rent too.

www.beach-huts.co.uk – great site, providing you want to buy or rent a beach hut.

www.cityscope.co.uk – flashy website from this London specialist.

www.easier.co.uk – free, no-hassle advertising also has a finance section.

www.findaproperty.com – 184,000 properties listed, biased to the South East.

www.heritage.co.uk – covers listed buildings only for sale plus information on their upkeep.

www.hol365.com – really good site design and a massive range of services and properties from thousands of estate agents nationwide.

www.houseweb.co.uk – highly rated with comprehensive advice and thousands of properties for sale.

www.itlhomesearch.com – independent home search and advice site that also covers Spain and Ireland – rent or buy.

www.knightfrank.com – world-wide service, easy-to-use site.

www.land-property-grab.com – track down and nab yourself some unclaimed property ... legally!

www.naea.co.uk – National Association of Estate Agents with their code of conduct, links and the latest property news.

www.primelocation.co.uk – one of the biggest property search engines.

www.propertyfinder.com – Britain's biggest house database, excellent site with lots of advice, information, houses and associated services.

www.property-platform.com – home of the Guild of Professional Estate Agents with a property search facility.

www.rightmove.com – very clear information site with a good property search engine.

www.smartnewhomes.com – search engine dedicated to new homes.

www.themovechannel.co.uk – an OK portal site. Each agent or property site gets a review and a link. Better than it looks at first glance.

www.ukpad.com – details of property auctions in the UK.

www.ukpropertyshop.com – claims to be the most comprehensive estate agent directory covering 3,000 towns in the UK.

www.vebra.com – above-average property search engine, much faster than most.

Renting

www.landlordzone.co.uk UK

RENTAL PROPERTY KNOWLEDGE
Very useful for landlords and tenants alike with the latest news
available and lots of advice too. It's great for links and easy to
navigate though a bit advert heavy.

See also:
www.arla.co.uk – home of the Association of Residential Letting
Agents with lots of useful information.

http://uk.easyroommate.com UK

FIND A FLATMATE
This service is available in 18 countries, including the UK.
Simply select your town from the pull down list, enter your
details and preferences and they'll search for available
matches – simple.

See also:
www.flatshare.com – great for London.
www.shareflatmates.com – also US, Canada and Australia.

Property Abroad

www.french-property.com UK

NO.1 FOR FRANCE
If you are fed up with the UK and want to move to France this is
the first port of call. They offer properties for rent or for sale in all
regions and can link you with other estate agents.

www.overseaspropertyonline.com UK

MOVING ABROAD
This site was formerly **www.spanish-property-online.com** and
remains a good starting point if you want to find property and
advice on buying in Spain. However, it has extended its range to
cover Europe, the Caribbean, North America, Australia and New
Zealand.

See also:
www.adhspain.com – excellent site from this Spanish property
specialist.
www.bulgariandreams.com – it's the place to be, apparently.
www.buy-property-dubai.com – Dubai property.

www.fopdac.com – home to the Federation of Overseas Property Developers, a trade association site that has some useful advice and contact information.

www.french-property-news.com – a poorly designed site, but good advice and links.

www.islandsforsale.com – yes, buy yourself a whole island!

www.latitudes.co.uk – French property specialists.

www.prestigeproperty.co.uk – links with estate agents in nine countries.

www.property-abroad.com – a site covering Spain, Italy, Greece and Florida.

www.realestateslovakia.net – beautiful chateaux in Eastern Europe.

www.worldclasshomes.co.uk – properties in Spain, Portugal, France and Bahamas …

Storage and Removal

www.reallymoving.com   UK

MAKING MOVING EASIER

A directory of sites and help for home buyers including mortgages, removal firms, surveyors, solicitors, van hire and home improvements. You can get online quotes on some services and there's good regional information. The property search is fast and has plenty of choice. For a helpful directory of removal and storage companies with information and advice try **www.helpiammoving.com** and also the British Association of Removers has an informative site at **www.removers.org.uk**

www.removal-companies.co.uk   UK

FIND THE BEST REMOVAL FIRM

An easy way of getting quotes from several removal companies in one go, just follow the simple instructions.

www.packnmove.co.uk   UK

ALL BOXED UP

Here you're offered a wide range of packaging options each designed to help you move your stuff in the most efficient way, whether you have a one room flat or a mansion. It includes calculators too, so you order the right quantity. See also **www.a1box.co.uk**, **www.removalboxes.co.uk** and **www.removal-boxes.com**

Radio

You need a decent downloadable player such as RealPlayer or Windows Media Player before you start listening. The downside is that quality is sometimes affected by Net congestion although that's becoming less of a problem these days as broadband becomes more common. See page 385 for information on Podcasts and page 355 for RSS. It will be interesting to see how this area of the Internet develops as people are increasingly able to tailor their listening according to their tastes.

www.mediauk.com/directory   UK

DIRECTORY OF RADIO STATIONS

Excellent site. You can search by station, presenter or by type, there's also background on the history of radio and articles on topics such as digital radio. The site also offers similar information on television and magazines.

See also:

http://dir.yahoo.com/News_and_Media/Radio – Yahoo's list of nearly 7,000 stations and related sites.

http://windowsmedia.com/Mediaguide/Radio – home to Microsoft's media listings, which is very comprehensive.

www.comfm.com/live/radio – a French site with access to thousands of stations.

www.icecast.org – download the player and get access to radio stations and video streams.

www.live365.com – good-looking site with thousands of radio stations to choose from and it's easy to customise to your tastes too. The basic service is free, but for CD-quality sound and to broadcast your own radio station, you have to pay.

www.publicradiofan.com – ugly site with thousands of stations listed but they are listed by time-zone so you should be able to find something you like playing at any one time.

www.radio-locator.com – a huge directory of radio, US-oriented.

www.radio-now.co.uk – radios to buy, listen live, plus lots of links.

www.shoutcast.com – another huge selection using the Winamp player. If you fancy yourself as a DJ, it's free to join in and broadcast here.

www.virtualtuner.com – tune in to a vast number of stations at this good-looking site, the top 500 is interesting in itself. They promise that you will also be able to record and watch any US TV station, free by the time this book comes out.

www.radioacademy.org UK

UK'S GATEWAY TO RADIO

Radio Academy is a charity that covers all things to do with radio including news, events and its advancement in education and information. It has a list of all UK stations including those that offer web casts. You get more from the site if you become a member.

www.bbc.co.uk/radio UK

THE BEST OF THE BBC

Listen to the news and the latest hits while you work, just select the station you want. If you've missed a programme, no problem, you can access it for up to a week and download many as podcasts. There's also information on each major station, as well as a comprehensive listing service. Some features such as football commentary on certain matches will be missing due to rights issues. Most of the stations have some level of interactivity, with Radio 1 being the best and most lively, you can also tap into their local stations and, of course, the World Service.

www.virginradio.co.uk UK

VIRGIN ON AIR

Excellent, if slightly cluttered site with lots of ads plus plenty of stuff about the station, its schedule and stars. There's also a good magazine with the latest music news. You can listen if you have Windows Media Player, RealPlayer, iTunes, WinAmp or Ogg media players.

Other independent radio stations online are:
www.capitalfm.com – Capital Radio.
www.classicfm.com – classical music and background information.
www.coolfm.co.uk – Northern Ireland's number one.
www.galaxyfm.co.uk – good range of dance music.
www.heart1062.co.uk – London's heart.
www.jazzfm.com – live broadcasts, cool site too.
www.lbc.co.uk – two stations providing the voice of London.
www.resonancefm.com – London-oriented arts station.

www.mercora.com US

CREATE YOUR OWN STATION

The idea here is to download the program and effectively create a radio station that matches your tastes and those of your friends. It's still free, at time of writing anyway although the Mercora download for your smartphone or pocket PC costs about £25 per year.

Railways

These are sites aimed at the railway enthusiast. For information on trains and timetables see pages 516 and 558 while for railway modelling go to page 272.

www.nrm.org.uk UK
NATIONAL RAILWAY MUSEUM
An excellent museum site packed with information and details on their collection, you can even take a virtual tour. See also Great Western's very informative museum site at **www.steam-museum.org.uk**

www.heritagerailways.com UK
HERITAGE RAILWAY ASSOCIATION
This site offers an online guide to the entire heritage railway scene in the UK, including details of special events and operating days for all heritage railways with lots of links world-wide.

www.narrow-gauge.co.uk UK
NARROW GAUGE
The new and improved Narrow Gauge Heaven (formerly Narrow Gauge on the Web) steams in with latest news and a better photo gallery plus all the narrow gauge information you'll need. You can also contribute your own articles or just browse.

See also:
www.drcm.org.uk – good site on the Darlington Railway Museum.
www.gensheet.co.uk – keep up to date with timetable changes and diversions.
www.heritagerailway.co.uk – geared to selling the mag but plenty of links and some archive material.
www.icrs.org.uk – home of the Inter-City Railway Society with an informative, highly comprehensive and useful site.
www.mylinkspage.com/rail.html – the train resource centre.
www.pcrail.co.uk – a rail enthusiast's dream: simulations of railway operations and journeys. The site is well designed and

simulations cost around £30 although the downloadable software is free.

www.railcentre.co.uk – the Stockton and Darlington railway.

www.railfaneurope.net – information on European trains.

www.railpictures.net – lots of pictures of mainly American trains.

www.railway-technology.com – the latest industry news.

www.rpsi-online.org – Ireland's Railway Preservation Society.

www.steamlocomotive.com – steam trains in the US.

www.steamtrain.info – a spectacular Scottish railway with puffa puffa sound.

www.trackbed.com – in excess of 2,500 pages on Britain's railway heritage, a labour of love.

www.trainorders.com – a US rail community site, there's a lot here with particularly lively discussion forums.

www.trainspotters.de – a good site from a German rail fan.

www.trainweb.org – an ugly directory of train- and railway-related sites.

www.uksteam.info – a well-organised site covering steam train preservation.

www.vintagetrains.co.uk – home of the Birmingham Railway Museum.

Reference and Encyclopaedias

If you are stuck with your homework or want an answer to any question, then this is where the Internet really comes into its own. With these sites you are bound to find what you are looking for. For schoolwork, also refer to the education section, page 117.

You should also check out your County/Borough library site, which gives you access to a huge amount of free online reference material. This includes sites such as Oxford Reference Online (including the entire OED), The Britannica Online, The Times Digital archive, the Naxos Music Library and more. Most of these sites are not available for free public use, but the library services have come to an agreement with the publishers and they are accessible to anyone with a library card. You may have to call into your local library to get an access number.

www.refdesk.com   US
    THE BEST SINGLE SOURCE FOR FACTS
    Singled out for its sheer size and scope, this site offers
    information and links to just about anything. Its mission is 'only

about indexing quality Internet sites and assisting visitors in navigating these sites'. It has won numerous awards and it never fails to impress. Users outside the US may find it too biased towards that country.

www.about.com   US

IT'S ABOUT INFORMATION
A superb resource, easy to navigate and great for beginners learning to search for information. Experts help you to find what you need every step of the way. It offers information on a wide range of topics from the arts and sciences to shopping.

www.ipl.org   US

THE INTERNET PUBLIC LIBRARY
Another excellent resource, there are articles on a vast range of subjects, its particularly good on literary criticism. Almost every country and its literature is covered. If there isn't anything at the library, there is invariably a link to take you to an alternative web site. Check out their children's section 'kidspace' for first class children's reference materials and 'teenspace' for teenagers.

See also:
www.archive.org – an excellent resource in the making. The 'Wayback Machine' is fun, though it has a serious side; it catalogues old sites so that they may never be lost.
www.factbites.com – a Google-style search engine that offers up results based on facts that match whole topic, rather than just spotting words that happen to appear on random, less relevant web pages. It is good for general searches and it is better than Google in some ways, although it comes with a big US bias.
www.plymouth.gov.uk/cyberlibrary – librarians have compiled a really useful set of reference links, organised alphabetically, of course.
www.ibiblio.org – holds a huge collection of textual, audio and software resources.
www.libraryspot.com – is similar in scope to IPL, but has a more literary emphasis and an entertaining trivia section for those obsessed by top 10s and useless facts.
www.questia.com – claims to be the biggest online library with over 67,000 books and 1.5 million articles. You can preview the books for free but have to join for full access (£55 per year). Excellent search facility.

www.theanswerbank.co.uk UK

QUESTIONS ANSWERED

Just go to any one of the listed categories and type in your question, and you'll get a list of articles and links relating to your query. Some results returned are quite odd so you have to be quite specific. It may be better to use a search engine such as **www.ask.co.uk**

www.homeworkelephant.co.uk UK

LET THE ELEPHANT HELP WITH HOMEWORK

A resource with some 5,000 links and resources aimed at helping students achieve great results. There's help with specific subjects, hints and tips, and help for parents and teachers. It's constantly being updated, so worth checking regularly.

See also:

www.channel4.com/learning/microsites/H/homeworkhigh/ – Channel 4's excellent homework help site. Shame they've lost the shorter URL.

www.kidsclick.org – more than 600 topics and subjects covered.

Encyclopaedias

www.wikipedia.org US

 THE FREE ENCYCLOPAEDIA

In an amazingly short time Wikipedia has become something of an Internet phenomenon. Basically, it's an encyclopaedia created by anyone who wants to contribute. The English version has more than 1.6 million entries and although the quality varies, it's a great place to go for researching. Although it's wise to double check your facts, a recent study found that its quality was up there with the best.

http://encarta.msn.com US

THE ENCARTA ENCYCLOPAEDIA

Even though the complete thing is only available by subscription, there is access to thousands of articles, maps and reference notes via the concise version. It's fast and easy to use, though navigating it is a bit of a pain.

Other useful encyclopaedias:

http://encyclozine.com – wide range of topics covered plus good use of games, quizzes and trivia.

http://i-cias.com/e.o/index.htm – Encyclopaedia of the Orient – for North Africa and the Middle East.

www.babloo.com – interactive encyclopaedia aimed at kids.

www.bartleby.com – one of the best. It offers access to a huge amount of reference work, but also fiction, verse and narrative non-fiction, largely with an American bias.

www.eb.com – *Encyclopaedia Britannica* – they are really cagey about the cost, though. Remember, you can access this via your local library website.

www.encyclopedia.com – possibly the most comprehensive free encyclopaedia on the net, nice design too. Check out the Highbeam library with access to huge amounts of data, from newswires to books, maps and images. You have to subscribe to get full access, although there are some free articles and you can preview texts for free.

www.infoplease.com – the biggest collection of almanacs, plus an encyclopaedia and an atlas.

www.seop.leeds.ac.uk – UK mirror site for Stanford Encyclopaedia of Philosophy.

www.si.edu/resource – encyclopaedia and links to the massive resources of the Smithsonian.

www.spartacus.schoolnet.co.uk – Spartacus Encyclopaedia is excellent for history homework.

www.utm.edu/research/iep – the Internet Encyclopaedia of Philosophy.

www.wsu.edu/DrUniverse – ask Dr Universe a question, any question …

Specialist Reference Sites

Classics and Literature

www.eserver.org   US

THE ENGLISH SERVER

A much-improved humanities site, which provides a vast amount of resource data about almost every cultural topic. There are some 34,000 texts, articles and essays available on subjects from the arts and fiction through to web design.

http://classics.mit.edu   US

THE INTERNET CLASSICS ARCHIVE

An excellent site for researching into the classics, it's easy to use and fast, with more than enough information for homework whatever the level. See also the excellent **www.bibliomania.com** for a wider range of resource materials.

www.perseus.tufts.edu   US
PERSEUS DIGITAL LIBRARY
An excellent source of data for ancient classics and mythology, history and early science. It also offers most of Shakespeare and Marlowe and, although it concentrates largely on pre-1600, it's ever expanding.

See also:
www.mythweb.com – an enjoyable and informative site devoted to Greek mythology.
www.pantheon.org – which contains over 6,000 definitions covering mythology, legends and folklore.

Dictionaries and Words

For information on grammar, pronunciation, plain English and learning English see the English usage section on page 131. For language and translation go to page 298.

www.askoxford.com   UK
ASK OXFORD UNIVERSITY
A pretty decent effort at making a dry subject interesting. You can ask an expert, get advice on how to improve your writing and, of course, use the famous dictionary and thesaurus. See also **www.oed.com** where you subscribe to the *Oxford English Dictionary* at a cost of £50 for 3 months or access via your local library website (see introductory notes). At **www.bbc.co.uk/balderdash** you can actually participate in writing the OED.

http://dictionary.cambridge.org   UK
CAMBRIDGE UNIVERSITY
This site has seven dictionaries: English, American English, idioms, phrasal verbs, a learner's dictionary, French/English and Spanish/English – all free.

www.onelook.com   US
DICTIONARY HEAVEN
Onelook claim to offer access to 1001 dictionaries and over 7½ million words, at a fast, user-friendly site. It also offers a translation facility and reverse dictionary facility, where you describe a concept and it gets back to you with related words.

www.thefreedictionary.com   US

DICTIONARY, ENCYCLOPAEDIA AND THESAURUS ... FREE
A clear layout, good responses and with the adverts quite subtly
placed, the Free Dictionary is a pleasure to use.

See also:
www.allwords.com – a well-categorised portal site on everything
to do with words, including help with crosswords and
translation.
www.collins.co.uk/wordexchange – Collins dictionary with
several useful word tools including a Scrabble dictionary.
www.crossword-dictionary.com – here you can type in the word
you're looking for, with the gaps, and the dictionary will come up
with a list of suggestions; while at **www.oneacross.com** you can
type in the pattern and the clue to get your answer.
www.dictionary.com – here you can play word games as an
added feature.
www.wordorigins.org – the origins of some 400 words and
phrases explained.
www.wordspy.com – the latest on how words are being used
and new words.
www.worldwidewords.org – international English from a British
point of view, new words and phrases analysed.
www.yourdictionary.com – very comprehensive, the last word in
words, apparently.

www.thesaurus.com   US

IF YOU CAN'T FIND THE WORD
Based on *Roget's Thesaurus*, this site will enable you to find
alternative words – useful but not worth turning your PC on for
in place of the book. The site is related to **www.dictionary.com**
and has several other facilities including translation into 11
languages.

www.visualthesaurus.com   US

THE VISUAL THESAURUS
If you get bored looking up words or looking for alternative
meanings for words in the usual way, then check out the Visual
Thesaurus. It's fun to use, if a bit weird. Unfortunately, it now
requires a subscription after the free trial.

www.peevish.co.uk/slang   UK

DICTIONARY OF SLANG
A comprehensive dictionary of English slang as used in the UK,

with good articles and search facility. See also
www.urbandictionary.com for a listing of the words allegedly
used by today's yoof.

www.acronymfinder.com   US
WHAT DO THOSE INITIALS STAND FOR?
If you don't know your MP from your MP3, here's where to go.
With over 475,000 acronyms it should help you find what
you're looking for.

www.symbols.com   US
WHAT DOES THAT SYMBOL MEAN?
Here you can find the meaning of over 2,500 symbols, with
articles on their history.

www.techweb.com   US
THE TECHNOLOGY DICTIONARY
Get the latest business and technology news plus an excellent
technology encyclopaedia. For a dictionary that specialises in
jargon and Internet terms only go to either **www.jargon.net** or
www.netdictionary.com for enlightenment.

Other word-related sites:
www.ag.wastholm.net – if you need an aphorism, it's probably
here.
www.identifont.com – identify any font and find one that you
like, also has information on the many different types available.
www.rhymezone.com – type in a word, up pop all those that
rhyme with it.
www.word-detective.com – a magazine devoted to words and
wordplay.

R

Maths and Numbers

*For a great conversion tool and calculator, it's worth visiting Microsoft's
download centre and searching Calculator Plus, which is free.*

www.mathsisfun.com   UK
MATHS RESOURCES
A good site devoted to the basics of maths, it covers all the
bases and was started by a British maths teacher. All is
well explained with lots of diagrams. See also the helpful
www.amathsdictionaryforkids.com which provides a useful
visual dictionary of mathematical terms.

www.onlineconversion.com   UK
CONVERSION CHARTS
Converts just about anything that can be converted. From the usual length, weight and currency to international clothing sizes, cooking volumes, astronomical light – it will even calculate your retirement date.

See also:
www.easymaths.com – Key Stage maths help.
www.google.com/help/features.html@lculator – this link takes you to Google's very useful calculator function.
www.math.com – a very comprehensive US maths site.
www.mathguide.de – a German maths portal and search engine.
www.math-net.de/links – maths links.
www.megaconverter.com/mega2 – annoying design but some useful converters.
www.scenta.co.uk/tcaep – if you need details on a particular equation, it's almost certain to be here.
www.univie.ac.at/future.media/moe – a useful collection of advice, tools and information.

Geography, Atlases and International Statistical Data

See also the section on Geology on page 341.

www.nationmaster.com   US
WORLD STATS
A well-designed site, which is excellent for comparative statistics on countries and people. The great benefit to this one is that it also includes access to a good encyclopaedia.

www.ntu.edu.sg/Library/Collections/Databases   SINGAPORE
STATISTICS AND MORE STATISTICS
Free information and statistics about national economies – not that easy to use at first, but it's all there.

www.internetgeographer.com   UK
GEOGRAPHY WEB RING
A good source of information on geography for all ages with quizzes and a population clock which enables you to see the population grow before your eyes. An alternative portal on

physical geography can be found at **www.geog.le.ac.uk/ cti/phys.html** which includes climatology, geomorphology, hydrology, oceanography and volcanology.

www.atlapedia.com US
THE WORLD IN BOTH PICTURES AND NUMBERS
Contains full colour political and physical maps of the world with statistics and very detailed information on each country. It can be very slow, so you need patience, but the end results are worth it.

www.geographyiq.com US
THE WORLD LISTED
A great site covering all the information you'd expect. List freaks will love the rankings pages: they cover everything from largest to oldest to richest. Great for homework.

http://platial.com US
MAKE YOUR OWN MAPS
Calling itself the People's Atlas at Platial, you can create maps that are tailored to your interests and needs. It's quite easy to set up and once you get the hang of it quite addictive. All the maps that have been created can be accessed by everyone and part of the fun is seeing what others have been mapping out.

See also:
http://earth.google.com – Google's excellent resource.
http://plasma.nationalgeographic.com/mapmachine – home of the *National Geographic*'s Map Machine where you can zoom in to any part of the world.
www.cia.gov/cia/publications/factbook – the CIA's famous fact book.
www.citypopulation.de – a really impressive site with a world population database including maps and flags.
www.geohive.com/index.html – population statistics combined with information on other key economic factors.
www.geosense.net – a good geography quiz game.
www.plcmc.org/forkids/mow – where you can find depicted all the flags of the world.
www.population.com – has a huge amount of data and information.
www.prb.org – the Population Reference Bureau holds masses of data on the world as well as on the US.
www.statistics.gov.uk – great for statistics on the UK.

R

> **www.worldatlas.com** – a pretty comprehensive world atlas and
> gazetteer.

Practical Skills

www.ehow.com   US
> HOW TO DO THINGS
> A directory and search site that provides information on how to
> do a mass of jobs and everyday tasks – categorised by subject.

Religion

*In this section we've attempted to list sites that are of general interest
and try to explain the philosophy of the religions, rather than those
sites that simply reflect the opinions of those who preach.*

www.omsakthi.org/religions.html   US
> RELIGION WORLD-WIDE
> This site provides a clear description of each world religion
> including values and basic beliefs with links to books on
> each one. For links see also the Religion Gateway at
> **www.academicinfo.net/religindex.html** and the extensive
> **www.adherents.com** who offer statistics on some 4,200
> religions and religious bodies.

> *More general information sites about religion:*
> **http://about.com/religion** – About has an excellent overview
> of the major religions and some minor ones. It also offers a
> selection of topical articles and covers areas such as spirituality
> too.
> **http://virtualreligion.net/vri** – Rutgers University has made
> available an excellent portal on religions, ethics, religious
> philosophy and psychology.
> **www.bbc.co.uk/religion** – the BBC's excellent site on religion
> and ethics.
> **www.beliefnet.com** – a wide-ranging and multi-faith approach
> to spirituality.
> **www.divinedigest.com** – a good overview of the major religions.
> **www.interfaith.org.uk** – promoting good inter-faith relations.
> **www.religioustolerance.org** – an organisation devoted to
> religions co-operating with each other, it has good information
> on all major faiths and attempts to explore controversial issues
> from various viewpoints.

The Key Religions and Philosophies

Buddhism

http://buddhanet.net – the world-wide Buddhist information and education network. A huge site with, one would guess, everything you need to know.
www.allspirit.co.uk – sacred writings and meditations.
www.ciolek.com/wwwvl-Buddhism.html – the Buddhist studies virtual library.

Christianity

www.anglicancommunion.org – the world-wide Anglican Communion.
www.anglicansonline.org – a huge resource site devoted to Anglicanism with over 10,000 links.
www.biblegateway.com – a searchable Bible in 35 languages.
www.catholic.net – a slick site devoted to the Catholic religion; here you'll find everything on the religion, and it seems very comprehensive.
www.cofe.anglican.org – home of the Church of England.
www.crosssearch.com – a directory of Christian web sites.
www.methodist.org.uk – the official line in Methodism.
www.newadvent.org/cathen – the Catholic encyclopaedia.
www.pres-outlook.com – a magazine site covering all forms of Presbyterianism; US orientated.
www.quaker.org.uk – information on what it is to be a Quaker.
www.russianorthodoxchurch.ws/english – for those outside Russia, with the latest news.
www.salvationarmy.org.uk – excellent site with lots of background information.
www.ship-of-fools.com – excellent radical Christian magazine.
www.thetablet.co.uk – a well-designed Catholic news site.
www.vatican.va – the official site of the Vatican, slow but informative.

Druidism/Paganism

www.druidnetwork.org – an overview of Druid beliefs with links and database.
www.ukpaganlinks.co.uk – web links and other information.

Hinduism

www.hindu.org – a good overview of this complex religion with an excellent directory.

www.hindulinks.org – an impressive number of links at this site.

Islam

www.al-islam.org – informative site with good information and links.

www.islamicity.com – a newsy site aimed at explaining Islam and creating more awareness of the religion.

www.islamonline.net – very comprehensive and interesting news and Islamic information site.

www.islamworld.net – a good overview of Islam.

www.salaam.co.uk – wide-ranging site covering all aspects of Islamic culture.

www.ummah.net – an excellent Muslim directory site.

www.usc.edu/dept/msa/reference/glossary.html – a glossary of Islamic terms and concepts.

Judaism

http://shamash.org/trb/judaism.html – a good overview of Judaism plus lots of links.

www.chiefrabbi.org – the official site of the Chief Rabbi.

www.jewfaq.org – an encyclopaedia devoted to Judaism.

www.ritualwell.org – ceremonies for Jewish living.

Scientology

www.scientology.org.uk – comprehensive site on Scientology and what it is.

Sikhism

www.panthkhalsa.org – information on the Sikh nation.

www.singhsabha.com – understanding the religious and philosophical teachings of Sikhism.

Humanism and Secularism

www.freethinker.co.uk – founded in 1881, this magazine has a long history of championing secular humanism.

www.humanism.org – a simple introduction to humanist principles.

www.humanism.org.uk – good introductory site; what humanism is and what they stand for, with information about their campaigns, policies and how to join a group. You can also arrange humanist ceremonies.

www.humanism-scotland.org.uk – the site for Scottish humanists.

www.infidels.org – a serious starting point for sceptics, check out the library for links to sites on atheism and humanism.

www.secularism.org.uk – the National Secular Society campaigns for a secular approach to society. There is a plethora of news features, information about their activities, their parliamentary submissions, the opportunity to join them and buy the T-shirt.

Science

The Internet was originally created by a group of scientists who wanted faster, more efficient communication and today, scientists around the world use the Net to compare data and collaborate. In addition, the layman has access to the wonders of science in a way that's never been possible before, and as for homework – well now it's a doddle.

Pure Science

www.scirus.com   US
SCIENCE SEARCH
A straightforward and easy-to-use search engine devoted to scientific information only.

www.royalsoc.ac.uk   UK
THE ROYAL SOCIETY
An attractive site where you can learn all about the workings of the society, how to get grants and what events they are running. They've improved the content to include more links and more interactivity.

www.scicentral.com   US

LATEST SCIENCE NEWS
Apart from being a very good portal, this site offers the latest news in the major categories of science, plus a searchable database of articles gleaned from papers and magazines around the world.

http://scienceworld.wolfram.com   US

PURE SCIENCE EXPLAINED

Eric Weisstein's World of Science contains encyclopaedias and detailed information written in accessible language on astronomy, scientific biography, chemistry, maths, physics and astronomy. The design is easy on the eye and the site is logical to use.

See also:
www.firstscience.com – accessible and colourful, good for older children.
www.plos.org – the Public Library of Science provides (free of charge) the world's scientific and medical literature online.
www.treasure-troves.com – an eccentric site on various aspects of science, quite fun in places too.

Magazines and Blogs

www.newscientist.com   UK

NEW SCIENTIST MAGAZINE

Much better than the usual online magazines because of its creative use of archive material, which is simultaneously fun and serious. It's easy to search the site or browse through back features, however, you have to subscribe to get access to premium content and the online archive of over 60,000 articles. For a more traditional science magazine site go to *Popular Science* at **www.popsci.com** – great for information on the latest gadgets.

www.sciencemag.org   US

SCIENCE MAGAZINE

A serious overview of the current science scene with articles covering everything from global warming to how owls find their prey. The tone isn't so heavy that a layman can't follow it and there are plenty of links too. You need to register to get the best out of it.

See also:
http://vlib.org/Science – the Virtual Library's natural science and maths links page.
www.blacktriangle.org – excellent blog on the latest science news.
www.discover.com – articles from *Discover* magazine.
www.raygirvan.co.uk/apoth/thought.htm – the Apothecary's Drawer, an eclectic blog with news, trivia and information.

www.scitechdaily.com – the latest science news.
www.visions-of-science.co.uk – marvel at the winners of the
photographic awards for scientific pictures.

Popular Science

www.sciencemuseum.org.uk   UK
> THE SCIENCE MUSEUM
> An excellent site detailing the major attractions at the museum
> with 3-D graphics and features on exhibitions and forthcoming
> attractions. You can also shop and browse the galleries. You
> can't help feeling they could do more though. See also
> **www.exploratorium.edu**, a similar but more child friendly site
> by an American museum.

www.discovery.com   US

> THE DISCOVERY CHANNEL
> A superb site for science and nature lovers, it's inspiring as well
> as educational. Order the weekly newsletter, get information on
> the latest discoveries as well as features on pets, space, travel,
> lifestyle and school. The 'Discovery Kids' section is very good
> with lots going on.

www.howstuffworks.com   US

> HOW STUFF REALLY WORKS
> An outstanding and popular site, it's easy to use and truly
> fascinating. There are sections ranging from the obvious, like
> engines and technology, through to food and the weather. Check
> out the helpful 'how to' guides and the featured video. It's written
> in a very concise, clear style with lots of cross-referencing.

www.si.edu/science_and_technology   US
> SMITHSONIAN SCIENCE AND TECHNOLOGY
> Another excellent set of pages from the outstanding Smithsonian
> site, which cover everything from biology to flight and there are
> some really well-written and interesting articles and sections too.

www.extremescience.com   US

> ULTIMATE SCIENCE EXPERIENCE
> Not sure that it really lives up to its billing, but it is a really
> entertaining site with lots of useful and useless facts to bamboozle
> your brain. Features include a time portal where you can learn
> the effects of relativity and other sections on weather, maps,
> technology, nature and the earth. It uses the word 'cool' a lot.

S

www.dangerouslaboratories.org   US

DON'T DO IT YOURSELF

Science with a smile: here you get details of various
'experiments' in a range of scientific fields. It all looks very
amateur and fun as well as educational too.

www.electricmuseum.com   US

… AND DON'T TRY THIS AT HOME!

A highly-charged site with sections on lightning and
atmospheric electricity, a high voltage zone, related articles
and some weird and wonderful images. It has the feel of a site
under development.

www.science-frontiers.com   US

SCIENTIFIC ANOMALIES

Science Frontiers is a bimonthly newsletter providing digests of
reports that describe scientific anomalies – 'those observations
and facts that challenge prevailing scientific paradigms'. There's
a massive archive of the weird and wonderful; it takes patience
but there are some real gems.

www.world-mysteries.com   US

WEIRD SCIENCE

All the mysteries and unexplained phenomena are here,
rationalised, discussed and illustrated in a fairly unbiased way.
It makes for an interesting browse.

www.improbable.com   UK

THE IG NOBLE AWARDS

These awards are for those inventors whose project initially
makes others laugh, then makes them think about the science
behind it. To quote the site, they 'celebrate the unusual and
honour the imaginative'. The site also offers much in the way
of unusual scientific gems.

http://whyfiles.org   US

SCIENCE BEHIND THE NEWS

If you've ever wondered why things happen and what's the real
story behind what they tell you in the papers, then a visit here
will be rewarding. With in-depth studies and brief overviews
Why Files is easy to follow and you'll get the latest news too.

See also:
www.badscience.net – the very entertaining blog of *Guardian* science journalist, Ben Goldacre.
www.scienceagogo.com – a popular science discussion and news site.
www.unmuseum.org – a site devoted to the unexplained and natural phenomena. There's some good stuff, but the busy site design gets in the way.

Scientists

www.nobelprize.org   NORWAY

NOBEL PRIZE
Excellent site on the prize with lots of background information and biographies of the winners.

See also:
http://galileo.rice.edu – excellent site on Galileo.
www.aip.org/history/curie – Marie Curie.
www.mos.org/leonardo – the most useful Leonardo Da Vinci site.
www.newton.cam.ac.uk/newton.html#ini – Isaac Newton.
www.rutherford.org.nz – Ernest Rutherford.
www.thomasedison.com – Edison.
www.westegg.com/einstein – Einstein online.

Biology

www.cellsalive.com   US
CELLS UNDER THE MICROSCOPE
The work of one biologist with a fascination for computer enhanced images of living cells. Fantastic pictures, video and accompanying explanations.

S

www.innerbody.com   US
INTERACTIVE BODIES
All the body's systems illustrated. Pull your mouse over one of the images to activate labels, which can in turn activate text. The animations are worth checking out.

www.wellcome.ac.uk/en/genome   UK
IN THE GENOME
Excellent site explaining in some detail how the human gene works and its implications for biology, medicine and society. The 'interactive centre' is particularly fascinating.

www.rbgkew.org.uk/scihort/index.html　　　　　　UK
BOTANY
Look under 'scientific research' for information on most aspects
of botany and information about research being undertaken at
Kew.

Chemistry

www.webelements.com　　　　　　US
THE PERIODIC TABLE
So you don't know your halides from your fluorides, with this
interactive depiction you can find out. Just click on the element
and you get basic details plus an audio description, all in all, a
great teaching aid. See also **www.chemicool.com** which does
much the same thing.

www.chemsoc.org　　　　　　UK
CHEMICAL SOCIETY
A really creative site that covers not only industry issues, but
also educational ones, all in a very entertaining style. The
timeline is especially well written and there is a very useful
links page too. For more chemistry links go to **www.liv.ac.uk/
Chemistry/Links/links.html**

www.chem4kids.com　　　　　　US
NOT JUST FOR KIDS ...
A very well put together overview of the subject with special
sections on atoms, matter, biochemistry and more. It's fun too
and explained in a non-patronising way.

Physics

www.physicscentral.com　　　　　　US
HOW THE WORLD WORKS
A good place to start when looking for an answer to a physics
question. It has high-quality information and illustrations,
physics news, some interesting writing, a good search
engine and links. For an alternative approach try
http://particleadventure.org which is both comprehensive
and well-written.

http://superstringtheory.com　　　　　　US
THE OFFICIAL WORD ON STRING THEORY
If you're curious about theoretical physics, but find it all a bit

perplexing, or even if you've a good level of understanding, this is the site for you. It explains theoretical physics at a basic or advanced level with good illustrations, a virtual lecture theatre and well-categorised links.

See also section on Space, page 441, and for general physics try:
http://demoroom.physics.ncsu.edu – lots of physics experiments on video.
http://physicsweb.org – online edition of the magazine for up-to-the-minute publications.
www.physics.org – a searchable database, plus a few frills.

Practical Science and Science for Children

www.doscience.com   US
EXPERIMENTS: FUN AND SERIOUS
A slightly messy but entertaining site that has a number of experiments to try both at home and outside. It's informative and most of the experiments seem easy to do.

www.planet-science.com   US
FAST FORWARD TO THE FUTURE
A visually gratifying site with lots to offer by way of helping children (and adults for that matter) to learn about science in an interactive and entertaining way.

www.madsci.org   US
THE LAB THAT NEVER SLEEPS
A site that successfully combines science with fun. You can ask a question of a mad scientist, browse the links list or check out the archives in the library.

See also:
http://insideout.rigb.org – a good, if a little dull, educational e-zine from the Royal Institute.
www.amasci.com – for the science hobbyist, an ugly site.
www.cafescientifique.org – Café Scientifique is a forum for those interested in science; find a café near you, or find out how to start one.
www.extremescience.com – a science education site with an emphasis on the biggest, baddest and best in the world of extremes.
www.funsci.com – a serious site with many experiments to try, both hard and easy.

www.instructables.com – creativity shared. There's some wacky projects here such as the 3-D chocolate printer made from Lego, but also some serious science projects.

www.practicalphysics.org – over 330 practical physics experiments.

www.scienceboffins.com – a group of children's entertainers who do their stuff using science.

www.spartechsoftware.com/reeko – a quirky site, but a great source of science and chemistry experiments designed to inspire school children; will appeal to kids of all ages.

www.thinkingfountain.org – aimed at kids but good for adults too, basically a list of galleries, science facts, projects and recommended books.

www.tryscience.org – bright site aimed at children, with a few experiments.

Innovation, Invention and Technology

www.21stcentury.co.uk   UK

YOUR PORTAL TO THE FUTURE

A stylish site that gives an overview of the latest technology put over in an entertaining style. Whether you're using it for homework or just for a browse, it's useful and interesting. They have 12 categories from cars through to humour, people and technology and they even cover fashion.

www.nesta.org.uk   UK

THE CREATIVE INVENTOR'S HANDBOOK

The National Endowment for Science Technology not only helps inventors get their ideas off the ground with support and guidance, but also encourages creativity and innovation. They'll also inspire you, as a visit to this well-designed site will show. See also the creatively designed **www.inventorlink.co.uk**

www.invent.org   US

THE INVENTOR HALL OF FAME

This outstanding and beautifully designed site features advice on how to patent inventions and gives details of those who have been inducted into the Hall of Fame. If for no other reason, just go to appreciate the web site design.

www.gadgets.co.uk   UK

GAGETS FOR ALL OCCASIONS

Split into 15 different categories, there are hundreds of things

here that you didn't now you wanted. More of the same is
available at **www.paramountzone.com** or **www.firebox.com**

www.robotstoreuk.com UK
ROBOSHOP
A store devoted to selling robot parts and designs, including
kits and a useful introduction to robotics. See also
www.superdroidrobots.com where you can buy parts as
well as kits.

Science Fiction and Fantasy

*Science fiction and fantasy deserves its own section given that so many
top movies and books are based on science fiction or fantasy. Here are
a few of the massive number of sites that are around.*

Directories and Reviews

www.uksfbooknews.net UK
FORMERLY ALIEN ONLINE
A relaunched site with Sci Fi, fantasy and horror book news plus
comics and graphic novel news, all with a UK flavour. There are
still interviews, film reviews, events listings as before and there's
the associated blog at **www.thegenrefiles.com**

See also:
www.feministsf.org – comprehensive, dour offering on the role
of women in Sci Fi.
www.lablit.com – an entertaining site run by scientists rallying
against the stereotypical perceptions of scientists in the media
and literature.
www.locusmag.com – the online version of US *Sci Fi* magazine
Locus. Dull but authoritative.
www.scifisource.com – a directory of all things Sci Fi, not pretty
or easy to navigate but it seems comprehensive.
www.sfrt.com – good for reviews, links and forums.
www.sfsite.com – the dated design doesn't detract from the fact
that this is one of the most comprehensive review sites you can
find; it's quite dense so you need time to digest it.
www.sfx.co.uk – the official site one of the most popular Sci Fi
magazines, it offers plenty of content, although is geared to
selling the mag.

S

Awards and Organisations

www.sfwa.org   US

SCI FI WRITERS OF AMERICA

A helpful and informative site from the SFWA including details of their prestigious Nebula awards. If truth were told it's not a great site but the links and writing advice are good.

See also:

www.appomattox.demon.co.uk/acca – home of the UK's Arthur C Clarke Awards.

www.asfa-art.org – the Association of Sci Fi and Fantasy Artists with an index of artists and galleries.

www.bsfa.co.uk – this chatty site represents the British Science Fiction Association.

www.wsfs.org – an amateur-looking site from the World Science Fiction Society, home of the Hugo awards and with details of the World Science Fiction Convention.

TV and Movies

www.sciflicks.com   US

SCI FI FILM REVIEW

A comprehensive listing of Sci Fi films with reviews, links, descriptions, cast listing and so on. There's plenty of detail and there is also information on forthcoming movies.

www.scifi.com   US

THE SCI FI CHANNEL

An excellent site from the Sci Fi Channel with a very strong emphasis on film and television, although it also includes books, games and other products. It's beautifully designed, easy to navigate, and there is a wealth of extra features, including weekly newsletters.

www.sfon.tv   UK

SCI FI ON TV

A very good site featuring everything Sci Fi on television from the famous and obscure. Dr Sci Fi will even attempt to answer your Sci Fi questions. There's also a good movie review section.

See also:

http://exclamationmark.typepad.com – check out the excellent B movie blog.

www.greatlink.org – a UK-oriented site devoted to all things Trek.

www.sadgeezer.com – great for fans of Sci Fi cult TV, though pretty difficult to navigate, it has plenty of other Sci Fi resources too; you should be aware that it is possible to access some adult oriented content.

www.startrek.com – everything you need to know about Star Trek and its spin off series.

www.starwars.com – outstanding official Star Wars site.

www.superherohype.com – lots of stuff on super heroes plus interviews from those involved in the films and downloads too.

www.timelord.co.uk – Dr Who and much more.

The Writing

http://isfdb.tamu.edu/sfdbase.html   US

INTERNET SPECULATIVE FICTION DATABASE
This excellent resource is an encyclopaedic guide to authors of 'speculative fiction', which includes every Sci Fi, fantasy and horror writer you could think of. The trouble is that it looks more like a library catalogue than a modern web site.

See also:
http://sff.onlinewritingworkshop.com – advice and courses to improve your writing.

www.fantasticmetropolis.com – this good-looking and acclaimed site is dedicated to 'new wave' alternative authors; it includes fiction, essays, interviews, reviews and more. It also has an excellent links section.

www.infinityplus.co.uk – original fiction and non-fiction by many top names.

www.sff.net – somewhere amongst the commercial bits there's a really good website, you just have to be patient and sign up.

www.sfnovelist.com – a writing group who believe in Sci Fi based on hard science; some good short stories, but you need to be a member really.

www.technovelgy.com – a fun site devoted to the inventions of Sci Fi writers and whether they would really work and what they would look like.

S

The Writers

www.lordoftherings.net   US
LORD OF THE RINGS
Slick on the movie trilogy, including information on the films,
interviews, picture galleries, trailers and other downloads. Best
accessed on broadband. See also **www.tolkien.co.uk** which is
home to the official UK web site from Tolkien's publishers,
including a biography, his books, artwork, downloads and other
information. Ordering facility through Amazon.

www.discworldmonthly.co.uk   UK
TERRY PRATCHETT
Probably the best of the many sites devoted to this massively
popular author and his Discworld creation with lots of links and
regular articles and updates.

Other key authors:
Clive Barker – **www.clivebarker.com**
Terry Brooks – **www.terrybrooks.net**
Peter F. Hamilton – **www.peterfhamilton.co.uk**
Katherine Kerr – **www.deverry.com**
Stephen King – **www.stephenking.com**
George RR Martin – **www.georgerrmartin.com**
Garth Nix – **www.garthnix.co.uk**
Christopher Paolini – **www.alagaesia.com**
Philip Pullman – **www.philip-pullman.com**
Alastair Reynolds – **http://members.tripod.com/~voxish**
Tad Williams – **www.tadwilliams.com**

Below is a list of key Sci Fi and fantasy publishers:
www.2000adonline.com – home to the venerable British comic,
featuring Judge Dredd.
www.marvel.com – great interactive site from Marvel Comics
with all their major characters suitably involved.
www.orbitbooks.co.uk – home of authors such as Robert
Jordan and Iain Banks, it's an attractive, frequently updated site
with author pages, new releases, sample chapters, a monthly e-
mail newsletter and exclusive offers.
www.titanbooks.com – the UK's largest publisher of graphic
novels – also features information on their range of film and TV
tie-ins.
www.voyager-books.co.uk – home of HarperCollins' Fantasy
and Sci Fi publishing. It's a classy-looking site, with author

profiles, news, new titles, sample chapters, interactive features
and extras such as downloadable screensavers.

Search Engines

*The best way to find what you want from the Internet is to use a search
engine. Even the best don't cover anywhere near the number of
available web sites, so if you can't find what you want from one, try
another. These are the best and most user-friendly. For children's
search engines see page 94.*

www.searchenginewatch.com   US
> A GUIDE TO SEARCHING
> This site rates and assesses all the search engines and it's a
> useful starting point if you're looking for a good or specific
> search facility. There's a newsletter and statistical analysis plus
> strategies on how to make the perfect search. See also
> **www.searchengineshowdown.com** who do much the same
> thing but it's less comprehensive.

General Searching

www.google.co.uk   US/UK
 BRINGING ORDER TO THE WEB
> Google is a massive success story and is one of the most useful
> sites around. Apart from the simple search facility, it also has a
> host of other features which are covered in our Google feature on
> page 226. If you want to get the best out of Google then pay a
> visit to the non-affiliated but very helpful **www.googleguide.com**

http://search.msn.co.uk   US/UK
> MSN SEARCH
> A minimal approach, this search engine is supposed to be
> Microsoft's answer to Google. It's very fast and it seems to be
> the business. You also get access to the Encarta Encyclopedia
> too.

www.ask.co.uk   UK
> ASK
> The famous old butler Jeeves has been ditched but, although
> less fun, it works very well; it's great for beginners and reliable
> for old hands too. See also **www.askforkids.com** which is the
> child-oriented version.

It's Not Just About Google

The Good Web Site Guide's Top 10s
of the Internet

1. **www.a9.com** – a search engine that uses many reference resources
2. **www.dmoz.org** – the most comprehensive site directory on the net
3. **www.mirago.co.uk** – great if you want a UK biased result to your search
4. **www.refdesk.com** – information and links, very impressive
5. **www.about.com** – fantastic, with expertly written pages on virtually any topic
6. **www.onelook.com** – access to almost 1,000 online dictionaries
7. **www.howstuffworks.com** – if it moves, it's explained
8. **www.nationmaster.com** – information and stats on virtually every country
9. **www.wikipedia.org** – the people's encyclopedia
10. **www.ehow.com** – instructions on how to do virtually anything

http://uk.yahoo.com   US/UK
FOR THE UK AND IRELAND
The UK arm of Yahoo is the biggest and one of the most established search engines. It's now much more than just a search facility as it offers a huge array of other services: from news to finance to shopping to sport to travel to games. You can restrict your search to just UK or Irish sites too.

www.lii.org   US
THE LIBRARIANS' INDEX TO THE INTERNET
This is a search engine with a difference in that all the source material has been selected and evaluated by librarians specifically for their use in public libraries. This doesn't stop you using it though, and it is very good for obscure searches and research – like putting together a web site guide, for example.

www.dmoz.org   WORLD-WIDE
THE OPEN DIRECTORY PROJECT
The goal is to produce the most comprehensive directory of the
web and relies on an army (some 71,000) of volunteer editors
to do so; if you want to get involved it's easy to sign yourself up.
If it can't help with your query, it puts you through to one of the
mainstream search engines.

*Finding the search engine that suits you is a matter of personal
requirements and taste. Here are some other very good, tried
and trusted ones:*
http://uk.altavista.com – limited but very efficient, offers up a
list of related options on every search.
www.accoona.com – a good alternative to Google, it allows you
to prioritise your searching easily.
www.alltheweb.com – no frills, similar to Google.
www.bbc.co.uk – BBC's search engine is simple to use.
www.copernic.com – download a free search program.
www.dogpile.com – straightforward and no mess … US
oriented.
www.factbites.com – results come with some context and
explanation, which is more helpful than most; strong US bias.
www.infoplease.com – good for homework, one of the best for
research.
www.looksmart.com – good, all sites handpicked.
www.pluck.com – a useful little free program that can be used
as a search tool, it's also got a useful news feed facility.
www.spurl.net – a search program enhanced with the ability to
manage links and bookmarks in a proactive way.

Clustering Search Engines

*Clustered search engines sort and categorise search results, which is
great, but we've yet to find a really good one that isn't US oriented.*

www.vivisimo.com   US
CLUSTERING TECHNOLOGY
With Vivisimo instead of the usual list, you get your search
results back categorised by subject, or clustered. It makes for
easy researching and is one of the three search engines I most
use. See also **www.clusty.com**

www.mamma.com   US
THE MOTHER OF ALL SEARCH ENGINES
Mamma have technology enabling them to search the major
search engines thoroughly and get the most pertinent results to
your query – it's fast too, your query comes back with the
answer and the search engine it came from.

www.A9.com   US
THE WEB AND BEYOND
A9 uses Google to search the web but enhances that search
with information from the Internet Movie Database, Amazon's
Search inside the book service and other reference sources. It's a
little slow but you get quality results.

See also:
http://turbo10.com – claims to search the bits of the Internet
where the major search engines don't go, this is one of the most
impressive results-wise.
www.37.com – a bit of a mess but can search 37 other search
engines in one go.
www.clusteredhits.com – clutter free, good for technical,
scholarly and corporate data although US oriented.
www.metacrawler.com – uses similar technology to Mamma
and is a popular choice.
www.search.com – a solid performer from CNet.

http://eurekster.com   US
SEARCHING WITH FRIENDS
Here you get the usual search facility with clustered results but
you can also sign up with a group of friends, then when one of
them does the same search your preferred result will appear
higher up their list of results. It's excellent if you share a
particular hobby or interest.

UK-oriented Searching

www.mirago.co.uk   UK
THE UK SEARCH ENGINE
Mirago searches the whole web but prioritises the search for UK
families and businesses. It's very quick, easy to use and offers
many of the services you get from Yahoo. You can tailor your
search very easily to exclude stuff you won't need.

For other UK-oriented search sites try:

http://UK20.co.uk – a good-looking site, it's OK as a search engine too.

www.4ni.co.uk – a good search engine serving Northern Ireland.

www.britishinformation.com – well designed and comprehensive.

www.clickclick2.net – odd design and more of a directory.

www.lifestyle.co.uk – a massive directory of specially selected sites for the UK.

www.lycos.co.uk – easy to use and popular, good for highlighting offers.

www.searchinwales.com – does what it says in the title (i.e. searches relevant to Wales).

www.searchsaint.com – good looking and easy to use.

www.searchscotland.net – does what it says.

www.wotbox.co.uk – excellent for UK-oriented searches, each site is denoted with its flag of origin.

www.watchthatpage.com   US
CHANGES ON THE WEB
Not strictly a search engine but if you have specific interests you can download the program, input the URLs and it will let you know when the site or page has been updated. You can also use it to search and hunt out specific articles.

Security

Keeping your computer, its contents and those who use it safe is one of the biggest priorities for any user, although it's unlikely you'll have any major problems. Here's a list of sites that will help you keep secure and some protection software and information that's available for nothing. If you've found yourself with an infection, then running some of these programs can, hopefully, identify and destroy the malicious files.

*Visit **www.download.com** for a selection of free and rated programs that can help with securing your PC, while at **www.microsoft.com/security** you can get updates to ensure your system is working properly. For Apple users try **www.apple.com/macosx/features/security** for the latest information on keeping your Mac safe. If you're running a business and worried about security, then you might try **www.cisecurity.org** which is a non-profit organisation and has plenty of advice as to the best way to look after your system.*

www.getsafeonline.org UK

EXPERT ADVICE

A great place to start to learn about online security. It gives information on personal safety, PC safety and has a businesses section. Much of the advice is suitable for beginners, but old hands can learn something as well. For a site aimed at young people try **www.thinkuknow.co.uk** which is an excellent site dedicated to online safety.

www.firewallguide.com US

HOME PC FIREWALL GUIDE

A firewall is a piece of filtering software that protects your PC and prevents unknown users from sending material to it. But which is the best one? Find out here. For a good and well-regarded firewall program that has a free trial version available go to **www.zonelabs.com** and if you can't get on with that a good alternative can be found at **www.agnitum.com** and also the highly rated **www.comodo.com**

There are plenty of sites advocating the best virus software, but not many of them are truly independent, below is a list of sites and programs that you may find helpful.

> **www.avast.com** – one of the most reliable free anti-virus programs.
> **www.clamxav.com** – a free virus checker for Macs.
> **www.f-secure.com** – one of the newer security companies.
> **www.free-av.com** – another good free-trial-only, anti-virus program.
> **www.grisoft.com** – for free trial of the AVG anti-virus scanner.
> **www.kaspersky.com** – home of the top-rated anti-virus program, offers free online virus scan and free trials.
> **www.macafee.com** – security specialists.
> **www.softscan.co.uk** – excellent for e-mail security.
> **www.symanteccom.com** – where to go for Norton products.
> **ww.pandasecurity.com** – another top-rated program.
> **www.viruslist.com** – if you're really interested in viruses, then go here where you'll find a virus encyclopaedia.

*It's always worth visiting a site like **www.download.com** (where you can find a great security section) to see how they rate security programs and to keep up with the latest versions and news. Pests such as spyware, malware and trojans are not always picked up by the virus scanners, so here is a list of other security sites and programs worth checking out …*

www.ccleaner.com – home of an excellent and free little
program that you can use to clean your system.
www.lavasoftusa.com – home of the excellent AdAware
program which gets rid of spyware and trojans.
www.microsoft.com/security/ – Microsoft's security section is
always worth checking out.
www.microsoft.com/security/malwareremove – check out
whether your PC system is infected.
www.microsoft.com/athome/security/spyware/software/default.
mspx – home of the anti-spyware program Windows Defender.
www.naomifilter.org – home of Naomi, a very good internet
filtering program aimed at families with children. It stops all sorts
of nasties from getting to your kids and your computer, and it's
free.
www.safer-networking.org – home of SpyBot, a useful spyware
destroyer.
www.spywarewarrior.com – more information, background and
downloads.
www.unwantedlinks.com/macsupport.htm – free download of
their spyware program for Macs, plus links to other security
programs for Macs.
www.webroot.com – home of the excellent Spy Sweeper
program.

Other areas of concern …

www.cookiecentral.com   US
COOKIES EXPLAINED
An excellent site dedicated to explaining the workings of that
mysterious animal the 'cookie' and how you can deal with them.

www.nclnet.org/technology/essentials   UK
PRIVACY
An informative site giving an overview of security and privacy
issues on the Internet, it has plenty of helpful advice and links to
related sites.

www.windowsstartup.com   UK
START UP PROBLEMS
A useful little program that helps with cleaning up your PC's
start up.

S

Ships and Boats

For shipping and boating enthusiasts here are a few sites that may interest you. Sailing is listed under Sport, page 471, and water-borne holidays can be found in the Travel section, page 508.

Boats

www.totallyboaty.co.uk   UK
BOATING DIRECTORY
A very good portal site devoted to all things boating, it's easy to find what you're looking for and it's developing fast; see also **www.aboard.co.uk** which offers a similar service and also **www.boatlinks.com** which is a well-categorised, US-oriented directory.

http://boatbuilding.com   UK
THE BOAT BUILDING COMMUNITY
If you want to repair or build a boat then here's where to go, with features and discussion forums to help you on your way. There's also a very good directory of links to suppliers and resource sites.

www.boatshop24.co.uk   UK
BOAT TRADER MAGAZINE
Primarily a vehicle to get you to subscribe to the magazine, the site offers information on brokers and over 23,000 adverts. See also the well-designed **www.boats.com** and for information of what you are buying **www.whatboat.com**

See also:
www.boatingnews.com – news and classifieds.
www.boatingontheweb.com – an American boating directory.
www.boatlaunch.co.uk – a mapping service showing all the places in the UK where you can launch your boat.
www.uscgboating.org – a good site for advice and information on safe boating.

Ships and Navy

www.royal-navy.mod.uk   UK
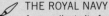
THE ROYAL NAVY
An excellent site from the Royal Navy giving details of the ships,

submarines and aircraft and what it's like to be a part of it all. There's a video gallery featuring highlights from the fleet and details of all the Royal Navy ships. Apart from all the information, you can have a go on the interactive frigate and take part in a strategic game.

www.hazegray.org US

NAVAL HISTORY AND PHOTOGRAPHY
A well-categorised and comprehensive site featuring naval histories, background on the world's ships and navies and also shipbuilding. It's oriented to the US.

More naval and historical sites:
www.mightyseas.co.uk – a history site on the boats and ships from NW England.
www.naval-history.net – a messy site, but good for the 20th century and links.
www.navsource.org – a thorough unofficial overview of the US navy.
www.nmm.ac.uk – a good site from the National Maritime Museum in Greenwich.
www.skipper.co.uk – nautical publishers and booksellers.
www.tallship.co.uk – a magazine-related site with articles and photo gallery.

www.red-duster.co.uk UK

RED DUSTER MAGAZINE
Red Duster is a merchant navy enthusiasts' site offering lots in the way of history covering sail, steam and shipping lines. There's also a section on the history of customs. To find out what the current merchant navy are up to go to **www.merchantnavyofficers.com** where you can find information and links.

www.maritimematters.com UK

OCEAN LINERS AND CRUISE SHIPS
An informative site with data on over 100 ships from the earliest liners to the most modern, each has its own page with quality pictures and some virtual tours. It is also good for news and links to related sites.

S

Other Watercraft

www.hovercraft.org.uk　　　　　　　　　　　　　　　UK
　　HOVERCRAFT
　　If you're into hovercraft or are just interested, here's the place to
　　look with three sections – Britain, Europe and the world, which
　　just about covers it all.

www.jetskier.co.uk　　　　　　　　　　　　　　　　　UK
　　JET SKI
　　Home of *Jetskier* magazine and while it's geared to sell the
　　mag, the site does offer much in the way of links and advice.
　　For more tips, forums and chat go to the US-oriented
　　www.jetskinews.com

www.rontini.com　　　　　　　　　　　　　　　　　UK
　　SUBMARINE WORLD NETWORK
　　A directory site with over 1,000 links all devoted to the world of
　　submarines. It covers everything from navies to models.

　　See also:
　　www.lr.org – Lloyd's register.
　　www.nao.rl.ac.uk – home of the Nautical Almanac Office.
　　www.paddling.net – for buying canoes and kayaks.
　　www.tpl.lib.wa.us/v2/nwroom/ships.htm – the Tacoma public
　　library has a searchable database of some 13,000 ships.

Shopping

*To many people shopping is what the Internet is all about, and it does
offer an opportunity to get some tremendous bargains. Watch out for
hidden costs such as delivery charges, import duties or finance deals
that seem attractive until you compare them with what's available
elsewhere. For help on finding comparative prices, see the price
comparison sites on page 386, in fact, starting your shopping trip at a
site like **www.kelkoo.co.uk** may prove to be a wise move. There is also
a section on consumer information on page 103 for the low-down on
your rights and what to do when things go wrong. For shopping
ethically see the section on page 139. The Introduction on page 9
contains more information on safe shopping on the Internet.*

Treat Yourself

The Good Web Site Guide's Top 10s
of the Internet

1. **www.which.net** – the consumer's friend
2. **http://froogle.google.co.uk** – if looking for something specific try here first
3. **www.dooyoo.co.uk** – get an impartial review before you buy
4. **www.amazon.co.uk** – the most popular online retailer
5. **www.kelkoo.co.uk** – a great price checking site
6. **www.ebay.co.uk** – bid for it
7. **www.ukshopsearch.com** – excellent directory of shops
8. **www.johnlewis.co.uk** – the UK's most loved retailer
9. **www.shopperuk.com** – online shopping from over 2,000 stores
10. **www.pricerunner.co.uk** – you know you can get it cheaper

---

www.tradingstandards.gov.uk   UK

TRADING STANDARDS CENTRAL

Find out where you stand and what to do if you think you're being ripped off or someone is not trading fairly – you can even take a quiz about it. There are advice guides to print off or download and there is help and advice to businesses and schools as well as consumers.

Two other consumer-oriented sites worth checking out are:
www.dti.gov.uk/consumers/fact-sheets – useful range of consumer factsheets from the Department of Trade and Industry.
www.howtocomplain.com – advice on how to go about airing your grievances and getting a result.

www.which.net   UK

WHICH? MAGAZINE

A good place to start your shopping experience but you have to be a member to get the best out of it. There is limited free information on their consumer reports featuring a wide range of goods and services from dishcloths to cars to personal finance. They provide quality consumer and health advice; you can also read about and join their campaigns.

S

www.dooyoo.co.uk UK

MAKE YOUR OPINION COUNT
Media darling Doo Yoo is a site where you the consumer can
give your opinion or a review on any product that's available to
buy, this way you get unbiased opinions about them – in theory.
They cover a wide range of 'products' from books to TV shows
and it's easy to contribute. See also **www.ciao.co.uk** where you
can actually get paid a small amount of money for your opinion
and also **www.epinions.com**

The Virtual High Street

www.marks-and-spencer.co.uk UK

CLOTHES AND GIFTS
A clear, attractive site that has a good selection of products from
clothes to gifts for all, as well as fashion advice and a quick
order facility.

www.boots.com UK

BOOTS
An online shop that reflects what you see when you visit the real
store and there are now lots of offers to tempt you. There's lots
of choice and it's well categorised, functional too.

www.whsmith.co.uk UK

WHSMITH
The Smith's site has a clean, easy-to-navigate format, with the
emphasis on offers and best-sellers. There is a great deal here
including the usual books, music, mags, games, stationery and
DVDs. You can avoid the delivery charge if you collect the goods
from your nearest store, which sort of defeats the object of
buying online, but you can also claim loyalty points with online
purchases.

www.woolworths.co.uk UK

WELL WORTH IT
A bright and breezy site from Woolworths with all you'd expect in
terms of range and prices. They are particularly good on kids' stuff
with strong prices on movies, chart music, clothes and games.

www.argos.co.uk UK

ARGOS CATALOGUE
Argos offers an excellent range of products (some 16,500)
across twelve different categories as per their catalogue. There

are some good bargains to be had. You can now reserve an item
at your local store, once you've checked that they have it in
stock. There's a good search facility and you can find a product
via its catalogue number, if you've a catalogue handy that is.
Returns can be made to your local store.

www.debenhams.com UK
AWARD-WINNING FAMILY SERVICE
Debenhams have a very good site aimed at their retailing
strengths: gifts, weddings and fashion. They've introduced a
nice range of furniture that is not only available online.

www.johnlewis.co.uk UK
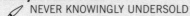
NEVER KNOWINGLY UNDERSOLD
A really attractive and usable site with a wide range of products
and some good offers too. Delivery costs start at £3.95, free
over £100. Especially good if you haven't got one of their
excellent stores near by. For more upmarket gear check out
www.selfridges.com which has interesting site designs and
products to match.

www.virginmedia.com/shopping UK
LIFESTYLE AND SHOPPING GUIDE
Virgin's shopping guide is comprehensive covering all major
categories while allowing retailers to feature some of their best
offers. It also attempts to be a complete service for entertainment
and leisure needs with excellent sections on music, travel and
cinema in particular.

Other high street names ...
www.bhs.co.uk – no online shopping but they do have a store
locator.
www.houseoffraser.co.uk – good store directory but you can
only buy vouchers online.

General Retailers, Directories and Online Department Stores

http://froogle.google.co.uk UK
SHOPPING SEARCH ENGINE
A very useful facility from Google: just type in what you want to
buy and up pops a list with prices and links to relevant shops.
It's quick but the search results don't appear in price order.

www.shopperuk.com UK

UK SHOPPING DIRECTORY
A very commercial directory of UK shops both specialist and
general. It's well categorised by both type and alphabet; a
genuinely useful site with each store having a write up and a list
of related stores alongside. There is also a product search facility.

www.edirectory.co.uk UK

IF IT'S OUT THERE, BUY IT HERE
A nice-looking directory of some 900 shops, it has a good
reputation for service as well as being topical.

www.catalink.com UK

CATALOGUES GALORE
If you love shopping via a catalogue then here is the place to
start, there are hundreds listed.

See also:
http://theukhighstreet.com – a good UK directory, with the
shops rated by you the customer.
www.abound.co.uk – an excellent site offering a wide range of
clothes and leisure and electrical products; it's well executed and
has some good offers too.
www.buy4now.ie – an Irish shopping portal with a massive
selection of goods with prices now quoted in Euros.
www.i-stores.com – a very good store search engine and
directory.
www.letsbuyit.com – claiming over a million members and the
best prices.
www.mailorderexpress.co.uk – excellent for toys and kids' stuff.
www.shoptour.co.uk – links to hundreds of secure shops in 14
categories, with a price comparison tool.
www.ukshopsearch.com – above average search engine and
quality design make this stand out from the crowd.
www.ukshopsnet.com – well-designed and well-categorised
store directory site and search engine.
www.worthaglance.com – great-looking shop with some
outstanding bargains.

TV Shopping Channels

www.qvcuk.com UK

TV SHOPPING ONLINE
As a shopping channel on satellite or cable, QVC was already

successful; this well-put-together site shows off the breadth of their range and has some good offers. In total they display some 10,000 products.

See also:
www.bestdirect.tv – loads of bargains and celebrity endorsements.
www.idealworld.tv – just details of their channels and presenters, not much to buy.
www.price-drop.tv – the shop with lots of offers, and you can watch it live too.
www.screenshop.co.uk – very limited range on offer.
www.simplyshoppingtv.co.uk – with emphasis on health and home.

Value for Money

www.thesimplesaver.com   UK
WHERE TO GET THE BEST DEAL
What started off as a simple e-mail conversation about where to go for savings has snowballed into a web site. You now have to register your details and select the category of goods that interest you and they will send you details of offers on a weekly, fortnightly or monthly basis.

www.gooddealdirectory.co.uk   UK
THE BARGAIN HUNTER'S BIBLE
Based on the book of the same name, this is basically a searchable directory of discount shops and sales. It's easy to use and the information seems comprehensive.

British Shopping

S

www.british-shopping.com   UK
UK SHOPPING LINKS AND DIRECTORY
An excellent comprehensive portal site specialising in British shops; it also has plenty of related links and information.
www.somucheasier.co.uk also offers a comprehensive UK-oriented shop listing.

For more quintessentially British shops check out these sites:
www.brooksandbentley.com – classy British gifts.
www.classicengland.co.uk – the best British products on a fun-looking and easy-to-use site.

www.distinctlybritish.com – a British shop directory with a wide range of food, clothing, gift and children's retailers on offer.

www.harrods.com – a selection of their products available to buy from an attractive-looking site.

www.pasttimes.com – gifts inspired by the past.

www.scotsmart.com   UK
SCOTTISH

A Scottish directory of sites, not just for shopping but covering most areas; you can search by theme or category and the shopping section is split into books, clothing, food, gifts and highland wear. See also **www.scotch-corner.co.uk** which is Scottish through and through.

www.wales-direct.com   UK
WALES DIRECT

A well-categorised shop devoted to all things Welsh, it has a wide range and some offers too, as well as a good links section.

The Good Web Site Guide's Gift Guide

The following sites should help you find the perfect gift!

www.hard2buy4.co.uk   UK
GIFT IDEAS

Excellent gift shop with a wide range of unusual products including celebrity items, activities and gifts for men, women and children in separate sections, some good offers too.

See also:

http://shop.christianaid.org.uk – give a gift to help the world's poor and needy.

www.baby-gifts.co.uk – personalised gifts for the very young.

www.beautifulthings.co.uk – retail therapy from your desk apparently, you can shop by star sign too.

www.boysstuff.co.uk – gifts and products aimed at boys of all ages, has a section for girls too.

www.buyagift.co.uk – activities and experiences for those who have everything.

www.cafepress.com – personalised gifts for all, well most occasions!

www.craft-fair.co.uk – a site devoted to bringing UK-made craft goods to market.

www.find-me-a-gift.co.uk – gifts, both products and special experiences, can be found here, loyalty scheme and wish lists thrown in too.

www.hawkin.com – odd design but good for range for children and the unusual.

www.indiangiftsportal.com – beautiful and unusual gifts from India.

www.iwantoneofthose.com – for more unusual gifts and stuff you don't need but would really like; it has a great gift finder.

www.jun-gifts.com – Japanese gifts and other products, excellent for the unusual.

www.maleorder.co.uk – presents for the man in your life.

www.michaelajdavies.co.uk – a great example of a showcase site with some nice gifts from around the world. If you're a retailer, they'll even make a range especially for you.

www.mumstheword.com – so that mums-to-be can feel beautiful.

www.needapresent.com – very good site with some out-of-the ordinary gifts.

www.placesafar.com – African arts and crafts with info on the techniques and bios of some of the artists.

www.presentcorrect.com – create a gift list for yourself, your friends and family. It's good for suggestions for those difficult-to-buy-for people.

www.presentprovider.com – for all those things that you never knew existed and never really wanted; gifts for people you don't really like.

www.prezzybox.com – good selection including garden games.

www.rebirth.co.za – authentic African art and gifts.

www.recyclenow.com/shopping/index.html – shop with an easy conscience with loads of gifts and products made from recycled material.

www.thedoghouse.co.uk – the gift reminder service and online shop, never forget that anniversary again.

www.thesharperedge.co.uk – some good stuff in amongst the tat.

www.voucherexpress.co.uk – the place to buy gift vouchers, including nearly all the major retailers.

So you can't be bothered to buy?

www.anythingforhire.co.uk   UK

HIRE IT!

A comprehensive directory of goods and services for hire across the UK, well laid out and easy to use. Alternatively, try **www.thehirehub.co.uk** who also let you offer stuff you own for hire, nice site and nice idea, but you wonder if it will catch on …

Skiing and Snowboarding

These sites tend to include information on both skiing and related travel, so we've moved it from Sports to create a combined section devoted to all things snowy.

www.fis-ski.com UK

INTERNATIONAL SKI FEDERATION
Catch up on the news, the fastest times and the rankings in all forms of skiing at this site. Very good background information and a live online section enabling events to be monitored as they happen.

www.ski.co.uk UK

THE PLACE TO START – A SKI DIRECTORY
Straightforward site, the information in the directory is useful and the recommended sites are rated. The sections include holidays, travel, weather, resorts, snowboarding, gear, fanatics and specialist services. See also **www.skicentral.com**

www.1ski.com UK

COMPLETE ONLINE SKIING SERVICE
With a huge number of holidays, live snow reports, tips on technique and equipment, and the ultimate guide featuring over 750 resorts, it's difficult to go wrong. The site is well laid out and easy to use. There's a good events calendar too.

Other good ski and snowboarding sites:
www.descent.co.uk – specialists in luxury alpine holidays.
www.flexiski.co.uk – tailor-made skiing holidays.
www.ifyouski.com – comprehensive skiing site that has a very good holiday booking service with lots of deals.
www.igluski.com – holiday specialists with lots of variety and offers.
www.inghams.co.uk – travel operator with a good reputation for skiing holidays.
www.mountainzone.com – great for features, articles and ski adventurers.
www.natives.co.uk – aimed at ski workers, there's info on conditions, ski resorts, a good job section, where to stay and links to other cool sites all wrapped up on a very nicely designed site.
www.skiclub.co.uk – Ski Club of Great Britain with lots of offers and information too.

www.skidream.com – skiing and snowboarding in America and Canada.

www.skireunited.com – a Friends Reunited but for skiing holidays and workers.

www.skisolutions.com – one of the oldest travel companies specialising in skiing holidays, with a huge range of holidays and expertise.

www.skiweekend.com – ski weekend specialist.

www.snow-forecast.com – weather forecasts for snow areas.

www.snowlife.org.uk – very good directory come advice centre.

www.snowrental.net – online equipment rental, all seems very easy.

www.boardtheworld.com   UK
SNOWBOARDING

Masses of information and links covering the world of snowboarding, the site is well designed and doesn't seem to miss out any aspect of the sport.

See also:

www.boardz.com/snowboard/snowboardcentral.html – the snowboarding e-zine from Boardz.

www.goneboarding.co.uk – the UK boarding community with lots of information and chat.

www.mcnabsnowboarding.com – snowboarding camps and holidays.

www.snowboardinguk.co.uk – forums and snowboarding chat.

Social Networking

Here's how to start up a social network with your friends and consequently with their friends. It's a great way to share experiences, data or photos and particularly good for clubs or if you're fed up with the traditional dating sites. Here are some of the best and most useful sites, however many more are listed on Wikipedia's social networking pages at http://en.wikipedia.org/wiki/List_of_social_networking_websites

www.friendster.com   US
COMMUNITY

A very easy-to-use set up with clear instructions and design; it's oriented towards dating but it's really adaptable.

www.faceparty.com   UK

BIGGEST PARTY ON EARTH

A combination of dating agency, party organiser and chat site.
You download your details and photo to create your own profile,
then just join in.

www.myspace.com   UK

MORE THAN SOCIAL NETWORKING

While social networking you can play games, watch short films,
go blogging and, of course, stream music. This site has
developed as a showcase for new bands, film producers and
artists – but be aware that you give up your rights on posted
material, which Myspace can potentially exploit as they please.

See also:

http://twitter.com – social networking site combined with
blogging and text messaging.

www.bebo.com – very popular social networking site, originally
for schools and colleges now much expanded.

www.blackplanet.com – a very popular site for the black
community.

www.facebook.com – networks created around a company,
school, college or area.

www.furl.net – not really a social networking program but its
facilities make it useful for sharing internet information in this
context.

www.last.fm – share your music taste with friends and listen to
personalized radio.

www.linkedin.com – popular especially in the business
community.

www.meetup.com – easy to use and well designed.

www.profileheaven.com – popular social site for young people.

www.zorpia.com – photo journals and sharing.

Software, Upgrades, Debugging and Widgets

*If you need to upgrade your software, then these are the sites to go to.
Shareware is where you get a program to use for a short period of time
before you have to buy it, freeware is exactly what you'd think – free.
Debugging programs fix problems in established programs that weren't
previously identified.*

www.softwareparadise.co.uk   UK

THE SMART WAY TO SHOP FOR SOFTWARE
With nearly 30 thousand products and excellent offers, this site
should be your first stop. It's a bit messy but easy to use;
there's a good search facility and plenty of products for Mac users.

www.download.com   US

CNET
A superb site covering all types of software and available
downloads. There are masses of reviews as well as buying tips
and price comparison tools; it also covers handheld PCs, Linux
and Macs.

www.softseek.com   US

ZDNET
Another excellent site with a huge amount of resources to
download, it's all a little overwhelming at first but the download
directory is easy to use and there's lots of free software available.

www.tucows.com   US

TUCOWS
Probably less irritating to use than ZDNet and CNet, the software
reviews are also entertaining in their own right, the best thing
about it though is that it's quick.

If you feel like shopping around a bit more see also:
http://freshmeat.net – lots of shareware, also good for Linux
fans.
www.annoyances.org – a good site devoted to fixing problems in
Microsoft Windows.
www.completelyfreesoftware.com – hundreds of free programs
for you to download, from games to useful desktop accessories;
if it's available free, then it's here. Membership is essential
costing under £10 per year.
www.computeractive.co.uk – this good UK-based magazine
offers free access to its software reviews and archives.
www.freewarehome.com – a great selection of free programs,
well classified and comprehensive.
www.handango.com – a good site specialising in downloads for
handheld PCs.
www.kidsfreeware.com – Internet freebies for kids.
www.neatnettricks.com – an archive of useful tips and
downloads with regular updates, you need to subscribe though,
which costs about £7 per year.

www.netscape.com – if you're a Netscape fan then you can improve its performance with 'plug-ins' from this site.

www.versiontracker.com – a massive selection, particularly good for Mac software.

www.vnunet.com – UK-orientated review and download site.

www.winplanet.com – specialises in software downloads and reviews for small businesses.

www.wired.com – popular technology magazine with all the latest news and reviews.

www.winzip.com   US

KONFABULATOR

Winzip allows you to save space on your PC by compressing data, making it easier to e-mail files and unlock zipped files that have been sent to you. It takes a few minutes to download. For Macs go to **www.allume.com** where you'll find Stuffit.

Widgets

Widgets are fun, small but useful programs (mini-applications) that sit on your desktop and quickly impart some piece of specific or useful (sometimes not so useful) information. Apple has integrated them into the new Dashboard as part of their Tiger operating system; at the blog program Typepad you can integrate them into your blog; and Opera has made them part of their browser too. They will become a more common sight, especially as they are so simple to create.

http://widgets.yahoo.com   US

KONFABULATOR

The original widgets program was the Konfabulator: you download the Widget Engine, which comes with several free widgets such as clocks and the weather forecast, then you can explore the widget gallery (**www.widgetgallery.com**); for thousands more, the radio ones are particularly good.

See also:

www.apple.com/downloads/dashboard – for more Mac widgets.

http://en.wikipedia.org/wiki/Widget_(computing) – for a more detailed explanation of widget programs.

www.versiontracker.com/macosx/cat/widgets – excellent for Mac owners, they are rated too.

www.widgetopia.net – a site in development but one that has got potential.

Space

E-zines and Reference Sites

www.space.com US

MAKING SPACE POPULAR
An education-oriented site dedicated to space; there's news, mission reports, technology, history, personalities, a games section and plenty of pictures. The science section explores the planets and earth.

www.spacedaily.com US

YOUR PORTAL TO SPACE
A comprehensive newspaper-style site with a huge amount of information and news about space and related subjects. It also has links to similar sister sites covering subjects like Mars, space war and space travel. See also the eccentric **www.astspace.demon.co.uk** – a good portal, once you find it.

www.astronomynow.com UK

THE UK'S BEST-SELLING ASTRONOMY MAG
Get the news and views from a British angle, plus reviews on the latest books. The store has widened out to include patches, T-shirts and videos as well as the magazine and posters.

www.windows.ucar.edu US

WINDOWS TO THE UNIVERSE
A well-designed site that provides information about the earth, solar system and universe at three levels of detail, making it suitable for everyone from children to the most serious-minded. There are interesting sections exploring the link between the world's mythology and space, and history and space. There are also sections on geology, space exploration and art.

www.heavens-above.com US

IT'S ABOVE YOUR HEAD
Type in your location and they'll give you the exact time and precise location of the next visible pass of the International Space Station or space shuttle. They also help you to observe satellites, flares from Iridium satellites and start charts customised to your location. You have to register now, but that means they keep the details of your location for your next visit.

S

The Final Frontier

The Good Web Site Guide's Top 10s
of the Internet

1. **www.space.com** – outstanding site on all things spacey
2. **www.nasa.gov** – informative with excellent multimedia
3. **www.heavens-above.com** – track satellites, learn stuff
4. **http://hubblesite.org** – awesome pictures
5. **www.redcolony.com** – what could happen when we colonise Mars
6. **www.solarviews.com** – great collection of views of the planets
7. **www.seds.org/images** – pay homage to the space images archive
8. **www.bbc.co.uk/science/space** – another outstanding site from the BBC
9. **www.windows.ucar.edu** – windows to the universe
10. **www.astronautix.com** – encyclopedia astronautica

See also:
http://skytonight.com formerly **www.skypub.com** – a magazine-related site with shop, archive and the latest news.
www.astronautix.com – a comprehensive encyclopaedia of astronomy.
www.astronomy.ac.uk – study astronomy.
www.bbc.co.uk/science/space – superb pages on space from the BBC with interactive features.
www.beagle2.com – a simple presentation on the Beagle 2 mission.
www.deepcold.com – a dark view of the space race, on an interestingly designed site.
www.kidsastronomy.com – astronomy site for kids, simple information, games and sky maps; however, marred by an over-busy site design.
www.spacescience.org – an American space education site.
www.universetoday.com – a space news-gathering service.

S

Space Organisations

www.nasa.gov   US

 THE OFFICIAL NASA SITE
This huge site provides comprehensive information on the US
National Aeronautical and Space Administration. There are
details on each NASA site, launch timings, sections for news,
kids, project updates, and links to their specialist sites such as
the Hubble Space Telescope, Mars and Earth observation. The
site has become more vocal since we last visited and there are a
range of multimedia activities including NASA TV.

www.esa.int   FRANCE

EUROPEAN SPACE AGENCY
Learn about the Agency's activities, the specific missions and
what's planned to come.

See also:
www.aerospaceguide.net – detailed site with information on the
space projects and space craft.
www.arianespace.com – attractive site from the makers of the
Ariane rocket.
www.bnsc.gov.uk – Britain's place in space, with links and
details of missions and the latest news.
www.iki.rssi.ru/eng – Russian space research.
www.isro.org/space_science – the Indian space programme.
www.jpl.nasa.gov – the goings on at the Jet Propulsion Lab with
excellent photography.
www.russianspaceweb.com – a good overview of the Russian
space programme with a history and the latest news.
www.sinodefence.com – look under 'nuclear weapons & space
program' for information on China's national space programme.

The Solar System and Beyond

www.seds.org/billa/tnp   UK

THE NINE PLANETS
A multimedia tour of the nine planets, stunning photography;
interesting facts combined with good text.

http://hubblesite.org   US

THE HUBBLE TELESCOPE
An action-packed site covering the photographs and discoveries
made by the Hubble Telescope, which has been orbiting the

earth for several years now. It contains some amazing and staggeringly beautiful pictures, some of which you can download.

www.redcolony.com US

MARS

A superb site all about the red planet. There is a synopsis of its history, plus details on past and future space missions with a focus on the colonisation of Mars. There's a great deal of information on things like terra forming and biogenesis, it's all taken very seriously too. See also the equally imaginative **www.exploremarsnow.org** where you can find a plausible manifestation of what a Mars mission could look like, backed up with outstanding graphics. At **http://marsrovers.jpl.nasa.gov** you can learn about the latest Mars missions.

For more planetary resources try:
http://astro.nineplanets.org/twn – a site about Nebulae with some beautiful pictures.
http://chandra.harvard.edu – learn all about space exploration with x-rays here.
http://exoplanets.org – an interesting site on those planets found outside our solar system.
http://moon.google.com – explore the Moon.
http://planetary.org – home of the Planetary Society.
www.asi.org – an organisation campaigning for the colonisation of the Moon.
www.fourmilab.ch/earthview – views of the Earth and the Moon from space.
www.solarviews.com – excellent encyclopaedic site on the planets.
www.spaceweather.com – a detailed site on solar activity with excellent links pages.
www.the-planet-jupiter.com – excellent site devoted to the solar system's largest planet. Substitute Jupiter with the names of any of the other planets and you'll find equally good sites on those too.
www.the-solar-system.net – great for pictures and links, you can also test yourself by taking the quiz.

Is There Life Out There?

www.setiathome.ssl.berkeley.edu US

GET IN TOUCH WITH AN ALIEN

To borrow the official site description 'SETI@home is a scientific experiment that uses Internet-connected computers in the Search for Extraterrestrial Intelligence (SETI).' You can participate by running a free program that downloads and analyses radio telescope data. Millions have participated and 5 billion potential signals have been located; they're pointing their scopes at the most promising now. There's still time for you to be the first! See also NASA's detailed site relating to the search for life at **http://planetquest.jpl.nasa.gov/SIM/sim_index.cfm**

www.ufoevidence.org   US
THEY'RE HERE!
A collection of 'evidence' showing that aliens regularly visit our planet. There's loads of links and sections on the UK government cover-up and various other conspiracy theories. See also **www.ufodigest.com** Both sites are advert laden.

Miscellaneous and Specialist Sites

www.spaceadventures.com   US
SPACE TOURISM
OK so you want to be an astronaut? Well now you have a golden opportunity, so long as you have $2 million! Having said that there are actually some cheaper options including shuttle tours and a trip to the edge of space. For more extra-terrestrial travel opportunities see **www.spaceislandgroup.com** – space tourism is on its way!

www.badastronomy.com   US
DEBUNKING THE MYTHS
A site devoted to exploring some of the myths and stories that surround astronomy and science fiction. It gives the facts in a straightforward and (because the site owner sometimes gets on his 'high horse') entertaining way.

www.lpl.arizona.edu/impacteffects   US
WHAT HAPPENS WHEN AN ASTEROID HITS …
A cheery little site, you input all the data about the size and related details of your asteroid or meteor, then the site tells you what will happen when it hits and whether you'll survive. Some of it is very technical but it's mostly explained well.

www.telescopeplanet.co.uk   UK
TELESCOPE SHOP
A wide range of telescopes for sale, plus accessories and some

good offers too. See also **www.skyviewoptics.co.uk** and
www.rothervalleyoptics.co.uk

Spectacles is now under Opticians, page 356.

Sport

*One of the best uses of the Internet is to keep up-to-date with how
your team is performing, or if you're a member of a team or
association, keep each other updated.*

General Sport Sites

www.sporting-life.com   UK

THE *SPORTING LIFE*
A very comprehensive sport site, with plenty of advice, tips,
news and latest scores. It's considered to be one of the best, and
is good for stories, in-depth analysis and overall coverage of the
major sports.

www.bbc.co.uk/sport   UK

BBC SPORT COVERAGE
They may have lost the right to broadcast many sporting events
but their coverage at this level is excellent – much broader than
most and it's always up to date.

http://home.skysports.com   UK

THE BEST OF SKY SPORTS
Excellent for the Premiership and football in general, but also
covers other sports very well particularly cricket and both forms
of rugby. Includes a section featuring video and audio clips, and
there are interviews with stars. You can vote in their polls, e-mail
programmes or try sports trivia quizzes. Lots of adverts spoil it.

www.rivals.net   UK

THE RIVALS NETWORK
Independent of any news organisations, Rivals is basically a
network of specialist sites covering the whole gamut of major
and some minor sports. Each site has its own editor who is
passionate about the sport they cover. In general, its promise is
better than the delivery, but what there is, is excellent with good
quality content and pictures.

With Sport in Mind

The Good Web Site Guide's Top 10s
of the Internet

1. **www.sporting-life.com** – a great overview of the major sports
2. **www.bbc.co.uk/sport** – hard to beat
3. **www.cricinfo.com** – outstanding site on cricket
4. **www.fishing.co.uk** – whether you consider angling a sport or not, this is excellent
5. **www.football365.co.uk** – the best football e-zine, probably
6. **www.racingpost.co.uk** – excellent and informative
7. **www.scrum.com** – a great rugby union site
8. **www.mountainzone.com** – if it's outdoors it's covered here
9. **www.1ski.com** – the best for snow sports
10. **www.kitbag.com** – whatever the sport get the gear here

www.sportonair.com   UK

HEAR ALL ABOUT IT ...
If you can't see it then you can always come here to listen to it, this site offers up lots of audio content including interviews and commentary from most of the major sporting events. There's a good archive and most major sports are covered.

http://sport.telegraph.co.uk   UK

THE *DAILY TELEGRAPH*
Very comprehensive and well written with lots of archive material. All the major sports are covered and with contributors like Mike Atherton, Henry Winter and Sebastian Coe, you know it has authority.

S

www.realbuzz.com   UK

GET SPORTY
Aimed at the amateur participant, their stated purpose is to help everyone to get more out of life by providing an increasing number of pages on sports, health, fitness, the great outdoors, charity adventures and travel. There is a buzzing online community too. Nice site.

Other good all-rounders and sites with good links:
http://dmoz.org/sports – links galore at the Open Directory project.
http://sport.independent.co.uk – good all-round coverage from the *Independent* newspaper.
http://sport.scotsman.com – Scottish sport covered.
http://sportsillustrated.cnn.com – the latest in American sport from CNN.
www.EL.com/elinks/sports – list of American-oriented sports links.
www.eurosport.com – the world of European sport.
www.sikids.com – *Sports Illustrated* for kids, excellent for US-based sports.
www.sportsline.com – excellent coverage from CBS.
www.theage.com.au/sport – good coverage of Australian sport.

Miscellaneous

www.culture.gov.uk/about_us/sport   UK
WHAT THE GOVERNMENT IS UP TO
Here's where to go to find the latest policies, what the minister for sport does and how they are helping sport develop in the community at large. A fairly dull site though. See also
www.uksport.gov.uk

www.sportengland.org   UK
THE NATION'S BIGGEST SUPPORTER
An attempt to get the English off their backsides and to find health and happiness through sport. And a very nice site too.

See also:
www.sportsci.org – interesting site covering sports science.
www.sportspubs.co.uk – directory of pubs where you can watch sport. You can search by sport or by region and there's a good links section too.
www.streetplay.com – covering the development of sports that have just sprung up in cities and parks all over America.
www.wada-ama.org/en – home of the World Anti-Doping Agency.

Sites on Specific Sports

American Football

www.nfl.com   US

NATIONAL FOOTBALL LEAGUE
American football's online bible with a talking homepage, it's a
huge official site with details and statistics bursting from every
page. It's got information on all the teams, players and likely
draft picks; there's also information on NFL Europe and links to
other key sites. All it really lacks is gossip!

See also:
http://football.espn.go.com/nfl/index – ESPN's site is
authoritative and offers links to other sports.
www.hot-iron.co.uk – a very good Scottish e-zine.
www.nfleurope.com – thorough coverage of the European league.
www.nflplayers.com – for the latest news and background on
all the key people in the game plus nostalgia from ex-players.
www.gridironuk.co.uk – the UK-oriented view of the game.

Archery

www.archery.org   UK

INTERNATIONAL ARCHERY FEDERATION
Get the official news, events listings, rankings and records
information from this fairly mundane site.

See also:
www.bownet.com – *Bow International Archery* magazine.
www.scottisharchery.org.uk – the Scottish Archery Association.
www.theglade.co.uk – an entertaining and chatty site, basically
an e-zine, devoted to all forms of archery.

S

Athletics and Running

www.iaaf.org   UK

INTERNATIONAL ASSOCIATION OF ATHLETICS
FEDERATIONS
The official site of the IAAF is a results-oriented affair with
lots of rankings in addition to the latest news. There's also a
multimedia section where you can see pictures, listen to
commentary or watch videos of the key events. There's a good
links page and information on the organisation's activities.

www.ukathletics.net UK

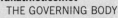

THE GOVERNING BODY
Many official 'governing body' sites are pretty boring affairs, not
so UK Athletics which contains lots of features, is newsy and
written with an obvious sense of enthusiasm. There are details
on forthcoming events, reports on aspects of the sport, records,
biographies of key athletes and advice on keeping fit. Somehow
you get the impression the site is sponsored ...

www.athletix.org UK

THE ATHLETICS SITE
A statistics and results-led site with coverage of all the
major events and some minor ones. It covers international
competitions as well as having a good gallery and biographical
details of some of the major athletes, it's also good for links.

www.runnersworld.com US

RUNNER'S WORLD MAGAZINE
A rather dry site with tips from getting started through to
advanced-level running. There's lots of information, news and
records plus reviews on shoes and gear. See also the redesigned
and comprehensive **www.runnersweb.com**

See also:
www.athleticsweekly.co.uk – *Athletics Weekly* magazine.
www.bal.org.uk – results from the British Athletics League.
www.boja.org – a great site for young athletes; there's not much
to look at but it contains lots of information.
www.british-athletics.co.uk – a boring site but it has a directory
of clubs and regional events. It's good for links to newsgroups
though.
www.gbrathletics.com – great for statistics and rankings.
www.marathonguide.com – all you need to know about
marathons with news and advice.
www.nuff-respect.co.uk – see what Linford Christie is up to
these days.
www.realrunner.com – now part of realbuzz, see under general
sports sites above.
www.runnersworld.ltd.uk – on equipment advice.
www.runtrackdir.com – details of all the UK's running tracks
and their facilities.
www.trackandfieldnews.com – all the latest from *Track & Field
News*. US bias.

Australian Rules Football

www.afl.com.au   AUSTRALIA
AUSTRALIAN FOOTBALL LEAGUE
A top-quality site covering all aspects of the game including
team news, player profiles and statistics as well as the latest
gossip and speculation. See also **www.footypedia.com** and
www.allthestats.com

Baseball

www.mlb.com   US
MAJOR LEAGUE BASEBALL
This now opens with a 'fastcast' bringing you up-to-date with the
latest news while you look at information on the top teams and
the World Series. It's not the best-designed site but there's good
information, statistics on the game and notes about the key
players as well as related articles and features.

See also:
www.baseball1.com – very detailed.
www.baseball-links.com – easy to use and has over 11,000
links.
www.gbbaseball.co.uk – all about the game in the UK.

Basketball

www.nba.com   US

NATIONAL BASKETBALL ASSOCIATION
A comprehensive official site with features on the teams, players
and games; there's also an excellent photo gallery and you can
watch some of the most important points if you have the right
software.

See also:
www.basketball.com – really extensive coverage including the
women's game.
www.basketball365.co.uk – comprehensive overview of the
game with news of what's going on both sides of the Atlantic.
www.bbl.org.uk – the official site of the British Basketball
League.
www.eurobasket.com – information on the European leagues.

S

Bobsleigh

www.bobteamgb.org UK

The British Bobsleigh Association has a newsy site with lots of pictures and information on the team and how you can get involved. For more pictures, movie clips to inspire you to take the plunge yourself visit **http://bobsleigh.gb.com**

Bowls

www.bowlsengland.com UK

ENGLISH BOWLING ASSOCIATION

A straightforward design making it easy to find out all you need to know about lawn bowls in England, including a good set of links to associated sites.

www.eiba.co.uk UK

ENGLAND INDOOR BOWLING ASSOCIATION

A pretty basic site giving an overview of the game, links and background information on competitions and rules.

See also:
www.bowlsclub.info – a portal site devoted to lawn bowls.
www.bowlsinternational.com – home of a bowls magazine, good for links.
www.esmba.org.uk – informative site from the English Short Mat Bowling Association.
www.short-mat-magazine.com – aimed at selling the mag, but has information on the Irish, English and Welsh games.

Boxing

www.boxinginsider.com US

BOXING INSIDER

An effective site with lots of information on the sport plus chat and stats. There's a bout-by-bout guide, lots of links and the writing is pretty good too.

See also:
www.bbc.co.uk/boxing – great for the latest news and background information.
www.boxrec.com – a statistician's nirvana here at this Wiki-based site. You'll find virtually any boxing statistic; however it is a little cumbersome to use and it has quite a few adverts.

www.heavyweights.co.uk – who cover the hype around heavyweight boxing.

www.ibhof.com – the International Boxing Hall of Fame has information on the best-ever boxers, it's great but could still do with more photos.

www.secondsout.com – excellent magazine and portal site for fight fans everywhere.

For the different boxing authorities:
www.aiba.net – the official site from the Amateur International Boxing Association.

www.wbaonline.com – the WBA has an OK-looking and functional site.

www.wbcboxing.com – a straightforward site from the World Boxing Council – that is after the sentimental musical introduction!

www.wbu.cc – the World Boxing Union covers the sport well from an unusual site.

www.womenboxing.com – a very comprehensive site devoted to women's boxing.

Clay Shooting

www.clayshooting.co.uk   UK

CLAY SHOOTING MAGAZINE
A good introduction to the sport with a beginner's guide to start you off and a good set of links to key suppliers and associated sites. There's also an online shop where you can buy essential kit. Serious shooters can go to the comprehensive
www.hotbarrels.com

Cricket

www.cricinfo.com   UK

THE HOME OF CRICKET ON THE NET
The best all-round cricket site on the Internet, with in-depth analysis, match reports, player profiles, statistics, links to other more specialised sites and live coverage. There's also a shop with lots of cricket goodies.

www.lords.org   UK

THE OFFICIAL LINE ON CRICKET
A pretty measly site these days with basic information, ticket sales details and fixtures, plus a top line history of the place. See

also **www.play-cricket.com** which is home to the English Cricket Board and a fine source of information and statistics on the game.

www.webbsoc.demon.co.uk UK
WOMEN'S CRICKET ON THE WEB
There are not many sites about women's cricket; this is probably the best, with features, news, fixture lists, match reports and player profiles. Nothing fancy, but it works.

www.theprideside.com UK
CRICKET TO THE ROOTS
A good attempt at encouraging young people to take an interest in cricket with an overview of the game on a really interesting and interactive site.

See also:
http://sport.guardian.co.uk/cricket – good-looking and up-to-the-minute site from the *Guardian* newspaper.
www.334notout.com – a history of the Ashes and the 'bodyline' controversy.
www.cricketonly.com – a comprehensive and news-oriented cricket enthusiasts' site.
www.cricketrecords.com – one for the statistics freaks, lots of pop up adverts too.
www.cricketsupplies.com – a good-looking online store specialising in cricket gear.
www.cricnet.co.uk – the Professional Cricketers' Association official site.
www.windiescricket.com – keep up to date with the West Indies team here, it also covers the game by island too.

Cycling

These are sites aimed at the more serious sportsman, for more leisurely cycling see page 107 and for holidays turn to page 506.

www.bcf.uk.com UK
BRITISH CYCLING FEDERATION
The governing body for cycling, their site has become more comprehensive: you can get information on events, rules, clubs and rankings, as well as contact names for coaching and development, plus a news service.

www.bikemagic.com   UK
IT'S BIKETASTIC!
Whether you're a beginner or an old hand, the enthusiastic and engaging tone of this site will convert you or enhance your cycling experience. There's plenty of news and features, as well as reviews on bike parts and gadgets, a classified ads section and a selection of links to other biking web sites, all of which are rated.

www.letour.fr   FRANCE
TOUR DE FRANCE
Written in English and French this site covers the Tour in some depth with details on the teams, riders and general background information.

www.mtbbritain.co.uk   UK
MOUNTAIN BIKING
Routes, tips, advice and gear; it's all here whether you're a real enthusiast or just a weekender. See also **www.dirtworld.com** which also offers news on events and is more sports-oriented.

See also:
http://uk.sports.yahoo.com/cy/index.html – keep up-to-date with the latest news.
www.cyclesport.co.uk – home of *Cycle Sport* magazine.
www.cyclingnews.com – race results and more.
www.grahamwatson.com – cycling photography.
www.levileipheimer.net – be inspired with news, history, cuttings and a video diary.

Darts

www.planetdarts.co.uk   UK
PROFESSIONAL DARTS CORPORATION
A messy site but one that has lots of league information, statistics, news, articles and rules.

See also:
www.bbc.co.uk/darts – basic information only.
www.cyberdarts.com – a darts e-zine, which contains lots of information such as articles, chat, forums and rules too.
www.dartbase.com – rules, techniques and equipment advice.

S

Diving

www.ukdiving.co.uk   UK

DIVING RESOURCE

A very good resource site with the latest news. It seems to cover
all aspects of the sport with some good articles, useful advice
and is good for links too. The wreck of the week is particularly
intriguing.

See also:

www.bsac.com – the British Sub Aqua Club, a basic site with
info on what they do.

www.cmas2000.org – the World Underwater Federation with
an odd but informative site.

www.divegirl.com – a magazine site about women and scuba.

www.padi.com – the place to start when you want to learn to
dive.

www.saa.org.uk – home of the Sub Aqua Association with links
and information.

Dog Racing

For the gambling side of dog racing, see page 198.

www.thedogs.co.uk   UK

BRITISH GREYHOUND RACING BOARD

A well-designed site offering an overview of the sport, the top
dogs and track information, also has help for owners and all the
results. See also **www.retiredgreyhounds.co.uk** where you can
find out how to adopt a retired greyhound.

Equestrian

www.bhs.org.uk   UK

BRITISH HORSE SOCIETY

A charity that looks after the welfare of horses. Here you can get
information on insurance, links, riding schools, competitions,
events and trials.

For more information try:

http://horses.about.com – About.com's excellent suite of pages
devoted to all things equestrian.

www.badminton-horse.co.uk – background and information on
the famous horse trials with lots of extra features and links.

www.britishdressage.co.uk – very good site covering this aspect of the sport.
www.britisheventing.com – an attractive, largely text-based site with details on the sport and links.
www.horseandhound.co.uk – excellent magazine site from the leading authority.
www.horseselect.co.uk – buying and selling competition horses.

Extreme Sports

www.extreme.com   US
EXTREME SPORTS CHANNEL
The official site of the Extreme Sports Channel is hi-tech but quite slow; however, once downloaded it's got lots to offer in terms of information, shopping and the latest headlines.

See also:
www.adventuredirectory.com – useful activity-by-sport portal site.
www.allextremesports.com – good for links and a wide range of sports.
www.expn.go.com – excellent extreme sports magazine with a US bias.
www.extremepie.com – good extreme sports gear shop.
www.extreme-sports-world.com – very useful portal site.

Fishing

www.fishing.co.uk   UK
 HOME OF UK FISHING ON THE NET
A huge site that offers information on where to fish, how to fish, where's the best place to stay near fish, even fishing holidays. There's also advice on equipment, a records section and links to shops and shop locations. Shop on-site for fishing books and magazines.

See also:
www.anglersnet.co.uk – good magazine site with lots of information and chat.
www.anglers-world.co.uk – great for fishing holidays.
www.bdaa.co.uk – home of the British Disabled Anglers Association and a comprehensive offering it is too.
www.fishandfly.co.uk – another good magazine site, this one devoted to fly fishing.
www.fisheries.co.uk – excellent for coarse fishing and links.

www.nfsa.org.uk – home of the National Federation of Sea Anglers with lots of links and information.

www.pacgb.com – the Pike Anglers Club, a bit specialist perhaps, but a good site nonetheless.

www.specialist-tackle.co.uk – excellent store for equipment plus much more in the way of chat and information.

www.tackleuk.co.uk – extensive online shop.

www.thefishfinder.com – yes it's a fish search engine and a pretty good one at that.

Football

www.football365.co.uk   UK

FOOTBALL NEWS
Probably still the best of the football e-zines in terms of the combination of looks, quality writing and features, although it can be a bit dense at times.

http://www.goal.com   UK

GOAL!!
Excellent portal and news site with lots of articles and coverage of the latest gossip; it also covers many of the European leagues as well.

www.teamtalk.com   UK

CHECK OUT THE TEAMS!
The most respected place to go if you want all the latest gossip and transfer information. It's opinionated but not often wrong. They have many top journalists on their books, so the information is likely to be on the ball.

www.soccerbase.com   UK

SOCCER STATISTICS
The site to end all pub rows, it's described as the most comprehensive and up-to-date source of British football data on the Internet.

www.footballgroundguide.co.uk   UK

FOOTBALL GROUNDS
Details of all 92 English league football club grounds, locations and facilities, incredibly useful for all away supporters. Excellent for team links too. For information on the new Wembley stadium including a tour, web cams, find your seat in 3-D, events and history check out **www.wembleystadium.com**

It's worth having a look at the sites listed below; just pick the one you like best.

http://pinkfootball.com – a girls' guide to football.

http://skysports.planetfootball.com – news, information and OPTA statistics on the world game, now part of the Sky Sports site.

www.4thegame.com – a messy and commercial football news site.

www.conferencefootball.tv – coverage of some of the key conference clubs including replays.

www.e-soccer.com – hundreds of links and the latest news.

www.fansfc.com – gossip and rumours, plus fans' forums for chat and debate.

www.footballchants.org – an advert laden catalogue of football chants, not exactly a riot of wit it has to be said …

www.football-rumours.com – the latest transfer gossip and detailed information on the players.

www.footballtransfers.co.uk – very detailed transfer information and likely moves.

www.guardian.co.uk/football – great writing and irreverent articles, uncluttered design.

www.icons.com – site host to many major players, lots of background info plus the latest news.

www.laughfc.co.uk – a humorous look at the game, good for jokes and chants, some adult content.

www.linkupfootball.com – over 3,700 football-related links in 83 categories.

www.pureworldcup.com – a fun and informative look at the World Cup.

www.ratetheref.co.uk – where you can get your revenge on the ref if you feel mistreated.

www.soccerbot.com – great for basic information, with interesting interactive league tables.

www.soccerhighway.com – a strange site but good for links.

www.soccernet.com – well-put-together by ESPN, comprehensive but a bit boring.

www.wsc.co.uk – home of the magazine *When Saturday Comes*.

www.footballaid.com   UK

FOOTBALL CHARITY

Football aid is a charity that helps good causes by running football events, you can sign on to play for the team of your choice or just send a cheque.

Football Authorities

www.fifa.com   SWITZERLAND

FIFA

This is FIFA's magazine where you can get information on what they do, the World Cup and other FIFA competitions. For the UEFA go to **www.uefa.com** where you can see how everyone is faring in the Champions League and UEFA cup.

See also:
www.irishfa.com – the Irish Football Association with a pretty standard site on the game in Northern Ireland.
www.leaguemanagers.com – the League Manager's Association.
www.premierleague.com – the official site of the Premier League, covering the latest news and information.
www.scotprem.co.uk – a comprehensive offering with links too.
www.thefa.com – home of English football, see 'England' for the official take on the team; also sections on the women's and grassroots game.
www.welsh-football.net – an independent magazine on the Welsh soccer scene.

Golf

www.golftoday.co.uk   UK

THE PREMIER ONLINE GOLF MAGAZINE

An excellent site for golf news and tournaments with features, statistics and rankings, also a course directory. It's the best all-round site covering Europe. There are also links to sister sites about the amateur game, shops and where to stay. GolfToday.com also hosts a comprehensive site on the amateur game; you can find it at **www.amateur-golf.com**

www.golfweb.com   US

PGA TOUR

The best site for statistics on the PGA, and keeping up with tournament scores, it also has audio and visual features with RealPlayer. For the official word on the tour go to **www.pga.com** while for the European tour go to **www.europeantour.com** and for a good overview of the Ryder Cup visit **www.rydercup.com**

www.golf.com   US

THE AMERICAN VIEW

Part of NBC's suite of web sites, this offers a massive amount of information and statistics on the game, the major tours and players, both men and women.

www.golfingguides.net   UK
UK GOLF COURSES

Detailed information on selected golf courses classed as 'gems', plus contact information on those lesser courses. A good search facility rounds it off, plus the fact it's pretty well designed.

www.uk-golfguide.com   UK
GOLF TOURISM

A useful directory of courses and hotels with courses, with links to travel agents for the UK and abroad, you can also get information on golf equipment suppliers and insurance. See also **www.whatgolf.co.uk**

www.onlinegolf.co.uk   UK
GOLF EQUIPMENT

A good-looking and comprehensive golf store with lots of offers and a good range, it has a ladies' section and a good search facility.

See also:
http://golfbidder.co.uk – store for second-hand clubs and equipment.
www.golflinks.co.uk – a large, UK-oriented site database.
www.lorringolf.com – for summer camps for junior golfers, corporate golf and golf tours.

Gymnastics

www.gymmedia.com   GERMANY
GYMNASTIC NEWS

A bilingual site giving all the latest news, it covers all forms of the sport and offers lots of links to related sites.

See also:
www.british-gymnastics.org – an official site offering lots of information and advice.
www.intlgymnast.com – the latest news from *International Gymnast* magazine.
www.scottishgymnastics.com – comprehensive coverage but tied to the magazine, so it's not all it could be.

Hockey

www.englandhockey.co.uk UK

THE ENGLISH HOCKEY ASSOCIATION

A slick site covering the English game with information and chat on the players, leagues and teams for both the men's and the women's games. For the Scottish game go to **www.scottish-hockey.org.uk** and for the Welsh **www.welsh-hockey.co.uk**. The latter is not great on design but both give all the relevant information.

See also:

www.fieldhockey.com – advert-laden with a dull design but has all the latest news.

www.hockeydirect.co.uk – good equipment store.

www.hockeyweb.co.uk – chat, news and links.

www.talkhockeyradio.co.uk – a state-of-the-art web radio programme and magazine site.

Horse Racing

For sites that cover the gambling side of horse racing go to page 196.

www.racingpost.co.uk UK

THE RACING POST

Superb, informative site from the authority on the sport, every event covered in depth with tips and advice. To get the best out of it you have to register, then you have access to the database and more.

www.bhb.co.uk UK

BRITISH HORSE RACING BOARD

A very well-put-together site offering up information and background on the sport including interviews, details of the latest meetings and horse ownership advice.

www.racenews.co.uk UK

RACING, COURSES AND BETTING

A slightly different spin from Racenews, they have three main sections: their news service, a course guide and a tipsters column. There's also an excellent links section covering racing world-wide.

www.flatstats.co.uk
UK

FLAT RACING STATISTICS

This site contains masses of detailed and unique statistics – horse, trainer, jockey, sire and race statistics, favourites analysis, systems analysis and much more. You have to be a member to get the best out of it; subscription costs £25 per month.

www.thejockeyclub.co.uk
UK

THE JOCKEY CLUB

A campaigning site aimed at promoting confidence in racing. It has news, details on the rules and how stewarding works, as well as links and sporting guidelines. See also **www.jockeysroom.com** which has an A–Z of jockeys with biographies and pictures.

Other sites worth a visit are ...
www.attheraces.co.uk – live action, tips and the latest news plus great design.
www.bbc.co.uk/racing – the BBC's excellent race pages.
www.ownaracehorse.co.uk – experience the ups and downs of owning your own horse or a part of one anyway.
www.racecall.co.uk – hear all the action on your phone.
www.teletext.co.uk – the information pages have gone, but under 'mobile services' you can sign up for racing alerts direct to your phone.

Ice Hockey

www.nhl.com
US

NATIONAL HOCKEY LEAGUE

Catch up on the latest from the NHL including a chance to listen to and watch key moments from past and recent games.

S

www.icehockeyuk.co.uk
UK

ICE HOCKEY UK

The official site with bags of information and background on the game. It's well designed and great for beginners and those who want to find out more about the sport.

See also:
www.azhockey.com – home of the encyclopaedia of ice hockey.
www.crazykennys.com – ice hockey equipment suppliers.
www.icehockeyhistory.co.uk – a sparse site covering the history of the game in the UK.

Ice Skating

www.frogsonice.com/skateweb   US

LINKS

Not a great design but it offers lots of links to all aspects of skating.

See also:

www.iceskating.org.uk – the official site of the National Ice Skating Association of the UK; good-looking site covering all aspects of ice skating.

www.iceskatingintnl.com – for competitive skating news, US bias.

www.iceskatingworld.com – comprehensive US site with excellent links and the latest news.

www.sisa.org.uk – the Scottish Ice Skating Association.

www.skating-shop.co.uk – for all your skating gear.

Martial Arts

www.martial-arts-network.com   US

PROMOTING MARTIAL ARTS

Possibly qualifies as the loudest introduction sequence, but once you've skipped the intro, the site offers a great deal in terms of resources and information about the martial arts scene, including *Black Belts* magazine and new this year, podcasts. Its layout is a little confusing.

www.britishjudo.org.uk   UK

JUDO

Judo has a proud tradition in the UK, and if you want to follow that you can get all the information you need at the British Judo Association site. It gives a brief history of judo, a shop and event information. For a broader view go to **www.judoinfo.com**

See also:

http://physical-arts.com – a site in the making, more a way of life than combat.

http://uk.dir.yahoo.com/recreation/sport/martial_arts – a huge number of links.

www.martialinfo.com – slow but comprehensive site with an online magazine.

www.practical-martial-arts.co.uk – useful advice on techniques and an overview of key combat types, there are also forums where you can have your say.

www.ryoku.co.uk – where to go for your gear.
www.kungfuscience.org – wacky site explaining the physics
behind chopping blocks with bare hands.

Motor Sport

www.crash.net   UK
MOTOR SPORT PORTAL
An excellent but very commercial news and directory site
covering the major motor sports and most of the minor ones too.
There's an online shop selling motor sport merchandise amongst
other things and there's a good photo library.

www.ukmotorsport.com   UK
INFORMATION OVERLOAD
This site covers every form of motor racing; it's got lots of links to
appropriate sites covering all aspects of motor sport. There are
also chat sections and forums plus links to product and service
suppliers. Could do with an updated message to customers.

www.msportuk.com   UK

UK MOTOR SPORT
A good site covering all aspects of motor sport in Britain,
highlights include the 'must see' section (I wish more sites had
one) and the links page. As they've kept out clutter, it's fast to
use.

www.autosport.com   UK
AUTOSPORT MAGAZINE
Excellent for news and features on motor sport plus links and an
affiliated online shopping experience for related products such as
team gear, books or models.

www.linksheaven.com   US
FORMULA 1 BLOG
They've kept their links in an extensive directory, but they've
mutated into a popular, stylish blog and forum site.

www.worldmotorsport.com   UK
MOTOR SPORT DEBATE
Many forums covering all aspects of racing. If you want a say or
get something off your chest then here's where to go.

S

Sites Covering Specific Types of Racing

www.itv-f1.com   UK

F1 ON ITV

This web site is excellent, it doesn't miss much and there is plenty of action. There's all the background information you'd expect plus circuit profiles, schedules and a photo gallery. See also **www.f1-world.co.uk** with more information and background plus links too.

www.formula1.com

THE OFFICIAL SITE

Keep up to date with downloads to your mobile, read about the teams and the drivers past and present, find out about the circuits via the interactive maps and lastly book tickets.

www.fota.co.uk   UK

FORMULA 3

Formula 3 explained plus info on the teams, drivers and circuits. It's the breeding ground for F1 drivers of the future which adds to the excitement reflected in the energy of this site.

www.indycar.com   US

INDY CARS

A comprehensive offering with coverage of all that goes on in the Indy car scene.

www.rallysport.com   UK

COVERING THE WORLD RALLY CHAMPIONSHIP

Good for results and news on rallying in the UK and across the world. See also **http://rally.racing-live.com/en** which has all the latest news, plus follow races stage by stage and **www.rallyzone.co.uk** – a comprehensive international e-zine.

www.btccpages.com   UK

BRITISH TOURING CAR CHAMPIONSHIP

This site offers a great deal of information and statistics on the championship, driver and team profiles, photos and links to other related sites. There are also a number of forums you can get involved with if you feel like chatting to fellow enthusiasts.

www.karting.co.uk UK
GO KARTING
A well-laid-out portal site to all things karting in the UK, with
links and directories covering the tracks, manufacturers,
events and a photo gallery plus the latest news. See also
www.gokartingforfun.co.uk

www.monstertrucks.net US
TRUCKS
All aspects of truck racing, exhibitions and shows, if you like
your motor sport large, then go here.

Motorcycling

www.motorcyclenews.com UK
 NEWS AND VIEWS
A very good magazine-style site giving all the latest news, gossip
and event information, there are also sections on buying a bike,
where to get parts and the latest gear, off-road biking and a links
directory. There's also a chat room and a good classified section.

www.acu.org.uk UK
AUTO-CYCLE UNION
The ACU is the governing body for motorcycle sports in the UK
and this site gives information on its work and the benefits of
being a member. There are also links and details of their
magazine.

www.motogp.com UK
TRACK AND OFF-ROAD
A well-laid-out magazine site, covering the world of Moto Grand
Prix with results, background and biographical details. Available
in eight languages.

www.british-speedway.co.uk UK
SPEEDWAY
Provides information on the leagues as well as the latest news,
there's also an events calendar and links to related sites.

www.motocross.com US
MOTOCROSS
An authoritative site covering the sport but it's centred on the
US, although it has got some information on the European
scene. See also **www.motolinks.com**

Mountaineering and Outside Sports

www.mountainzone.com US

FOR THE UPWARDLY MOBILE

Thoroughly covers all aspects of climbing, hiking, mountain biking, skiing and snowboarding with a very good photography section featuring galleries from major mountains and climbers.

www.ukclimbing.com UK

CLIMBING NEWS

Excellent and very informative site covering all aspects of climbing, it has plenty of opportunities for chat along with the latest news. There's also weather information and a very good database of climbs with comments and essential information for each one.

www.rockrun.com UK

ALL THE RIGHT EQUIPMENT

Excellent equipment shop covering climbing and walking gear, which is also pretty comprehensive on the information front too. See also **www.gearzone.co.uk** who have a similar offering.

Other good climbing sites:

www.blacks.co.uk – good camping and equipment store.

www.bouldering.com – revamped site and a good job they've done too, there's a wide range of gear as well.

www.climb-guide.com – the guides are pretty basic but there's a good links page.

www.cruxed.com – nice-looking site with advice on techniques and training, good links.

www.onward-outward.co.uk – a good outdoor clothing store with a wide range and the best brands.

www.outdoorgear.co.uk – everything you need for the outdoors.

www.thebmc.co.uk – good all-round climbing and hill-walking magazine-style site from the British Mountaineering Council with good links pages.

www.ukcrags.com – some good guides to popular climbs, but the site was for sale at time of visiting.

www.upandunder.co.uk – a Welsh mountaineering store with a good links section.

Have an Adventure

The Good Web Site Guide's Top 10s
of the Internet

1. **www.adventuredirectory.com** – find an adventure
2. **www.madadventurer.com** – get inspired by sport
3. **www.ecovolunteer.com** – do it for nature
4. **www.africatravelresource.com** – go on a safari
5. **www.lonelyplanet.com** – choose where to go
6. **www.ctc.org.uk** – get on yer bike
7. **www.polartravel.co.uk** – go on a polar expedition
8. **www.tenrag.com** – charter a yacht
9. **www.divechannel.co.uk** – take a dive or two
10. **www.visitbritain.co.uk** – find an adventure at home …

Netball

www.netball.org   UK
> INTERNATIONAL FEDERATION OF NETBALL
> ASSOCIATIONS
> Get information on the work of the federation and the rules of
> the game, plus rankings and the events calendar. See also
> **www.netballcoaching.com** which is good for advice and links.

Olympics

www.olympics.org/uk   UK
> BRITISH OLYMPIC ASSOCIATION
> An expanded site featuring highlights of the Torino Winter Games
> and looking forward to Beijing in 2008 and, of course, London
> in 2012. You can learn more about 300 Olympic heroes, access
> an athlete's medal tally and learn more about the sports featured
> in the games. There's information for collectors and also the
> doping policy. For a history of the games there's the Olympic
> museum link and links to sports federations and committees.

S

www.london2012.org UK

IT'S OFFICIAL

Find out what's planned and where, download the interactive map, see artists' impressions of the Olympic Park, learn about the business links and you can sign up to be a volunteer or even get a job.

See also:

www.olympianartifacts.com – good site featuring an Olympic memorabilia store.

Rowing

www.ara-rowing.org UK

AMATEUR ROWING ASSOCIATION

This site offers information on the history of the sport, plus the latest news, coaching tips and links.

See also:

www.steveredgrave.com – Sir Steve's official site offers biographical information, training instruction and tips, links and background on the sport.

www.total.rowing.org.uk – a good rowing portal site.

Rugby

www.scrum.com UK

RUGBY UNION

An excellent site about rugby union with impressively up-to-the-minute coverage. For a similar but lighter and more fun site go to **www.planet-rugby.com** which has a comprehensive round-up of world rugby with instant reports, lots of detail and information on both union and league. **www.rugbyheaven.com** is also worth checking out. For the history of rugby union go to the **www.rugbyfootballhistory.com** which is also good for links.

www.rfu.com UK

RUGBY FOOTBALL UNION

Masses of features, articles and news from the official RFU site, it's got team news and information, links and a shop where you can buy gear.

www.rleague.com UK

WORLD OF RUGBY LEAGUE

Another very comprehensive site, featuring sections on Australia, New Zealand and the UK, with plenty of chat, articles, player profiles and enough statistics to keep the most ardent fan happy. See also the magazine site **www.totalrugbyleague.com** and also **www.ozleague.com**

www.rugbyrelics.com UK

RUGBY MEMORABILIA

A good memorabilia store covering most countries and aspects of the game, everything from autographs to ties and programmes.

Sailing

www.madforsailing.com UK

THE DAILY SAIL

An informative and well-laid-out site covering all aspects of sailing both as a sport and as a hobby. There are some really good and well-written articles, video clips and features such as a crew search facility and weather information.

www.ukdinghyracing.com UK

UK DINGHY RACING

Devoted mainly to this one aspect of sailing, it covers the sport comprehensively and gives advice on buying, and hosts links to auctions, specialist shops as well as an excellent set of general sailing links.

www.ellenmacarthur.com UK

ELLEN MACARTHUR

An interesting and well-put-together site where you can find out what Ellen is up to as well as biographical details. When she is sailing, you can follow her progress, access the charts and weather forecasts while listening to her latest transmission.

See also:

www.rya.org.uk – a good advice-laden site from the Royal Yachting Association, very informative at all levels.
www.sailing-411.com – excellent American sailing portal.
www.uksail.com – a sailing portal site offering some 1,000 links.
www.yachtsandyachting.com – a good yachting magazine site.

Skiing and Snowboarding – see page 436.

Skateboarding

www.skateboarding.com   US

Good skateboarding magazine with lots of videos, pictures and trick tips. For a scientific approach to the subject investigate **www.exploratorium.edu/skateboarding**. To buy kit online try **www.popcornskate.co.uk** who also provide instructions on making your own board. See also Extreme Sports on page 457.

Snooker

www.worldsnooker.com   UK

THE SITE OF THE PROFESSIONALS

An informative site, which is run by the game's governing body, World Snooker has all the latest news, tournament up-dates, the low-down on the players plus photos, videos of highlights and free live scoring. There's a lot here for everyone, but members get added extras, and its free.

See also:
www.snooker.net – great for the latest news and gossip.
www.snookersports.co.uk – a snooker equipment shop.

Tennis and Racket Sports

Tennis

www.lta.org.uk   UK

 LAWN TENNIS ASSOCIATION

An excellent and attractively designed all-year tennis information site run by the Lawn Tennis Association, it has information on the players, rankings and tournament news, as well as details on clubs and coaching courses. There's also an online tennis shop where you can buy merchandise and equipment. Check out their portal **www.totaltennis.net** for chat, news and resources to download. See also **www.atptour.com** which gives a less UK-biased view of the game, with excellent sections on the players, tournaments and rankings.

www.wimbledon.org   UK
THE OFFICIAL WIMBLEDON SITE
Very impressive, there's a great deal here and not just in June, but
you need to be patient. Apart from the information you'd expect,
you can download screensavers, visit the online museum and
eventually see videos of past matches. The shop is expensive.

Other tennis sites worth a look:
www.cliffrichardtennis.org – excellent site aimed at encouraging
children to take up the game.
www.itftennis.com/juniors – for the junior game in the UK.
www.juniortennis.com – keep a watch on international young
hopefuls.
www.pwp.com – a comprehensive tennis and racket store.
www.tennis.com – good magazine, with gear guides, tips and
hot news.
www.tennisnews.com – the latest news updated daily and e-
mailed to you.

Badminton

www.badders.com   UK
BADMINTON COMMUNITY NETWORK
A very good example of a site that pulls together an interest
group. It's excellent for news and chat as well as links and
information on the sport.

See also:
www.badzone.co.uk – a pretty comprehensive offering,
interesting design!
www.baofe.co.uk – the site of the Badminton Association of
England with all the latest news.
www.internationalbadminton.org – home of the International
Badminton Federation.

Squash

www.squashplayer.co.uk   UK
 WORLD OF SQUASH AT YOUR FINGERTIPS
A really comprehensive round-up of the game, with links galore
and a great news section; there's also a section for the UK,
which has club details and the latest news. See also
www.worldsquash.org for a good site on what's going on
world-wide.

Table Tennis

www.ittf.com   UK
INTERNATIONAL TABLE TENNIS FEDERATION
A messy site but one that covers most aspects of the sport
around the world. See also **www.ettu.org** for the European view.

Tenpin Bowling

www.btba.org.uk   UK
BRITISH TENPIN BOWLING ASSOCIATION
The home of the game in the UK with rules, information on
clubs and background on what the governing body does. See
also **www.probowluk.co.uk** – a serious site with useful tips and
links.

Water Sports and Swimming

Swimming

www.swimnews.com   US
SWIMMING NEWS
It's up to date and offers a wide coverage of news, with other
features such as rankings, events calendar, shopping and
competition analysis.

www.pullbuoy.co.uk   UK
UK SWIMMING
A good site that covers the UK scene. You can find unusual
features such as a job finder and time converter. It's great for
links too.

Other good swimming sites:
www.learn-to-swim.co.uk – learn-to-swim holidays.
www.swiminfo.com – US magazine site with articles,
information and results.
www.swimmersworld.com – pretty average site with news and
links.
www.webswim.com – forums, articles and help.

Surfing

www.coldswell.co.uk   UK

SURFING THE UK COAST
Includes forecasts for weather and surf, satellite images, live surf
web cams from around the world and a complete directory of
surfing web sites.

www.thesurfingmuseum.co.uk   UK
FOR SURF BUMS
The museum in Brighton is now open and you'll find information
about it here. Online there's also news, exhibitions (including
surfers' stories and videos), campaign issues (e.g. surfers
against sewage and support the lifeboats) and the history of
surfing. The shop has a disappointing range of goods on offer.
Interesting design too.

See also:
www.britsurf.co.uk – home of the British Surfing Association.
www.coastalwatch.com – great, if you're in Australia.
www.surfline.com – check out weather, sea conditions, the
latest gear – essentially, all you need before you go.
www.surfstation.co.uk – for links, shopping and surf speak.
www.troggs.com – good for surfing gear.

www.2xs.co.uk   UK
WINDSURFING IN THE UK
Where to go windsurfing, plus tips and the latest sports news,
shopping, weather information and advice.

Water-skiing

www.waterski.com   US
WORLD OF WATER SKIING
An American site which features information about the sport,
how to compete, news, tips, equipment and where to ski.
See also **www.bwsf.co.uk** although not an attractive site, it
does have UK-based information on places to ski, clubs,
competitions and a message board. Another good site is
www.planetwaterski.com – an American site with a global
guide to places to ski.

S

Wrestling

www.wwe.com   US
WORLD WRESTLING ENTERTAINMENT
Whether you think it's sport or soap opera, here you can keep
up with the twists and turns plus all the action at this exciting
site, which has news, clips and of course a merchandise shop.

See also:
www.amateurwrestlingnews.com – amateur wrestling scene
with US bias.
www.prowrestling.com – all the latest news and controversy.
www.wrestlingusa.com – a more serious and credible magazine
site.

Sports Clothes and Merchandise

www.sweatband.com   UK
SHOP BY SPORT
A wide-ranging shop that supplies equipment for many sports,
but it's especially good for tennis, rugby and cricket. Delivery
costs depend on the weight of your parcel. See also
www.newitts.com which is comprehensive.

www.kitbag.com   UK
SPORTS FASHION
Football kits and gear galore from new to retro; it covers cricket
and rugby too. Costs on delivery vary according to order. Also
offers shopping by brand and a news service.

www.sportsbooksdirect.co.uk   UK
TAKING SPORT SERIOUSLY
Sportspages and Sports Books Direct have joined forces to
create an online book store that also stocks video and DVD.
Concentrating on sport, they offer a wide range at OK prices,
even signed copies. Great for that one thing you've been unable
to find.

www.sportsworld.co.uk   UK
SPORT TRAVEL
Specialists in making travel arrangements to sporting events; at
this site you can book tickets and find out about future events.
It's particularly good for corporate hospitality; they seem to feel
the need to talk to you on the phone though!

www.newoxygen.co.uk   UK
ACTIVEWEAR FOR WOMEN
Nicely designed site for surf gear for women, all the kit for
the beach and the bar. There's a good selection of organic
pampering products to get the salt out of the skin too.

www.sportingheritage.co.uk   UK
SPORTING GIFTS
A selection of prints, gifts and collectibles available to buy from
this well-laid-out site and they cover all the major sports.

Stationery

www.stationerystore.co.uk   UK
STATIONERY STORE
A well-designed and easy-to-use stationery store supplying
everything from paperclips to office machinery. There are also
sections on green stationery, electronics and lots of offers.

www.staples.co.uk   UK
NOT JUST STAPLES
A good all-rounder with a wide range and some good offers; next
day delivery is available, in the past this site was reserved for
business use, however, now all it takes is a basic registration
and anyone can order online.

For other stationery stores try:
www.cardcorp.co.uk – good place to go for your business cards
and other printing needs.
www.katespaperie.com – to some it's just 'paper with bits in'
but for those who pay regular homage to the New York stores,
Kate's Paperie represents the best in hand-made stationery.
Delivery is expensive.
www.michaelajdavies.co.uk – fashion stationery.
www.paperchase.co.uk – you can't buy online but it looks great
and you can order by phone – bless.
www.papershed.com – delicious hand-made paper, creative
supplies and wedding stationery.
www.penhome.co.uk – for pens and pen repairs.
www.theperfectcardcompany.co.uk – handmade cards, photo
albums, guest books and keepsake boxes.
www.viking-direct.co.uk – excellent range, now serving
everyone, not just business customers.

www.whsmith.co.uk/stationery – part of the WH Smith site
with some offers and multi-buys but a limited range, which does
include some of their fashion stationery.

http://rps.gn.apc.org   UK
TOTALLY RECYCLED
For all your stationery needs from computer paper to art
supplies, all recycled and several ranges to choose from. They
will also print your letterheads and customise promotional
goods. There's lots of information on paper making and recycling
too. For more, try **www.greenstat.co.uk**

See also:
www.paper-caper.co.uk – nice range of notebooks and gift
stationery – all fair trade.
www.remarkable.co.uk – for pencils made from recycled plastic
cups.

Student Sites

*There's masses of information for students on the Internet. Here are
some sites worth checking out. The links are generally very good, so if
the topic isn't covered here, it should be easy to track down.*

Universities and Colleges

www.ucas.co.uk   UK
THE UNIVERSITY STARTING BLOCK
A comprehensive site listing all the courses at British universities
with entry profiles. You can view the directory online and order
your UCAS handbook and application form. If you've already
applied, you can view your application online. There are links to
all the universities plus really good links to related sites. There is
good advice too. If you want to learn a language you can try
finding a course through **www.edunet.com**

www.nusonline.co.uk   UK

STUDENTS UNITE
Lots of relevant news and views for students on this really good-
looking site. You need to register to get access to their discounts
directory and special offers. Once in, you can send e-cards and
use their mail and storage facilities too.

www.studential.com UK
STUDENT UNIVERSITY HELP
A growing resource aimed at helping students through the minefield of applying to universities and coping with the first year, excellent advice and links too.

See also these other useful sites:
www.braintrack.com – a comprehensive directory of links to universities world-wide.
www.britishcouncil.org/education – the student section is full of options for further education and training.
www.careers-portal.co.uk – tasters of their comprehensive selection of books on surviving university and finding a career. You can buy the books too.
www.findaphd.com – find a PhD, Masters or Post Doc course.
www.hotcourses.com – a very good database of courses for students at all levels, with careers and money advice thrown in.
www.slc.co.uk – home of the Student Loan Company.

Working Abroad and Job Finding

www.gapyear.com UK
COMPLETE GUIDE TO TAKING A YEAR OUT
Whether you fancy helping out in the forests of Brazil or teaching in Europe you'll find information and opportunities here. There's loads of advice, past experiences to get you tempted, chat, a message board, competitions and they'll help you find a travel mate.

www.payaway.co.uk UK
FIND A JOB ABROAD OR A WORKING HOLIDAY
A great starting place for anyone who wants to work abroad. There is an e-zine with reports from travellers, and you can register with their online jobs service. They've missed nothing out in their links section from embassies to travel health.

www.anyworkanywhere.com UK
JOBS IN THE UK AND WORLD-WIDE
A bright and breezy site with jobs and all the right advice, plus links.

See also:
www.bunac.co.uk – combine work and travel with these programmes from an experienced specialist.

S

www.world-challenge.co.uk – take part in any one of a number of expeditions. They're age ranged and vary greatly in scope, so there should be something for everyone.

www.yearoutgroup.org – a mass of information and help for both those taking a gap year and their parents too.

Careers

www.prospects.ac.uk   UK
   CAREER OPTIONS
   Home of the official graduates' careers guide offering a huge amount of information, which is all packed into a pretty dense site.

Discounts

www.istc.org   UK
   INTERNATIONAL STUDENT TRAVEL CONFEDERATION
   Get your student and youth discount card as well as info on working and studying abroad. Also help with such things as railpasses, phonecards, ISTC registered travel agents worldwide, plus e-mail, voice mail and fax messaging. For a wide range of discounts sign up for a card at **www.isiccard.com** and be sure to get a European youth card for discounts within the EU at the cool **www.euro26.org**

   If you've got time, also checkout:
   www.discounts4students.net – the 'definitive' directory for student discounts.
   www.sellstudentbooks.com – sell your books and look for bargains.
   www.s-k-i-n-t.co.uk – for discounts, offers, competitions, quizzes and more.
   www.studentcomputers.co.uk – for good deals on refurbished laptops and cheap computers, good prices on cartridges too.
   www.studentfreestuff.com – for all kinds of freebies.
   www.student-subscription-service.co.uk – claim to get as much as 76% off magazine subscriptions.
   www.studentbookworld.com – discounted books.

Student Life

www.studentuk.com   UK

STUDENT LIFE

A good-looking, useful and generally well-written student's e-zine featuring news, music and film reviews, going out, chat, even articles on science and politics. There's also some excellent advice on subjects such as gap years, accommodation and finance. For an alternative look at the same information, and learn how to survive boring lectures, see **www.funky.co.uk**

www.good2bsecure.gov.uk   UK

FIGHT CRIME AGAINST STUDENTS

Students are more likely to be victims of crime than any part of society, here you can get advice on security and keeping safe.

www.studenthealth.co.uk   UK

CLICK IT BETTER

Written by doctors for students, this site offers excellent printable advice on hundreds of topics along with a health problem page. There are also comprehensive links for further advice, support groups and health centres.

www.accommodationforstudents.com   UK

ACCOMODATION SEARCH ENGINE

A searchable database for students in need of accommodation. As well as providing information about accommodation available, you can find/rent out a room or advertise for housemates via their noticeboard.

See also:

www.capitalstudents.com – from clubbing to jobs for students in London with e-mail and chat.

www.studenttimes.org – online version of the free, independent student newspaper written for students by students.

www.wrecked.co.uk – the perils of drinking (not just for students).

www.studenthampers.com   UK

STUDENT SURVIVAL

One for parents and friends really, send hampers filled with good quality goodies, there are general foodstuffs, curry and pasta hampers, tuck boxes, even an exam hamper and a celebratory one for after it's all over. If it's cleanliness you're worried about, there is one of those too, and a selection of stationery boxes.

Links and information

www.lazystudent.co.uk   UK
> SITE LISTING
> The perfect site for those who can't be arsed to look things up
> properly. It's well categorised and has listed virtually any site that
> a student might need.

www.whatnow.co.uk   UK
> INFORMATION AND ADVICE
> Excellent, well-constructed site giving information for young
> people on everything from sex to careers. You can make an
> enquiry directly to them or chat with people who have similar
> issues. There's also a good links section.

Teenagers

*Here's a small selection of the best sites aimed at teenagers. Many of
the most hyped sites are just heavily disguised marketing and sales
operations, treat these with scepticism and enjoy the best, which are
generally done for the love of it, or through a genuine desire to help.
We've also indicated the sort of age group that the magazines are
aimed at, although sometimes the content does seem quite mature
for the site's targeted age range. We should add our thanks to all
those who keep writing in to us suggesting sites for this section.
Don't forget your personal safety if you chat online, see page 79 for
details or go to **www.thinkuknow.co.uk** for a look at the issues and
www.whatnow.co.uk for information and advice.*

Teenage Magazines

www.globalgang.org.uk   UK
> WORLD NEWS, GAMES, GOSSIP AND FUN
> See what the rest of the world gets up to at Global Gang. You
> can find out what kids in other countries like to eat, what toys
> they play with, chat to them or play games. Lastly you get to find
> out how you can help those kids less fortunate than yourself. *10
> plus*

www.girland.com   UK

> GIRL AND ...
> An excellent, really attractive and well-put-together site aimed at
> teenage girls. It has chat forums, news and lots of features, but

you do have to register. It has won loads of awards and the environment is safe. *11 plus*

www.mykindaplace.com UK
IT'S MY KINDA PLACE
Excellent site for teens, with the latest news, gossip and celebrity features. Aimed squarely at girls it seems to have everything, including lots of adverts! *13 plus*

www.dubit.co.uk UK

GAMES, ARTICLES – THE LOT
Dubit combines 3-D graphics with chat, games, video, music and animations in a fun and interactive way. It's a completely different approach to the normal teen magazine. It needs a little patience but it's worth it in the end. Registration is required, which is a pity as it is a pain and very slow. *12 plus*

www.teentoday.co.uk UK
FOR TEENAGERS BY TEENAGERS
Get your free e-zine mailed to you daily or just visit the site: which has much more games, chat, news, entertainment, free downloads, ringtones and message boards. It's well designed and genuinely good with not too much advertising. *13 plus*

www.bbc.co.uk/teens UK
E-ZINES FOR BOTH SEXES
This site keeps on changing. There is now a link to **www.bbc.co.uk/slink** a slick magazine site for girls 13–16, which gives good quality magazine-style entertainment along with good health advice, ask a Dr, blogs, mail, photos and more. Back on the main teen site, the BBC also provides a link to **www.bbc.co.uk/blast** an art, dance, music, film and writing showcase where you can upload and share your talent, read articles and advice, learn about other artists and join in the message board. The teens page also gives links to Radio 1, 1Xtra for the best in new black music, sportdaq, the sports stock exchange, Bitesize revision, *EastEnders* and *Wannabes*, the teen drama homepage. *13 plus*

T

www.alloy.com US
ALLOY MAGAZINE
On the face of it, this is great; it's got loads of sections on everything from personal advice to shopping albeit a bit American. But with too many adverts, it all seems to be geared

to getting your name for marketing purposes and selling stuff. *13 plus*

www.cheekfreak.com   US
FOR THE FREAK IN ALL OF US
Best for stories, blogging and reviews. It's got chat sections, forums and a search engine. Some of the forums are devoted to serious topics such as suicide, sexual hang-ups and family break-up, as such they may prove helpful in dealing with teenage angst. *13 plus*

www.cyberteens.com   UK
CONNECT TO CYBERTEENS
One of the most hyped sites aimed at teenagers, it contains a very good selection of games, news, links and a creativity section where you can send your art and poems. *13 plus*

www.teentoday.co.uk   UK
TEEN TODAY
A UK-oriented magazine site aimed at teenagers. It covers all the things you'd expect: quizzes, music, films, plus chat and free SMS. Not bad. *13 plus*

www.student.com   US
13 TO 24
A comprehensive magazine site aimed at school and college students. Has all the usual stuff – blogs, forums, entertainment, advice, plus a useful teen directory and a really good resources section for advice on all aspects of teen life. There is also teen trivia, teen jokes and teen travel. There's a strong American feel here, but there is some good stuff for UK teens here too. *13 plus*

www.4degreez.com   US
INTERACTIVE COMMUNITY
A friendly and entertaining site with reviews, poetry, jokes, polls and links to other related sites. You have to become a member to get the best out of it though. *15 plus*

Directories

www.ipl.org/div/teen   US
TEEN SPACE
Part of the Internet Public Library, these pages offer a directory of

links for help and information on everything from careers, homework, issues, technology and entertainment.

See also:

http://directory.google.com/Top/Kids_and_Teens – good directory from Google.

www.kidgrid.com – well laid out and easy to use, with a US bias.

www.kidsclick.org – massive database of sites put together by a group of librarians.

www.surfnetkids.com – a comprehensive directory put together by an American journalist.

Advice

www.worriedneed2talk.org.uk   UK
CRUELTY TO CHILDREN MUST STOP!
A site from the NSPCC aimed at helping teenagers and children cope and deal with violence, family problems and drug advice. Also available in Welsh.

www.mindbodysoul.gov.uk   UK
GET THE LOW-DOWN ON HEALTH
A health site for teenagers. It covers all you'd expect, all wrapped up in good-looking graphics; it's also not too densely written or too patronising.

www.trashed.co.uk   UK
R U THINKING ABOUT IT?
Excellent site on sex and sexuality. There is well-balanced information on contraception, sexually transmitted infections, the law and about where to go for help and advice. Sections devoted to girls and lads give a gender-based perspective too. See also the US-based **www.teenwire.com** and also **www.thehormonefactory.com**

T

www.thesite.org.uk   UK
THE SITE
This site offers advice on a range of subjects: careers, relationships, drugs, sex, money, legal issues and so on. Aimed largely at 15 to 24 year olds, it's well laid out and very informative.

www.no-ur-rites.com UK
KNOW YOUR RIGHTS

A basic but useful information site providing legal information on everything from drugs to online shopping. As it's put together by a local trading standards authority, the information should be current. See also **www.youthinformation.com** which aims to serve as an 'information toolkit' for young people.

http://teenadvice.about.com US
QUESTIONS AND ANSWERS

An agony aunt service of sorts, it's a bit of a jumble but the quizzes are entertaining. Parents should check out **http://parentingteens.about.com**

www.horsesmouth.co.uk UK
FIND A MENTOR

If you feel the need for advice and long term help from someone who has been in the same place as you and can understand your specific issues, then you could do worse than try Horsesmouth.

See also:

www.click4tic.org.uk – aimed at teenagers, this site provides information on cancer.

www.teenissues.co.uk – discussion site on the big topics of the day.

www.ukyouth.org – the place to go to raise your aspirations and really do something worthwhile.

www.youthaccess.org.uk – not a great site, but lots of links and info.

www.youthinformation.com – excellent US-based information site.

Telecommunications

In this ever-changing section there's information on ADSL and computer-related communications, where to go to buy mobiles, get the best out of them and even have a little fun with them. For phone numbers see the section entitled Finding Someone on page 161. For broadband see page 58.

www.ofcom.org.uk UK
THE REGULATOR

Ofcom is the regulator for the UK communications industries, with responsibilities across television, radio, telecommunications and wireless communications services. Theirs is a useful site with the latest news and consumer information surrounding this complex world. If you have a complaint, here's where to seek redress. See also **www.icstis.org.uk** for the Independent Committee for the Supervision of Standards of Telephone Information Services, and the Telecommunications Ombudsman at **www.otelo.org.uk**

www.magsys.co.uk/telecom UK
COMPARE TARIFFS

A potentially useful site if you want to see how your tariff compares with those of other phone companies; it's not exactly user friendly though. For a site that is campaigning against expensive telephone lines have a look at **www.saynoto0870.com**

Mobile Phones

www.carphonewarehouse.com UK
CHOOSING THE RIGHT MOBILE

You need to take your time to find the best tariff, then take advantage of the numerous offers. Excellent pictures, details of the phones and the information is unbiased. There's a shop that also sells handheld PCs and delivery is free too. You can download a wide range of new phone ring tones, from classical to the latest pop tunes.

www.mobileedge.co.uk UK
MOBILE INFORMATION

A quirkily designed site with help on buying the right mobile, it also offers information on health and mobiles, links and contact numbers, pre-pay deals, global networks, ring tones, shop and much more.

See also:
www.dialaphone.co.uk – another phone shop. They'll match anyone else's prices though; let's hope they continue to survive.
www.expansys.com – dense site with masses of information and competitive prices.
www.mobilefun.co.uk – a huge range of phones and accessories.
www.mobileshop.com – nice design and lots of offers.
www.onestopphoneshop.com – nicely designed site with a deal finder. Also promise to match competitors' prices.

Recycling

www.oxfam.org.uk/what_you_can_do/recycle/phones   UK

SEND YOUR OLD MOBILES HERE

If you have all your old mobiles hanging around the house then go here to find out how you can put them to good use. **www.helptheaged.org.uk** and **www.actionaidrecycling.org.uk** have similar schemes.

Ring Tones and Text Messaging

www.treasuremytext.com   UK

SAVING YOUR TEXTS

Here you can store your text messages online, even create a mobile blog and share your text conversations with your friends.

See also:

www.onmymob.com – offering hundreds of free ring tones and logos.

www.ringtones2go.co.uk – massive selection, all the latest tunes.

www.chatlist.com/faces.html   UK

TEXT MESSAGING

Confused about your emoticons? %-) Here's a list of several thousand for you to choose from.

Accessorising Your Phone

www.theaccessoryphoneshop.com   UK

FOR COMPLETE MOBILE COVERAGE

Covers, body pouches, chargers, batteries, cables, memory cards – all the kit for all the phones. Sat nav, Bluetooth, PSP and iPod accessories too. Clear and well organised.

Services

www.verilocation.com   UK

MOBILE PHONE TRACKING

Use a phone tracking service if, for example, you're Big Brother or a parent wanting to keep track of your kids or you're a business wanting to co-ordinate sales teams. You can choose your level of surveillance from a simple web-based to a full GPS system. **www.followus.co.uk** offer a similar

service, while **www.mobilelocate.co.uk** also run an offshoot
service called **www.childlocate.co.uk**. For the low down see
also **www.mapaphone.co.uk**

www.jiwire.com   US
WIFI
A very useful site if you travel with a laptop and need to know
the location of the nearest WiFi spots. There is also a great deal
of advice on how to get the best out of it and keep secure too.

Faxing

www.efax.com   UK
FAX USING E-MAIL
A paid-for service that makes it easy for you to send faxes via
your e-mail service. See also **www.j2.com** who offer a similar
service. For more information go to **www.tpc.int** and it's also
worth checking out **www.download.com** for fax programs.

Lowering the Costs

*Broadband users can take advantage of Voice over IP (or VoIP), the
technology that allows the transfer of conversations over the Internet
at vastly lower prices than we're used to paying over the normal land
lines. Wikipedia has a thorough overview of the subject, which can
be found at **http://en.wikipedia.org/wiki/Voip**. A full listing of sites
that sell or use VoIP can be found at **www.dmoz.org/Business/
Telecommunications/Services/VoIP/***

www.skype.com   US

FREE CALLS
Now owned by eBay, this one allows you to make free calls
using the Internet to other Skype users, quality is pretty good but
you have to pay to call someone not using Skype.

See also:
www.18866.co.uk – cheaper international calls plus VoIP too.
www.bt.com – with details of its own VoIP system, which is
charged for but you get good quality lines.
www.freeworlddialup.com – one of the best for features.
www.voiponline.com – a directory and VoIP news service.
www.vonage.co.uk – a subscription service, which, on the face
of it, looks good value.

Technology

www.bluetooth.com US
OFFICIAL BLUETOOTH
A superb official Microsoft site devoted to Bluetooth technology;
it's amazing how fast it's become so widespread and so old hat.

www.3g.co.uk UK
3G
Excellent site devoted to bringing you the latest information and
developments in this technology.

See also:
www.gprshelp.co.uk – helpful site covering GPRS.
www.tmcnet.com – dense site devoted to telecommunications
technology.

Television

*TV channels, listings and your favourite soap operas are all here, some
have great sites, others are pretty naff, especially when you consider
they're in the entertainment business. Television now shares a
regulator with telecommunications in general. See Ofcom below.*

www.ofcom.org.uk UK
OFCOM
Ofcom is the regulator for the UK communications industries
including television, radio, telecommunications and wireless
communications services. If you've a complaint, here's the place
to go – they've made it quite easy.

www.tvlicensing.co.uk UK
TELEVISION LICENCE
All you need to know about your TV licence, how to pay and
how to deal with problems.

Channels and Digital

www.bbc.co.uk UK
 THE UK'S MOST POPULAR WEB SITE
The BBC site deserves a special feature, it is huge with more
than 2 million pages and it can be quite daunting. It has
sections covering everything from business to the weather and

there are also regional sections, a web guide, as well as tips on how to use the Internet and you can subscribe to a newsletter. The BBC is well into podcasting and you can listen again to many of their radio programmes, and you can watch news and sports features with more to follow. There are feature sites on all their major programmes and most of the minor ones too, it's a fantastic site and more than a useful resource.

www.itv.com   UK
ITV NETWORK
ITV has a pretty straightforward site with links to all the major programmes, soaps, topics and categories, their related web sites and a TV Guide, plus a few extras such as quizzes. For a history of Independent Television go to **www.itw.org.uk**

www.citv.co.uk   UK
CHILDREN'S ITV
A bright and breezy site that, as well as features on the programmes, has loads of interactive activities including a galley of uploaded art, story writing, competitions and games – should keep the kids amused for hours.

www.channel4.co.uk   UK
CHANNEL 4
A cool design with details of programmes and links to specific web pages on the best-known ones. There are also links to other initiatives such as E4, More4, 4radio and the acclaimed Filmfour. You can also download TV programmes via the 4oD section.

www.channel5.co.uk   UK
CHANNEL 5
The usual programme information, scheduling details, news and competitions. There are also some useful programme related factsheets and a bright and breezy children's section featuring the *Milkshake* magazine.

www.sky.com   UK
SKY TV
Links to the main Sky sites – news, sport etc, plus information on their digital packages.

www.nick.com   US
  NICKELODEON
  Bright doesn't do this site justice – you need sunglasses! It's got
  info on all the top programmes plus games and quizzes.

www.freeview.co.uk   UK
  FREEVIEW
  Details of the Freeview service and where it's available in the
  UK.

www.wwitv.com   US
  WORLD-WIDE INTERNET TV
  Watch several international channels, the BBC and listen to
  radio too. Probably best for broadband users. See also the
  excellent **www.liketelevision.com** which is very much geared
  to broadband.

TV Downloads and Streaming

*You can get access to lots of TV programs through sites like YouTube
but be careful that it's not illegal or, if it's legit, then a poor quality
substitute. See also movie downloads on page 314.*

www.broadband-television.com   US
  STREAMING TV
  A huge range of channels available to view including music as
  well as TV. You have to download the free software but the
  results are generally worth the effort. It's making a selection
  that's the difficult part.

  See also:
  http://worldwiredtv.com – access to some 3,000 channels
  through your PC, costs seem vague at time of writing but there
  was an offer to get the lots for $40. See also the similar
  http://fasttvdownloads.com
  www.elitetvdownloads.com – excellent site with masses of
  content all well categorised, it works on a subscription basis.
  www.tvcentral.org – especially good if you're a Linux user.
  www.tvtonic.com – watch specially made programmes and
  podcasts, it's fun and good value too.

TV Fans and Nostalgia

www.sausagenet.com   UK
CULT AND CLASSIC TV
An outstanding nostalgia site devoted to popular children's TV
programmes from the past 40 years. You can download theme
tunes or buy related merchandise via the excellent links
directory. See also **www.sadgeezr.com** which is Sci Fi-oriented.

www.uktvadverts.com   UK
TV ADVERTS
A collection of TV adverts and background information, now you
can find out who did that voiceover. See also **www.adwatch.tv**
who offer a similar collection. And about that piece of music you
can't remember ... **www.commercialbreaksandbeats.co.uk** is
the place to go.

See also:
http://epguides.com – a massive database of episode guides
covering a wide variety of US and some UK TV shows and
series.
http://tv.cream.org – great for nostalgia from the 70s and 80s.
www.625.uk.com – a personal celebration and overview of the
rights and wrongs of British telly, with downloads of logos and
even public information films.
www.animus-web.demon.co.uk – eclectic look back on several
shows from the 70s; the Blue Peter section is very good.
www.apts.org.uk – history of Alexander Palace where it all began.
www.beonscreen.com/uk/index.asp – the chance to appear on
your favourite show.
www.british-tv-history.co.uk – fact-oriented site with a timeline
of sorts, great for checking information.
www.clappers-tickets.co.uk – be part of the TV show audience,
free tickets for selected shows.
www.geocities.com/TelevisionCity/1011 – home of 'Watched it',
a look back on Children's TV.
www.kaleidoscope.org.uk – an organisation devoted to
preserving classic TV; it puts on events and shows too.
www.offthetelly.co.uk – a good e-zine about telly.
www.petford.net/kaleidoscope – the site of a voluntary
organisation devoted to the appreciation of classic TV, lots of
links and information to be found here.
www.saturdaymornings.co.uk – great site about those
programmes that used to be shown on Saturday mornings.

T

www.sitcomsonline.com – a huge amount of information on US sitcoms.

www.thetvroom.com – if you want to know anything about TV presenting go here.

www.transdiffusion.org/emc – selection of articles, sites and links which look back at television history, diverse and not easy to navigate but there's some excellent stuff here especially in the Halcyon Days section.

www.tv-ark.org.uk – another excellent archive site.

www.tvfetish.net – a good site, and they promise a revamp in 07 which should sort out the navigation problems, there's a lot here for those looking to reminisce.

www.tvradiobits.co.uk – an excellent excerpt and clips site.

www.ukgameshows.com – an encyclopaedic site about games shows.

www.waveguide.co.uk – keep up to date with what's going on in the world of TV.

www.whirligig-tv.co.uk – a great site for 50s TV nostalgia.

TV Review and Listings Sites

www.digiguide.co.uk   UK

THE DOWNLOADABLE GUIDE

If you have Sky digital, you'll be familiar with this guide. It follows a similar format, although you can customise it. Simply download the program and you get 14 days, forward programming for up to 200 channels, masses of links and background information. It costs £8.99 per annum.

www.radiotimes.com   UK

THE *RADIO TIMES*

Excellent listings e-zine with a good search facility for looking up programme details, plus competitions, links and a cinema guide. There are also sections on the best-loved TV genres – children's, sci-fi, soaps and so on.

See also:

www.onthebox.com – a simple and effective daily TV guide. Lots of pop-up ads.

www.thecustard.tv – a personal, fun and well-put-together TV and listings guide, which deserves to succeed.

Theatre

*Here's a great selection of sites that will appeal to theatre goers
everywhere. Be aware that some online ticket services charge large
processing fees for the privilege plus postage as well. Check the invoice
carefully before you commit yourself.*

www.whatsonstage.com   UK
HOME OF BRITISH THEATRE
A really strong site with masses of news and reviews to browse
through plus a very good search facility and booking service
(through a third party), a real theatre buff's delight. For more
information try out the British Theatre Guide at
www.britishtheatreguide.info

www.aloud.com   UK
ONLINE TICKET SEARCH
You can search by venue, location or by artist, it's fast and pretty
comprehensive and there's a hot events section – it mainly
covers music and festivals nowadays though it's good for
comedy. The review section is good and you can buy tickets.

www.officiallondontheatre.co.uk   UK
SOCIETY OF LONDON THEATRES
The latest news, a show finder service and hot tickets are just
a few of the services available at this great site. You can also
get a Theatreland map, half price tickets and they'll even fax
you a seating plan. See also **www.thisislondon.co.uk** who
have a good theatre section and also **www.thisistheatre.com**
which lists all the London shows.

*For alternative sites and more theatrical reviews and gossip try
the following:*
www.theatrenet.com – catch the new shows, search their
archives for information on past productions and learn how to
become a theatre angel. There's discount ticket club too.
www.uktheatre.net – whether you're a fan or an actor this site
is a useful source of information and as a good site directory.
www.uktw.co.uk – cheerful site offering information on theatre
plus amateur dramatics, jobs, chat, competitions and just gossip.

To book online also try the following sites:
www.lastminute.com

>   www.londontheatretickets.com
>   www.ticketmaster.co.uk
>   www.uktickets.co.uk

www.rsc.org.uk   UK
THE ROYAL SHAKESPEARE COMPANY
Get all the news as well as information on performances and
tours. You can book tickets online although it's via a third party
site. There is also loads of information about the life and times of
the Bard and synopses of his plays.

www.reallyuseful.com   UK
ANDREW LLOYD WEBBER
At this attractive, hi-tech site you can watch video clips and
listen to top audio clips, download screen savers and wallpaper,
take part in competitions and chat. There's also a good kids'
section plus details on the shows.

www.nt-online.org   UK
THE NATIONAL
Excellent for details of their shows and forthcoming plays with
tour information added. You can now buy tickets online.

www.dresscircle.co.uk   UK
THEATRE SHOP
A long-established supplier of music, books and products related
to the theatre, with links and the latest news.

www.uktheatrebreak.co.uk   UK
THEATRE BREAKS
A useful site and booking service that allows you to combine
your trip to the theatre with a short holiday or overnight stay.

Travel and Holidays

*Travel is one of the biggest growth areas on the Internet, from holidays
to insurance to local guides. If you're buying, then it definitely pays to
shop around and try several sites, but be careful, it's amazing how fast
the best deals are being snapped up. You may find that you still spend
time on the phone, but the sites are constantly improving. The amount
of information available is staggering and it's no wonder this is the
biggest section in the book.*

Travel Sites that Make You Want to Go There

The Good Web Site Guide's Top 10s
of the Internet

1. **www.africatravelresource.com** – on East Africa, excellent design
2. **www.travelCanada.ca** – attractive and informative
3. **www.franceway.com** – culture, history and travel
4. **www.jnto.go.jp** – great site from the Japanese Tourist Association
5. **www.nepal.com** – making the most of what nature has given them
6. **www.tourspain.es** – colourful and a great overview
7. **www.visitbritain.com** – comprehensive or what!
8. **www.seeamerica.org** – great for links and information
9. **www.ecuadorexplorer.com** – awesome and the Galapagos too
10. **www.sg** – at least you'll remember the URL, a great portal on Singapore

When checking out travel sites, you should be aware that the same company may own many sites, for example Lastminute.com (owned by Expedia) has interests in sites covering everything from skiing holidays to general travel and even ferry bookings. These sites will be listed under their specialist area.

*If you are concerned about a particular company and want to check, nearly all sites have company information hidden away, usually at the bottom of the page, or you can quickly check them out at Companies House: **www.companies-house.gov.uk***

Information for disabled travellers can be found on page 115.

Starting Out

www.ukpa.gov.uk   UK

UK PASSPORTS

Pre-apply for your passport online and get tips on how to get the best passport photo amongst other very useful information.

www.uk.cibt.com UK

QUICK VISA

This service will get you your visa in double quick time, for a price.

www.hmce.gov.uk UK

HM CUSTOMS AND EXCISE

All you need to know about visiting the UK, exporting and importing and the regulations surrounding what you can bring back with you from your holidays.

www.abta.com UK

ABTA

Make sure that the travel agent you choose is a member of the Association of British Travel Agents as then you're covered if they go bust halfway through your holiday. All members are listed and there's a great search facility with links for you to start the ball rolling. See also the Air Travellers Licensing home page **www.caa.co.uk** which is part of the Civil Aviation site.

www.brochurebank.co.uk UK

BROCHURES DELIVERED TO YOUR HOME

Holiday brochures from the major and specialist travel companies can be selected then delivered to your home, free of charge. The selection process is easy and the site is fast. Delivery is by second class post.

Health, Safety and Tips

www.fco.gov.uk/travel UK

 ADVICE FROM THE FOREIGN OFFICE

Before you go, get general advice or safety or visa information. Just select a country and you get a run-down of all the issues that are likely to affect you when you go there, from terrorism to health.

www.travelhealth.co.uk UK

STAY HEALTHY

An authoritative site with sections on general health advice and disease prevention, a shop and links.

For more health and safety travel information and tips …
http://nomadtravel.co.uk – store with very good health and advice pages.

www.bloodcare.org.uk – the Blood Care Foundation offers a wide range of advice and tips for many illnesses and situations.
www.cdc.gov/travel – official American site giving sensible health information world-wide.
www.cyborlink.com – international etiquette and facts covering 120 countries. Designed for business users but useful for the traveller too.
www.first48.com/guide/features/muslimcode.php – clothing advice for women travelling to Muslim countries.
www.flyana.com – good advice from an experienced traveller.
www.masta.org – authoritative health advice and an online shop to get your medicines.
www.medicalert.org.uk – buy a bracelet that contains all your essential medical details.
www.tripprep.com – country-by-country risk assessment covering health, safety and politics; it can be a little out of date so check with the foreign office as well.
www.who.int/en – statistics and health information country by country.

Family Travel Advice

www.family-travel.co.uk   UK
PRACTICAL INFORMATION
A wide-ranging site covering every aspect of travelling with children, including health, hotels, culture, products and just getting to your destination.

See also:
www.familytravelforum.com – an American site offering lots of information and advice.
www.flyingwithkids.com – sensible air travel advice for those travelling with babies and small children.
www.babyflying.co.uk – bright and breezy design but it could have more content, still some good ideas and travelling tips for parents though biased to England.
www.opfh.org.uk – good information for single-parent families, but turn the sound off ...
www.smallfamilies.co.uk – a wide range of holiday options for single-parent families.
www.thefamilytravelfiles.com – a US-oriented e-zine with lots of advice and links.
www.themeparkinsider.com – reviews theme and amusement parks world-wide.

www.tinytravelers.net – a well-designed and attractive site offering tips, product reviews and travel advice.
www.travellingwithchildren.co.uk – good for ideas and advice.

Travel Services

www.whatsonwhen.com   UK
WORLD-WIDE EVENTS GUIDE
An easy-to-use site with information on every type of event you can think of from major festivals to village fêtes.

www.worldtimezone.com   US
TIME ZONE MAP
Useful time zone mapping, although it's heavily advert laden.
See also **www.timeanddate.com**

www.kropla.com   US
PHONE HELP
Here you can find out about where to plug in your modem, if your mobile will work, international dialling codes, even TV standards.

Also worth checking out for more information:
http://cybercaptive.com – a directory of world cyber cafés.
http://mytravelrights.com – an American site devoted to travellers' rights abroad.
www.cybercafes.com – over 4,000 cyber cafés listed throughout the world.
www.jiwire.com – locate wireless hotspots worldwide.
www.tipping.org – good advice on how much to tip around the world.

While You're Away

All these companies offer similar services looking after your home, pets or plants while you're away – so there's no need to worry.

www.home-and-pets.co.uk – wide-ranging service.
www.homesitters.co.uk – for a premium service.
www.minders-keepers.co.uk – pet-oriented service.

www.holiday-companions.com   UK
TO KEEP YOU COMPANY
If you need a companion to go away with you, then start here.

See also **www.people-connection.co.uk** and
http://travelmatesonline.com

Luggage and Travel Gear

www.bags123.com   UK
BUYING LUGGAGE
A wide range and with some good offers, this store is worth a
visit if you have to replace that tatty old case.

http://nomadtravel.co.uk   UK
SHOP AND GET INFORMED TOO
Exceptional travel store that not only offers a good range of
equipment and medical supplies but also a whole mass of
advice and travel information too.

www.excessluggage.co.uk   UK
EXCESS LUGGAGE
For problems concerning excess baggage, here's the place
to go. There are lots of options and it's best to discuss your
requirements with them.

www.holidayadditions.co.uk   UK
ESSENTIAL ITEMS
A bright and breezy shop that offers a small range of 'essential'
travel-oriented products from padlocks to mosquito repellents.

Travel Money

www.xe.net/ucc   UK
 ONLINE CURRENCY CONVERTER
The Universal Currency Converter could not be easier to use,
just select the currency you have, then the one you want to
convert it to, press the button and you have your answer in
seconds. See also **www.oanda.com**

www.onlinefx.co.uk   UK
FOREIGN CURRENCY DELIVERED
A pretty straightforward and potentially hassle-free way of
getting your currency, just order with your card and it gets
delivered the next working day. They charge a flat rate £4.95
handling fee, but no other commission or service fee. They
also offer financial services such as international transfers at a
very competitive rate.

Insurance

Unfortunately there isn't one site for collating travel insurance yet, it's a question of shopping around. These sites make a good starting point offering a range of policies for backpackers, family and business travel.

www.costout.co.uk – well-rated insurance and good value.
www.direct-travel.co.uk – nice design and some good offers too, online quotes.
www.dogtag.co.uk – great concept in insurance that covers you for even the most extreme activities.
www.moneysupermarket.com/travelinsurance – compare policies and pick the best one for you.
www.saga.co.uk/finance/travelinsurance – if you're of a certain age, travel insurance is often difficult to get. Check out Saga's policies for over 50s.

Travel Shops and Agents

www.travel-lists.co.uk   UK
TRAVEL OPERATORS' DIRECTORY
A largely subscription-based service but with free access to their database of travel specialists and agents. Each entry has a link, contact number and a short overview of what they do.

www.expedia.co.uk   US/UK

THE COMPLETE SERVICE
This is the UK arm of Microsoft's very successful online travel agency. It offers a huge array of holidays, flights and associated services, for personal or business use, nearly all bookable online. Its easy and quicker than most, and there are some excellent offers too. Not the trendiest, but it's a good first stop. As with all the big operators, you have to register. They've also got sections on travel insurance, mapping, guides, ferries and hotels.

www.lastminute.com   UK
DO SOMETHING LAST MINUTE
Last Minute has an excellent reputation not just as a travel agent, but as a good shopping site too. For travellers there are comprehensive sections on hotels, holidays and flights, all with really good prices. There is also a superb London restaurant guide and a general entertainment section. Mostly, you can book online, but a hotline is available.

www.thomascook.com UK
THE WIDEST RANGE OF PACKAGE HOLIDAYS
This site is easy to use and well laid out and, with over one thousand destinations to chose from, you should be able to find something to your liking. You can also browse the online guide for ideas or search for cheap flights or holiday deals.

www.e-bookers.com UK
FLIGHT BOOKERS
Acclaimed travel agents specialising in getting good flight deals, but also good for holidays, special offers and insurance.

www.travel.world.co.uk UK
FOR ALL YOUR TRAVEL REQUIREMENTS
A massive, comprehensive site, it basically includes most available travel brochures with links to the relevant travel agent. It concentrates on Europe, so there are very few American sites, but provides links to hotels, specialist holidays, cruises, self-catering and airlines.

www.uk.mytravel.com UK
SEARCH FOR THE RIGHT DEAL
This site has got an excellent search engine that enables you to find a bargain or just the right holiday. There are also good offers and the Late Escapes holiday auction site.

www.priceline.co.uk UK
LET SOMEONE ELSE DO THE WORK
Although they now offer a discounted travel service, Priceline still offer the facility to let someone else do the travel searching for you. You provide details of the trip/flight/hotel you want and how much you're willing to pay, then they try to find a deal that will match your requirements. If you're flexible about timing then there are some great offers. Priceline want your credit card details before you agree to any transaction so you may feel more comfortable using the more traditional route.

www.budgettravel.com UK
BUDGET TRAVEL
Rubbish design but masses of links and information for the budget traveller plus advice on how to travel on the cheap. It can be difficult to navigate but the information is very good.

See also:

www.aito.co.uk – offers and information from the Association of Independent Tour Operators, excellent for the unusual.

www.bargainholidays.com – probably the best for quick breaks, excellent for late availability offers.

www.dreamticket.com – the usual holiday offers, but the site also offers much in the way of information too.

www.firstchoice.co.uk – bargains from First Choice holidays.

www.holiday.co.uk – a portal offering a massive number of package holidays and a wide range of other options from all the major operators.

www.opodo.co.uk – slick site from some of the major airlines, worth checking out for flight offers and discounts on hotels.

www.packageholidays.co.uk – late bargain holidays and flights from a wide range of tour operators including Airtours, Cosmos, and Thomson.

www.thefirstresort.com – a good general site with some good deals and a price promise, owned by Tui UK, formerly Thomsons.

www.thisistravel.co.uk – in association with the newspaper group that publishes the *Daily Mail*, this is a comprehensive offering with some good offers. Lots of pop-up ads too.

www.thomson.co.uk – for a wide range of package holidays as well as low-cost flights on their airline.

www.travelagents.co.uk – another all-rounder, nothing special but competent.

www.travelbag.co.uk – straightforward and easy-to-use long haul flight and holiday finder. Part of same group as ebookers.

www.travelcareonline.com – loads of deals and honest information from the UK's largest independent. Winner of the British Travel Awards 2004 'Best Online Travel Agent'.

www.travelmood.com – individual design and long haul destinations.

www.travelocity.com – one of the oldest online travel agents; it's similar to Expedia, comprehensive with plenty of advice and background information.

Short and City Breaks

www.eurobreak.com – click on the map for your destination and you get presented with lots of options including hotel details and online booking.

www.shortbreaks.com – hotel breaks in the UK, Europe and US; arranges theatre breaks too.

www.shortbreaksbyair.com – a good selection of city breaks from this specialist operator.

www.superbreak.com – great site, great prices; includes theatre, concert and attraction breaks in the UK and abroad.

www.railbookers.com/breaks – short breaks in Europe by train.

www.webweekends.co.uk – specialists in weekend breaks both in the UK and abroad.

Luxury and Tailor-made Holidays

Here's a list of the best known luxury holiday specialists and a few we've had recommended to us ...

www.abercrombiekent.com – one of the most experienced luxury travel operators with a very competent site.

www.amanresorts.com – exclusive hotels and villas in gorgeous locations.

www.audleytravel.com – tailor-made itineraries for escorted groups.

www.balesworldwide.com – for something special, tailor-made holidays to the exotic parts of the world. This hi-tech site is excellent especially now you can book online.

www.carrier.co.uk – luxury holiday specialists, nice looking site too.

www.caz-loyd.com – specialists in the more exotic destinations.

www.coxandkings.co.uk – a slightly disappointing site from one of the oldest travel companies.

www.essentialescapes.com – exclusive luxury spa holidays.

www.exsus.com – tailor-made luxury adventures.

www.hayesandjarvis.co.uk – long-haul holiday specialists, lots to choose from.

www.itcclassics.co.uk – luxury everything basically.

www.jeffersons.com – taking a holiday with your own private jet ...

www.jewelholidays.com – India, Turkey, Red Sea and Asia.

www.journeysbydesign.co.uk – tailor-made African specialists.

www.luxurylink.com – luxury holiday auctions.

www.originaltravel.co.uk – holidays for activity and well-being, outstanding site design too.

www.pura-aventura.com – active holidays in comfort, mainly Latin America and Spain.

www.rbrww.com – opulence and fishing.

www.seasonsinstyle.co.uk – world-wide luxury in the world's finest hotels.

www.tailor-made.co.uk – basic site but the holiday options look good.

www.tripsworldwide.co.uk – despite the name, it specialises in Latin America and the Caribbean. Some beautiful photography enhances the site.

www.vjv.co.uk – Voyages Jules Verne with an excellent selection of luxury activity holidays.

Cruises

www.discover-cruises.co.uk   UK
CRUISE INFO

A clear, new site put together to encourage people to take cruise holidays featuring 35 cruise lines. Factsheets are provided to enable you to find the perfect trip, whoever you are and whatever you want from your cruise. If you can't find information here, there's a good collection of links.

See also:

www.cruisedeals.co.uk – easy to use, a little sparse on info but some good offers.

www.cruisedirect.com – information, advice and good prices.

www.cruiseline.co.uk – a great site from one of the UK's leading specialist cruise companies.

www.cruisesandvoyages.com – a cruise specialist with a basic site and some good deals.

www.psa-psara.org – useful information from the Passenger Shipping Association.

www.shiphappens.co.uk – entertaining forum site for cruise goers, lots of advice and comment for everyone, from newbies to experienced enthusiasts.

Activity and Sporting Holidays

Cycling Holidays

www.ctc.org.uk   UK
WORKING FOR CYCLING

The CTC have a great travel section with routes, tours, offers, links and directories. It's a great place to start your search for the perfect cycling holiday.

Also check out:

www.backroads.com – a US-based specialist with a wide range of options.

www.bicycle-beano.co.uk – Bicycle Beano have a good site covering cycling holidays in Wales and the borders.

www.bikemagic.com – go to the travel pages for an excellent section on where Bike Magic have got partners who'll supply flight deals for cyclists or rail travel and holidays.

www.byways-breaks.co.uk – a nice-looking site, Byways Breaks arrange cycling and walking holidays in the Peaks, Shropshire and Cheshire countryside.

www.cycleactive.co.uk – excellent for action-packed cycle holidays.

www.cyclebreaks.co.uk – cycling holidays in Suffolk, Norfolk and now Europe.

www.cycle-rides.co.uk – a very good selection of biking tours through Europe and further afield.

www.discoveradventure.com – a great selection of biking holidays for the more adventurous.

www.rough-tracks.co.uk – a wide range of active adventure holidays for beginners and experts.

www.scotcycle.co.uk – Scottish Cycling Holidays are specialists in cycling holidays in Scotland obviously. Nice site too.

www.skedaddle.co.uk – one of the best for variety, everything for the beginner or expert. It covers most of the world too.

www.sustrans.co.uk – the National Cycle Network is featured as part of this campaigning charity site.

Diving Holidays

www.aquatours.com – the site isn't up to much but they offer a world-wide service.

www.divechannel.co.uk – excellent site specialising in diving holidays and travel.

www.divequest.co.uk – lots of detail, prices and choice make this a good site to visit.

www.regaldive.co.uk – learn to dive in the best diving locations.

Golfing Holidays

www.golfbreaks.com – a travel agent specialising in holidays for golfing nuts.

www.lorringolf.com – high level golfing holidays, an academy and corporate events.

www.prosolgolf.com – holidays on the Costa del Sol, the laboured English is somewhat endearing.

Hobby and Culinary Holidays

www.shawguides.com   US

LOOKING FOR SOMETHING TO DO?
A massive database of cultural, hobby and learning holidays, mostly American but you can find UK-based ones if you search hard enough.

See also cookery courses on page 175 and ...
www.arblasterandclarke.com – wine tours world-wide.
www.epiculinary.com – culinary holidays.
www.martinrandall.com – cultural travel with expert lecturers.
www.holidayonthemenu.com – as well the usual European offerings, you can learn to cook in Australia, Indonesia, Jordan, Vietnam ... Part of **www.onthegotours.com**, holidays for the semi-independent who want to mix culture and fun.
www.theinternationalkitchen.com – cookery vacations in France, Italy, Spain and Morocco.

Language Learning

See the Languages section on page 298.

Riding Holidays

www.equineadventures.co.uk – a good agent for riding holidays.
www.equitour.co.uk – a wide range of riding holidays available for all levels of rider.
www.horsebackholidays.com – a similarly broad selection of places and types of holiday for the enthusiastic rider.
www.inthesaddle.com – a good-looking site covering a variety of holiday options.
www.ranchweb.com – excellent site on all forms of ranch holidays mainly in the US.

Sailing

www.sunsail.com   US

SAILING AND WATERSPORT HOLIDAYS
A wide-ranging and informative site with lots to offer whether you're an enthusiast or a beginner, plenty of special offers too.

See also:

www.allafloat.com – lots of choice and online booking.

www.bootoo.co.uk – the luxury yacht Bootoo takes you around the Caribbean.

www.compass24.com – a good shop for sailing enthusiasts, over 14,000 products.

www.elitesailing.co.uk – learn to sail.

www.neilson.com – award-winning operator, they run a sailing training school and a wide variety of other water-based holidays too.

www.sailingholidays.com – specialists in Greece and Croatia.

www.sea-trek.co.uk – specialist in Greece, learn-to-sail holidays too.

www.tenrag.com – charter your own yacht.

Solo Travel

http://solotravelonline.co.uk – excellent site for single travellers with lots of information, background and holiday options; also ads from likely travel companions.

www.justyou.co.uk – comprehensive offering from the market leader in solo travel.

Backpacking and Adventure

www.adventuredirectory.com   UK

THE ADVENTURE DIRECTORY

A huge directory of sites devoted to adventure, just click on the world map or search and away you go …

See also:

http://couchsurfing.com – one for the idealists but if you sign up and buy into it, then there's the chance of free accommodation.

http://retiredbackpackers.com – if you're too old, too poor or just too knackered to carry on backpacking, then try this site where you can be matched with like-minded travellers.

www.backpackeurope.com – aimed at Americans but useful for Europeans too.

www.footprint-adventures.co.uk – birding, trekking and wildlife all over the world.

www.highplaces.co.uk – treks in high places in some 20 countries.

www.iexplore.com – a high-quality offering with a huge amount of information for the adventure traveller.

T

www.igougo.com – more of an information exchange for global travellers, but you can book trips through them. There are plenty of features and the IgoUgo awards too.

www.madadventurer.com – excellent site design with loads of mad adventures to choose from while helping community development in 23 countries.

www.spicemcr.com – vibrant activity and social club with holidays to match.

www.theleap.co.uk – similar approach to Mad Adventurer but based in Africa.

www.trailsource.com – excellent resource covering the world's great trails, categorised by mode of transport.

www.transitionsabroad.com – excellent for long-term travelling and working holidays.

Eco-tourism and Nature

For holidays by train see pages 516 and 558.

www.responsibletravel.com   UK
GIVE THE WORLD A BREAK
Endorsed by Anita Roddick, this site provides a huge range of travel experiences all selected for their sensitivity to the local environment and its people. You can search by destination, activity or accommodation type. If you become a member, you can receive their monthly magazine. There are a several campaigns to join too ranging from protecting wildlife to outlawing child sex tourism.

www.tourismconcern.org.uk   UK
ETHICAL TOURISM
If you're concerned about the impact of your trip, then come here for advice or help with one of their campaigns. It all goes to ensuring that the poorest holiday workers are not exploited.
http://ecofriendlytourist.com deals in the same issues, gives good practical advice especially on how to avoid greenwashing (appearing to be green).

See also:
http://travel.guardian.co.uk/tag/green – articles from the *Guardian*'s Green Travel pages.
www.btcv.org – conservation holidays.
www.changingworlds.co.uk – worthwhile working holidays.

www.coralcay.org – 'providing resources to help sustain livelihoods and alleviate poverty through the protection, restoration and management of coral reefs and tropical forests'.
www.csv.org.uk – information for volunteers.
www.discoveryinitiatives.co.uk – responsible wildlife holidays.
www.ecoclub.com – a network providing a wealth of information about all aspects of ecotourism.
www.eco-res.com – make a reservation at an eco-friendly lodge, camp or reserve.
www.ecotourism.org – the International Ecotourism Society.
www.ecotravel.com – a US-based site with a magazine and an excellent search facility.
www.ecovolunteer.com – if you want to give your services to a specific animal benefit project.
www.exodus.co.uk – specialist agents and winners of the 'Best Tour Operator' in the Responsible Travel Awards 2004.
www.inntravel.co.uk – specialists in walking and cycling holidays, excellent, informative site.
www.naturetrek.co.uk – excellent nature holiday specialists.
www.northsouthtravel.co.uk – a small travel agent which channels much of the profit into aid projects in the third world.
www.sacredearth.com – ethnobiology and eco-travel to South America, for those seriously interested in nature.
www.thetravelfoundation.org.uk – information on the effect of tourism and how you can help.
www.traveltree.co.uk – for eco-sensitive volunteer work overseas.
www.wildshots.co.uk – wildlife photography holidays.

Healthy Holidays

If you want to lie back and relax then try one of these ...

www.bodyandsoulholidays.com   UK
SPA BREAKS AND HOTELS
A cool site where you can pick out your treatments or activities and they will select the resort or holiday to suit your needs. There's quite a bit of choice and some of the locations are stunning.

See also:
http://spas.about.com – a useful directory with tips and information on taking a spa holiday.
www.inspa-retreats.com – a combination of luxury and health.
www.nealsyardagency.com – healthy holidays.

www.thermalia.co.uk – one of the leading specialists in spa holidays.

Air Travel

With climate change in mind, you may wish to visit
www.carbonneutral.com *to calculate your emissions and buy trees to compensate for the carbon emissions your flight has generated.*

Airline Information and Flying

http://oag.com   UK
AIRLINE DATA
What was the Official Airline Guide is now a massive database of facts on flights, airlines and airports. It's also a good travel guide, magazine and you can even book hotels; however, airline information is its strength.

www.airlinequality.com   UK
RANKING THE AIRLINES
An independent ranking of all the world's airlines and their services, see who's the best and the worst and why. Each airline is rated using a number of stars (up to five) on criteria such as seat quality, catering and staff.

www.airfraid.com   US
CONQUER YOUR FEAR OF FLYING
A good place to go if you're of the opinion that getting on a plane is the last thing you'll ever do. There's advice gleaned from various reputable sources and details on how you can go on courses to help you overcome your fears. See also **www.aviatours.co.uk** which is a course backed by British Airways and also **www.freedomtofly.biz**

These sites might also prove useful:
http://airwise.com – on the face of it a pretty dull site but tucked away in the flight information page is a complete world flight schedule listing and it's free.
http://crankyflier.blogspot.com – an award-winning blog, Aircraft nut the Cranky Flier gives some forthright views on how it should be done.
http://seatguru.com – information and seating details for planes operated by many of the major airlines, it shows which are the

good seats and the bad, includes contact details and comparison charts too.

www.airlinemeals.net – all you need to know about airline stodge.

www.flightmapping.com – useful site, find out who flies from UK and Irish airports and where they fly to.

www.flyertalk.com – a US-based forum site where frequent flyers give their travel tips.

Airline and Flight Sites

www.traveljungle.co.uk   UK
FARE COMPARISONS
Travel Jungle have become very popular and it's easy to see why: here you can compare offers from 23 airlines and 7 travel agents so you should be able to get a great deal.

www.kayak.co.uk   UK/US
FLIGHT SEARCH
The UK version of one of the most popular travel sites in the US, Kayak allows you to search for flights from over 120 other sites. It's relatively fast and it's easy to adjust your itinerary. The 'Buzz' section is great for ideas and the latest travel gossip; there's also a lively forum section too.

www.cheapflights.co.uk   UK
NOTHING BUT CHEAP FLIGHTS
You don't need to register here to explore the great offers available from this site; you still need to phone some of the travel agents or airlines listed to get your deal although an increasing number have web links. If you're after a last-minute deal, they have a handy calendar that will search for deals from your local airport. See also

www.netflights.com   UK
THE AIRLINE NETWORK
Discount deals on over 100 airlines world-wide make the Airline Network worth checking out for their flight offers page alone. It's good for flights from regional airports. They also do all the traditional travel agent things and there are some good holiday bargains too.

www.openjet.com UK

NO FRILLS MADE EASY
This site searches the low-cost carriers to find you the best prices to European destinations and gives you the results for adjacent days to enable you to fly at the lowest possible price. See also **www.whichbudget.com** and also the basic but up-to-date **www.flycheapo.com**

See also these helpful sites ...

www.attitudetravel.com/lowcostairlines – now covering the world's low cost airlines and where they fly to.
www.bargainflights.com – good search facility and plenty of offers, but you need to be patient.
www.deckchair.com – a strong site where you can get some good flight bargains as well as plan the rest of your holiday. Now part of the Lastminute.com empire.
www.flightcentre.com – they guarantee to beat any genuine current quoted airfare!
www.skyscanner.net – excellent for Europe and comparing the budget airline offers.
www.travelselect.com – good flight selection and lots of different options available at this very flexible site.

The Key Airlines

www.aa.com – American Airlines, standard airline site.
www.aerlingus.ie – good, easy-to-use site.
www.airfrance.co.uk – plenty of offers.
www.airindia.com – good offers and travel information and destination guide.
www.alitalia.it – a no-nonsense site.
www.ba.com or **www.britishairways.co.uk** – easy-to-use, efficient site.
www.bmibaby.com – the low-cost arm of British Midland.
www.cathaypacific.com – comprehensive flight service and guide.
www.easyjet.co.uk – great for an ever increasing number of destinations, particularly good for UK flights.
www.emirates.com – no-frills design and flight booking facilities.
www.flybmi.com – British Midland, good offers for European destinations.
www.klm.com – good design with lots of offers.
www.lufthansa.co.uk – masses of information and express booking.

www.quantas.com – straightforward booking facility.

www.ryanair.com – very good for Ireland, northern Europe, Italy and France. Clear and easy-to-use web site, massive discounts.

www.flysilverjet.com – lower-cost, carbon-neutral, business class only flights from this new venture; London to New York only at present.

www.singaporeair.com – follows the formula but with the added extra of a multi-city flight planner.

www.united.com – United Airlines offers a good all-round service at this site.

www.virgin-atlantic.com – good online booking facility with some offers.

UK Regional Airlines

It's worth trying out regional airlines, not only because they may be cheaper, but also they might fly to your destination from a more convenient local airport. Here are the best of them.

www.airsouthwest.com – small airline offering great-value flights from the South West of England to London.

www.excelairways.com – an ambitious and service-oriented charter airline, they offer luxuries, such as leather seating, and fly to a wide range of European and Middle Eastern destinations.

www.flyglobespan.com – a Scottish low-cost airline, expanding into England and flying to European holiday destinations, Canada and the US.

www.jet2.com – flying from Leeds-Bradford, Manchester and Belfast to a select number of European destinations, Jet2 is offering seats at very low prices.

Airport Information

www.worldairportguide.com   GERMANY

WHAT ARE THE WORLD'S AIRPORTS REALLY LIKE?
It seems that no matter how out of the way, this guide has details on every airport – how to get there, where to park, facilities, key phone numbers and a map. There are also guides on cities, resorts and even world weather. See also **www.airportcitycodes.com**

www.baa.co.uk   UK

BRITISH AIRPORT AUTHORITY
Details on all the major UK airports that are run by the BAA, you

get all the essential information plus flight data, weather and shopping information.

www.a2bairports.com   UK
UK AND IRISH AIRPORTS
These pages from A2B Travel offer all the relevant information on all the major airports and lots of the smaller ones too. Another site with information on UK airports is **www.airport-maps.co.uk** which also has flight route information along with maps, facility details and related links.

www.sleepinginairports.net   UK
GUIDE TO SLEEPING IN AIRPORTS
Rated 'Good', 'Tolerable' or just 'Hell', here is a sleeper's guide for budget travellers on many of the world's airports. It's actually pretty funny too.

Airport Parking
www.uk-airport-car-parking.co.uk   UK
BOOK YOUR SPACE
Probably the best of the sites dedicated to helping you find somewhere to park your car while you're away. It offers more options and information than the others listed but it's always worth shopping around, so you should try these alternatives.

See also:
www.bcponline.co.uk – easy to use and with some good savings on airport car park rates.
www.holidayextras.co.uk – who are also good for parking, airport hotels, airport lounges and also have information on getting to airports by public transport.
www.ncp.co.uk – airport parking and more.
www.parking4less.co.uk – high-quality secured parking assured.
www.securedcarparks.com – as the title suggests, a useful guide to car parks nationwide with decent security.

Rail, Taxi and Coach Travel Abroad
www.seat61.com   UK
THE MAN IN SEAT 61
You can get timetables and book on many routes whether by train, ship or coach. You can compare costs and there's plenty of information and links too.

See also:

www.busabout.com – create your own trip through Europe by bus. Island explorer tickets available too.

www.busaustralia.com – for some really long road trips.

www.busstation.net – great links for bus info worldwide.

www.eurail.com – details of the Eurail ticket, information and prices, and you can now buy online.

www.eurolines.com – Europe's coach network, covering 500 destinations, 15- or 30-day passes available.

www.eurostar.com – through the Channel Tunnel … online booking plus timetables and offers.

www.eurotunnel.com – online passenger bookings.

www.greatrail.com – fabulous selection of railway journeys.

www.greyhound.com – the famous American coach company.

www.greyhound.com.au – Greyhound buses Australia.

www.holidaytaxis.com – book a taxi in a limited number of destinations, mainly in Europe but also USA.

www.orient-express.com – details of their holidays and routes.

www.railaustralia.com.au – for some of the world's great train holidays.

www.raileurope.co.uk – booking European rail travel.

www.taxisabroad.com – book taxis in a selection of European countries.

www.trainseurope.co.uk – European and North American trains with online booking.

www.trainweb.com – a huge train portal site, particularly good for Amtrak in the US and Via Rail in Canada.

Car Hire Worldwide

It's probably best to go to a price-comparison site before going to one of the car hire companies, that way you should get the best prices. One of the best is to be found at www.priceline.co.uk

www.holidaycars.co.uk   UK

WORLD-WIDE CAR HIRE
Over 4,000 car hire locations throughout the world means that this site is well worth a visit on your quest, you can get an instant online quote and you can book too. Very good for the US.

See also:

www.bnm.com – Breezenet, excellent for the US.

www.easycar.com – low-cost, online car hire specialist, part of the Easyjet group.

www.holidayautos.co.uk – excellent prices and a wide choice too.

www.insurance4carhire.com – who have a number of options to suit.

www.pelicancarhire.co.uk – competitive rates from this specialist in Europe.

Places to Stay

Hotels

www.hotelguide.com   UK

COMPREHENSIVE

With services available in nine languages and specialist sections such as golfing breaks, this site ranks amongst the best for finding the right hotel. It lists around 850,000 at time of writing.

www.from-a-z.com   UK

A–Z OF HOTELS

A well-designed British site with over 20,000 hotels to choose from in the UK, Eire and France and a further 40,000 world-wide; it's quick and easy to use and there's online booking available plus plenty of special discounts. See also **http://booking.com** which provides a huge database of hotels, especially good for Europe and some great discounts too; well worth checking out.

Other good hotel directory and booking sites:
www.all-hotels.com – 120,000 hotels listed with lots of options, American bias.

www.ase.net – some 150,000 listed properties here with many reviews.

www.best-inn.co.uk – another hotel/motel directory containing thousands of entries, very good for London and links to specialist accommodation.

www.discount25.com – great for hotel discounts, primarily in Spain but also the major European cities.

www.hotelchatter.com – excellent hotel review site. As it's American most of the reviewed hotels are situated there.

www.lowcostbeds.com – part of the Low Cost travel group, there are some serious bargains to be had here, especially in Europe but expect to end up on the phone.

www.mrandmrssmith.com – the place to find luxury hotels, excellent site too.

www.octopustravel.com – a huge number of rooms and deals available, one of the most used sites for hotel booking.
www.openworld.co.uk – a collection of links to hotel sites, just use the interactive world map.
www.placestostay.com – simple to use and provides a list of hotels, descriptions, prices, maps and an online reservation service.

Hostels

www.hostels.com   US

INTERNATIONAL HOSTELLING
An excellent resource for anyone looking for budget accommodation. Many of the hostels are reviewed and it's easy to find one using the click-through maps.

See also:
www.hihostels.com – a hostelling booking service with lots of information too.
www.hostellingworld.com – a hostelling club with online booking.
www.yha.org.uk – very good site from the Youth Hostels Association.

Villas and cottages

http://ownersdirect.co.uk – some 8,000 cottages and villas to be rented direct from their owners.
www.abercrombiekent.com – offer villas in their 'Independent Travel' section.
www.cvtravel.net – passionate about villas, mainly in Europe.
www.jamesvillas.co.uk – over 2,000 villas, mostly in the Med.
www.ownerssyndicate.com – a wide choice with some good offers.
www.thebigdomain.com – big houses for hire.

Travel Guides and Information

www.johnnyjet.com   US

TRAVEL PORTAL
A very detailed and comprehensive portal site devoted to all things travel. It's well categorised but has an American bias.

Travel Abroad

The Good Web Site Guide's Top 10s
of the Internet

1. **www.expedia.co.uk** – not always the cheapest but the best
2. **www.fco.gov.uk/travel** – essential advice from the Foreign Office
3. **www.xe.net/ucc** – the online currency converter
4. **www.e-bookers.com** – reliable and good value, especially for flights
5. **www.baa.co.uk** – information on the major UK airports and flights
6. **www.uk-airport-car-parking.co.uk** – book your parking in advance
7. **www.lonelyplanet.com** – superb for independent travellers
8. **www.mappy.co.uk** – get to where you're going
9. **www.brochurebank.co.uk** – order your brochures, get them delivered to you
10. **www.johnnyjet.com** – great travel portal

www.lonelyplanet.com   UK

LONELY PLANET GUIDES
A superb travel site, aimed at the independent traveller, but with great information for everyone. Get a review on most world destinations or pick a theme and go with that; leave a message on the Thorn Tree; find out the latest news by country; get health reports; read about the travel experiences of others – what's the real story?

www.bugbog.com   UK

TRAVEL INFORMATION
An outstanding and well-organised site offering information and advice on all aspects of travel, with guides and a good directory too.

www.tripadvisor.com   US

UNBIASED REVIEWS
An excellent site offering guidance on almost any destination with reviews and links. It includes magazine articles as well as guide book reviews and opinions from members.

www.roughguides.com UK

ROUGH GUIDES

Lively reviews on a huge number of places. In addition, there's general travel information, a place to share your travel thoughts with other travellers, or you can buy a guide. Excellent for links and you can get some good deals via the site. You can now order interactive city maps for your PDA or listen to world music on Rough Guides Radio.

www.fodors.com US

FODOR'S GUIDES

These guides give an American perspective, but there is a huge amount of information on each destination. The site is well laid out and easy to use. See also the comprehensive **www.mytravelguide.com**

http://kasbah.com US

THE WORLD'S LARGEST TRAVEL GUIDE

A site facelift for the worse. Ignore the travel agency stuff and head for the 'travel guide' section. Unfortunately, the search engine has also gone but if you find the alphabetical index at the bottom of the page you'll be able to access good quality information. The highlights on each destination are useful and the 'Global Travel Toolbox' provides info, telecommunications, maps, currency and more. What a pity they've made it all so difficult now.

www.packback.com AUSTRALIA

PACKBACK TRAVEL GUIDE

A good-looking and useful site with an independent travel guide, a growing membership and a reputation for quality reviews. It includes a discussion forum, travel tools and flight booking.

www.guardian.co.uk/travel UK

FROM THE *GUARDIAN* NEWSPAPER

A good reflection of the excellent *Guardian* weekly travel section with guides, information and inspiration throughout. There's also the latest news and links to sites with offers plus extra features such as audio guides and articles on parts of the UK. See also **www.ivebeenthere.co.uk** which is their very useful collection of travellers' tips, there are several hundred across lots of categories, nearly enough for a book!

www.gorp.com US

FOR THE GREAT OUTDOORS
A great title, Gorp is dedicated to adventure, whether it be
hiking, mountaineering, fishing, snow sports or riding the rapids.
It has an American bias, but is full of relevant good advice, links
and information.

www.bradmans.com UK

BRADMAN'S FOR BUSINESS TRAVELLERS
A really excellent city guide with none of your fancy graphics,
just a straightforward listing of countries and sensible
information on each one, includes restaurant reviews and
tips on orienting yourself in the city.

www.vtourist.com UK
THE VIRTUAL TOURIST
Explore destinations in a unique and fun way. Travellers describe
their experiences, share photos, make recommendations and
give tips so others benefit from their experience.

Other guides and sites worth checking out are:
http://away.com – lots of links and information hidden away
amongst the offers.
http://insideragency.com – get help from local inhabitants, find
your way around using their insights and expertise.
http://picturesofplaces.com – here you can find a huge number
of photos from around the world.
www.360travelguide.com – excellent use of technology, this is
an archive of those panoramic 360 degree shots you get from
hotel sites. There are thousands available from beaches to
monuments.
www.about.com/travel – a comprehensive travel directory from
About.com.
www.bootsnall.com – aimed at the independent traveller, it has
several guides and is packed with information, looks good too.
www.holidays-uncovered.co.uk – reviews of over 50,000
holidays and hotels, a very good resource but could do with a
good search facility.
www.officialtravelinfo.com – a directory covering the world's
official tourism sites.
www.nytimes.com/pages/travel/index.html – travel news and
information from the *New York Times*.
www.roadnews.com – help and information for those of us who
travel with a laptop computer.

www.thetravelportal.com – hotel reviews and an excellent set of links from a bigger web directory.

www.travelintelligence.net – excellent collection of travel writing to inspire you along with a hotel search and reservation service.

www.travel-library.com – less entertaining than some but combines recommendation with hard facts very well.

www.travel-rants.com – entertaining blog from a frustrated traveller.

www.wikitravel.org – an attempt to build an authoritative travel guide using the same technology as Wikipedia.

www.world-heritage-tour.org – a list and tour of World Heritage sites around the globe with panoramic views.

www.worldinformation.com – not specifically a travel guide but there is a mountain of information on the world's countries, their culture and advice about how to deal with issues like corruption.

City Guides

www.timeout.com   UK

TIME OUT GUIDE

A slick site with destination guides covering many European cities and an increasing number further afield such as New York and Sydney. Not surprisingly, it's outstanding for London. You can also book tickets and buy books via other retailers.

See also

http://gridskipper.com – stylish blog site aimed at the trendy urban traveller.

www.citypopulation.de – lots of information about cities and regions throughout the world.

www.citysearch.com – a listing for mainly US cities with entertainment and orientation guides.

Maps and Route Finders

www.multimap.com   UK

 GREAT BRITAIN

Outstanding design, easy to use, excellent for the UK, you can search using postcodes, London street names, place names or Ordnance Survey grid references. Once you've found what you're looking for, you can also see an aerial view of the area.

www.mappy.co.uk   UK
START HERE

Mappy has a great-looking site which is easy to use and has lots
of added features such as a personal mapping service where you
can store the maps you use most. The route finder is OK, and
business users can fill in their mileage allowance and Mappy
will calculate how much they should claim.

www.geograph.org.uk   UK
PHOTO MAP

An attempt to photographically represent the UK using OS map
grid references with some 50% covered. It looks like it's building
into a great resource.

See also:
http://maps.msn.com – excellent mapping and route-finding
service from MSN.
www.expedia.co.uk – select 'maps'; limited to the US, Canada,
France, Germany and UK. Modest route planner.
www.mapquest.com – find out the best way to get from A to B
in Europe or America, not always as detailed as you'd like, but
easy to use and you can customise your map or route plan.
www.mapsonus.com – it's notoriously difficult to find your way
around America, but using the route planner you should
minimise your risk of getting lost.
www.memory-map.co.uk – a useful range of downloadable
maps based on Ordnance Survey mapping.
www.ordnancesurvey.co.uk – a good site with mapping for sale;
links to the GPR service **www.gps.gov.uk**
www.stanfords.co.uk – travel book and map specialists.
www.uk.map24.com – excellent interactive and static mapping
but the directions are a little difficult to follow at times.
www.viamichelin.com – a good all-round travel site with an
improved route-finder service, which is OK.

www.theaa.co.uk   UK
AUTOMOBILE ASSOCIATION

A superb site that offers route-planning and traffic information,
a hotel and restaurant guide with a booking service, and help
with buying a car or even a GPS. There is also information on
insurance and other financial help.

www.rac.co.uk   UK

GET AHEAD WITH THE RAC

Great for UK traffic reports, this site has a very reliable route planner, which seems to be very busy and slow at peak times. There's also a good section on finding the right place to stay, and lots of help if you want to buy a car.

Destinations

www.antor.com   UK

ASSOCIATION OF NATIONAL TOURIST OFFICES

A useful starting point for information about the 90 or so countries that are members of the association. It also has very good links to key tourism sites. See also **www.towd.com** who list every official government tourist office and some unofficial ones too.

www.embassyworld.com   US

EMBASSIES AROUND THE GLOBE

Pick two countries, one for 'whose embassy' and one for 'in what location', press go and up pops the details on the embassy with contact and essential information.

Here's an alphabetical list of countries and regions to help you research your chosen destination and plan your holiday.

A

www.africatravelresource.com   UK

EAST AFRICA

An exceptional site that specifically covers Burundi, Kenya, Rwanda, Uganda and Tanzania plus the resorts of Lamu and Zanzibar. The level of detail is great but because the site is packaged so well, it doesn't overwhelm. A lesson in how a travel site should be set up.

See also:

http://i-cias.com – an excellent information site covering North Africa and the Middle East.

www.africaguide.com – detailed country-by-country guides, discussion forums, shopping, culture and a travelogue feature make this site a good first stop.

www.africa-nature-photography.com – how to take the best shots while on safari.

www.africanodyssey.co.uk – African and Arabian specialist agents.

www.africansafariclub.com – cruises and safaris a speciality.
www.backpackafrica.com – excellent site for backpackers with
over 400 links and advice on where to go and what to see.
www.ecoafrica.com – tailor-made safaris with the emphasis on
eco-tourism.
www.onsafari.com – good advice on what sort of safari is right
for you.
www.phakawe.demon.co.uk – safaris in Botswana.
www.sahara-overland.com – the trans-Sahara experience with
information and travellers' reports.
www.vintageafrica.com – awesome safaris and destinations
from this specialist travel agent, who will tailor-make holidays if
requested.
www.wilderness-safaris.com – specialises in providing safaris
that go to pristine wilderness.
www.wildnetafrica.net – an excellent travel and information
portal for safaris to south and south-east Africa.

www.turisme.ad   ANDORRA
ANDORRA
A nice little site extolling the many virtues of this tiny country.

www.polartravel.co.uk   UK
ARCTIC AND ANTARTICA
How to get to the Poles in safety and even enjoy yourself when
you get there!

See also:
www.arctic-experience.co.uk – spectacular holidays in the
Arctic.
www.arcticseakayakingadventures.com – experience the Arctic
waterways in kayaks.
www.iaato.org – International Association of Antarctic Travel
Operators, has links to all the major agents.
www.nunavik-tourism.com – the wild frontier of the Quebec
Arctic with a list of tour operators.

www.argentour.com   ARGENTINA
ARGENTINA
Outstanding (but very slow-loading) travel site with video clips,
regional information, history and slide shows of the major
cities. There's even a section on how to tango. See also
www.argentinatravelnet.com/indexE.htm

www.asiatravel.com   SINGAPORE
ASIA
A horribly designed site packed with travel information about all
the Asian countries and beyond. Fortunately, the quality of the
information is much better than the site design would suggest
and covers accommodation, travel and background facts on the
countries and what to buy while you're there.

www.austria-tourism.at   AUSTRIA
AUSTRIA
An excellent site covering all you need to know about the
country, with information on skiing and summer holidays too.
See also **www.tiscover.at**

www.australia.com   AUSTRALIA
DISCOVER AUSTRALIA
The Australian Tourist Commission offer a good and informative
site that gives lots of facts about the country, the people, the
lifestyle and what you can expect when you visit.

See also:
www.acn.net.au – a directory of Australian cultural and
recreational resources.
www.australianexplorer.com – excellent and well-illustrated site
with some 14,000 pages of information.
www.travelaustralia.com.au – informative site, good for regional
information.
www.travelmate.com.au – a comprehensive site with masses of
information, which is especially good if you're driving.
www.voyages.com.au – stay in luxury at Ayers Rock, or Uluru
as it's officially known now.
www.westernaustralia.com – comprehensive-tourist-oriented
site.
www.wilmap.com.au – excellent for Australian maps and links.

T

B
www.indo.com   INDONESIA
BALI ONLINE
This site covers Bali and its top hotels, but there's also plenty
of information on the rest of Indonesia and links to other
Asian sites.

www.virtualbangladesh.com   US
BANGLADESH
A colourful and atmospheric travel site that contains all the
practical information you need to start planning a trip written
in an informal, welcoming style. You can find out about the
people, customs, flora and fauna, and there is an interesting
section on the politics. For another general tourist site go to
www.discoverybangladesh.com

www.trabel.com   BELGIUM
BELGIUM
The Belgium Travel Network offers a site packed with
information about the country and its key towns and cities.
You can get information on hotels, travelling, an airport guide,
flight information and there's also a good links page. See
also the well-designed **www.belgium-tourism.net** and
www.visitflanders.co.uk

www.belize.com   US
BELIZE
A good general site covering the country. It's not just aimed at
tourists but it's incredibly useful for the visitor.

www.boliviaweb.com   US
BOLIVIA
A useful and well-put-together portal site.

www.botswana.com   SOUTH AFRICA
BOTSWANA
A well-illustrated site covering Botswana's exciting collection of
game lodges. It also offers links to hotel and services directories
too. See also **www.okavango.com**

www.brazil.com   BRAZIL
BRAZIL
A straightforward, no-nonsense guide, travelogue and listing site
for Brazil that also contains information on hotels and resorts.

See also:
www.brazil.org.uk – very informative site from the Brazilian
Embassy.
www.carnaval.com – you have to hunt for the information but
there's a very helpful site in there.
www.helisight.com.br – book your helicopter tour over Rio.

www.ipanema.com – outstanding site by people who really
know Rio, with masses of links and detailed cross referencing.
www.varig.co.uk – the national airline, good site with online
booking.

www.travel-bulgaria.com   BULGARIA
EXPLORE BULGARIA
A well-put-together portal site with all the information you
should need, Bulgaria is the hottest place for cheap property at
the moment. See also **www.bulgaria.com/travel** and the UK-
based specialist **www.balkanholidays.com**

C

www.cambodia-travel.com   CAMBODIA
HOME OF THE KHMER
A wide-ranging site with some interesting spelling! There
are sections on Angkor Wat, the Khmer and the usual
accommodation details. See also **www.eyeoncambodia.com**

www.travelcanada.ca   CANADA
 EXPLORE CANADA
Did you know that the glass floor at the top of the world's
tallest free-standing structure could support the weight of 14
large hippos? Find out much more at this wide-ranging
and attractive site, from touring to city guides. See also
www.canadianaffair.com who offer some excellent low-cost
flights and tours, and for an outdoor experience of the country go
to **www.playday.com**, Canada's recreation website. For cheap
flights check out Zoom at **www.zoomairlines.co.uk**

www.turq.com   US
CARIBBEAN
All you need to organise a great holiday in the Caribbean.
There's information on flights, hotels, cruises, a travel guide and
trip reports to the islands, all on a well-presented and easy-to-
use site.

See also:
www.antigua-barbuda.com – competent site from the Antiguan
High Commission.
www.barbados.org – great overview of the island with excellent
links.
www.caribbeandreams.co.uk – UK travel agent specialising in
the Caribbean.

www.doitcaribbean.com – information, booking and an
interactive map.
www.jamaicatravel.com – a pretty comprehensive site devoted
to the island with regional guides and help in planning your trip.
www.visittnt.com – basic information site on Trinidad and Tobago.

www.gochile.cl   CHILE
CHILE
A great overview of the country with all the holiday information
you'll need including details on Easter Island. See also
www.chile-hotels.com

www.chinatour.com   CHINA
CHINA
A comprehensive site stuffed with data on China: where to go
and stay, how to get there and what to see, maps and visa
application information. See also the China Travel System at
www.chinats.com who have a good-looking and very polite site
where you can book hotels and tours, get travel information and
chat to others who've experienced China.

See also:
www.chinapage.com/china.html – information on everything
from calligraphy to language to tattoos. Some historical
background information on major sites.
www.discoverhongkong.com – for Hong Kong.
www.haiweitrails.com – organised treks in SW China and Tibet.

www.croatia.hr   CROATIA
CROATIA
An excellent site covering the country and its virtues with
sections on events, attractions, background, accommodation
and an all-round travel guide. For villas and general info check
out **www.croatianaffair.com**

www.cubanculture.com   US
CUBA
A fast, easy-to-use site with the basic information about Cuba
and its heritage. There are lots of useful links too.

www.cyprustourism.org   CYPRUS
CYPRUS
A pretty basic site about the country, well the Greek-run bit
anyway.

www.czech-tourism.com CZECH REPUBLIC
CZECH REPUBLIC

A good directory site providing information and links in 15 categories from business to the weather including tour operators and a country guide. See also Czech It Out at **www.goaway.co.uk**

D

www.visitdenmark.com DENMARK
DENMARK

The official Danish tourist board site where you can get links to book a holiday and all the advice and information you'd expect from a well-run and efficient-looking site. See also **www.woco.dk** for an excellent site on Copenhagen.

E

www.ecuadorexplorer.com US

ECUADOR

A very well-put-together directory site covering all you need for a visit to one of the most beautiful countries on the planet. For specific sites on the Galapagos go to the thorough **www.galapagos-travel.com** and also the Galapagos Conservation Trust at **www.gct.org** which is full of information and good for links.

http://touregypt.net EGYPT
EGYPT

A pretty ugly but very comprehensive site covering the country and in particular its history. It's really a very good portal site as well as a travel guide.

See also:
www.ancient.co.uk – archaeological tours with this specialist operator.
www.discoveregypt.co.uk – a well-illustrated site from a UK-based specialist.
www.peltours.com – great site from an agent specialising in Egypt.

www.visitestonia.com ESTONIA
ESTONIA

Gushing with enthusiasm for the charms of this small Baltic state, this site gives you information on travel, accommodation, history, climate and money. For another view try the no-nonsense **www.estoniantravel.com**

www.eurotrip.com   UK
BACKPACKING EUROPE
Student and independent European travel with in-depth
information, facts, reviews, articles, discussion, live reports,
links and travel advice on a good-looking and well-designed site.
Also connects to a no-frills airline booking service and a section
with information on finding low-cost air fares.

www.eurocamp.co.uk   UK
SELF-CATERING EUROPE
The leading self-catering company with over 150 holiday parks
in 12 countries. Here you can find details of the accommodation
and book a holiday; there are some bargains too. See also
www.eurocampindependent.co.uk who offer a European
campsite reservation service.

www.visiteurope.com   US
EUROPEAN TRAVEL COMMISSION
A site aimed at Americans to encourage them to visit Europe. It's
informative and there's a section for each country.

F
www.visitfinland.com   FINLAND
FINLAND
Look under the 'Individual holiday planner' for good-quality
information on travelling around, accommodation and outdoor
activities. There are also organised tours available for the British
traveller. Don't miss out on Santa's homepage and arrange a
Christmas visit. See also **www.wildnorth.net** – a visual treat
with fishing and hunting tours.

www.franceway.com   FRANCE

VOILA LA FRANCE!
Excellent site giving an overview of French culture, history, facts
and figures, and of course, how to book a holiday. You can also
sign up for the newsletter.

See also:
www.brittanytourism.com – a good site on all that Brittany has
to offer.
www.cdt-nord.fr – useful site on northern France.
www.cheznous.com – holiday cottages in France.
www.corsica.co.uk – good site from a Corsican specialist.
www.franceguide.com – official French Government Tourist

Office portal site or **www.francetourism.com** the sister site aimed at US tourists.

www.francemag.com – really informative and useful e-zine devoted to France.

www.frenchconnections.co.uk – French holiday specialist.

www.gites-de-france.fr/eng – a wide variety of gite accommodation with online booking.

www.justparis.co.uk – details on how to get there and hotels for when you've arrived; cluttered design.

www.le-guide.com – a messy but informative guide to the South of France.

www.logis-de-france.fr – reliable guide to 3,000 hotels and restaurants throughout France.

www.magicparis.com – revamped, stylish guide to Paris with comprehensive information and beautiful pictures.

www.manchetourisme.com – what to do in La Manche, Normandy.

www.normandy-tourism.org – excellent and informative site on Normandy.

www.northernfrance-tourism.com – a scrappy site on northern France.

www.parishotels.com – a fast booking service for Paris hotels.

www.rhonealpes-tourism.co.uk– information and holidays.

www.vive-la-france.org – very comprehensive and good fun.

www.voiceofacity.com – sponsored by Eurostar, a number of Parisians give the insider's view of the city, quirky but interesting.

G

www.visitthegambia.gm   GAMBIA
GAMBIA
A good tourist site which promotes Gambia's wildlife and ecological sites with particular emphasis on the bird-life and waterways. See also **www.gambia.co.uk**

www.germany-tourism.de   GERMANY
 GERMANY – WUNDERBAR
As much information as you can handle with good features on the key destinations, excellent interactive mapping and links to related sites. For further information try **www.germany-info.org**

www.gibraltar.gi/tourism   GIBRALTAR
GIBRALTAR – THE ROCK
A good site devoted to the area with sections on the sights plus travel information.

www.gnto.gr   GREECE
GREEK NATIONAL TOURIST ORGANISATION
An attractive site with the official word on travelling in Greece,
also a good travel guide and information for business travellers
plus accommodation, advice and details on what you can do.

See also:
www.culture.gr – excellent site covering Greek culture and its
legends.
www.inntravel.co.uk/greece – good for unusual accommodation
in unspoilt corners of Greece.
www.gogreece.com – a search engine devoted to all things Greek.
www.greekisland.co.uk – an entertaining and personal view of
the Greek islands with over 200 links.
www.gtpnet.com – the Greek Travel Pages with the latest ferry
schedules for island hoppers.
www.islands-of-greece.com – another specialist operator with a
good site and features on the better islands.
www.travelalacarte.co.uk – specialists in holidays in the best of
the Greek islands.

H
www.holland.com   HOLLAND
HOLLAND IS FULL OF SURPRISES
A very professional site offering a mass of tourist information and
advice on how to have a great time when you visit. There are
sections on how to get there, what type of holiday will suit you
and city guides. For an unpretentious guide to Amsterdam
designed to be downloaded onto your mobile of PDA try
http://homepages.cwi.nl/~steven/amsterdam.html

www.gotohungary.com   HUNGARY
HUNGARY
All the information is here to enable you to plan your trip to
Hungary including information on the wide range of cultural
events taking place in Budapest. If it's restoration you're after,
there's an interesting section on Hungary's curative spas. See
also **www.budapest.com** and **www.hungarytourism.hu**

I
www.iceland.is   ICELAND
ICELAND
The official site of the Icelandic Ministry of Foreign Affairs with a
wealth of information about the country, the people and its

history. It's easy to navigate and there are good links to related sites. See also **www.iceland.com** which is more tourism oriented and also **www.icelandexpress.com** which is good for low-cost fares.

www.incredibleindia.org   UK
INDIAN TOURIST OFFICE UK

Essential tourist information and advice as well as cultural and historical background on the country and its diverse regions. It has a massive hotel database as well.

www.indiamart.com   INDIA
INDIA TRAVEL PROMOTION NETWORK

Basically a shopping site with diverse information including travel, hotels, timetables, wildlife, worship, trekking, heritage and general tourism. It's well organised and easy to use.

See also:
www.greavesindia.com – luxury holidays in India and Nepal.
www.hindustantimes.com – full of useful information, news and gossip.
www.indianrail.gov.in – passenger information and timetables for the largest rail network in the world.
www.india-travel.com – a really strong travel site with lots of information and guidance as well as essential links.
www.indiatraveltimes.com – great for links and the latest news.
www.mapsofindia.com – an excellent site with maps of the country and a rail timetable and route planner.
www.partnershiptravel.co.uk – specialist Indian travel agent.
www.rrindia.com – another good information site offering tour itineraries and hotel booking.
www.taj-mahal.net – explore the Taj Mahal.

www.tourismindonesia.com   INDONESIA
INDONESIA

A very good overview of the country and its people, with lots of useful information about travelling there and a good links section. See also **www.indo.com** and for trips to see the Komodo Dragon go to **www.komodotours.com**

www.shamrock.org   IRELAND
IRELAND

A wide-ranging site giving you the best of Ireland. Aimed at the American market, it really sells the country well with good links to other related sites. See also **www.ireland.ie** – the very good, official Irish Tourist Board site.

See also:
www.12travel.co.uk – Irish holiday specialists with lots of holiday options.
www.camping-ireland.ie – over 100 parks listed for caravanning and camping.
www.heritageireland.ie – exploring the history of Ireland.
www.iol.ie/~discover – a good travel guide plus lots of links.
www.irelandhotels.com – a good accommodation directory.
www.visitdublin.com – very comprehensive official guide to Dublin.

www.goisrael.com   ISRAEL
ISRAEL
Excellent site with information on the country, its sights and sites, how to get there and how to organise a tour. See also **www.infotour.co.il** and **www.e-israel.com**

www.italytour.com   ITALY
VIRTUAL TOUR OF ITALY
Good looking, stylish and cool, this site is essentially a search engine and directory but a very good one.

See also:
www.doge.it – a basic but informative site on Venice.
www.emmeti.it – slightly eccentric site with bags of good information, although it takes a while to find it. Very good for hotels, regional info and museums.
www.initaly.com – another 'Italian' site but generally well organised, informative and useful.
www.itwg.com – Italian hotel reservations with online booking.
www.travel.it – a messy information site but you can book online.
www.tuscanynow.com – villas for rent in Tuscany.

J
www.jnto.go.jp   JAPAN

JAPAN
This excellent site is the work of the Japanese Tourist Association. There's a guide to each region, the food, shopping and travel info with advice on how to get the best out of your visit.

See also:
www.jaltour.co.uk – travel agents specialising in Japan.
www.japan-guide.com – comprehensive information site about
Japan with links, culture notes, shopping and a hotel finder.
www.uk.emb-japan.go.jp – a site from the Japanese Embassy
with details on how to study or work in Japan, plus visa, tourist
and background information.

www.see-jordan.com   JORDAN
JORDAN

An attractive and interesting site from the Jordanian tourist
board. It is very cultural and informative with good links and a
photo gallery. See also **www.jtehome.com** where you'll find the
attractive site of the Jordan Travel Exchange.

K
www.visit-kenya.com   KENYA
KENYA

A slightly amateurish site with links and information on travelling
in Kenya. There are sections on Nairobi and the coast as well as
the expected safari information.

See also:
www.bwsafaris.com – a stunning site from this Kenyan safari
specialist.
www.kenya.com – good-looking site with a safari deal finder
and information on the country too.
www.kenyaweb.com – a good portal site on all things Kenyan.

L
www.lata.org   US
LATIN AMERICA

The Latin American Trade Association's text-based site has a
good country-by-country guide to the region plus links and
general information.

www.southamericanexperience.co.uk   UK
SOUTH AMERICA

Specialists on South America are hard to come by, but at this
site you can get tailor-made tours to suit you plus some scant
information on the countries and special offers. See also
www.adventure-life.com and **www.gosouthamerica.about.com**,
both are very informative and are good for links.

See the sites below, most of which also cover South America:
www.journeylatinamerica.co.uk – lots of tour and country options from this specialist agent.
www.lastfrontiers.com – tailor-made itineraries for holidays across the continent.
www.latinamericatraveler.com – great for links and information.
www.steppeslatinamerica.co.uk – from the Steppes group offering tailor-made packages.

www.nexteurope.com/tourism   LATVIA
LATVIA
A valiant effort with information on what to do when you get there and a good selection of links. They will also arrange for a translator/guide to show you around. For a second opinion go to **www.latviatravel.info**. For a good interactive site on Riga try **www.virtualriga.com**

www.destinationlebanon.com   LEBANON
THE LEBANON
The Lebanon is going through a resurgence and is successfully rebuilding itself. Written with the help of US-aid money to encourage tourism, this site successfully provides all the resources you need to organise a visit and see its many attractions.

www.tourism.lt   LITHUANIA
LITHUANIA
A straightforward offering from the State Department with basic tourist information.

www.luxembourg.co.uk   LUXEMBOURG
LUXEMBOURG
Comprehensive information on the Grand Duchy with good links to other sites. It could do with a few pictures to whet the appetite though.

M
www.malaysianet.net   MALAYSIA
MALAYSIA
Great for hotels in particular but you'll also find flight information and hidden away is a pretty good travel guide to the country. For air travel info see also **www.malaysiaair.com**

www.visitmaldives.com   MALDIVES
MALDIVES

A good overview of the islands and all the options available to tourists with links and a section on the capital Male.

www.visitmalta.com   MALTA
MALTA

A text-heavy but informative site about this beautiful island, with good details on accommodation and interactive mapping.

www.tourbymexico.com   MEXICO
MEXICO

A basic site, but there is a travel guide to Mexico plus information on tours, hotels, health, tips, links and sights. See also the bright and breezy European gateway into Mexico **www.mexicanwave.com/travel**

http://i-cias.com   NORWAY
THE MIDDLE EAST

Probably the best site for information on the Middle East, just click on the interactive map. There's really extensive information on selected countries including maps, statistics, history, plus the religious, economic and political state of each nation. See also **www.ancient.co.uk**

www.arab.net   SAUDIA ARABIA
RESOURCE FOR THE ARAB WORLD

A wide-ranging site covering North Africa and the Middle East with excellent country guides. See also **www.arabianodyssey. co.uk**

www.tourism-in-morocco.com   MOROCCO
MOROCCO

Take the guided tour and visit the major tourist sites in Morocco. There are also sections covering museums, tourist events, Moroccan culture and you can try out a recipe at home. The site provides links, but for more see **www.morocco.com** and **www.morocco-travel.com**

N
www.namibweb.com   NAMIBIA

NAMIBIA

Comprehensive as a description doesn't quite do this site justice, it seems to have covered everything. The result is a little messy but it's easy to find what you need, and it is a stunning country to visit.

www.nepal.com   US

NEPAL AND THE HIMALAYAS
A beautifully presented site showing Nepal in its best light. Business, sport, culture and travel all have sections and it's a good browse too. The travel section is not that comprehensive, it has a basic guide.

Specialist tour companies and information sites. Also check out entries under China and India in this section.
www.himalayankingdoms.com
www.nepaltravelinfo.com
www.rrindia.com/nepal.html
www.trans-himalaya.com

www.purenz.com   NEW ZEALAND
NEW ZEALAND
A good-looking and informative site about the country with a section devoted to recollections and recommendations from people who've visited. See also the comprehensive but **www.nz.com** and **www.newzealand.com**

www.nicaragua.com   US
NICARAGUA
On the face of it a comprehensive portal devoted to all things Nicaraguan, it's not what it seems, however, and only the guide book information seems useful.

www.visitnorway.com   NORWAY
NORWAY
The official site of the Norwegian Tourist Board offers a good overview of what you can get up to when you're there, from adventure holidays to lounging around in the midnight sun to cruising the coast. You need an up-to-date browser to get the best out of the site. See also **www.norway.org** which is the Norwegian Embassy's site and also **www.norwayshop.com**, great for dodgy patterned jumpers.

P

www.tourism.gov.pk   PAKISTAN
PAKISTAN
A pretty lightweight site but it has all the basic information
and a good set of links with a travel guide built in. See also
www.nicepakistan.com which has travel information and some
interesting sections on life in Pakistan and about its history.

www.enjoyperu.com   US
PERU
It's amazing how much there is to see in Peru and this site does
a good job of reflecting the country's assets. It has plenty of
tourist information and deals. See also the basic but useful site
of the Peruvian embassy **www.peruembassy-uk.com**

www.polandtour.org   US
POLAND
A basic overview of the country, tourist facilities and travel
information. For a portal site go to **http://poland.pl**

www.portugal-web.com   PORTUGAL
PORTUGAL
A complete overview of the country including business as well
as tourism with good regional information, news and links to
other related sites.

See also:
www.madeiratourism.org – all about Madeira although you
have to hunt for the English site, we found the link in the top
right of the Portuguese page.
www.portugal.com – a news and shopping site with a good
travel section.
www.portugal.org – well-designed information site with good
travel information.
www.portugalregional.pt – a shop devoted to Portuguese wine
and arts.
www.thealgarve.net – all you need to know about the Algarve.

R

www.rotravel.com   ROMANIA
ROMANIA
Good historical information, maps and regional guides backed
up with tourist services for both the independent traveller and

T

those wanting a ready-made tour, make this site a good starting point for the exploration of this central European gem. The Romanian National Tourist Office has a good web site at **www.romaniatourism.com**

www.russia-travel.com   RUSSIA
RUSSIA

The official guide to travel in Russia with good information on excursions, accommodation, flights and trains; there's even a slide show, plus historical facts and travel tips. See also **www.themoscowtimes.com/travel** which offers a more traditional approach. For links go to **www.russia.com**

www.rwandatourism.com   RWANDA
RWANDA

It's good to see Rwanda back on the tourist map and here at the Tourist Board site you can find out what the country has to offer including interactive mapping on the gorilla treks. For more on gorillas there's **www.rwanda-gorillas.com**

S
www.sey.net   US
SEYCHELLES, PARADISE – PERIOD

A good all-round overview of the Seychelles with background information on the major islands and activities. There are also links to travel agents.

See also:
www.seychelleselite.co.uk – specialists in the Seychelles.
www.seychelles-travel.co.uk – excellent site from another specialist agent.
www.seychelles.uk.com – informative and geared to a British audience.

www.sg   SINGAPORE
SINGAPORE

The shortest URL in the book brings up one of the most detailed and comprehensive sites – all you need to know about the country and its people. See also **www.satours.com** and the official uniquely Singaporean site **www.visitsingapore.com**

www.slovenia-tourism.si   SLOVENIA
SLOVENIA

A good introduction to the country, which is trying to establish a
tourist industry.

www.sacr.sk   SLOVAKIA
SLOVAKIA

The official word of the Slovak Republic on their tourist
attractions. For similar but more wordy information go to
www.slovakia.org/tourism who also have an audio guide to
common phrases in Slovak.

www.southafrica.net   SOUTH AFRICA
SOUTH AFRICA

Official tourist site with masses of information about the country
and how you can set yourself up for the perfect visit with
suggested itineraries.

See also:
www.gardenroute.org.za – excellent site covering the Garden
Route and south coast.
www.southafrica.com/travel – very good portal site with a
comprehensive travel section.
www.southafricanaffair.com – tailor-made itineraries, basic site
though.

South America – see Latin America on page 537.

www.tourspain.es   SPAIN
TOURIST OFFICE OF SPAIN

A colourful and award-winning web site that really makes you
want to visit Spain. Very good for an overview.

You could also try any of these listed below:
www.costablancaworld.com – Costa Blanca revealed.
www.iberia.com – the Iberian airlines site, with helpful advice
and offers.
www.majorca.com – great site about the island.
www.munimadrid.es – comprehensive site on Madrid.
www.okspain.org – nice all-round information and travel site.
www.red2000.com – a colourful travel guide, with a good
search instrument!

T

www.lanka.net   SRI LANKA

SRI LANKA
An exhaustive site, which isn't easy to navigate, but it has
loads of information and news on the country. See also
www.slmts.slt.lk for the Ministry of Tourism.

www.sverigeturism.se/smorgasbord   SWEDEN

SWEDEN
The largest source of information in English on Sweden. It's
essentially a directory site but there are sections on culture,
history and a tourist guide. For more details of Sweden's cities
see the very good **http://cityguide.se** and **www.visit-
sweden.com** and also **www.sweden.se**

www.switzerlandtourism.ch   SWITZERLAND

SWITZERLAND
An excellent overview of the country with the latest news,
travel information, snow reports and links. See also
www.myswitzerland.com

T

www.tanzania-web.com   TANZANIA
TANZANIA
Find your way around Tanzania with its wonderful scenery,
Mount Kilimanjaro, safaris and resorts with this very good and
comprehensive online guide from the official tourist board. For a
range of safaris and personalised tours try **bush2beachsafaris.
com**

www.thailand.com/travel   THAILAND
THAILAND
Another excellent portal site, which acts as a gateway to a mass
of travel and tourism resources. It covers some of South East
Asia too and it has a good search facility. The helpful **www.
tourismthailand.org** is the official tourist board site and is very
informative, as is **www.thaismile.co.uk** which is the official
tourist site.

www.tourismtunisia.com   TUNISIA
TUNISIA
A welcoming and easy-to-use site with lots of interactive links
that gives you a good introduction to the country, its tourist sites
and its people. There's information on hotels and restaurants –
plus what to eat when you get there and links to travel agencies.

www.allaboutturkey.com   TURKEY
TURKEY

The best-looking and most informative site on the country and
its people, though some sections are pretty odd. It's the work of
one professional tour guide.

See also:

www.exploreturkey.com – pretty boring but
comprehensive.

www.tourismturkey.org – great for links and basic information
from the Ministry of Culture and Tourism.

www.turkey.org – informative site from the Turkish Embassy in
Washington DC.

www.turkeycentral.com – a huge number of Turkish links.

U

www.uae.org.ae   UAE

UNITED ARAB EMIRATES

A useful guide to the seven states that make up the UAE, it
carries historical and social information as well as the usual
travel guide stuff – turn down your sound, though. See also
www.godubai.com

www.visituganda.com   UGANDA

UGANDA

A great site and directory from the Ugandan Tourist Board with
excellent-quality pictures.

www.ukraine.co.uk   UK
UKRAINE

A basic site with information on flights, the cities, mapping and
links. **http://travel-2-ukraine.com** has more of the same with
some information on what to expect from a Ukrainian hotel.

www.usatourism.com   US
US

A state-by-state guide to the US, just click on the interactive
map and you get put through to the relevant state site. See also
www.areaguides.net which is very detailed.

www.usembassy.org.uk   US
VISA INFO

This site gives a dull look at the latest tourist entry requirements
plus information on gripping topics such as driving. It also

provides some limited but useful links. For tourist information they send you to **www.visitusa.org.uk**

See also:
http://vijaydandapani.com – entertaining and well-written blog from a New York hotel industry insider.
www.americanadventures.com – great site devoted to budget adventure tours. Now merged with **www.trekamerica.com** to offer an even broader range of holidays.
www.americanroundup.com – ranch holidays for wannabe cowboys.
www.amtrak.com – rail schedules and fares across America.
www.cruiseamerica.com – rent an RV for your fly-drive holiday.
www.disneyworld.com – all you need to know about the world's number-one theme park.
www.eosairlines.com – travel to New York in style.
www.gocitykids.com – a family-friendly guide to some of the major cities in the US.
www.gohawaii.com – great site for checking out Hawaii and its many attractions.
www.greyhound.com – coach and bus schedules; for selected cities you can now buy tickets online using the 'will call' option and pick them up before boarding the bus. Beware the surcharge for those without a US address.
www.hawaii-tourism.co.uk – the official site of Hawaii's tourist board, excellent information on all the islands.
www.kidscamps.com – a massive directory of kids' camps, mainly in the US.
www.newyorkology.com – outstanding guide/blog on the Big Apple.
www.seeamerica.org – an excellent portal to American travel sites.
www.themeparksonline.org – over 200 of them, apparently.
www.usa-by-rail.com – the definitive guide book for touring the US by rail.
www.usahotelguide.com – reserve your room in any one of 55,000 hotels across the US.
www.us-national-parks.net – the fabulous US National Parks Service with plenty of info; use the online Reservation Centre to book accommodation.

V

www.vietnamtourism.com   US
VIETNAM

Vietnam is the hot destination, apparently. Here's the official tourism site, which is informative and good for links.

Z

www.zambiatourism.com   ZAMBIA

ZAMBIA

Comprehensive tourist site with loads of information about places to visit, where to stay and what to do when you get there.

www.allaboutzanzibar.com   TANZANIA
ZANZIBAR

An outstanding tourist site with concise (then very detailed if you need it) descriptions covering all the information you need, including accommodation and cultural stuff. Other tourism sites could learn a lot from this. See also **www.zanzibar.net** There are sections on the animals and birds you might see, plus maps and a good travel directory.

Travel in Britain

www.visitbritain.com   UK

HOME OF THE BRITISH TOURIST AUTHORITY

Selling Britain using a holiday-ideas-led site with lots of help for the visitor, maps, background stories, images, entertainment, culture, activities and a planner. There's also a very helpful set of links.

www.informationbritain.co.uk   UK
HOLIDAY INFORMATION

Where to stay and where to go with an overview of all the UK's main tourist attractions, counties and regions; it has good cross-referencing and links to the major destinations.

www.ukholidaybreaks.co.uk   UK
FIND YOUR PERFECT HOTEL

A directory of hotels in the UK, you find the one you want by drilling down through a series of maps or selecting by category. It's easy, although results are a bit hit and miss, but it claims to use the latest technology to find just the right break for you.

Travel UK

The Good Web Site Guide's Top 10s
of the Internet

TOP 10

1. **www.visitbritain.com** – all you need to know about us
2. **www.timeout.com/london** – probably the best guide to the capital
3. **www.sightseeing.co.uk** – information on what to see and how to get there
4. **www.nationaltrust.org.uk** – 350 homes, gardens and industrial relics
5. **www.ctc.org.uk** – the perfect site for cyclists
6. **www.traveline.org.uk** – all you need on public transport
7. **www.walkingworld.com** – great for the UK and abroad
8. **www.goodbeachguide.co.uk** – where to put the windbreak
9. **www.hebrides.com** – beautiful
10. **www.knowhere.co.uk** – a warts and all overview of our country

www.thetravelplanner.co.uk   UK
UK TRAVEL PLANNER
A good resource if you're planning a journey anywhere in Britain.
There are good links and it makes a useful addition to your
favourites list.

See also:
www.aboutbritain.com – attractive, well-laid-out and
comprehensive UK guide.
www.anothertravel.com – a good-looking site, a bit light on
information though.
www.atuk.co.uk – billed as the UK travel search engine,
unattractive design.
www.enjoybritain.com – useful links directory.
www.i-uk.com – useful information on the UK, mainly aimed at
visitors.
www.touristnetuk.com – a good regional guide.
www.ukguide.org – well-organised directory with a UK and a
London guide plus mapping.
www.ukvillages.co.uk – not a great design but has good
information on over 30,000 places.

www.knowhere.co.uk   UK
THE USER'S GUIDE TO BRITAIN
An unconventional 'tourist guide', which gives a warts-and-all
account of over 2,000 places in Britain; it's very irreverent and if
you are squeamish or a bit sensitive, then they have a good list
of links to proper tourist sites.

For the separate countries and regions:

England

http://themeparksofengland.com – reviews and information on
all of England's major theme parks.
www.enjoyengland.com – official tourist site with lots of
information and features.
www.travelengland.org.uk – nice online guide to everything
English, places to visit and accommodation.

English Holiday Regions

www.blackcountrytourism.co.uk – visiting the Midlands and the
Black Country.
www.cumbria-the-lake-district.co.uk – a good guide to the Lake
District.
www.dorset-newforest.com – Dorset and the New Forest.
www.peakdistrict.org – home of the Peak District Park Authority.
www.the-cotswolds.org – all about the honey-stoned world of
the Cotswolds.
www.visiteastofengland.com – for East Anglia and the Broads.
www.visitenc.com – visit England's North Country.
www.visitnortheastengland.com – nice site to entice visitors to
North East England.
www.visitenglandsnorthwest.com – the official tourist site of the
North West.
www.visitnorthwest.com – what to do in the towns and cities of
the North West.
www.visitpeakdistrict.com – good site on tourism in our oldest
National Park.
www.visitsoutheastengland – for history, gardens and more.
www.westcountrynow.com – official guide to England's West
Country.
www.yorkshirevisitor.com – get to know Yorkshire.

London

http://london.flavourpill.net – an excellent and entertaining London city guide which is updated weekly.
https://sales.oystercard.com – buy an Oyster card and reduce your travelling costs in London.
www.londonhotelreservations.com – some good deals on London hotels.
www.londontown.com – very comprehensive survival and holiday guide rolled into one, with sections on restaurants, hotels, attractions and offers. It is quite slow.
www.timeout.com/london – *Time Out* mag's excellent guide to the capital.

Northern Ireland

www.discovernorthernireland.com – Northern Ireland Tourist Board has an attractive site showing the best that the region has to offer. It has a virtual-tour holiday planner.
www.gotobelfast.com – excellent site on Belfast.
www.guide-to-nireland.com – a good directory site and guide.

Scotland

www.aboutscotland.com – excellent site with information on a broad range of accommodation and sights to see, it's fast too.
www.agtb.org – pour yourself a whisky, it's Aberdeen and the Grampians!
www.edinburgh.org – comprehensive offering on Edinburgh.
www.scotac.com – accommodation by region.
www.scot-borders.co.uk – what to do on the Scottish/English Borders.
www.scotland.com – nicely illustrated site with a good overview of the country.
www.scotland-info.co.uk – very good online guidebook covering Scotland by area; it's quite slow but the information is very good.
www.seeglasgow.com – excellent site on Glasgow.
www.visithebrides.com – a light and airy site with links and information relating to the islands. See also **www.hebrides.com** which offers beautiful photography.
www.visithighlands.com – all you need to know about the Scottish Highlands and more.
www.visitorkney.com – from the Orkney Tourist Board, a very informative and appealing site. See also **www.orknet.com**

www.visitscottishheartlands.com – Argyll, the Isles, Loch Lomond, Stirling and the Trossachs.

www.visitshetland.com – a definite green theme to this site devoted to Shetland, highlighting its outdoor life and spirit of adventure.

Wales

www.cadw.wales.gov.uk – historic monuments in Wales.

www.cardiganshirecoastandcountry.co.uk – great guide to West Wales.

www.data-wales.co.uk – not so much a tourist site, but excellent for history and culture and quite funny too.

www.nwt.co.uk – North Wales tourism.

www.southernwales.com – Cardiff and the south.

www.stayinwales.co.uk – for hotels, cottages, B&Bs, campsites, even bunkhouses.

www.valleyconnection.co.uk – a useful directory devoted to all things Welsh.

www.visitmidwales.co.uk – Wales' best kept secret.

The UK's Islands

www.alderney.net – a good-looking site devoted to the third largest Channel Island.

www.islandbreaks.co.uk – official site on the Isle of Wight.

www.isle-of-man.com – learn all about this unique island with help on where to stay and, of course, background on the famous TT races.

www.jersey.com – very slick site on Jersey.

www.jerseyhols.com – good-looking site with lots of information on where to stay and what to do.

www.sark.info – a lively site with all the information you need plus online booking for ferries.

www.simplyscilly.co.uk – specialists in travel to the Isles of Scilly with info on how to get there and what to do.

www.visitguernsey.com – all the information you need on Guernsey.

www.wightlink.co.uk – Isle of Wight ferries and holiday information.

Things to do in Britain and Ireland

www.daysoutuk.com   UK

 TAKE A DAY OFF
An excellent directory of venues and events with lots of search
options. It's easy to use and you can get discounts to many
attractions too. For a similar but more colourful site go to
www.daysout.co.uk which includes a useful section for the
disabled too.

www.gardenvisit.com   UK
GO TO A GARDEN
A basic text-based site, which lists some 2,000 gardens in the
UK and abroad, giving details of each, how to get there and how
they rate. There's also an excellent overview of garden history.
See also the section on Gardening, page 219.

www.nationaltrust.org.uk   UK

 PLACES OF HISTORIC INTEREST AND BEAUTY
The National Trust's site has an excellent overview of their
activities and the properties they own. There is a very good
search facility and up-to-date information to help with your visit.
See also **www.nts.org.uk** for the National Trust for Scotland.

See also:
www.castles-of-britain.com – informative and lively site on
Britain's castles.
www.english-heritage.org.uk – excellent, high-quality site with
information on their properties and an events calendar.
www.hrp.org.uk – pretty boring site devoted to five historic royal
palaces – the Tower, Hampton Court, Kensington, Kew and the
Banqueting House.
www.statelyhomes.com – comprehensive site devoted to our
stately homes, with links and an e-zine to keep you updated.

www.goodbeachguide.co.uk   UK
THE BEST BEACHES
From the Marine Conservation Society you can find out which
are Britain's worst and best beaches. It's set out regionally and
the site is updated regularly.

What to do With the Kids

www.babygoes2.com   UK
ESSENTIAL TRAVEL GUIDE FOR PARENTS
An excellent resource for parents who have children under five,
it covers a wide range of holiday options, plus plenty of advice,
guides and information.

For more ideas try:
http://babyfriendlyboltholes.co.uk – a great place to find self-
catering accommodation, all properties are stylish and provide
something extra for kids.
www.barracudas.co.uk – activity camp holidays.
www.butlins.co.uk – bright and breezy site from this popular
family-oriented company.
www.campbeaumont.co.uk – a summer camp covering
southeast England.
www.centerparcs.com – attractive site from this holiday village
specialist, covering the UK and parts of Europe.
www.kidscamps.com – a massive directory of kids' camps,
mainly in the US.
www.kidsdaysout.co.uk – a directory of things to do by county,
covering England, Scotland and Wales.
www.kidstravel.co.uk – up-beat design but it could have more
content, still some good ideas and travelling tips for parents
though biased to England.
www.pgl.co.uk – activity holidays for children with lots of
options.
www.xkeys.co.uk – specialist in residential camps for children
of all ages, excellent web site with lots of information and
references.

Holiday Cottages and B&B

www.bedandbreakfast-directory.co.uk   UK
B&B
A regional directory of B&Bs with a good search facility. Each
entry has contact details, a description and information such as
whether online booking is available.

www.special-escapes.co.uk   UK
SELF CATERING IN BRITAIN
Excellent site from Alastair Sawday, who selects and
recommends the best of British self-catering. Worth reading

just for the reviews; however, you should find something different here.

See also:
www.cottagesdirect.com – click on the interactive map and away you go, plenty of cottages to choose from.
www.goodcottageguide.com – a good selection from this established specialist.
www.nationaltrust.org.uk – look under holidays for cottages and b&b with a difference.
www.oas.co.uk/ukcottages – over 1,000 cottages available throughout the UK.
www.preferredplaces.co.uk – good site with a wide range of options.
www.pub-explorer.com – find a pub with rooms and a good pint.
www.pub-rooms.co.uk – stay in a pub, unfortunately most don't have websites, but you can e-mail.
www.seasidecottages.co.uk – all within 10 miles of the sea.
www.selfcatering-directory.co.uk – a very useful directory site listing hundreds of cottages with information and contact details.
www.thebigdomain.com – for those who want to hire a place for a big party.

Camping and Caravanning

Many of the sites listed specialise in Britain but some have information on camp sites abroad too.

www.camp-sites.co.uk   UK
FIND A SITE
Excellent regional listing of the UK's campsites with comprehensive details on each site and links to other related directories.

See also:
www.eurocampindependent.co.uk – excellent site if you want to go camping in Europe, some special offers and you can chat about your experiences too.
www.keycamp.co.uk – European specialist with sites in seven countries.
www.ukparks.com – directory site covering caravan and camping sites.

www.caravan.co.uk   UK
THE CARAVAN CLUB
This site offers help and advice, and has a huge listing of over
200 sites and some 2,500 other certified locations where you
can park up. There's also a European service. You can join the
club online and request any of the 50 or so leaflets they publish.

See also:
http://camping.uk-directory.com – a good regional sites
directory, with retailing links, caravans for sale and forums.
Camping in New Zealand is covered too.
www.campingandcaravanningclub.co.uk – an OK offering with
information on sites and technical help and advice too.
www.campinguk.com – a basic regional campsite directory for
campers and caravanners.
www.caravannersreunited.co.uk – forums, chat, information
and meeting up with old friends.
www.caravan-sitefinder.co.uk – listing of over 3,500 caravan
sites, with background information on a wide range of topics.
www.clicreports.co.uk – the Chat Line for Internet Campers
offers loads of advice in a fun and informative way.

Waterways

www.britishwaterways.co.uk   UK
BRITISH WATERWAYS
This organisation is responsible for maintaining a large part of
Britain's waterways and this excellent site details their work. On
two sites (also **www.waterscape.com**) it features interactive
mapping of the routes with a great deal of background
information, events, holidays, listings and history.

See also:
www.blakes.co.uk – a boating holiday specialist.
www.broads-authority.gov.uk – excellent overview of the
Norfolk Broads.
www.canalholidays.com – an easy way to book your
narrowboat holiday.
www.gobarging.com – luxury barging in Europe.
www.hoseasons.co.uk – great site from the specialists in
boating holidays, you can book online too.
www.waterways.org.uk – Inland Waterways Association site,
dedicated to keeping canals open and you can find out about
their organised activities too.

Adventure and Activity

Listed below are UK-oriented sites, see also page 509 for international adventure specialists.

www.sportbreak.co.uk   UK
THE SPORTS BREAK DIRECTORY
A good directory, apart from sports it covers all activity holidays including leisure breaks, health clubs, even stag and hen parties. They specialise in corporate entertaining too. It's easy to use and the information is well put over.

Other adventure holiday sites:
www.activityholsni.co.uk – Activity Holidays in Northern Ireland have a great site and lots to do.
www.adventuredirectory.com – for an excellent portal site.
www.adventureholiday.com – ProAdventure specialise in activity holidays in North Wales.
www.hightrek.co.uk – strenuous activities in the mountains of North Wales.
www.mountainandwater.co.uk – wide range of activities for adults and children in Wales.
www.sportstoursinternational.co.uk – sports holidays (mainly running, cycling and swimming) in the UK and abroad, but many to international events.
www.trailplus.com – the ultimate adventure, offering lifestyle experiences, adventure camps and much more.
www.uksurvivalschool.co.uk – learn new skills; learn how to survive in many different situations on the courses.

Walking and Rambling

www.ramblers.org.uk   UK
THE RAMBLERS' ASSOCIATION
News, strong views and plenty of advice on offer here, where you can find out about the Association's activities and even join a campaign. There are features on events and details of *The Rambler* magazine, shopping and holidays.

www.walkingbritain.co.uk   UK

BRITISH WALKS
Some 3,300 pages of information about walking in Britain, it mainly covers the National Parks but it is expanding to include less well-known areas. They provide decent route maps and

photos to guide you. There's also a list of handy links and a good photo gallery.

www.onedayhikes.com US

WHERE DO YOU WANT TO HIKE TODAY?
A great site, which is basically a directory of hikes that you can complete in a day; it's not just for the UK either, it covers the whole world. There's excellent information on each hike plus pictures and you get the chance to win a digital camera if you send in a report of a hike you've done and it gets accepted.

www.walkingworld.com UK

OVER 3,500 WALKS
Each walk has a detailed description and map, and it's easy to find a good one. In addition, there's advice on difficulty and what you can expect to see. The walks cost £1.50 or you can become a member for £17.45 per annum, then they're free.

For more sites for hikers try:
www.gelert.com – equipment for sale, a good-looking site, well worth a visit.
www.georgefisher.co.uk – another excellent equipment store.
www.hfholidays.co.uk – excellent specialist travel agent with walking holidays for all levels and all around the world.
www.ramblersholidays.co.uk – Ramblers Holidays specialise in escorted rambling holidays.
www.trailsource.com – the hiking section of this big site has some great walks and detailed mapping.

Train, Coach and Ferry Journeys

www.transportdirect.info UK

PUBLIC TRANSPORT INFORMATION
Excellent travel resource for public transport or the car driver. You opt for a quick journey plan or a more detailed door to door plan. If you just need to find a train, bus or coach or even a car route, this information is available too. There is information for travellers with disabilities, maps, live travel info and you can also link to your mobile or PDA. An alternative is **www.traveline.org.uk** although this site only finds journeys between major towns and cities. They do, however, provide timetables and links and details for all the major transport providers.

See also:
http://journeyplanner.tfl.gov.uk is very useful for travelling around London.
www.internet.xephos.com – a subscription service which offers a high degree of accuracy on train and bus timetables.

Railway Travel

www.rail.co.uk
UK

RAILWAY LINKS
A directory of useful links including timetables, operators and associated businesses.

www.nationalrail.co.uk
UK

NATIONAL RAIL
National Rail's site has all the latest information, timetables and links you need to plan a rail journey. It's very comprehensive with up-to-the-minute information on what's going on. The TrainTracker facility enables you to get departure/arrival board information via your mobile and enquiries are now enabled on PDA. They are trying …

www.thetrainline.com
UK

BUY TRAIN TICKETS
You have to log in first but you can book a ticket for train travel, whether business or leisure (except sleeper, Motorail, and ferry services). They have an up-to-date timetable and the tickets will be sent or you can collect. You can now buy European rail tickets and other travel services from the site. See also the fast-working **www.qjump.co.uk** which is similar. At both these sites there are a bewildering number of options and prices, a little help regarding ticket type and relative costs wouldn't go amiss.

See also:
www.gensheet.co.uk – information on unusual rail journeys in the UK.
www.networkrail.co.uk – what was Railtrack, some useful information.
www.seat61.com – the UK pages give extensive rail information.
www.traintaxi.co.uk – useful site if you need a taxi once you're off the train, with taxi company contact details and advice on whether there are usually taxis waiting.
www.youngpersons-railcard.co.uk – how to save as much as a third on your rail travel.

www.tfl.gov.uk   UK

LONDON TRANSPORT
Transport for London is an excellent and informative site featuring
the London Underground, DLR, buses, taxis and river transport
plus advice for travellers who come by car, use a bike or just
walk. At **www.thetube.com** you'll find lots of features, articles on
visiting London and links to related sites. There's a good journey
planner, tube maps and you can buy an Oyster card for low-cost
travel too. See also the Tube Planner at **www.tubeplanner.com**
which is a straightforward journey planner and a tube guide and
history at **http://owen.massey.net/tubemaps.html**

Coaches and Buses

www.nationalexpress.com   UK
BOOK COACH TICKETS
Organise your journey with this easy-to-use web site from
National Express, and then book the tickets. Also offers an
airport service, transport to events and tours. See also
www.stagecoachbus.com where you can find information about
Stagecoach services and buy tickets, and **www.citylink.co.uk** for
their Scottish Services.

www.megabus.com   UK
NO FRILLS
The coach equivalent of low-cost planes, Megabus is expanding
rapidly, currently they serve over 30 towns and cities. Tickets
can only be purchased online and all you need is your booking
reference to present to the driver on the bus. Tickets start from
£1 if you book soon enough, with only a 50p booking charge.

See also:
www.busabout.com – for independent travellers, mainly covers
Europe and North Africa.
www.wallacearnold.co.uk – coaching holiday specialist with
online booking.

Ferries

www.ferrysavers.com   UK
BOOK YOUR CROSSING
Low-cost ferry crossings and plenty of special offers on a number
of routes, you can book online but the price promise seems to
have disappeared.

T

See also:

www.boozecruise.com – for ferry tickets, guides to the French ports and maps for locating the hypermarkets and shopping areas.

www.brittany-ferries.co.uk – crossings to France and Spain with online booking and special offers, also cruises and holidays.

www.dfdsseaways.co.uk – details and offers on Scandinavian routes.

www.directferries.co.uk – claims to offer the widest choice of routes and crossings.

www.drive-alive.com – motoring holiday specialists who get good rates on channel crossings as part of their package.

www.eurotunnel.com – we know it's not a ferry; also has hotel and holiday deals.

www.ferrycrossings-uk.co.uk – a helpful site with offers and links, a shopping guide too.

www.hoverspeed.com – online booking and all the information you need to make the fastest channel and Irish Sea crossings.

www.irishferries.ie – excellent magazine-style site where amongst all the features you can find timetables and book tickets.

www.poferries.com – P&O with online booking, details of sailings and offers.

www.seafrance.com – bookings and information on their Calais–Dover service plus some special offers.

www.speedferries.com – a low-cost operator offering crossings on the Dover–Boulogne fast-ferry service. Book online to save admin fee.

www.steam-packet.com – get Sea Cat to destinations on the Irish sea.

www.stenaline.ferries.org – details of their routes and offers.

www.transmancheferries.com – the new boys on the south coast offering Newport to Dieppe at competitive prices.

Road Travel

For Mapping see page 523. Here are some sites that may help your journey to go smoother still.

www.5minutesaway.com   UK
JUST OFF THE MOTORWAY
An excellent site which lists by motorway junction the facilities that exist within a five minute's drive of the exit. It's excellent for those who hate motorway services. See also

www.offthemotorway.com which is still in development, although it does appear that they will charge for membership.

See also
www.gloveboxloo.co.uk – yes, it really exists.
www.moto-way.com – the company that runs most of the services.
www.motorwayservices.info – a feedback site where people give their views on motorway service stations.
www.welcomebreak.co.uk – book a hotel room and find out about their services.
www.westmorland.com – home of the Tebay services who show everyone how a motorway service station should be run.

Travel Writing and Travel Blogs

http://worldhum.com – a descriptive site derived from the rush people get from travelling. Some excellent writing.
www.exposedplanet.com – exceptional photography.
www.gridskipper.com – described as an 'urban travel guide', here you'll find a wide variety of personal views of the major cities around the world.
www.mytripjournal.com – here at this well-put-together site, you can find a huge number of personal travel sites and blogs covering most major destinations and many obscure ones too.
www.palinstravels.co.uk – an outstanding site from Michael Palin with his recommendations, excerpts from the books and video clips as well as competitions and links.
www.paultheroux.com – a biography and details on all his books.
www.randomhouse.com/features/billbryson – an official site from Bill Bryson's publisher, it has a short biography, his book lists and a forum. Given the breadth of material available it could be so much better …
www.timseverin.net – details about his life and his remarkable voyages.
www.travelwriters.com – the place to go if you want to become a travel writer, the place to go if you are one already.
www.wandalust.com – entertaining, gossipy and informative.
www.writtenroad.com – the inside scoop to the travel writers' world apparently, it's certainly a good resource for likely guide writers.

Utilities

Get the best prices on your gas, electricity and water and find out what the big suppliers are up to as well.

www.ofgem.gov.uk   UK

GAS AND ELECTRICITY SUPPLIER WATCHDOG
Data on the suppliers and companies. The comparison
information makes for interesting reading. There's also
background on how bills are made up, complaints, government
policy and how energy reaches your home. For more impartial
advice see also the independent watchdog Energywatch at
www.energywatch.org.uk

www.uswitch.com   UK

CUT YOUR BILLS – COMPARE PRICES
Take a few minutes to check the prices of the key utilities and
see whether you can save on your current bills, its easy and
quick. It also gives you the option to change to a green energy
tariff. In addition you can check out phones, broadband access,
digital TV and loans.

See also:
www.energylinx.co.uk – one of the best switch sites with a wide
range of options, particularly good on renewable energy.
www.greenelectricity.org – switch to green energy.
www.moneysupermarket.com/utilities – excellent comparison
tool.
www.switchandgive.com – switch energy suppliers and give to
charity at the same time.
www.switchwithwhich.co.uk – *Which* Magazine's impartial
switching site.
www.theenergyshop.com – very easy to use and fast results.
www.unravelit.com – savings on gas and electricity plus
numerous other services.
www.utilitydeal.com – helps business users as well as home
owners.

Electricity and Gas

*Here are the main energy sites, who owns them at the time of writing
and the highlights of the sites:*

www.british-energy.com – one of the largest electricity providers with a good-looking but not very useful site.

www.centrica.co.uk – owners of British Gas, this site aims to give information about the group, could be a lot more helpful.

www.esb.ie – messy site from an Irish supplier with online sign-up available.

www.house.co.uk – a comprehensive service from British gas with account viewing and offers.

www.hydro.co.uk – Scottish Hydro Electric has one of the sites most oriented to its customers.

www.edfenergy.com – a stylish site for London Energy, SWEB Energy, Seeboard Energy and Virgin Home.

www.nie.co.uk – Northern Ireland Electricity with customer information on their service, the rest is fairly corporate.

www.npower.com – nicely designed site with online application and the usual incentives to switch to their service.

www.powergen.co.uk – Powergen has a neat site with calculators and a switching service.

www.scottish-southern.co.uk – owner of Swalec, their site is aimed at shareholders and provides company information.

www.scottish-power.co.uk – a messy site from one of the cheaper suppliers.

www.swalec.co.uk – Swalec, useful information.

www.nationalgrid.com/uk   UK
FORMERLY TRANSCO, FOR GAS LEAKS
National Grid doesn't sell gas, but maintains the 24-hour emergency service for stopping gas leaks – call 0800 111 999 to report one.

www.trustcorgi.com   UK
COUNCIL OF REGISTERED GAS INSTALLERS
CORGI is the gas industry watchdog; the site has advice on gas installation and where to find a fitter or repairman.

www.calorgas.co.uk   UK
CALOR GAS
Information on your nearest stockists, how best to use Calor Gas and Autogas; there's also corporate background and customer services too. You can also order it online with payment collected on delivery.

U

Solid Fuel

www.solidfuel.co.uk   UK
>
> SOLID FUEL ASSOCIATION
> Information about solid fuels, about which is right for you and
> what appliances to buy; also covers suppliers and has a wealth
> of information and links.
>
> *See also*
> **www.coal.gov.uk** – information from the National Coal Authority.
> **www.ecodyfi.org.uk/energy/DyfiEcoWdFfinl.htm** – excellent
> overview of the different wood-based fuels.
> **www.euroheat.co.uk** – a variety of stoves, select according to
> fuel type.
> **www.nef.org.uk/logpile** – the National Energy Foundation's site
> that aims to 'promote and aid the use of wood as a source of
> renewable energy and sustainable heating'.
> **www.onlinelogs.co.uk** – order online with next day delivery.
> **www.stovesonline.co.uk** – stoves and more stoves ...

Saving Energy

www.nef.org.uk   UK
>
> NATIONAL ENERGY FOUNDATION
> Devoted to saving energy in order to benefit the environment.
> There's lots of advice and information to help save money too.
>
> *See also:*
> **www.banthebulb.org** – campaign blog aimed at promoting the
> use of energy efficient light bulbs.
> **www.battery-force.co.uk** – buying batteries at discounted prices
> including good prices on rechargeable ones.
> **www.ukace.org** – Association for the Conservation of Energy.

Alternative Energy

www.cat.org.uk   UK
>
> CENTRE FOR ALTERNATIVE TECHNOLOGY
> Get information on how to help save the planet and ease your
> conscience including strategies on how to be more energy
> efficient.
>
> *See also:*
> **www.british-hydro.org** – find out about hydro-power.

www.bwea.com/you/byo.html – build your own wind turbine.
www.diy.com – for B&Q's range of solar panels and wind power turbines.
www.clear-skies.org – information about grants for those installing renewable energy systems such as solar panels.
www.eaga.co.uk – the Energy Action Grants Agency.
www.energysaving.me.uk – energy saving products.
www.est.org.uk – home of the Energy Saving Trust.
www.greenelectricity.org – sign up for a greener tariff.
www.greenenergy.org.uk/sta – home of the Solar Trade Association.
www.greenshop.co.uk – sells green products and solar/wind power.
www.heatpumpcentre.org – all about heat pumps and geothermal power.
www.unlimited-power.co.uk – solar and wind power specialists.

Water

www.ofwat.gov.uk   UK
OFFICE OF WATER SERVICES
A relatively poor effort, especially when compared with the Ofgem counterpart's site; however, you can find out about what they do and you can contact them for advice. There's a search facility to help you navigate the site and all the contact details for the water companies are listed on the site.

www.wateraid.org   US
WATER FOR LIFE
A charity devoted to helping people for whom getting water is very difficult or almost impossible, you can find out about their work and how to help. See also **www.actionaid.org**

The Weather

www.met-office.gov.uk   UK
EXCELLING IN WEATHER SERVICES
Comprehensive information on our favourite topic of conversation: easy to use with interactive maps. Includes details on world weather and world weather news, UK weather headlines and flash-weather warnings, weather for aviators and sailors and you can see what the weather is like on their webcams. There's also a good selection of links and a mobile phone service.

W

www.bbc.co.uk/weather   UK
ANOTHER WINNER FROM THE BBC
Another page from the BBC site, it gives up-to-the-minute forecasts, and is very clear and concise. It features: 5-day forecasts by town, city or postcode; specialist reports such as ski resorts, pollution, sun index; world weather and the shipping forecast. There are also audio and video forecasts and links.

See also:
www.intellicast.com – a general weather guide from the US.
www.weather.com – geared to the US but has some really good articles and features.
www.weather.org.uk – basic but informative UK weather site.
www.weatherunderground.com – an entertaining site with colourful, interactive mapping.

www.weatherimages.org   US
SEE THE WORLD'S WEATHER – LIVE
Weatherimages is compiled by a true weather fan. Split into twenty or so areas of interest, there is plenty of information and loads to see. The best feature is the network of weather cams from which you can see the best and worst of the world's weather. See also the excellent **www.weather-photography.com**

Other interesting and useful weather sites worth checking out:
www.chasingstorms.com – home of the Storm Chasers and Spotters Association.
www.climateark.org – all the links you'll ever need on climate change.
www.cloudappreciationsociety.org – all you need to know about clouds and how to appreciate them; stunning photography too.
www.everythingweather.com – poor site but lots of information and links.
www.hurricaneadvisories.com – American hurricane information, loads of very annoying adverts.
www.hurricanes.net – information on tropical storms and their effects.
www.risingslowly.com – an entertaining blog devoted to weather in the UK, with lots of links and other related blogs.
www.spaceweather.com – for daily updates on solar winds and flares plus information on solar weather patterns in general.
www.stormstock.com – the world's premier storm footage library with some stunning clips.

www.stormtrack.org – another US storm-tracking site, very comprehensive.
www.torro.org.uk – the Tornado and Storm Research Organisation, an interesting UK-oriented site.
www.weatherbase.com – statistics on world weather, data on over 16,000 cities.
www.worldclimate.com – city weather data, averages and statistics.

Web 2.0

A somewhat controversial term, Web 2.0 has basically been applied to programs available online rather than as an application based on one computer. On one level, this enables you to access your work from anywhere and share it, as though it were a web-based operating system, rather than send files as attachments via e-mail. On another level, the term can be applied to a site where its users have a huge influence over the input of data and how the site is used. In such cases, there may be some aspects of the site that are available as a free service or can be accessed for the good of the public.

Whatever your views, here are some of the most useful programs that conform to the 'rules' of Web 2.0. Many can be found throughout the book, but look out for these as particularly good examples ...

www.writely.com   US
GOOGLE DOCS AND SPREADSHEETS
Now owned by Google and probably the most high profile Web 2.0 site, writely.com offers a fully functioning word processor, which is also a good blogging tool and there's an Excel-style spreadsheet program too. There are loads of functions that are generally associated with the Microsoft products and it's compatible with many other similar programs. Although a little slow to use, it's a very good free option. We also found the flexibility of **www.ajaxwrite.com** very impressive as a word processor.

See also:
http://del.icio.us – bookmark tagging par excellence.
www.mapquest.com – tailor-made mapping.
www.box.net – online storage.
www.flickr.com – online photo album.

www.myspace.com – possibly the best known example of how the technology can work.
www.wikipedia.org – the online encyclopaedia.
www.youtube.com – the popular video sharing site.

People are even starting to talk about Web 2.1 which encompasses sites with even more interactivity, watch this space …

Web Cameras

One of the most fascinating aspects of the Internet is the ability to tap into some CCTV or specially set-up web cameras from all around the world. It's almost inevitable that sites will contain adult material though.

www.camcentral.com   US
WEB CAM CENTRAL
An excellent selection of cameras, chosen for quality rather than quantity; the wildlife ones are very good in particular but there's a good search facility too.

See also:
www.bbc.co.uk/webcams – the BBC has a great selection of regional and world webcams.
www.camvista.com – web cam shots of the UK and the US from a web cam manufacturer, annoying pop-ups.
www.webcam-index.com – lists over 2,000 sites from around the world.
www.webcamsearch.com – excellent search engine and directory of web cams from around the world.

Web Site Guides and Directories

If you can't find the site you're looking for in this book, then rather than using a search engine such as Yahoo or Google (both of which have superb directories), you might want to check out one of these web sites.

W

www.uk250.co.uk   UK
1000S OF QUALITY SITES IN 250 CATEGORIES
Heavily advertised and hyped though this site has been, many people seem to think that it consists of just the top 250 sites,

but it's actually a very comprehensive database of Britain's most important and useful .co.uks and .coms. The sites listed are not reviewed but a one-liner gives a brief description of what they are about.

www.ukdirectory.co.uk UK
DEFINITIVE GUIDES TO BRITISH SITES
A massive database of web sites conveniently categorised into fifteen sections, they don't review, but there are brief explanations provided by the site owners.

www.bored.com US
IF YOU'RE BORED
Basically a directory of unusual and humorous sites to occupy you when you've nothing better to do; it's quite entertaining really.

www.thebrickwall.com UK
PICK A BRICK
An entertaining route to categorised directories. Each brick represents a category, clicking on a general category brick brings up more bricks and the sites you're looking for.

http://del.icio.us/ US
SOCIAL BOOKMARKING
Here you can create your own web directories and share them with your friends or the whole of the Internet; it's also a good way to discover new sites.

Weddings

An industry that has really embraced the Internet, these sites go from strength to strength, for information and sites on Civil Partnerships see page 221.

www.confetti.co.uk UK
YOUR INTERACTIVE WEDDING GUIDE
A good-looking and busy site designed to help you through every stage of your wedding with information for all participants. There are gift guides, planning tools, advice, a supplier directory and a shop. They don't miss much.

W

www.theknot.com   UK
PREPARATION
All (well nearly all) your wedding needs catered for, excellent
and attractive design too. You even get your own web pages and
a useful countdown to the day.

www.wedding-service.co.uk   UK
UK'S LARGEST WEDDING AND BRIDE DIRECTORY
A huge list of suppliers, service providers and information by
region, everything from balloons to speechwriters are listed. The
site is not that easy on the eye and it takes a little while to find
what you want.

Other good sites for weddings:
http://bridesandgrooms.com – a comprehensive guide and
community site.
www.bestman.co.uk – heavily advertised and a useful resource
for any nervous best man.
www.bipp.com – the home of the British Institute of Professional
Photographers and a good place to find one for your wedding
pics.
www.bridesmagazine.co.uk – excellent site from *Brides*
magazine; get all the latest in bridal fashion and a guide to
where to go on honeymoon.
www.hitched.co.uk – another good all-rounder with the added
feature of a discussion forum where you can swap wedding
stories.
www.lastnightoffreedom.co.uk – everything you need to
organise your stag or hen night.
www.limoshop.co.uk – reserve your stretch limo.
www.partydomain.co.uk – if you want to organise your own
party, then this is the site for you with some fairly naff offerings
for hen and stag nights.
www.printed4u.co.uk – invitation printing.
www.pronuptia.co.uk – illustrated details of the range and
stores, not much else.
www.thebridalconsultant.co.uk – organise an overseas
wedding.
www.trading-direct.co.uk – your wedding presents taken care of
with an online wedding list service.
www.webwedding.co.uk – lots of expert advice and inspiration,
you need to join up to get the best out of it.
www.weddingguide.co.uk – clean-looking site with shop,
directory, forums and advice plus a good search facility.

W

www.weddings-abroad.com – overseas wedding and honeymoon packages.
www.whitesandweddings.co.uk – for more overseas options.

Women

The following are a few sites of particular interest to women.

Equality Issues and Politics

www.womenandequalityunit.gov.uk   UK
THE WOMEN AND EQUALITY UNIT
Dedicated to promoting a 'vision of equality and opportunity for all'. Politics aside, the site provides useful information on how government policies impact on women's lives, covering hot topics such as encouraging women to become more involved in public life, balancing work and family, domestic violence, money, health and equal opportunities. Worth visiting for the useful links. For information on what the UN is doing to promote gender equality go to **www.un.org/womenwatch** where there is information on all their initiatives and international treaties. A dry but informative read.

www.eoc.org.uk   UK
EQUAL OPPORTUNITIES COMMISSION
Know your rights by checking here about sex discrimination in the workplace, sexual stereotyping in education or work, the legalities of part-time work, maternity leave, etc. A useful resource although not very user-friendly.

www.womensaid.org.uk   UK
UNTIL WOMEN AND CHILDREN ARE SAFE
Excellent site aimed at helping women (and children) cope with domestic violence. As you'd expect, there are plenty of links and help for anyone in distress.

See also:
www.now.org – The National Organisation for Women.
www.poptel.org.uk/women-ww – dedicated to supporting the rights of women workers world-wide.
www.wen.org.uk – the Women's Environmental Network campaigns and educates on environmental matters.

W

Aimed at Women

The Good Web Site Guide's Top 10s
of the Internet

1. **www.handbag.com** – the most useful place for women on the internet, apparently
2. **www.bbc.co.uk/radio4/womanshour** – excellent magazine spin off
3. **www.healthywomen.org** – get healthy, get informed
4. **www.journeywoman.com** – safe travel resource
5. **www.womengamers.com** – for a great selection of games
6. **www.ivillage.co.uk** – a great magazine site
7. **www.bintmagazine.com** – irreverent e-zine that takes no prisoners
8. **www.fashionangel.com** – all the fashion links you'll ever need
9. **www.womanmotorist.com** – proving that cars aren't just for men to enjoy
10. **http://shinyshiny.tv** – a girl's guide to gadgets

Working Women

www.everywoman.co.uk   UK
   NOT JUST FOR BUSINESS WOMEN
   A really useful site aimed at women business owners, but the
   'home' channel provides sound information on personal finance,
   family and well-being for all women.

www.womenatwork.co.uk   UK
   DIRECTORY OF WOMEN IN BUSINESS
   If you want to support local women in business, search the
   site for self-employed freelancers, consultants, home workers,
   tradeswomen or women running small businesses in your area. If
   you're one of those women, join here for networking and support.

   See also:
   www.busygirl.co.uk – a more serious site than the name
   suggests, their aim is to advance women by supporting the
   business and career needs of women.

W

www.equalitec.org.uk – helping women back into IT, electronics and communications jobs after a career break.

www.ivillage.co.uk/workcareer – useful advice and information on a range of employment issues for women.

www.positivepresence.com – take their image quiz found in the 'specials' folder.

www.scottishbusinesswomen.com – a good community site aimed at business women in Scotland.

www.the-bag-lady.co.uk – international women's trading portal with plenty of information and links for those in business.

www.womenintechnology.co.uk – information portal with careers advice, jobs and links for women who work in technology.

www.workingmums.co.uk – a job finding site for working mums.

Women and Their Families

Information on divorce, separation and family relationships is found on page 365.

www.timeforparenting.org   UK

FOR FULL-TIME MUMS

The site is an initiative of Full Time Mothers who aim to promote the status of stay-at-home mums and campaign for changes in taxation, the benefit system and employment policy to give women more choice. There is also information on how to join a local group, or set one up. See also **www.netmums.com** while for the working mother's perspective see **www.workingmother. com**, a campaigning e-zine for working mothers from the US and **www.motheratwork.co.uk**, a very useful e-zine for British mothers.

See also:

www.childlessstepmums.co.uk – a site for those who love him, but not his kids. Good problem sharing forum.

www.matchmothers.org – self-help support site for mothers separated from their children for whatever reason. There is useful information for all, but you need to join to get the most out of it.

www.mothers35plus.co.uk – support and information for older mothers.

www.mumsnet.com – a rather advert-laden site devoted to product reviews with advice and tips thrown in. You have to subscribe to get the best of it.

W

www.thebritishsecondwivesclub.co.uk – support for second wives and the problems they face.

www.thestepfamilycoach.com – help for newly formed families.

www.womensaid.org.uk – national charity working to end domestic violence against women and children.

Women Students

www.womanstudent.co.uk   UK

FOR WOMEN IN HIGHER EDUCATION

Loads of information for UK and international students with sections on money and careers, travel, health, leisure and universities. There is a helpful section for overseas women planning to come to British universities.

Magazines

www.handbag.com   UK

THE ISP FOR WOMEN

Described as the most useful place on the Internet for British women, Handbag lives up to that with a mass of information written in an informal style and aimed at helping you get through life. There's shopping and competitions too. For some it's a little too commercial though.

www.ivillage.co.uk   UK

WHERE WOMEN FIND ANSWERS

All the sections you'd expect in a women's magazine, the difference here is that they are trying, and succeeding, to create a community with a range of message boards, advice, a good section on work, even a dating service. Alternatively, visit MSN's Women's Channel at **www.msn.co.uk/womens**

www.bintmagazine.com   UK

ALWAYS A PLEASURE

An irreverent weekly that strives to turn the word bint into something better than its regular usage. It's fun, controversial and no prisoners are taken.

www.blackwomen.co.uk   UK

THE VOICE OF BLACK WOMEN

A serious magazine-style site which in addition provides a list of services targeted at Black women living in the UK. For the

W

'interactive magazine aimed at women of colour' visit
www.preciousonline.co.uk

www.asianamag.com

ASIANA

All the usual features of a women's magazine written for Asian
women. There are a number of forums, a wedding directory
and an online shop, which serves mainly to sell back issues
of the magazine. For a more tabloid magazine go to
www.asianimage.co.uk which, although aimed at the
Northwest, has some interesting and useful articles.

www.mookychick.co.uk   UK

THE ALTERNATIVE VOICE

A light-hearted, spirited e-zine for younger women with many of
the usual features but written with a distinctive voice. In addition
there's a section on 'tek stuff', action and travel, spirit, blogs,
forums, quizzes and more.

www.bbc.co.uk/radio4/womanshour   UK

WOMAN'S HOUR

An excellent magazine spin-off from the popular Radio 4
programme, you can listen to programmes, have your say and
go to sections such as those on food, health and history (which
includes a timeline).

www.e-women.com   UK

THE MULTICULTURAL WOMEN'S PORTAL

E-women aims to provide women world-wide with features and
links which are relevant to their lives. There are lots of women's
magazine-type features, a good range of forums, a shopping
directory but less serious comment than when previously
visited.

Other general women's e-zines and portals:
http://womensissues.about.com – features on a comprehensive
range of women's issues.
www.allthatwomenwant.com – a portal site which offers links
to sites covering a vast range of topics. It needs a search engine
though.
www.femina.com – a useful search engine for women-friendly
sites.
www.newwomanonline.co.uk – good representation of the
magazine.

W

www.wwwomen.com – US directory site for women, with extensive coverage.

Women's Health

Below are a few excellent sources of information on women's health issues. For more general health sites see page 232 and don't rely on web sites; see a doctor if you are unwell.

www.healthywomen.org   US
EDUCATING WOMEN ABOUT THEMSELVES
The layout doesn't do justice to the quality of information on this site provided by the American-based National Women's Health Resource Center. Go to the 'health center' and use the pull-down menu to select a topic such as breast cancer, acupuncture or menopause. The aim is to provide women with good information to help them make informed decisions about their health.

www.womens-health.co.uk   UK
OBS AND GYNAE EXPLAINED
A good starting point for information on obstetrics and gynaecology including pregnancy, infertility, complications and investigations. Has a good search facility and useful links.

www.fpa.org.uk   UK
FAMILY PLANNING
A really comprehensive web site from the Family Planning Association with information on all aspects of birth control written in a clear and helpful style. There is a useful page entitled 'I need help now' plus good links. For a more campaigning approach, try **www.mariestopes.org.uk** for a rundown on contraception choices and information on related topics such as health screening. You can even arrange for him to have a vasectomy online.

See also:
www.ein.org – European Infertility Network with information and advice.
www.fertilityfriends.co.uk – an online community offering support and information.
www.infertilitynetworkuk.com – advice, support and understanding for those pursuing infertility treatment.
www.menopausematters.co.uk – excellent site giving the latest information on the menopause and how to live with it.

www.miscarriageassociation.org.uk – for miscarriage support
and information. .

www.pms.org.uk – National Association for Premenstrual
Syndrome.

www.pni.org.uk – an American support site for those suffering
post-natal depression.

www.surreypnd.nhs.uk – written for women in Surrey, but
useful for everyone suffering from post-natal depression. There is
some excellent information, advice and personal stories from
those who've been there.

Travel

www.journeywoman.com   US
PREMIER TRAVEL RESOURCE FOR WOMEN
Dedicated to ensuring safe travel for women. Registering gets
you access to the free newsletter plus lots of advice, guidance
and tips from women who've travelled, travellers' tales and
health warnings. See also **www.poshnosh.com/swt** which is
aimed at the 50+ traveller.

www.hermail.net   .   US
CONNECTING WOMEN TRAVELLERS
Great idea, once joined up you can be put in e-mail contact with
women who have knowledge of the destination you're about to
visit. You can exchange e-mail messages about the weather,
restaurants or what to pack.

www.womenwelcomewomen.org.uk   UK
CIRCLE OF FRIENDSHIP
With 2,500 members in 70 countries, the aim is to foster
international friendship and understanding by enabling women
from different countries to visit one another. Members range in
age from teens to over eighties and visit each other's homes as
individuals or as part of organised gatherings.

See also:
http://thelmaandlouise.com – an online community of women
who use the site to find travel companions and share
information and stories.

www.christinecolumbus.com – travel tips for women plus the
opportunity to share the experiences of other women.

www.goodadventure.com – opportunities for adventurous travel
with other active women.

W

www.wildroseholidays.co.uk – holidays for single women in the UK and overseas.

Leisure and the Arts

www.wsf.org.uk   UK
WOMEN'S SPORT FOUNDATION
The voice of women's sport is committed to improving and promoting opportunities for women and girls in sport at every level. It does this by lobbying and raising the awareness of the importance of women in sport to the organisers and governing bodies. Here you can find out how to get involved or get help.

www.womengamers.com   US
BECAUSE WOMEN DO PLAY
The aim is to provide a selection of reviews and games geared specifically to a female audience (although it doesn't stop this being an enjoyable site for men to visit). It has up-to-the-minute reviews, really well-written articles, lots of content and high-quality design.

www.womeninmusic.org.uk   UK
WOMEN IN MUSIC
If you're a musician be it classical, jazz, folk or hip hop, then you'll find support and encouragement here. It seems particularly good for women composers. There's a very good 'what's on' section, one on competitions, links and a forum.

www.nmwa.org   US
NATIONAL MUSEUM FOR WOMEN IN THE ARTS
Take a tour of this New York-based museum dedicated to women artists. They have paintings and artefacts dating from the 16th century up to the present day with a reasonable collection available to view online. The shop is tempting, but remember delivery from the US is expensive.

http://digital.library.upenn.edu/women   US
A CELEBRATION OF WOMEN WRITERS
A site with a passion for the work of women writers; the quality and quantity of information on this site is tremendous with links to biographical and bibliographical information about women writers as well as providing complete books written by women.

For other sites on women's arts see:
http://web.ukonline.co.uk/n.paradoxa – feminist art journal with good links to artists and women's art associations.
http://womenwriters.net/links.htm – a guide to Internet resources as well as book reviews and features.
www.blackwomenart.org.uk – dedicated to black women in fashion, design, crafts and the performing arts.
www.society-women-artists.org.uk – join the Society of Women Artists, learn about their annual exhibition and see some of the exhibits.
www.the-womens-press.com – publishers of incisive feminist writing.

History

www.fordham.edu/halsall/women/womensbook.html   UK
WOMEN'S HISTORY SOURCEBOOK
Fabulous resource on women's history worldwide. It covers each country/time period looking at great women of the era, women's oppression, the structure of women's lives and gender construction. Unfortunately, not all the links work, but with so many on offer, you're bound to find a substitute. For more internet resources on women's history try the virtual library at
www.iisg.nl/w3vlwomenshistory

The following sites are also interesting on women in history:
http://womenshistory.about.com – About.com's pages, good on suffrage and has a good women's history picture gallery.
www.bbc.co.uk/history – the BBC's women's history section has disappeared, but you can use the search facility as all the information is still on the site. Shame on them.
www.distinguishedwomen.com – biographies and information on women's impact on history.
www.greatwomen.org – the US National Women's Hall of Fame, biographies of women who have made a difference.
www.lothene.demon.co.uk – Scottish women warriors from the 9th to the 18th century (with a lot of information about porridge!).
www.thewomenslibrary.ac.uk – an extensive collection of archives on women's history with some now available electronically. You can also see the catalogue and book a visit to the reading room.
www.womeninworldhistory.com – an limited educational site, but some good information.

W

Miscellaneous

http://shinyshiny.tv   UK

A GIRL'S GUIDE TO GADGETS

A fun blog which catalogues, gadgets and gifts that have
particular appeal to women. The authors have great taste and
the stuff featured is mostly gorgeous and desirable whoever you
are.

www.hintsandthings.co.uk   UK

PEARLS OF WISDOM

Not strictly for women, but it features serious hints and tips on
such things as not losing your children, bank statements and
computer viruses, but also some tongue-in-cheek information on
the rules of cricket and what to do with unwanted CDs. It's a
good place to visit for a coffee break.

Index